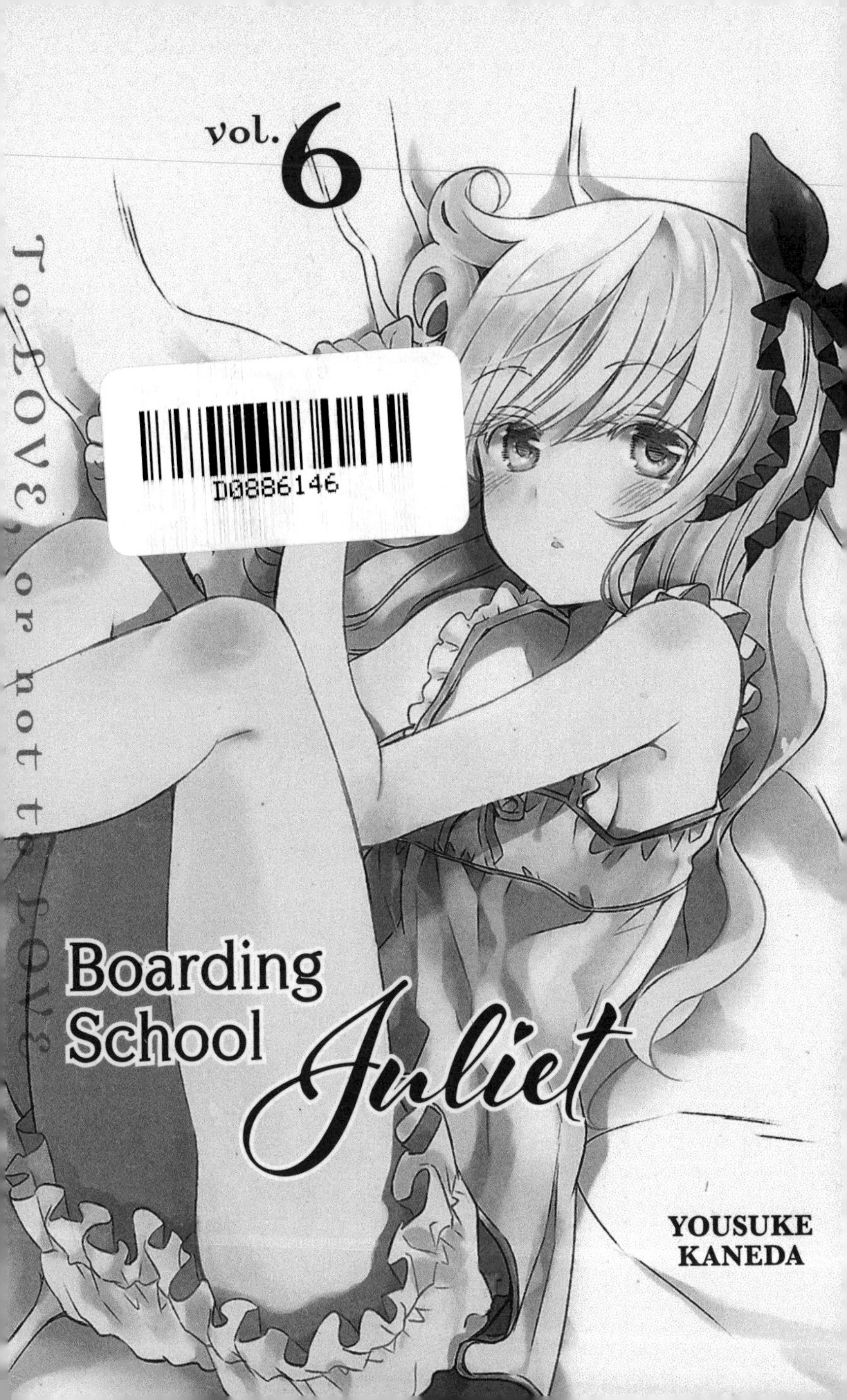
vol. 6
To LOVE, or not to LOVE
Boarding School
Juliet
YOUSUKE
KANEDA

THE PLAYERS

character

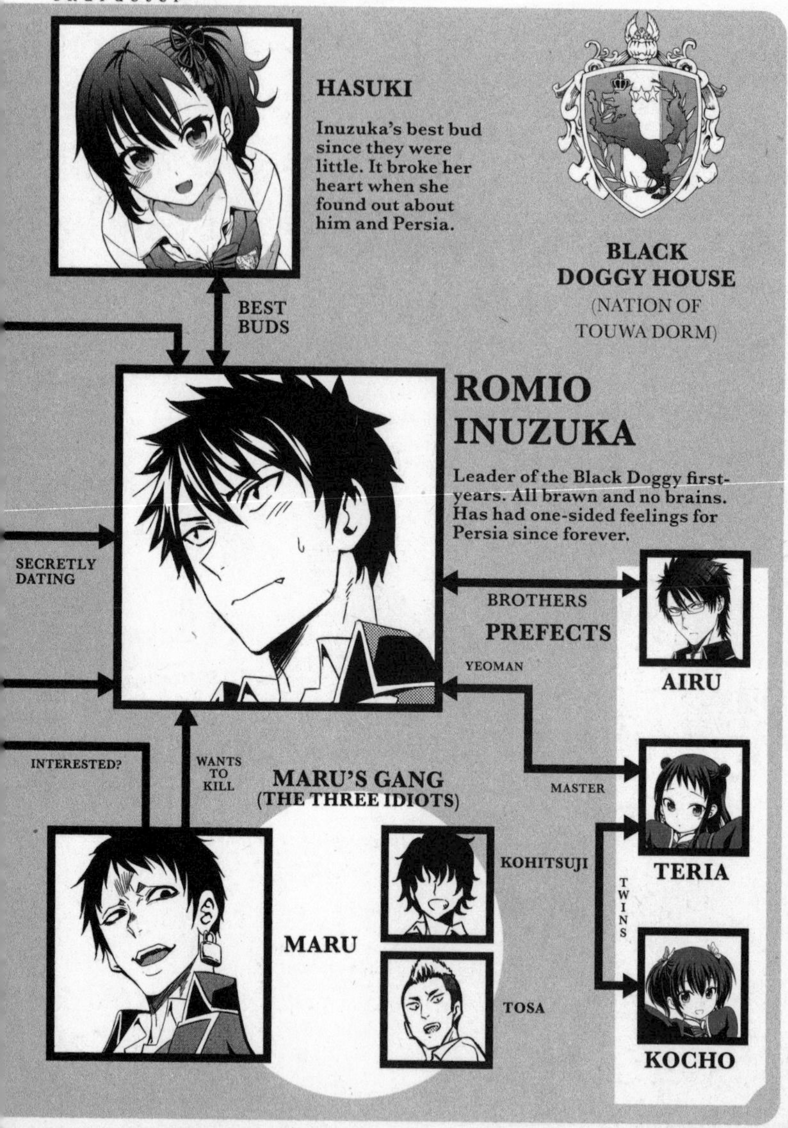

HASUKI
Inuzuka's best bud since they were little. It broke her heart when she found out about him and Persia.
BLACK DOGGY HOUSE
(NATION OF TOUWA DORM)
BEST BUDS
ROMIO INUZUKA
Leader of the Black Doggy first-years. All brawn and no brains. Has had one-sided feelings for Persia since forever.
SECRETLY DATING
BROTHERS
PREFECTS
YEOMAN
AIRU
INTERESTED?
WANTS TO KILL
MARU'S GANG (THE THREE IDIOTS)
MASTER
KOHITSUJI
TERIA
TWINS
MARU
TOSA
KOCHO

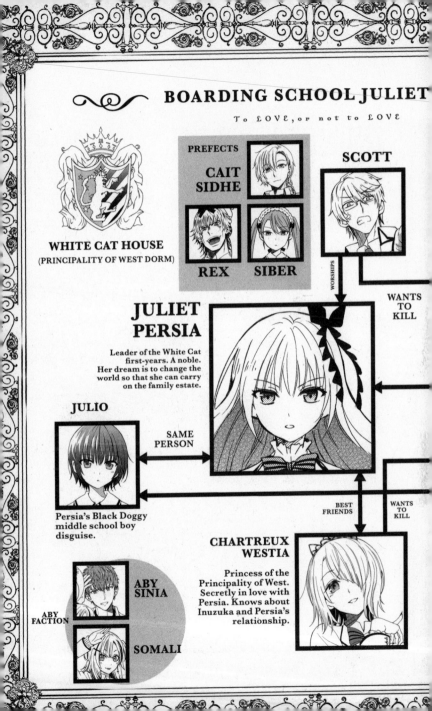

BOARDING SCHOOL JULIET

To LOVE, or not to LOVE

PREFECTS

CAIT SIDHE

REX   **SIBER**

SCOTT

WHITE CAT HOUSE
(PRINCIPALITY OF WEST DORM)

WORSHIPS

WANTS TO KILL

JULIET PERSIA

Leader of the White Cat first-years. A noble. Her dream is to change the world so that she can carry on the family estate.

JULIO

SAME PERSON

Persia's Black Doggy middle school boy disguise.

BEST FRIENDS

WANTS TO KILL

ABY SINIA

ABY FACTION

SOMALI

CHARTREUX WESTIA

Princess of the Principality of West. Secretly in love with Persia. Knows about Inuzuka and Persia's relationship.

contents

story

At boarding school Dahlia Academy, attended by students from two feuding countries, one first-year longs for a forbidden love. His name: Romio Inuzuka, leader of the Black Doggy House first-years. The apple of his eye: Juliet Persia, leader of the White Cat House first-years. It all begins when Inuzuka confesses his feelings to her. This is Inuzuka and Persia's star-crossed, secret love story...

By secretly teaming up with Persia, Inuzuka got a hit on Airu, and won back the first-year leader position he had lost in the Sports Festival. Overcoming a castaway incident during the seaside camp and the summer school from hell, among other obstacles, has rapidly drawn Inuzuka and Persia closer together...

DIIING
カラ〜〜ン

DOOONG
カラ〜〜ン

THIS IS THE LOVE STORY...

...OF A CERTAIN COUPLE AT A CERTAIN BOARDING SCHOOL.

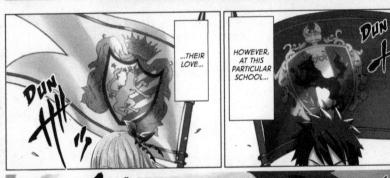

DUN ガガ ッ

...THEIR LOVE...

HOWEVER, AT THIS PARTICULAR SCHOOL...

DUN ガガ ッ

ガガ
DUNNN

...IS FORBIDDEN.

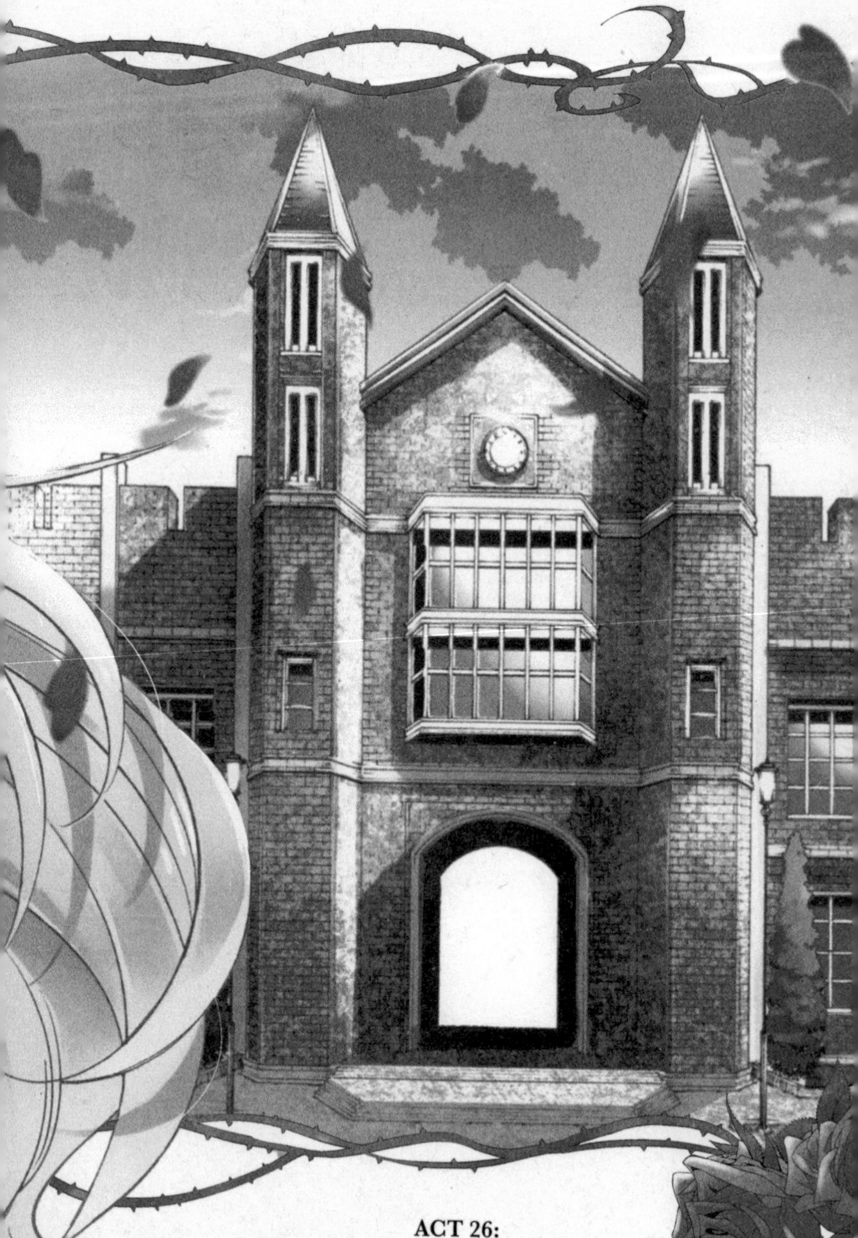

ACT 26:

ROMIO & JULIET & DAHLIA FIELD

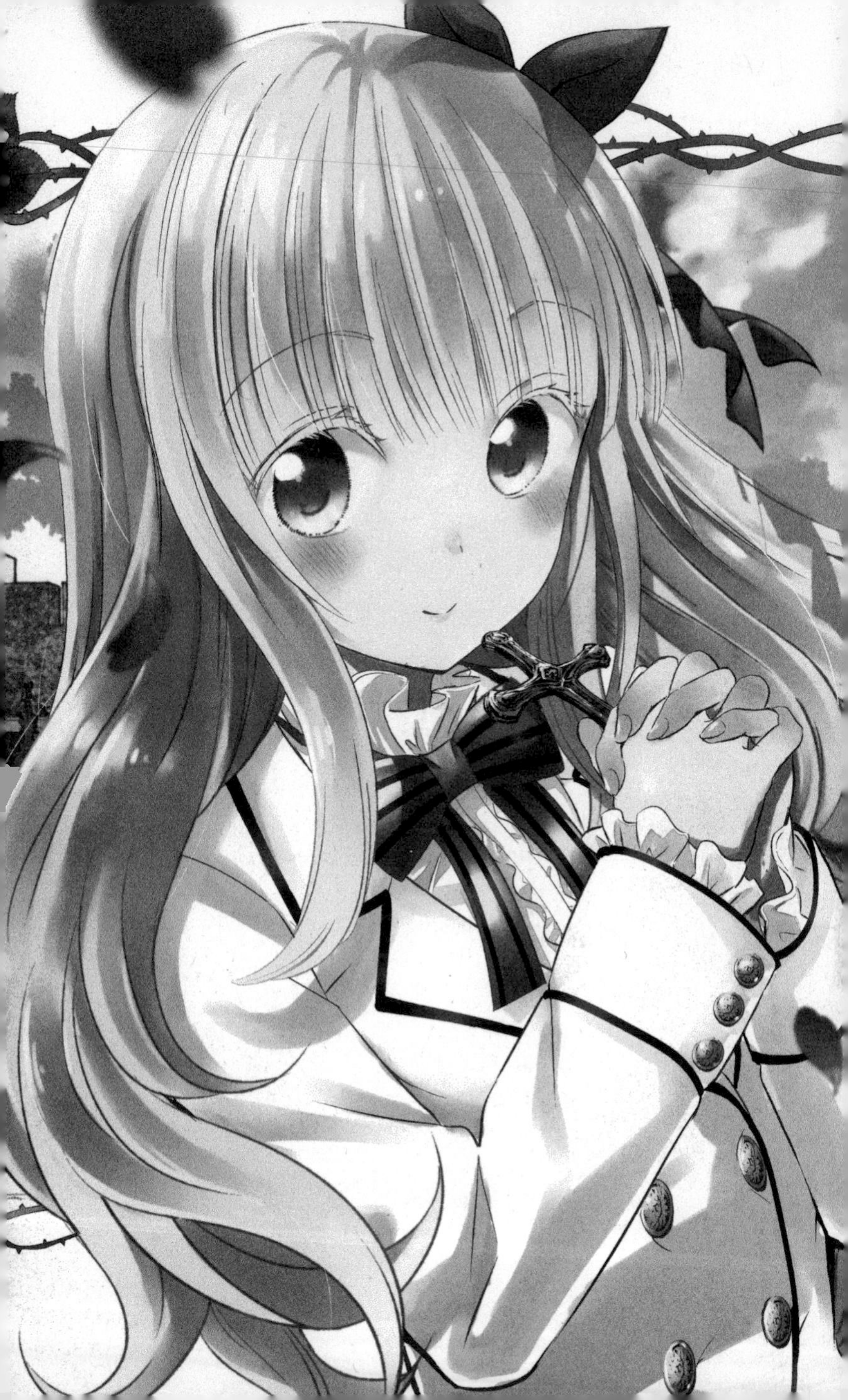

Allow me to explain why some of you may be getting déjà vu from these pages: beginning with this volume's chapters, *Boarding School Juliet* moved magazines. We used to be serialized in *Bessatsu Shonen Magazine*, and now we're in *Weekly Shonen Magazine*.

The opening pages of this volume are a quick catch-up for first-time readers, but the story and setting remain unchanged. Chronologically, this is the second school term.

Thanks for your understanding.

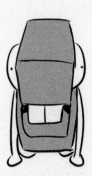

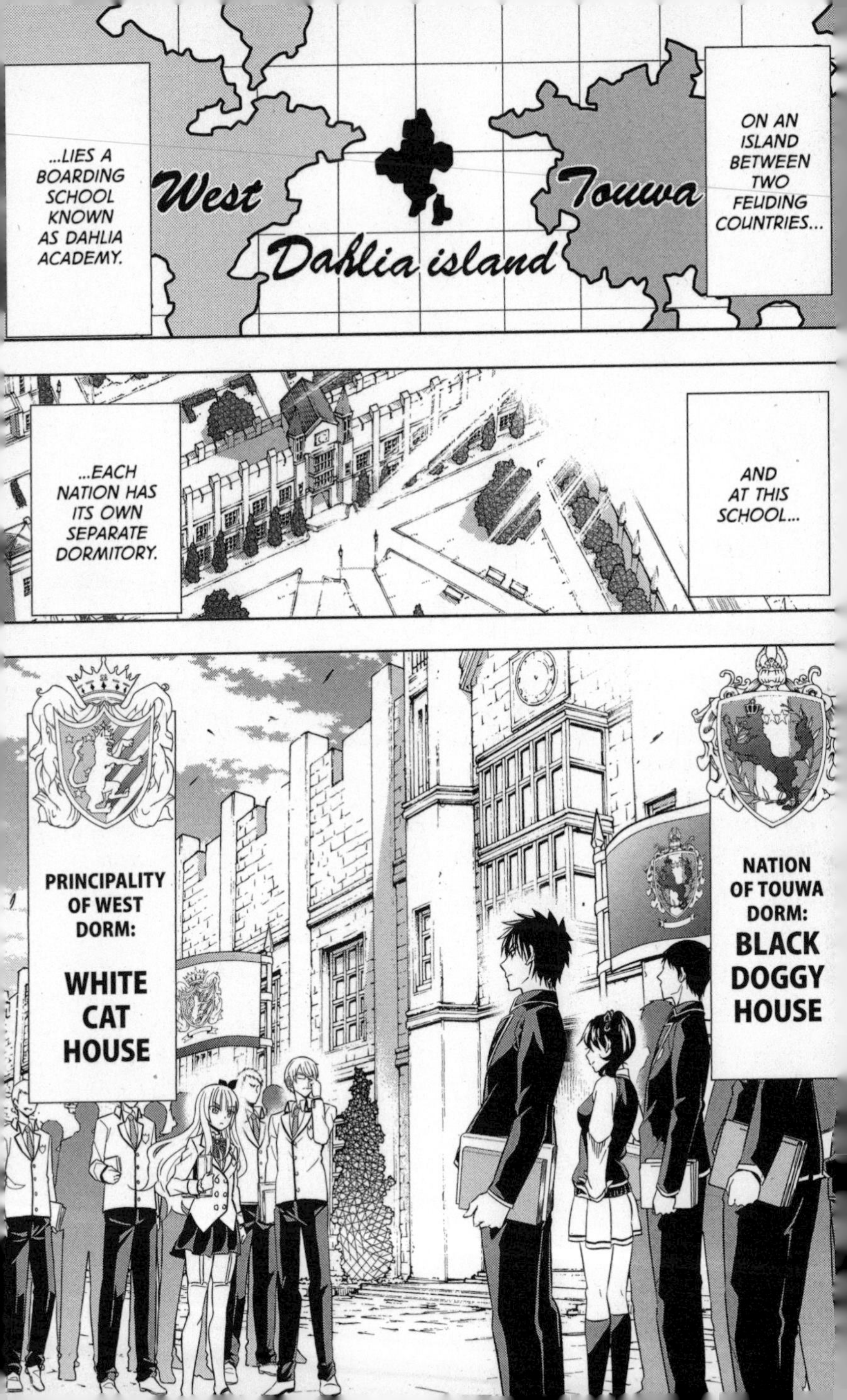
ON AN ISLAND BETWEEN TWO FEUDING COUNTRIES...
Touwa
West
Dahlia island
...LIES A BOARDING SCHOOL KNOWN AS DAHLIA ACADEMY.
AND AT THIS SCHOOL...
...EACH NATION HAS ITS OWN SEPARATE DORMITORY.
NATION OF TOUWA DORM:
BLACK DOGGY HOUSE
PRINCIPALITY OF WEST DORM:
WHITE CAT HOUSE

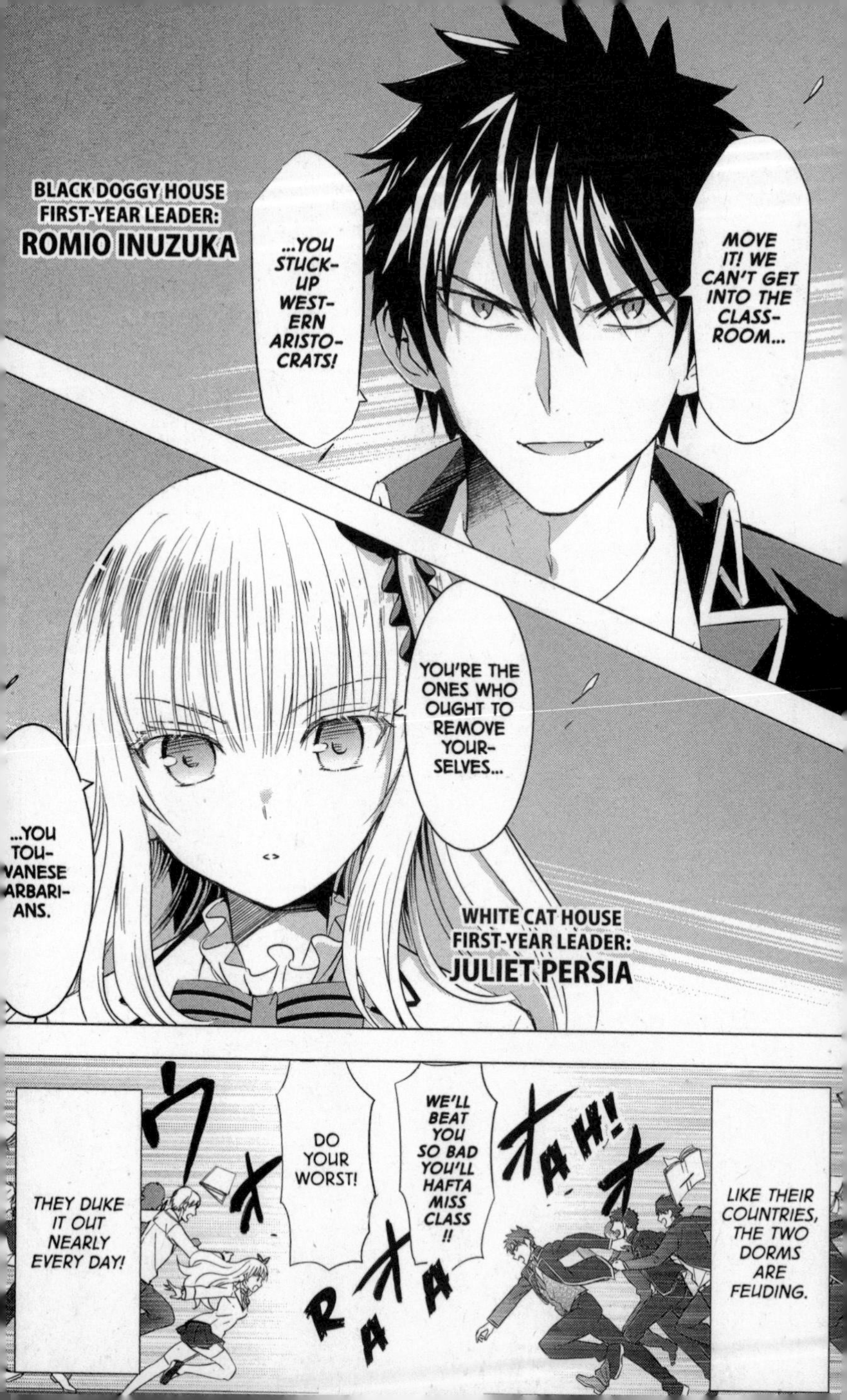
MOVE IT! WE CAN'T GET INTO THE CLASS-ROOM...
...YOU STUCK-UP WEST-ERN ARISTO-CRATS!
BLACK DOGGY HOUSE
FIRST-YEAR LEADER:
ROMIO INUZUKA
YOU'RE THE ONES WHO OUGHT TO REMOVE YOUR-SELVES...
...YOU TOU-VANESE ARBARI-ANS.
WHITE CAT HOUSE
FIRST-YEAR LEADER:
JULIET PERSIA
LIKE THEIR COUNTRIES, THE TWO DORMS ARE FEUDING.
AH!
WE'LL BEAT YOU SO BAD YOU'LL HAFTA MISS CLASS!!
DO YOUR WORST!
RAAA
THEY DUKE IT OUT NEARLY EVERY DAY!

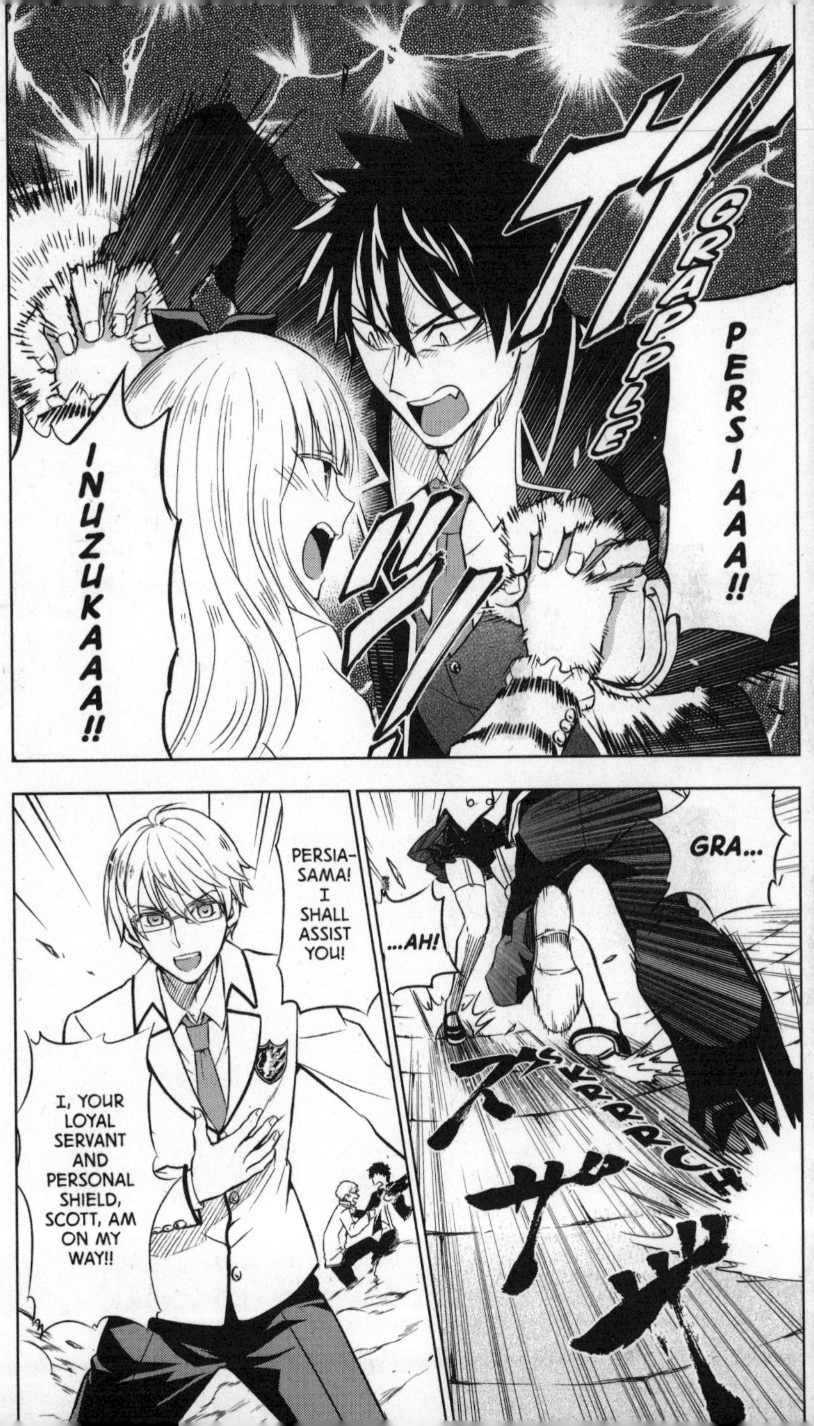
GRAPPLE
PERSIAAAA!!
INUZUKAAAA!!
GRA...
...AH!
SKRRRUCH
PERSIA-SAMA! I SHALL ASSIST YOU!
I, YOUR LOYAL SERVANT AND PERSONAL SHIELD, SCOTT, AM ON MY WAY!!

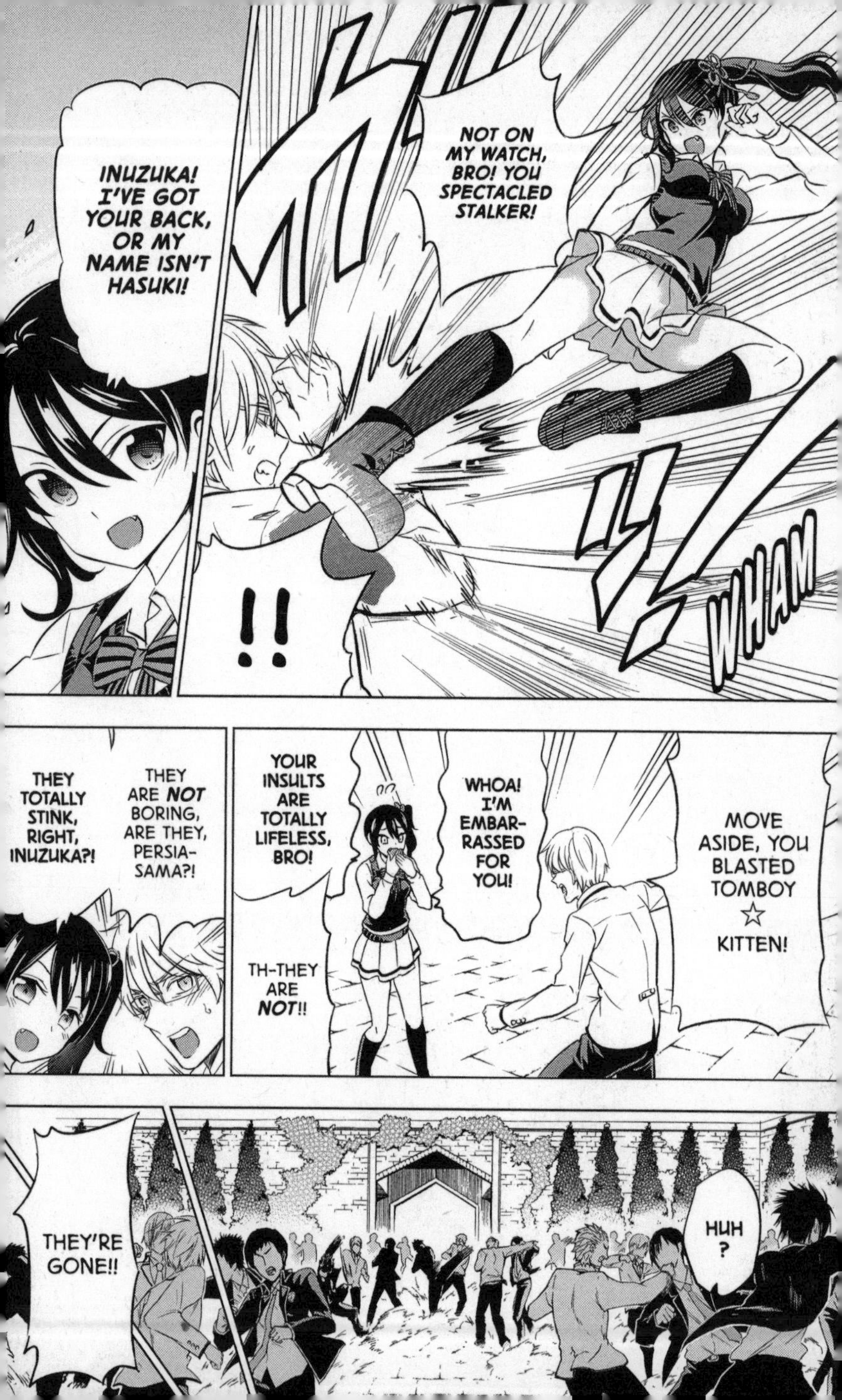
NOT ON MY WATCH, BRO! YOU SPECTACLED STALKER!
WHAM
!!
INUZUKA! I'VE GOT YOUR BACK, OR MY NAME ISN'T HASUKI!
MOVE ASIDE, YOU BLASTED TOMBOY ☆ KITTEN!
WHOA! I'M EMBAR-RASSED FOR YOU!
YOUR INSULTS ARE TOTALLY LIFELESS, BRO!
TH-THEY ARE NOT!!
THEY ARE NOT BORING, ARE THEY, PERSIA-SAMA?!
THEY TOTALLY STINK, RIGHT, INUZUKA?!
HUH?
THEY'RE GONE!!

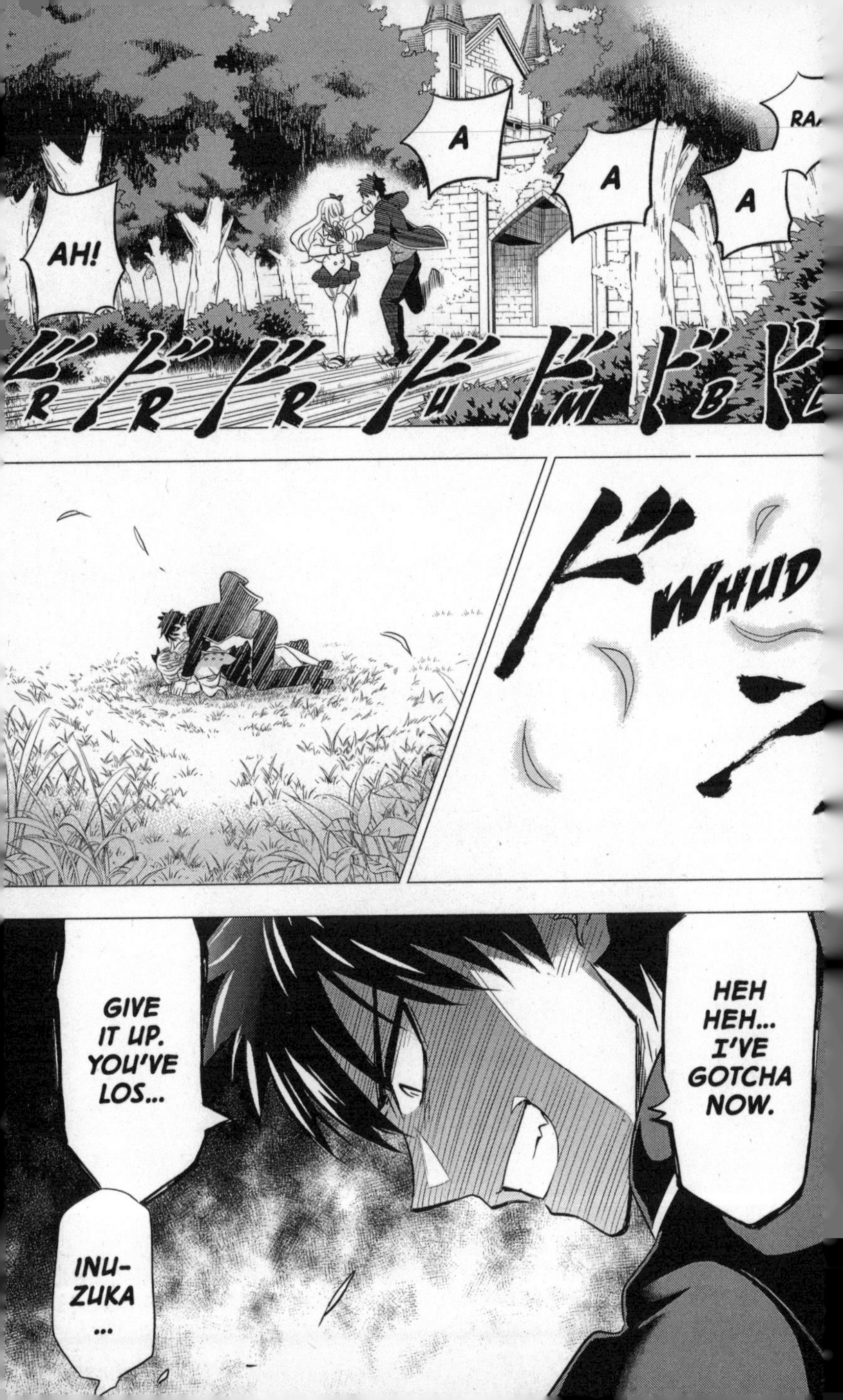
RA
A
A
A
AH!
RRRUMB
WHUD
HEH HEH... I'VE GOTCHA NOW.
GIVE IT UP. YOU'VE LOS...
INU-ZUKA ...

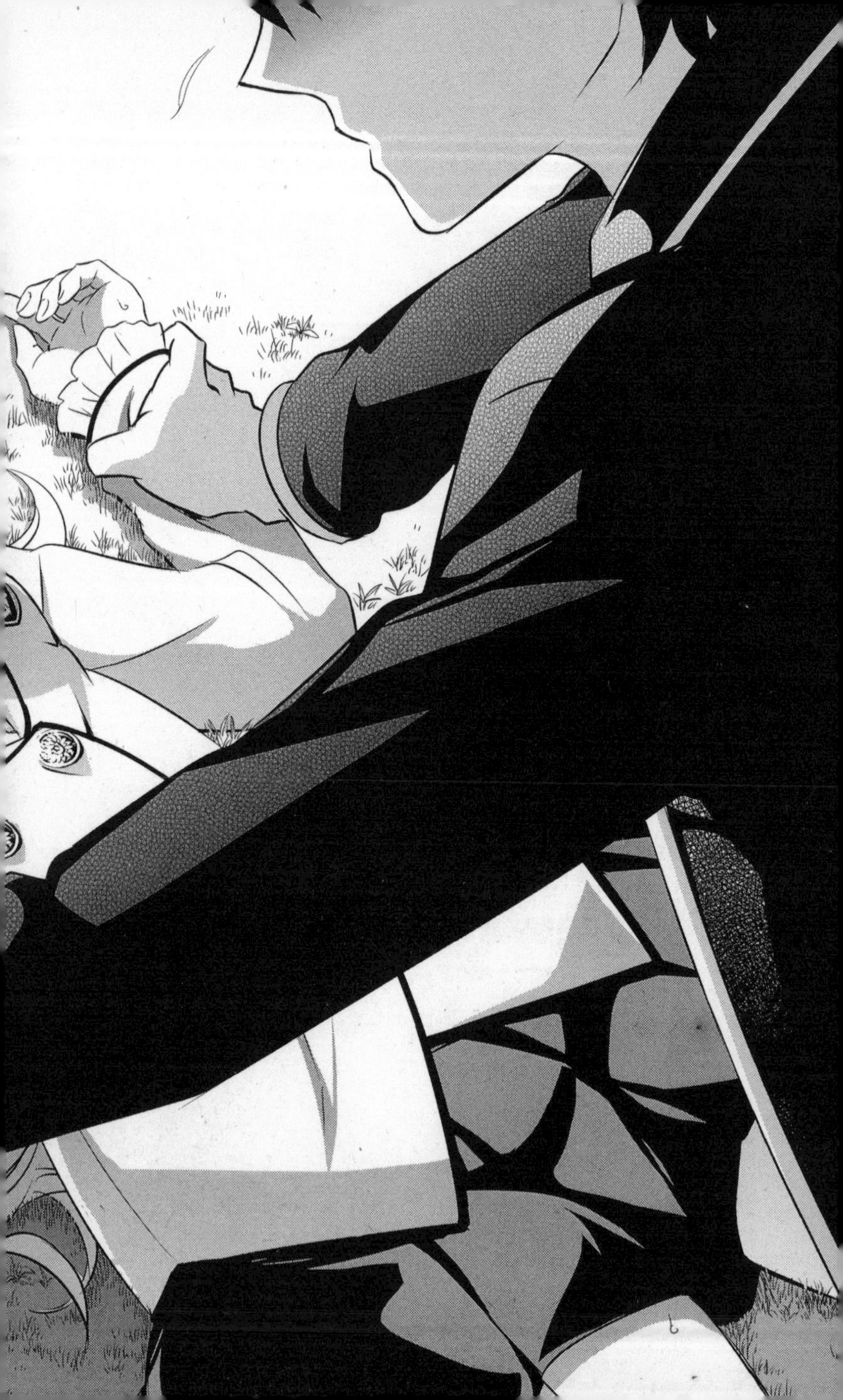

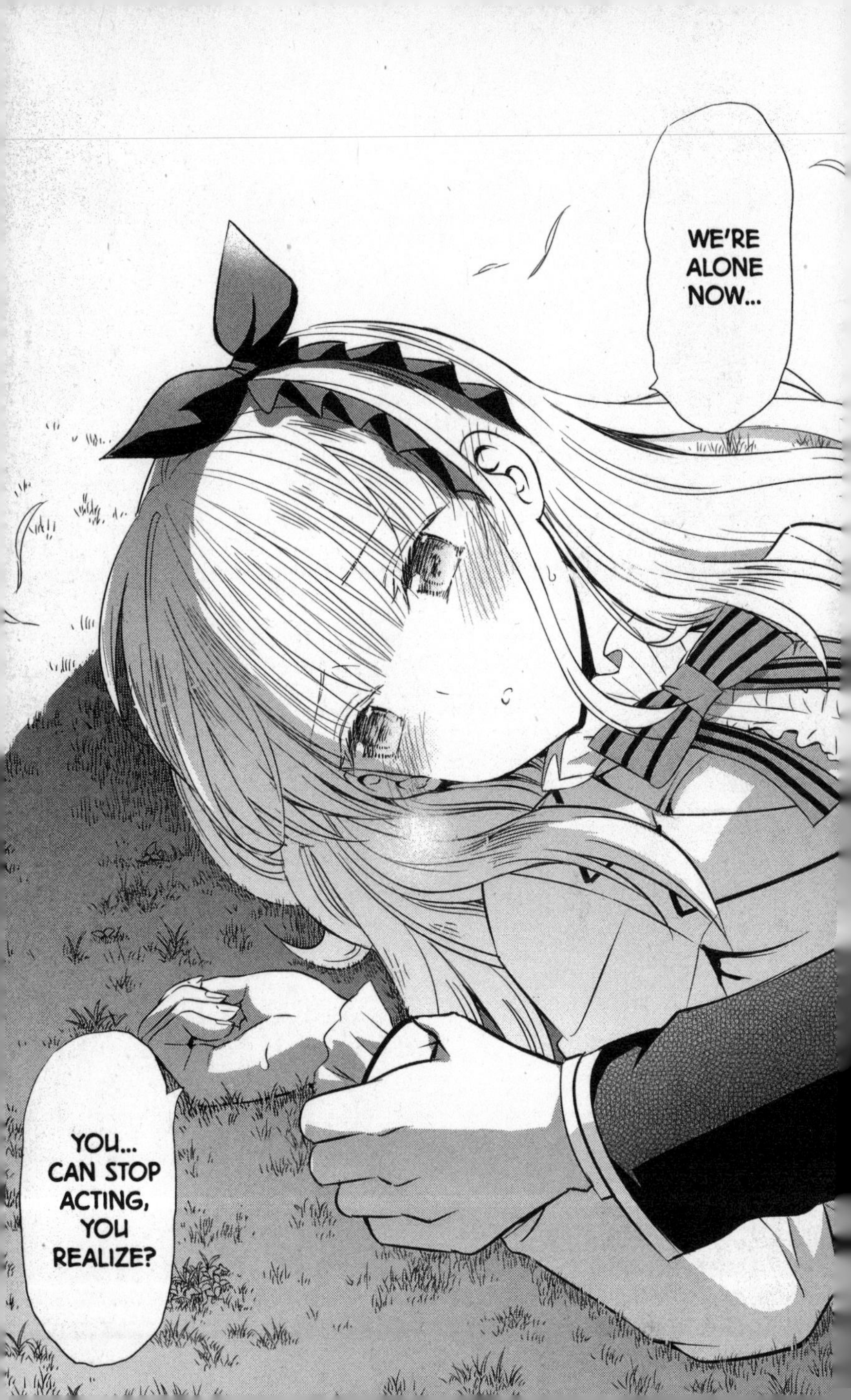
WE'RE ALONE NOW...
YOU... CAN STOP ACTING, YOU REALIZE?

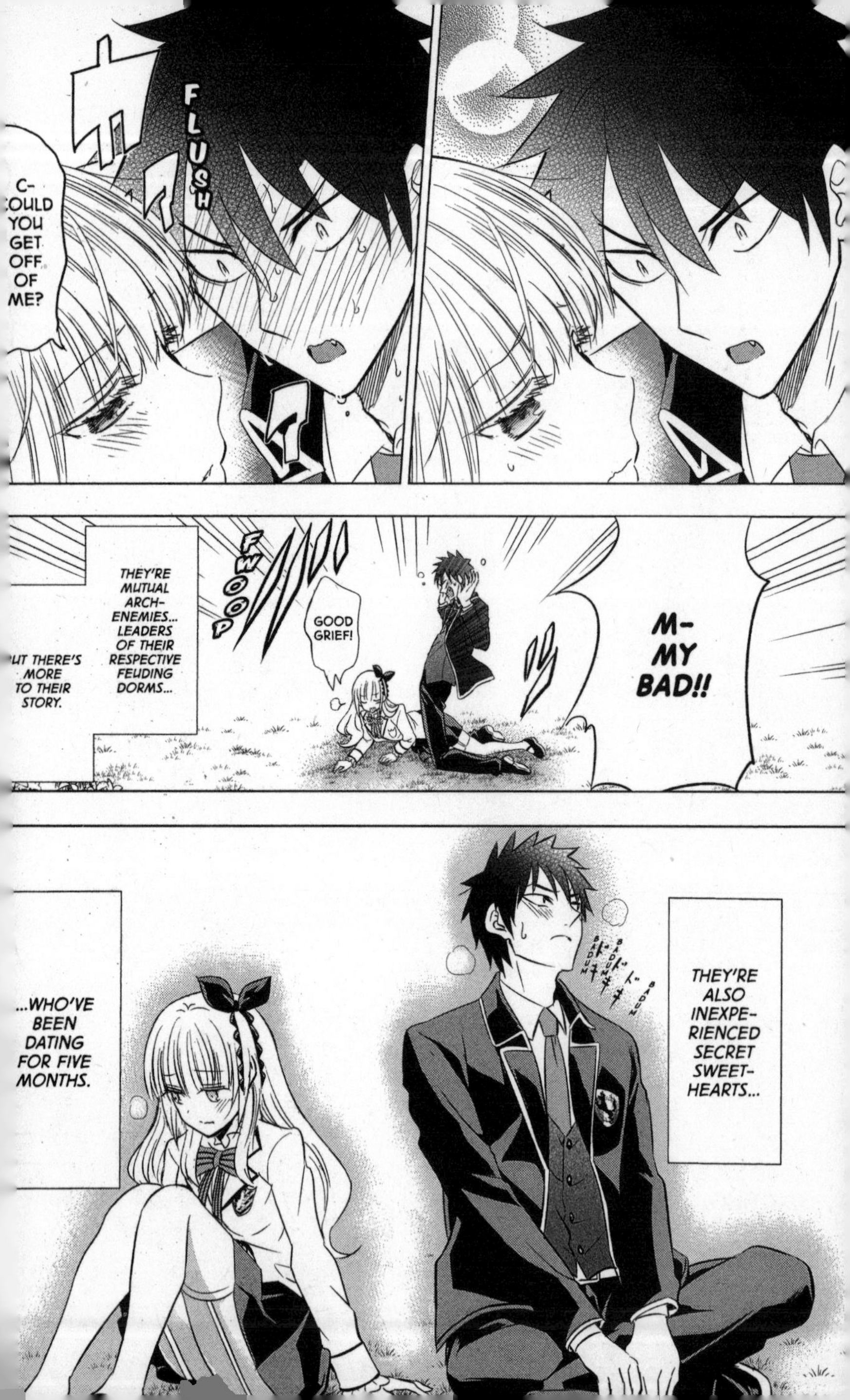

FLUSH
C- OULD YOU GET OFF OF ME?
M-MY BAD!!
GOOD GRIEF!
FWOOOP
THEY'RE MUTUAL ARCH-ENEMIES... LEADERS OF THEIR RESPECTIVE FEUDING DORMS...
UT THERE'S MORE TO THEIR STORY.
THEY'RE ALSO INEXPE-RIENCED SECRET SWEET-HEARTS...
BADUM BADUM BADUM
...WHO'VE BEEN DATING FOR FIVE MONTHS.

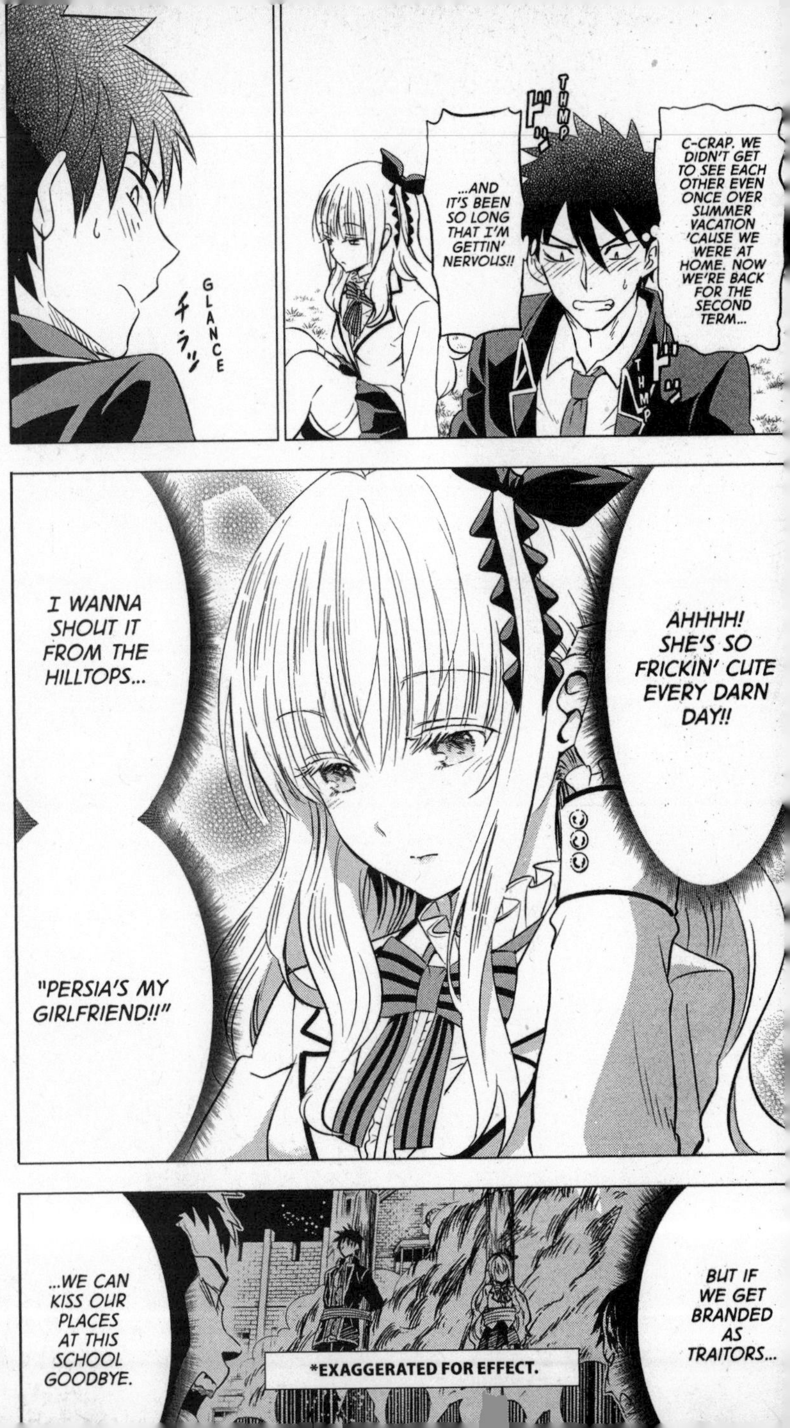
C-CRAP. WE DIDN'T GET TO SEE EACH OTHER EVEN ONCE OVER SUMMER VACATION 'CAUSE WE WERE AT HOME. NOW WE'RE BACK FOR THE SECOND TERM...
ドッ THMP
...AND IT'S BEEN SO LONG THAT I'M GETTIN' NERVOUS!!
ドッ THMP
チラッ GLANCE
AHHHH! SHE'S SO FRICKIN' CUTE EVERY DARN DAY!!
I WANNA SHOUT IT FROM THE HILLTOPS...
"PERSIA'S MY GIRLFRIEND!!"
BUT IF WE GET BRANDED AS TRAITORS...
*EXAGGERATED FOR EFFECT.
...WE CAN KISS OUR PLACES AT THIS SCHOOL GOODBYE.

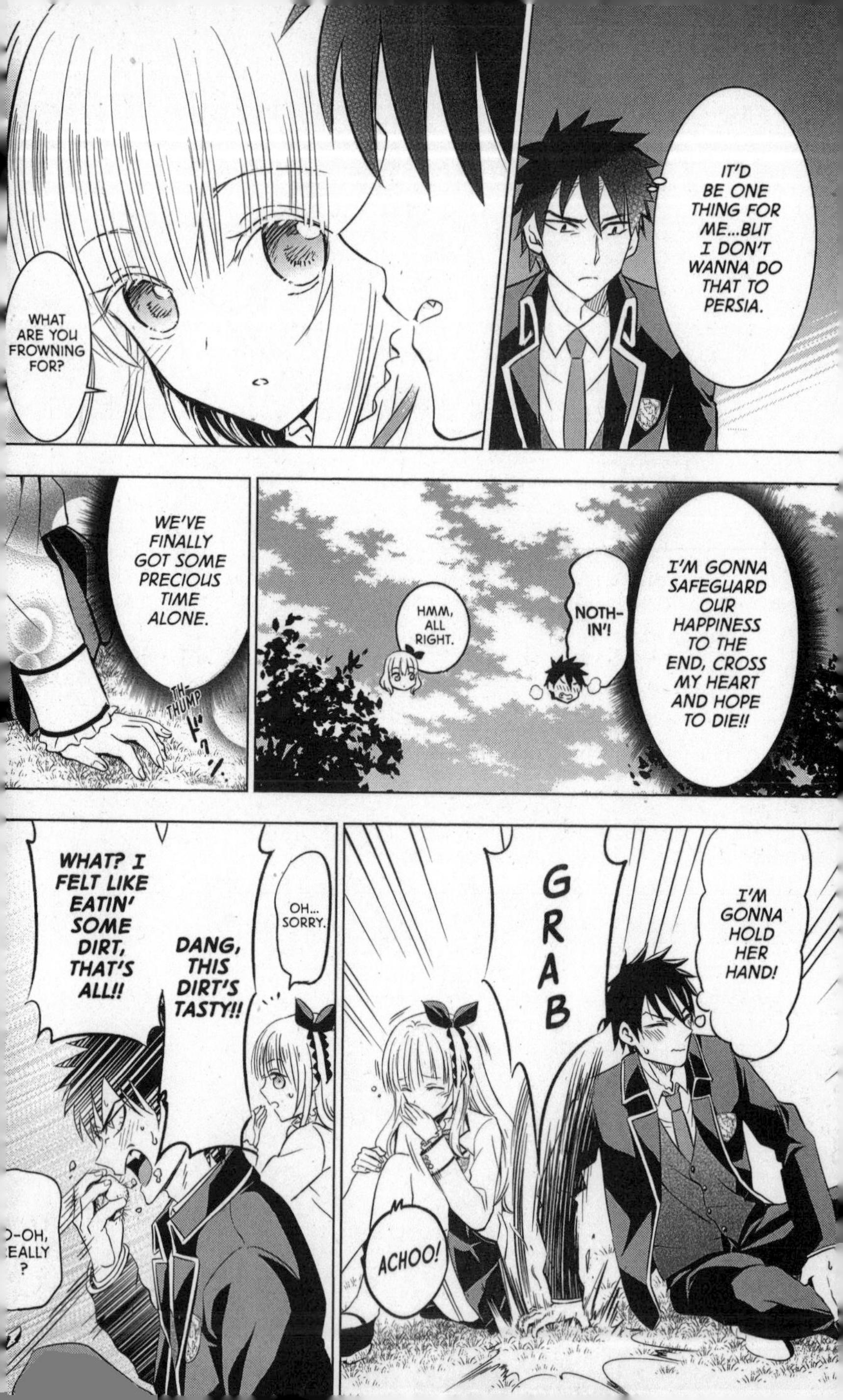
IT'D BE ONE THING FOR ME...BUT I DON'T WANNA DO THAT TO PERSIA.
WHAT ARE YOU FROWNING FOR?
I'M GONNA SAFEGUARD OUR HAPPINESS TO THE END, CROSS MY HEART AND HOPE TO DIE!!
NOTH-IN'!
HMM, ALL RIGHT.
WE'VE FINALLY GOT SOME PRECIOUS TIME ALONE.
TH-THUMP
I'M GONNA HOLD HER HAND!
GRAB
ACHOO!
OH... SORRY.
WHAT? I FELT LIKE EATIN' SOME DIRT, THAT'S ALL!!
DANG, THIS DIRT'S TASTY!!
-OH, EALLY ?

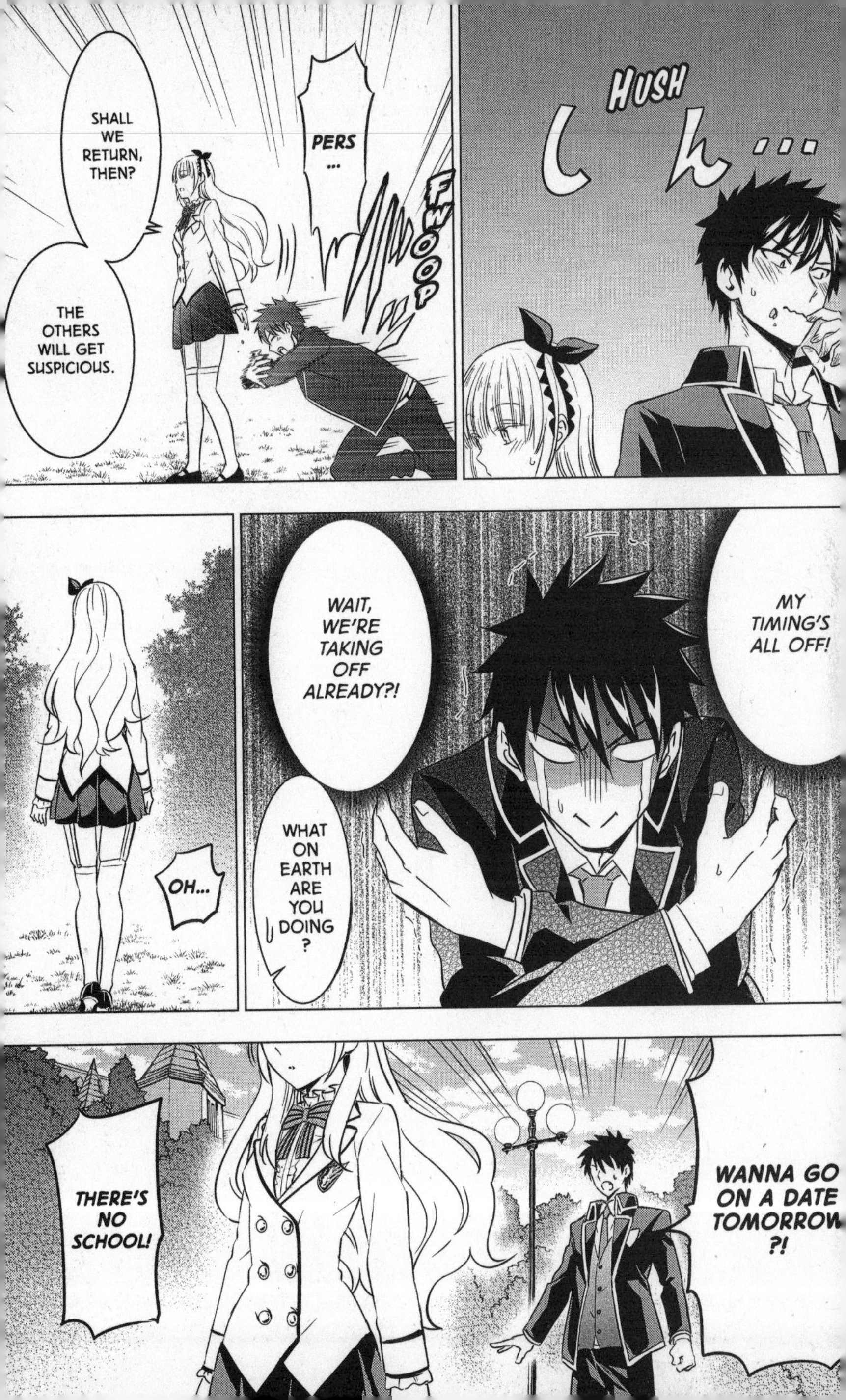
HUSH
しん…
PERS…
FWOOOP
SHALL WE RETURN, THEN?
THE OTHERS WILL GET SUSPICIOUS.
MY TIMING'S ALL OFF!
WAIT, WE'RE TAKING OFF ALREADY?!
WHAT ON EARTH ARE YOU DOING?
OH…
WANNA GO ON A DATE TOMORROW?!
THERE'S NO SCHOOL!

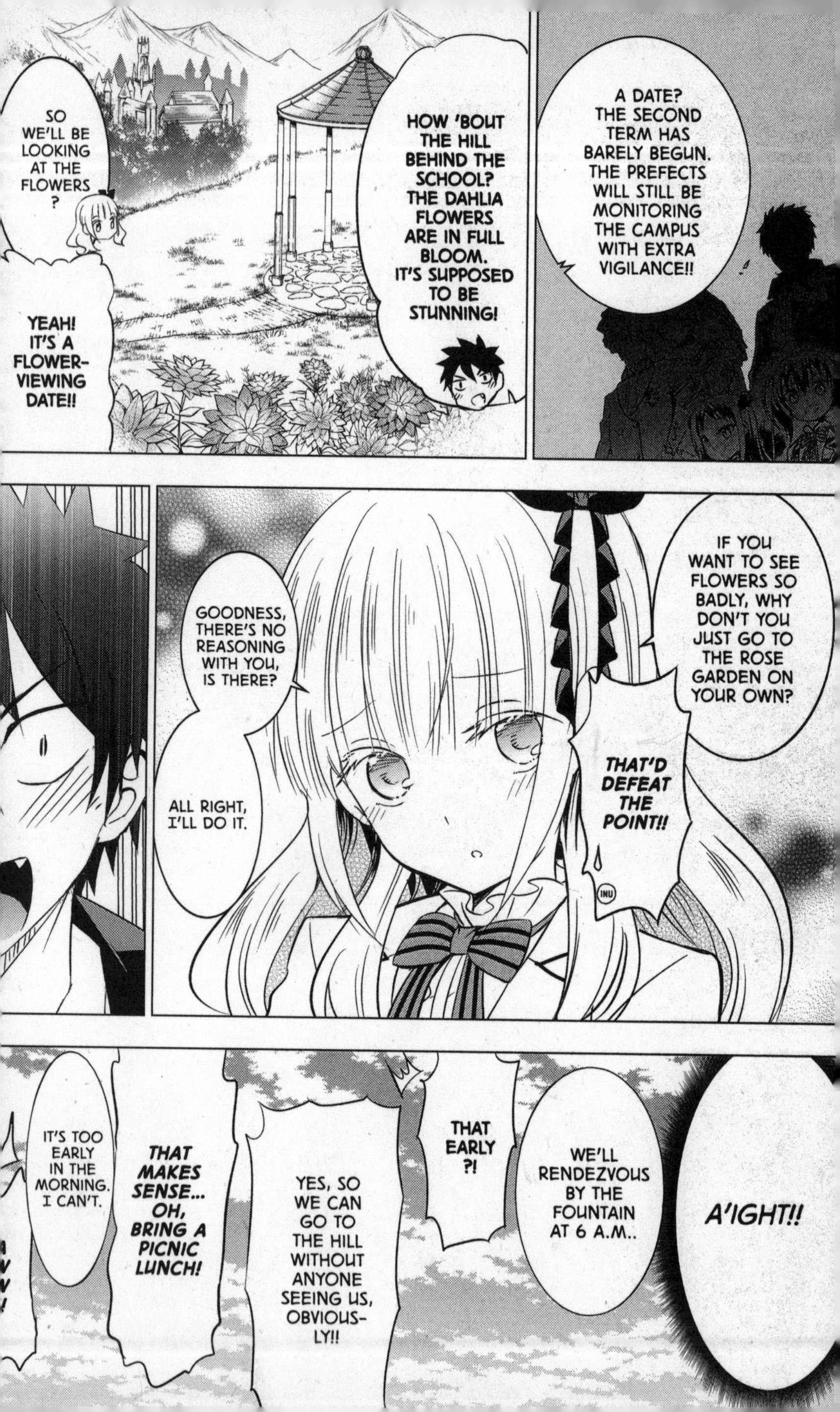
A DATE? THE SECOND TERM HAS BARELY BEGUN. THE PREFECTS WILL STILL BE MONITORING THE CAMPUS WITH EXTRA VIGILANCE!!
HOW 'BOUT THE HILL BEHIND THE SCHOOL? THE DAHLIA FLOWERS ARE IN FULL BLOOM. IT'S SUPPOSED TO BE STUNNING!
SO WE'LL BE LOOKING AT THE FLOWERS?
YEAH! IT'S A FLOWER-VIEWING DATE!!
IF YOU WANT TO SEE FLOWERS SO BADLY, WHY DON'T YOU JUST GO TO THE ROSE GARDEN ON YOUR OWN?
THAT'D DEFEAT THE POINT!!
GOODNESS, THERE'S NO REASONING WITH YOU, IS THERE?
ALL RIGHT, I'LL DO IT.
A'IGHT!!
WE'LL RENDEZVOUS BY THE FOUNTAIN AT 6 A.M..
THAT EARLY?!
YES, SO WE CAN GO TO THE HILL WITHOUT ANYONE SEEING US, OBVIOUSLY!!
THAT MAKES SENSE... OH, BRING A PICNIC LUNCH!
IT'S TOO EARLY IN THE MORNING. I CAN'T.

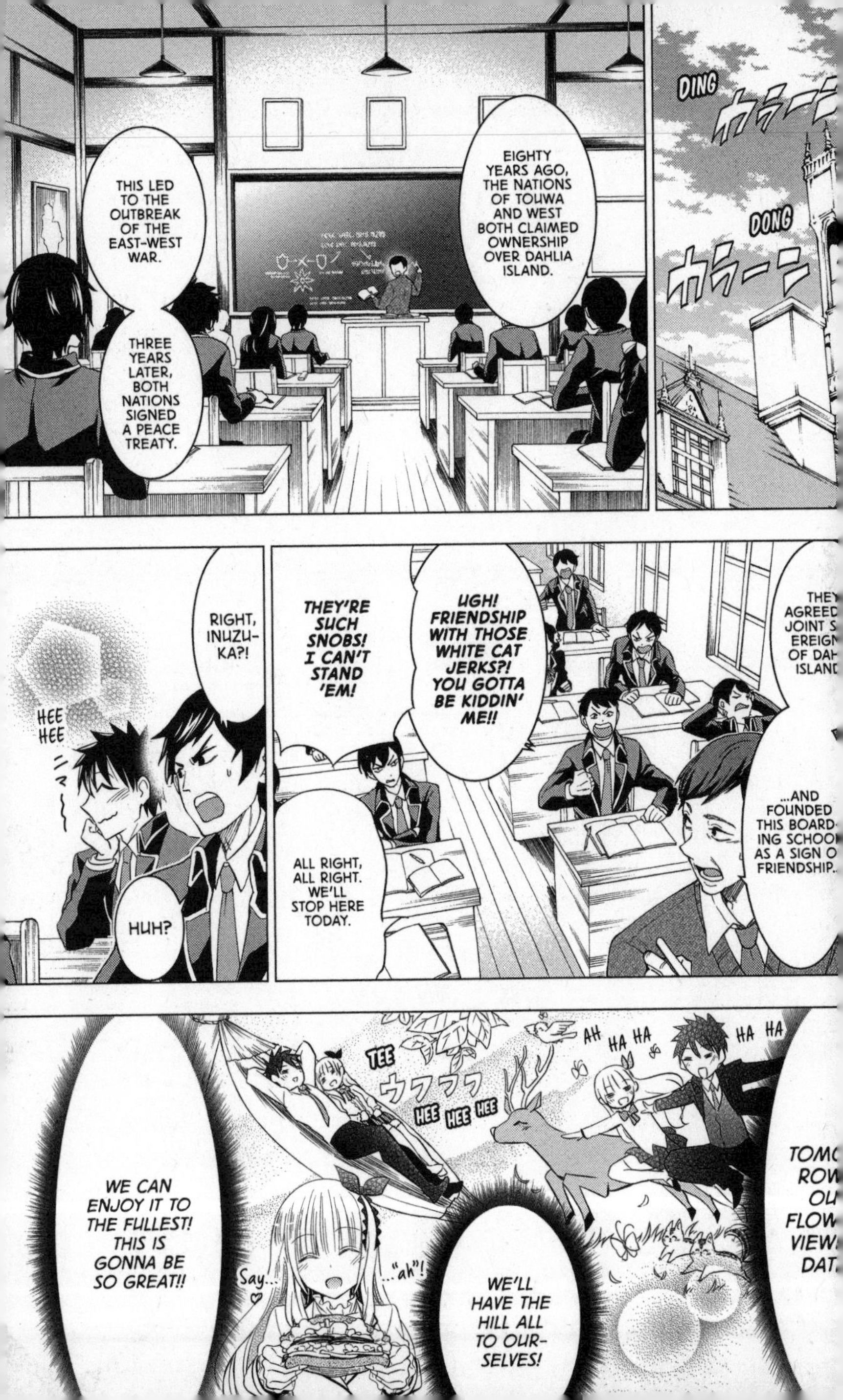
DING
ウラーン
DONG
ウラーン
EIGHTY YEARS AGO, THE NATIONS OF TOUWA AND WEST BOTH CLAIMED OWNERSHIP OVER DAHLIA ISLAND.
THIS LED TO THE OUTBREAK OF THE EAST-WEST WAR.
THREE YEARS LATER, BOTH NATIONS SIGNED A PEACE TREATY.
THEY AGREED JOINT S EREIGN OF DAH ISLAND
...AND FOUNDED THIS BOARD-ING SCHOO AS A SIGN O FRIENDSHIP...
UGH! FRIENDSHIP WITH THOSE WHITE CAT JERKS?! YOU GOTTA BE KIDDIN' ME!!
THEY'RE SUCH SNOBS! I CAN'T STAND 'EM!
ALL RIGHT, ALL RIGHT. WE'LL STOP HERE TODAY.
RIGHT, INUZUKA?!
HEE HEE
ニマ〜
HUH?
TOMO ROW OU FLOW VIEW DAT
HA HA
AH HA HA
TEE
ウフフフ
HEE HEE HEE
WE'LL HAVE THE HILL ALL TO OUR-SELVES!
Say...
..."ah"!
WE CAN ENJOY IT TO THE FULLEST! THIS IS GONNA BE SO GREAT!!

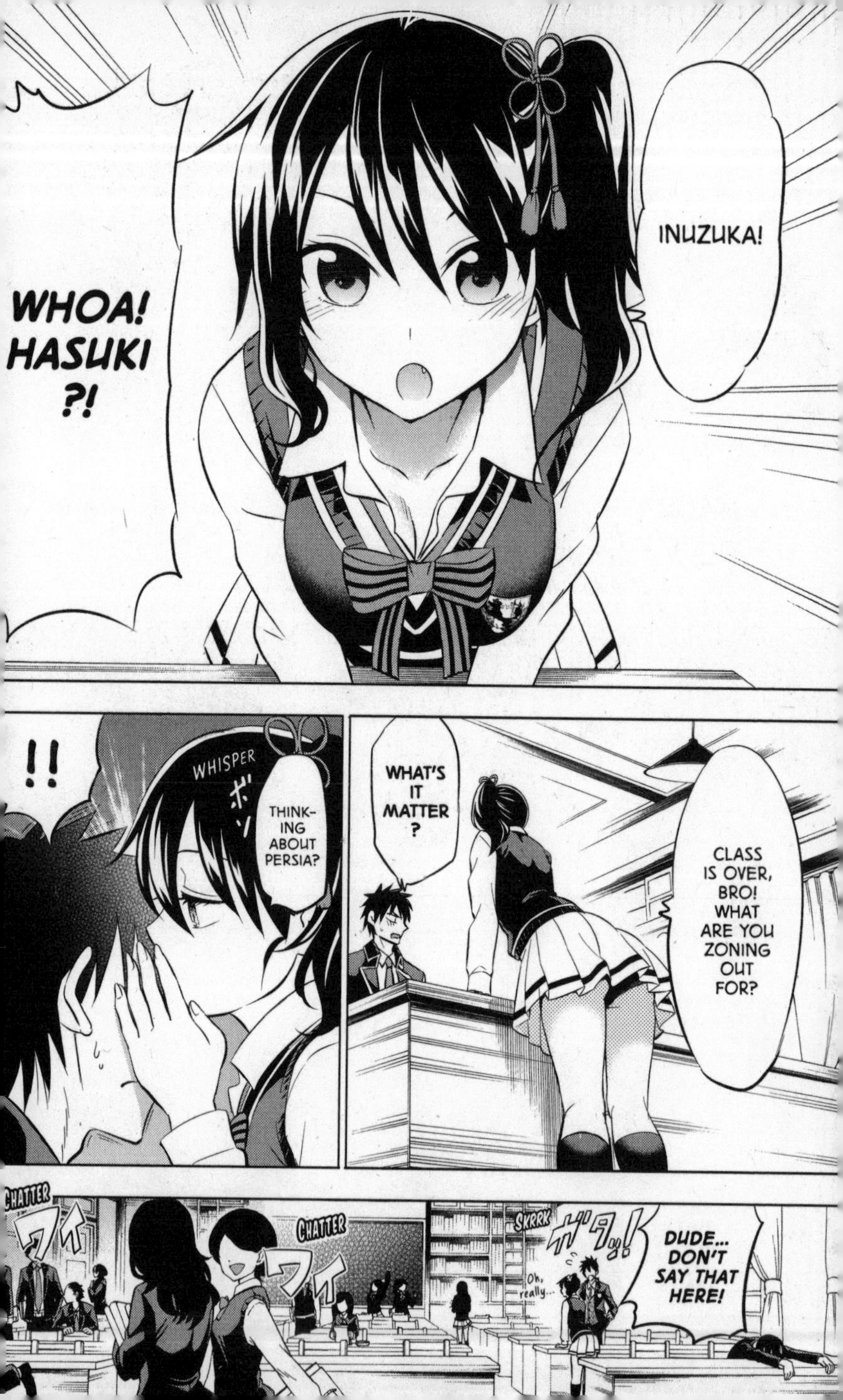
INUZUKA!
WHOA! HASUKI ?!
CLASS IS OVER, BRO! WHAT ARE YOU ZONING OUT FOR?
WHAT'S IT MATTER ?
THINKING-ING ABOUT PERSIA?
WHISPER
!!
DUDE... DON'T SAY THAT HERE!
SKRRK
Oh, really...
CHATTER
CHATTER

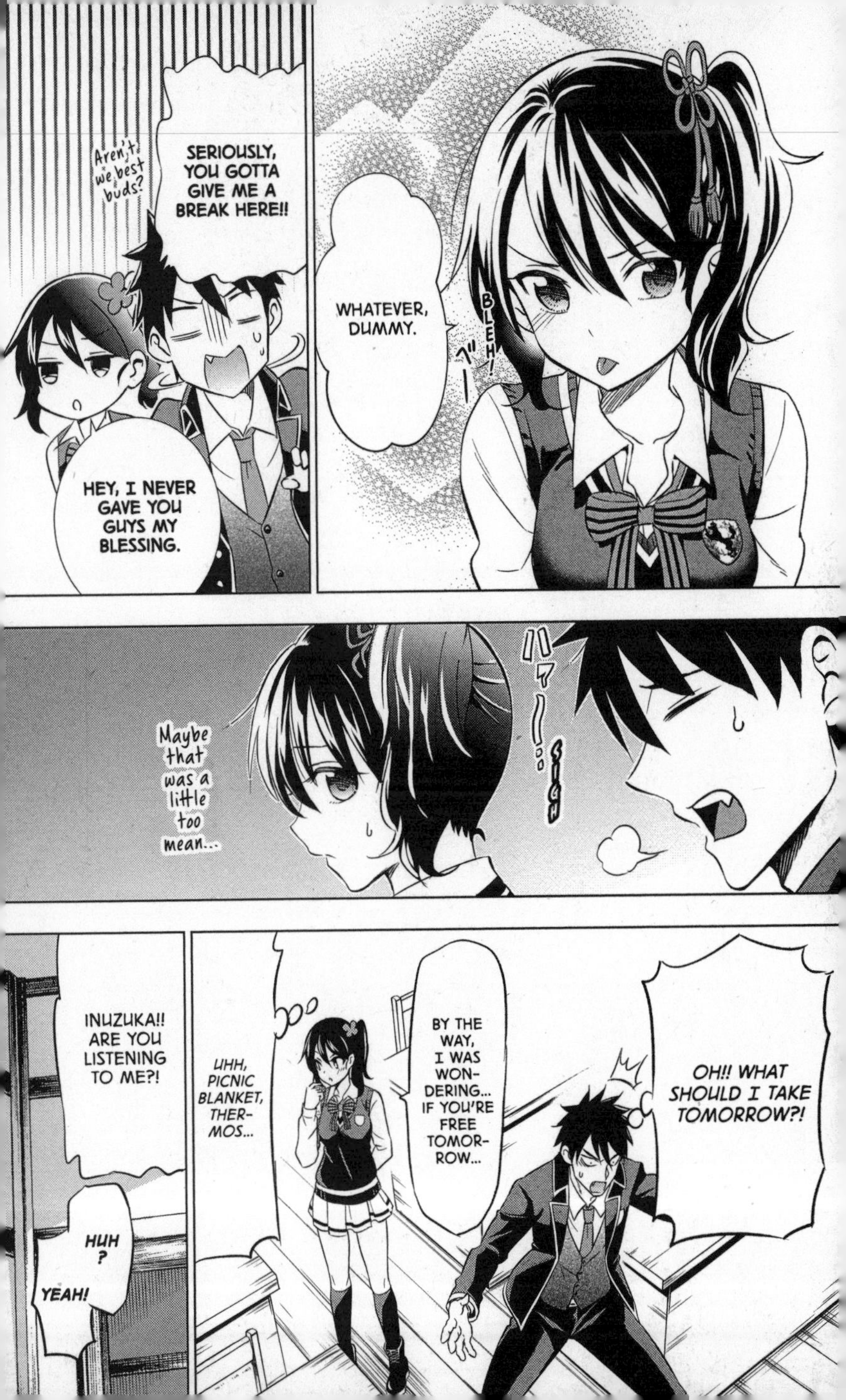
WHATEVER, DUMMY.
BLEH!
SERIOUSLY, YOU GOTTA GIVE ME A BREAK HERE!!
Aren't we best buds?
HEY, I NEVER GAVE YOU GUYS MY BLESSING.
SIGH
Maybe that was a little too mean...
OH!! WHAT SHOULD I TAKE TOMORROW?!
BY THE WAY, I WAS WON-DERING... IF YOU'RE FREE TOMOR-ROW...
UHH, PICNIC BLANKET, THER-MOS...
INUZUKA!! ARE YOU LISTENING TO ME?!
HUH?
YEAH!

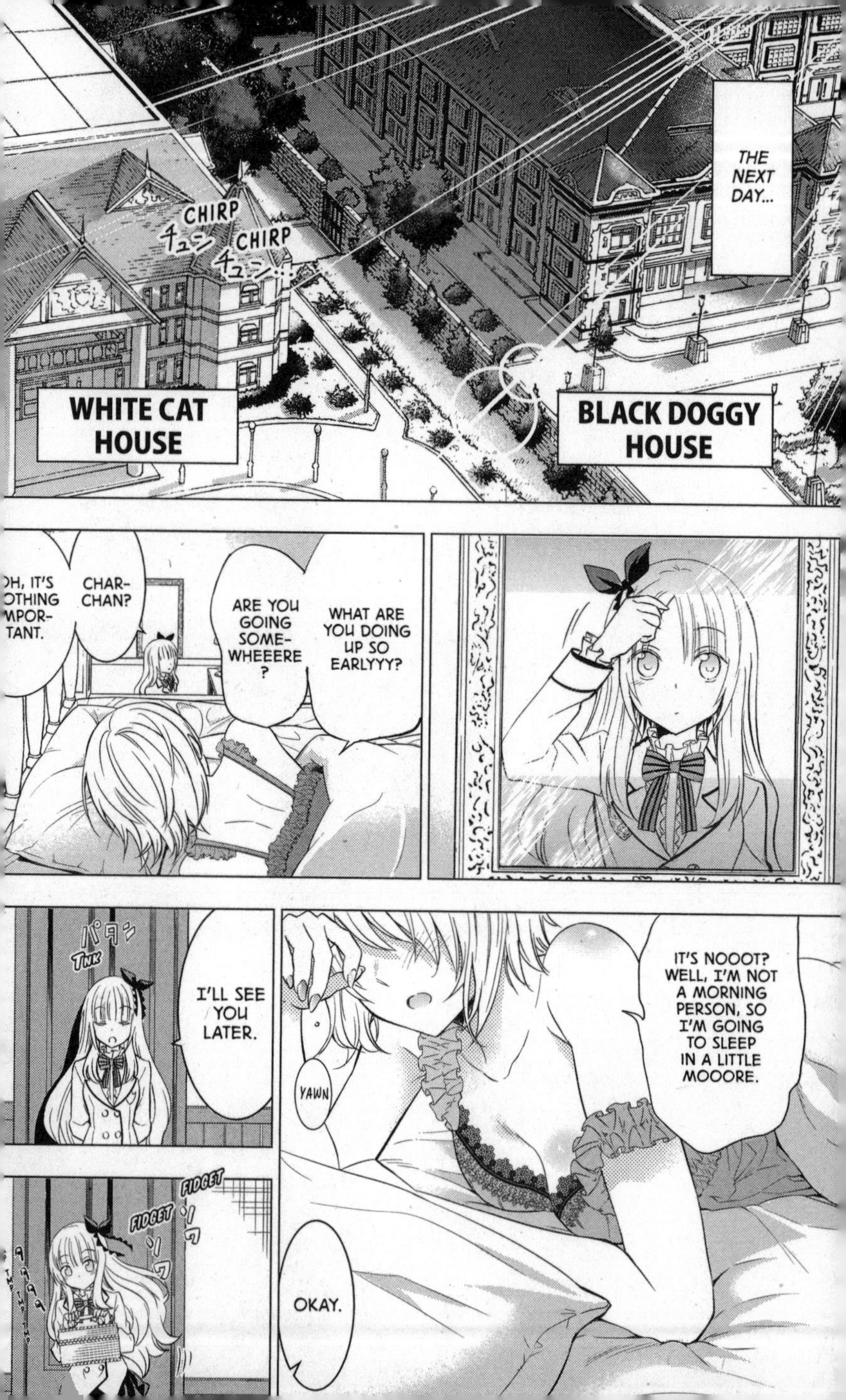
THE NEXT DAY...
BLACK DOGGY HOUSE
CHIRP チュン CHIRP チュン...
WHITE CAT HOUSE
WHAT ARE YOU DOING UP SO EARLYYY?
ARE YOU GOING SOME-WHEEERE?
CHAR-CHAN?
DH, IT'S OTHING MPOR-TANT.
IT'S NOOOT? WELL, I'M NOT A MORNING PERSON, SO I'M GOING TO SLEEP IN A LITTLE MOOORE.
YAWN
OKAY.
I'LL SEE YOU LATER.
パタン
TMK
FIDGET ソワ
FIDGET ソワ
タタタタ
THP THP THP

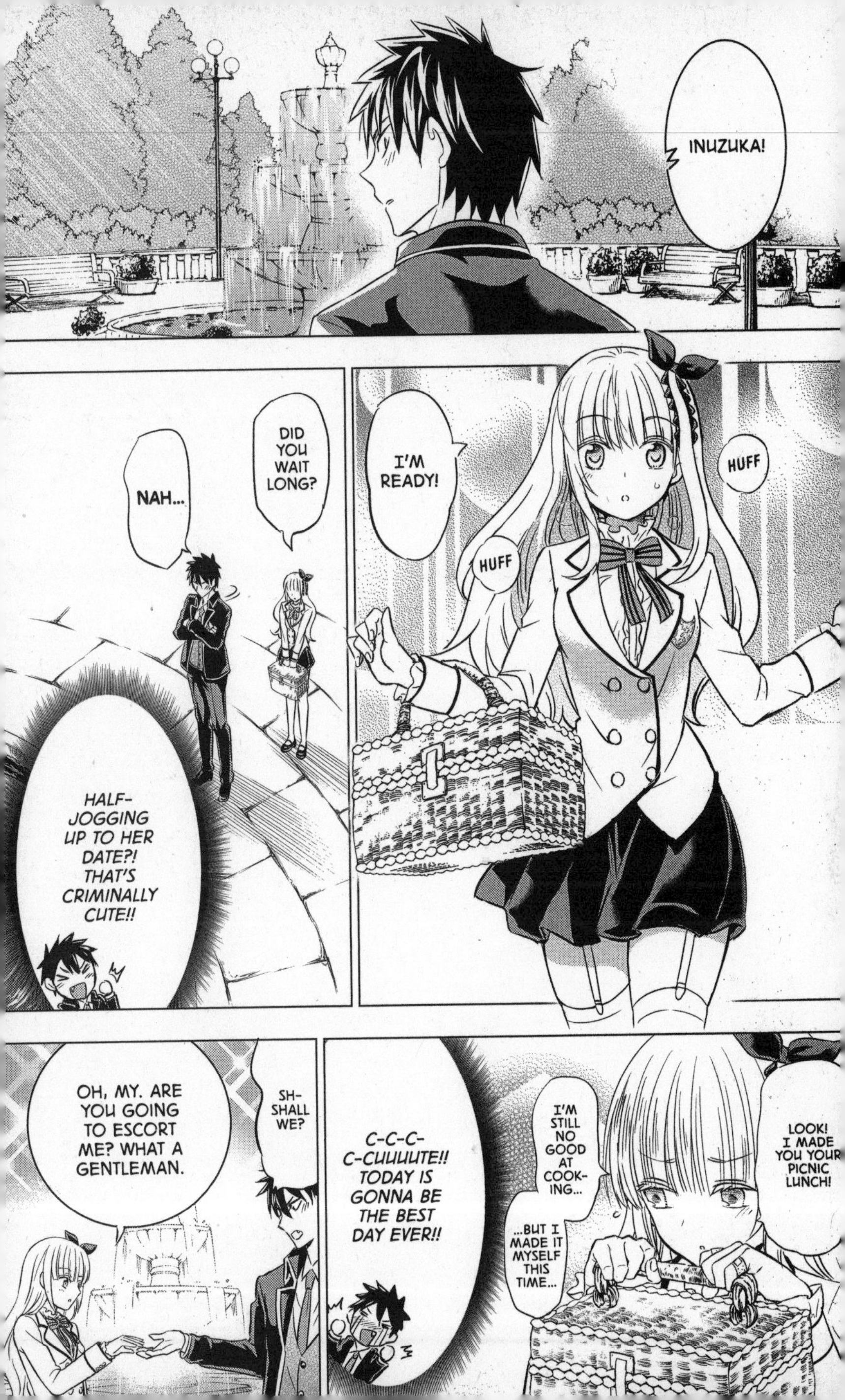
INUZUKA!
HUFF
I'M READY!
HUFF
DID YOU WAIT LONG?
NAH...
HALF-JOGGING UP TO HER DATE?! THAT'S CRIMINALLY CUTE!!
LOOK! I MADE YOU YOUR PICNIC LUNCH!
I'M STILL NO GOOD AT COOK-ING...
...BUT I MADE IT MYSELF THIS TIME...
C-C-C-C-CUUUUTE!! TODAY IS GONNA BE THE BEST DAY EVER!!
SH-SHALL WE?
OH, MY. ARE YOU GOING TO ESCORT ME? WHAT A GENTLEMAN.

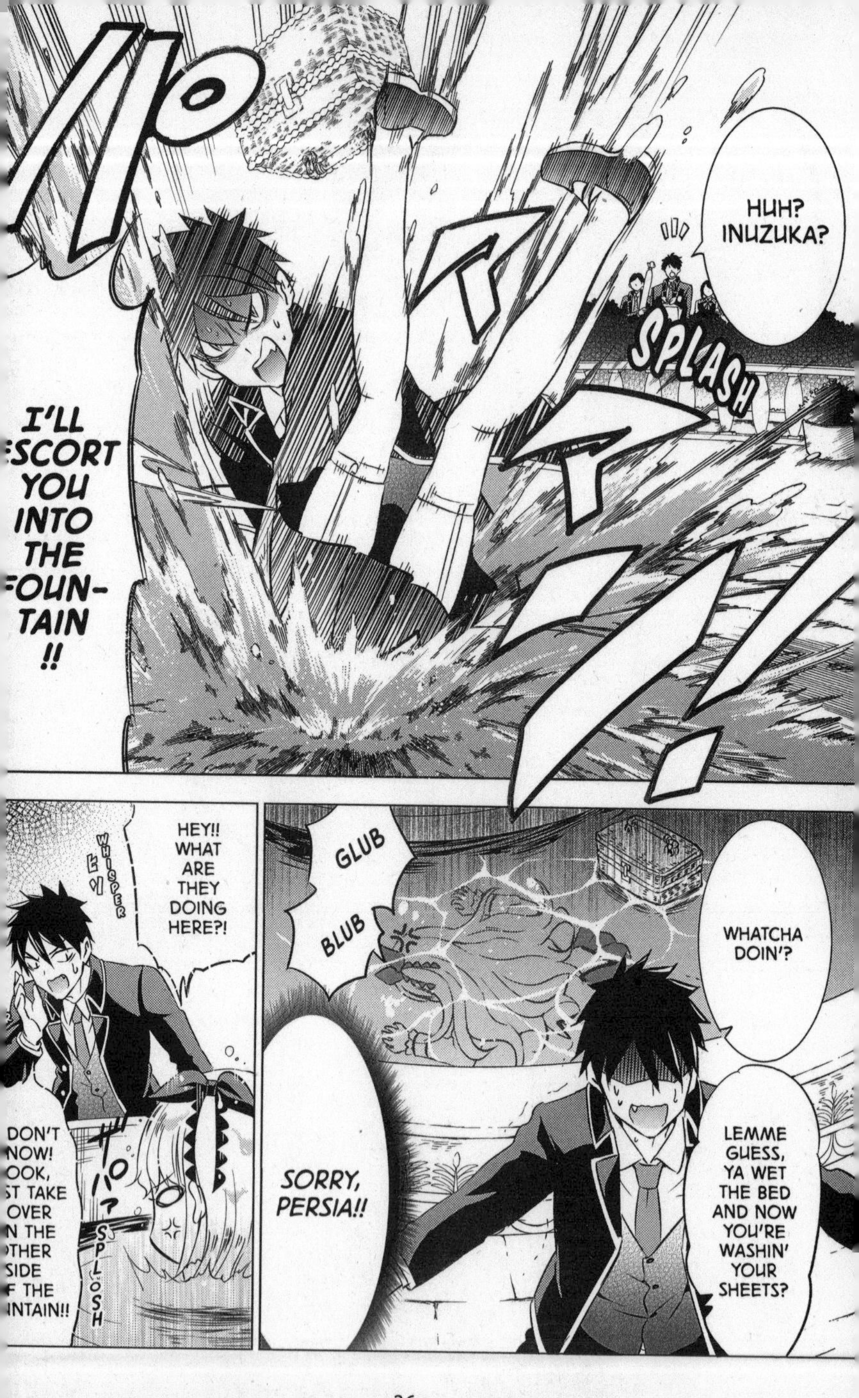
HUH? INUZUKA?
SPLASH
I'LL ESCORT YOU INTO THE FOUN-TAIN!!
WHATCHA DOIN'?
LEMME GUESS, YA WET THE BED AND NOW YOU'RE WASHIN' YOUR SHEETS?
GLUB
BLUB
SORRY, PERSIA!!
HEY!! WHAT ARE THEY DOING HERE?!
WHISPER
DON'T NOW! OOK, ST TAKE OVER N THE THER SIDE F THE NTAIN!!
SPLOSH

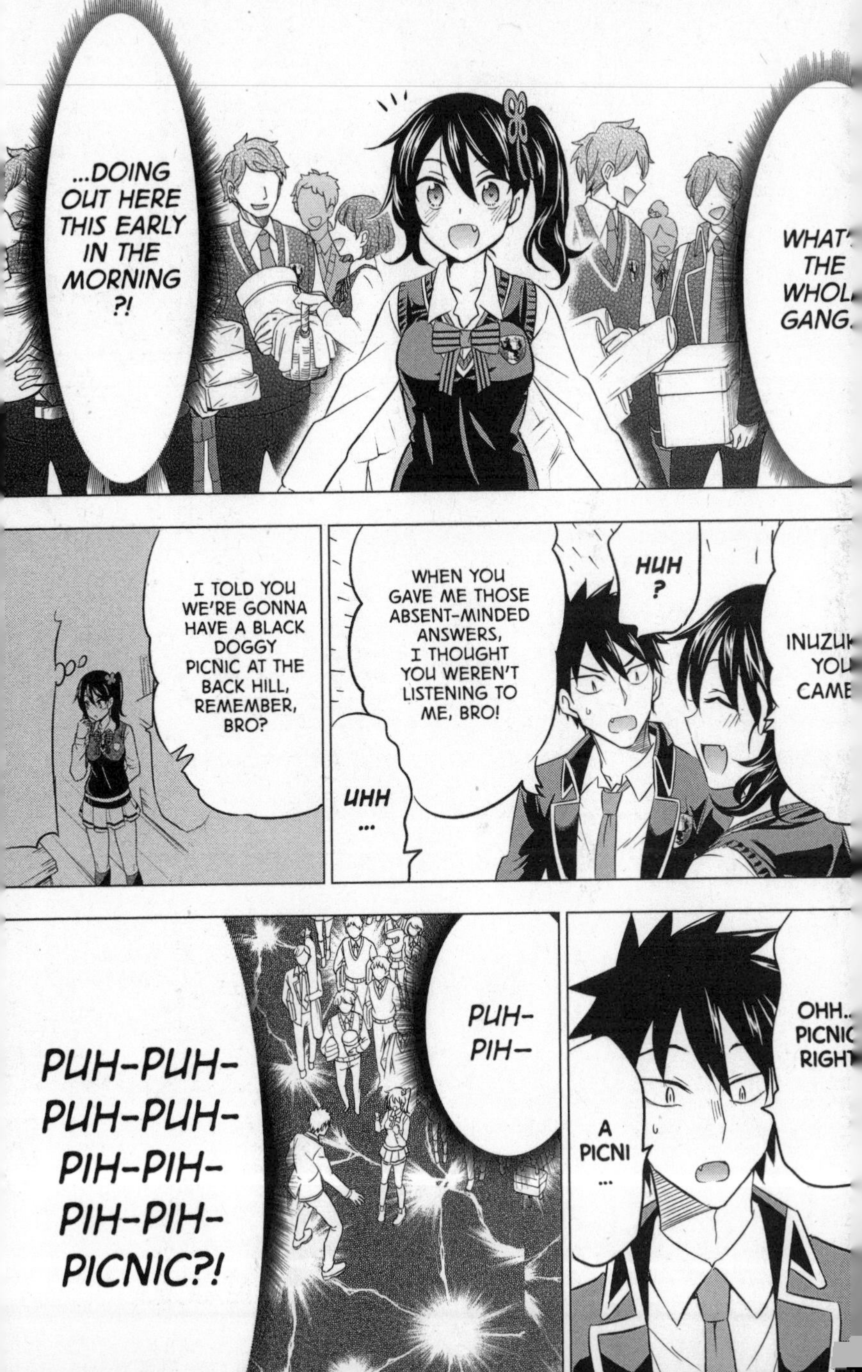
WHAT' THE WHOL GANG.
...DOING OUT HERE THIS EARLY IN THE MORNING ?!
INUZUK YOU CAME
HUH ?
WHEN YOU GAVE ME THOSE ABSENT-MINDED ANSWERS, I THOUGHT YOU WEREN'T LISTENING TO ME, BRO!
UHH ...
I TOLD YOU WE'RE GONNA HAVE A BLACK DOGGY PICNIC AT THE BACK HILL, REMEMBER, BRO?
OHH.. PICNIC RIGHT
A PICNI ...
PUH-PIH–
PUH-PUH-PUH-PUH-PIH-PIH-PIH-PIH-PICNIC?!

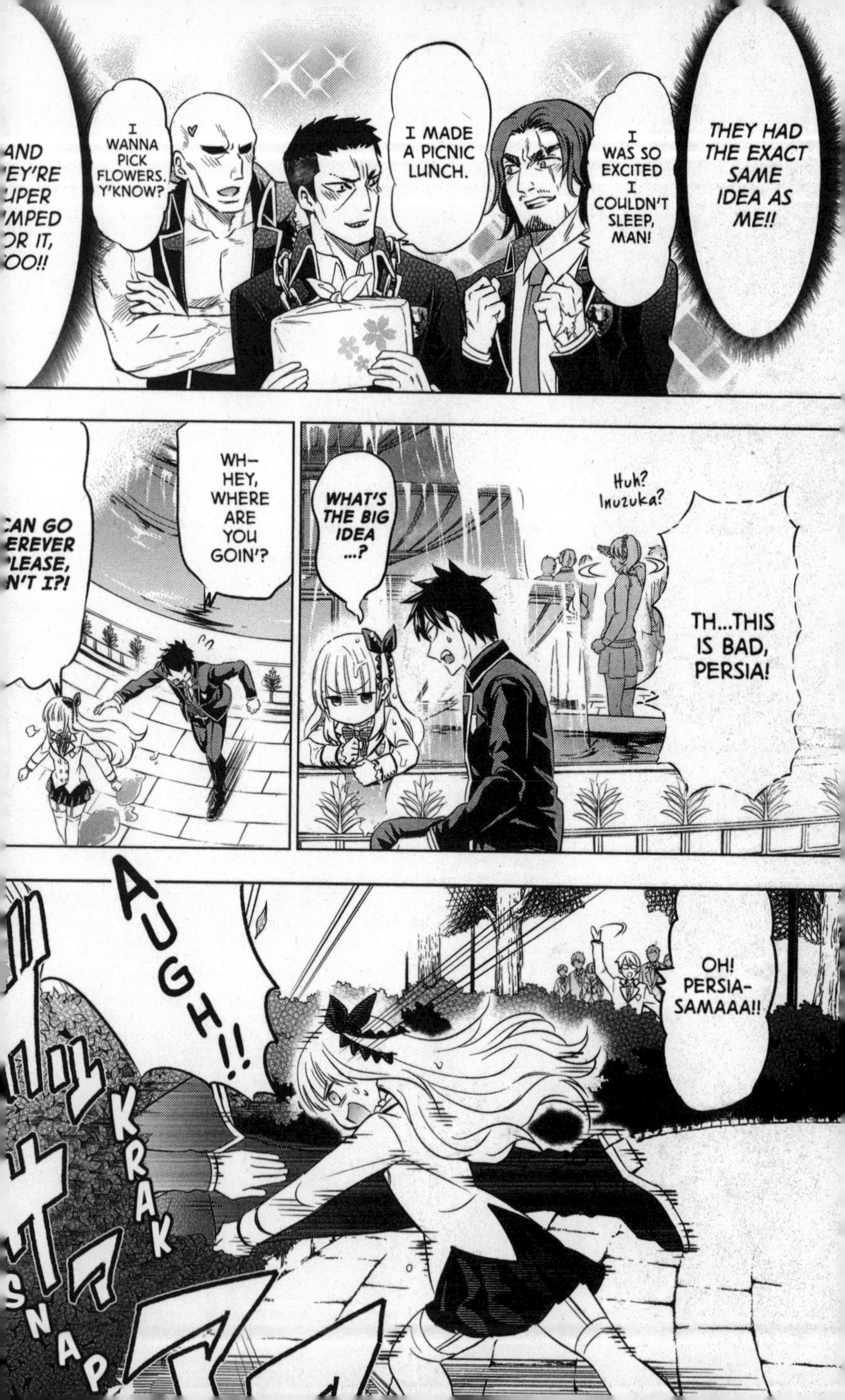
THEY HAD THE EXACT SAME IDEA AS ME!!
I WAS SO EXCITED I COULDN'T SLEEP, MAN!
I MADE A PICNIC LUNCH.
I WANNA PICK FLOWERS. Y'KNOW?
AND EY'RE UPER MPED OR IT, OO!!
TH...THIS IS BAD, PERSIA!
Huh? Inuzuka?
WHAT'S THE BIG IDEA ...?
WH— HEY, WHERE ARE YOU GOIN'?
CAN GO EREVER LEASE, N'T I?!
OH! PERSIA-SAMAAA!!
AUGH!!
KRAK
SNAP

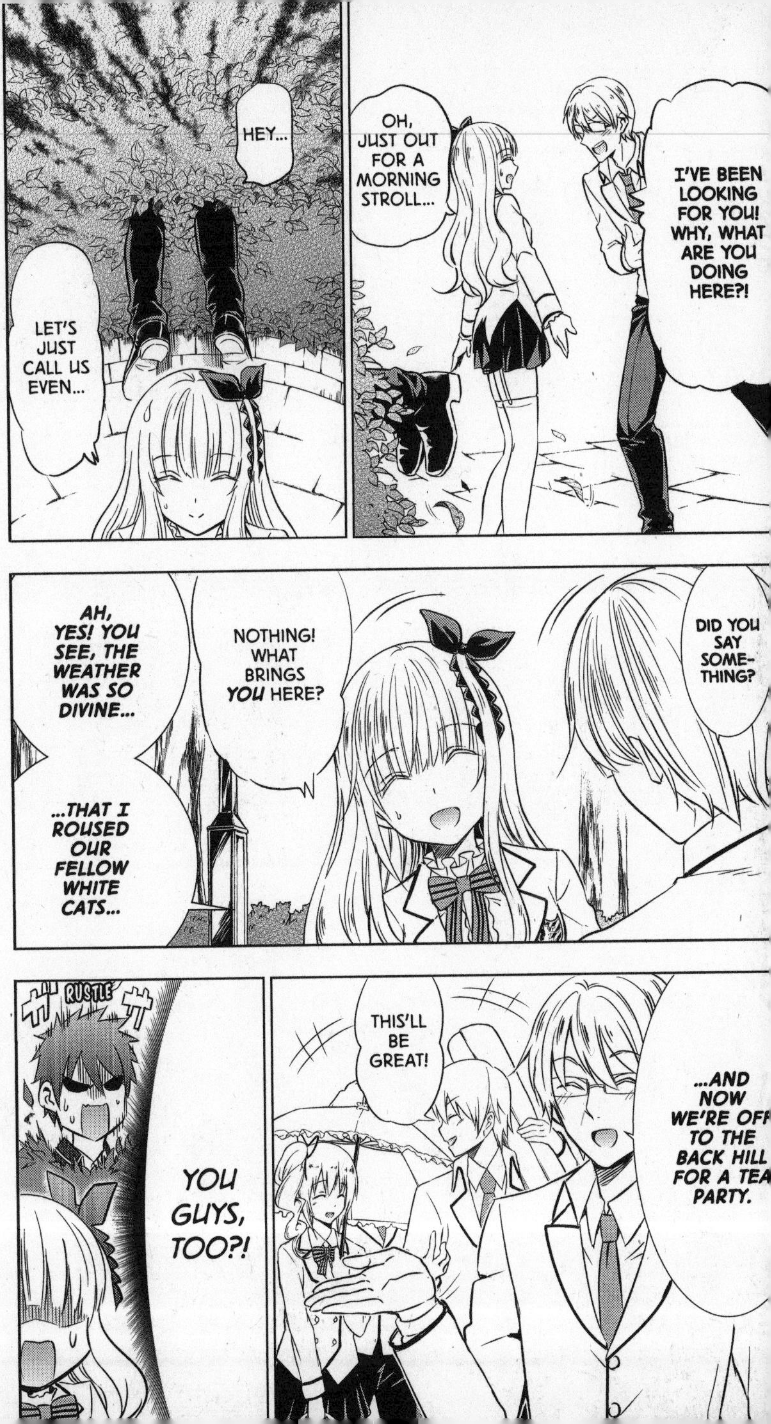
I'VE BEEN LOOKING FOR YOU! WHY, WHAT ARE YOU DOING HERE?!
OH, JUST OUT FOR A MORNING STROLL...
HEY...
LET'S JUST CALL US EVEN...
DID YOU SAY SOME-THING?
NOTHING! WHAT BRINGS YOU HERE?
AH, YES! YOU SEE, THE WEATHER WAS SO DIVINE...
...THAT I ROUSED OUR FELLOW WHITE CATS...
...AND NOW WE'RE OFF TO THE BACK HILL FOR A TEA PARTY.
THIS'LL BE GREAT!
RUSTLE
YOU GUYS, TOO?!

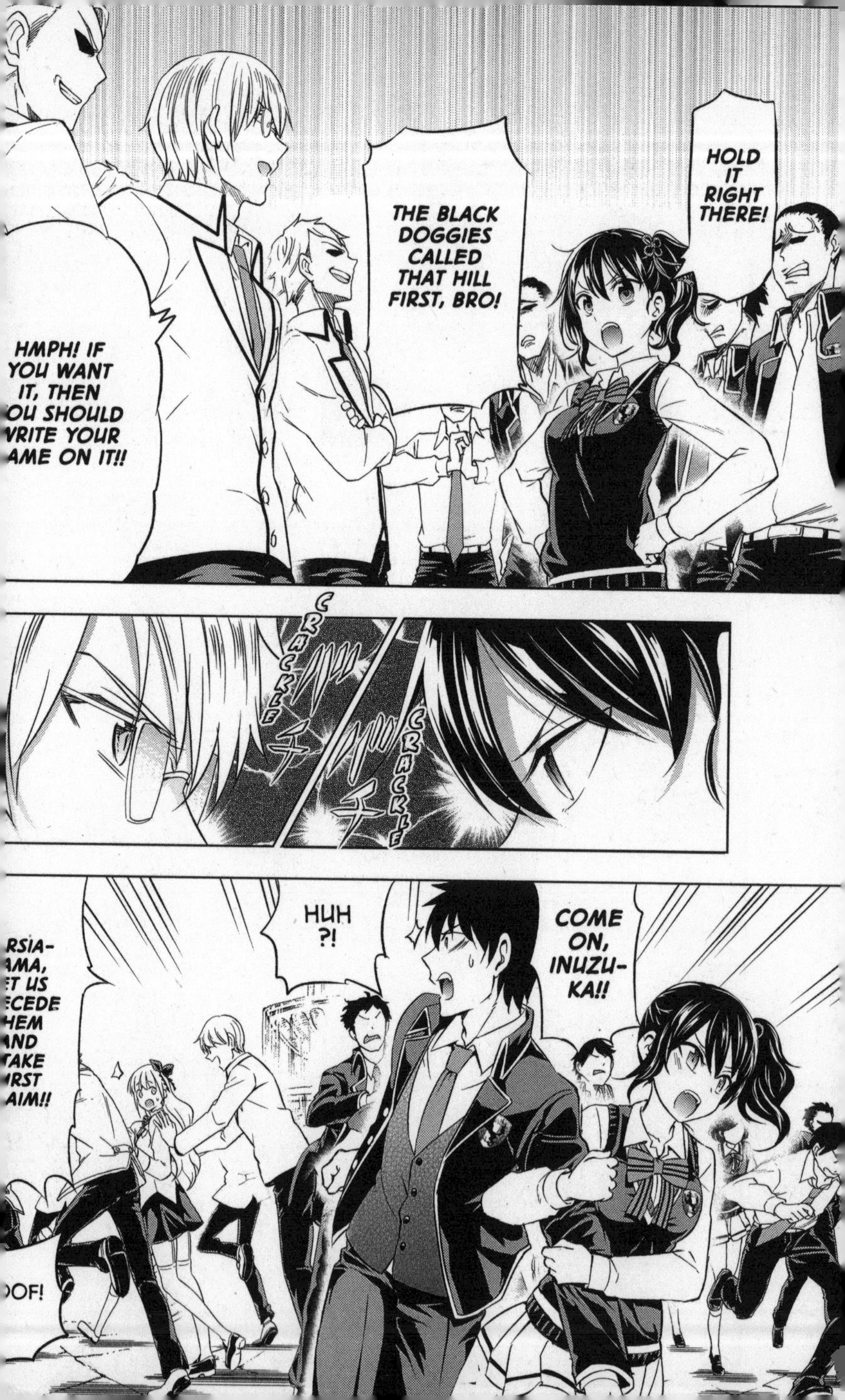

HOLD IT RIGHT THERE!
THE BLACK DOGGIES CALLED THAT HILL FIRST, BRO!
HMPH! IF YOU WANT IT, THEN OU SHOULD VRITE YOUR AME ON IT!!
CRACKLE
チ
CRACKLE
チ
COME ON, INUZU-KA!!
HUH ?!
RSIA-AMA, ET US ECEDE HEM AND TAKE IRST AIM!!
OOF!

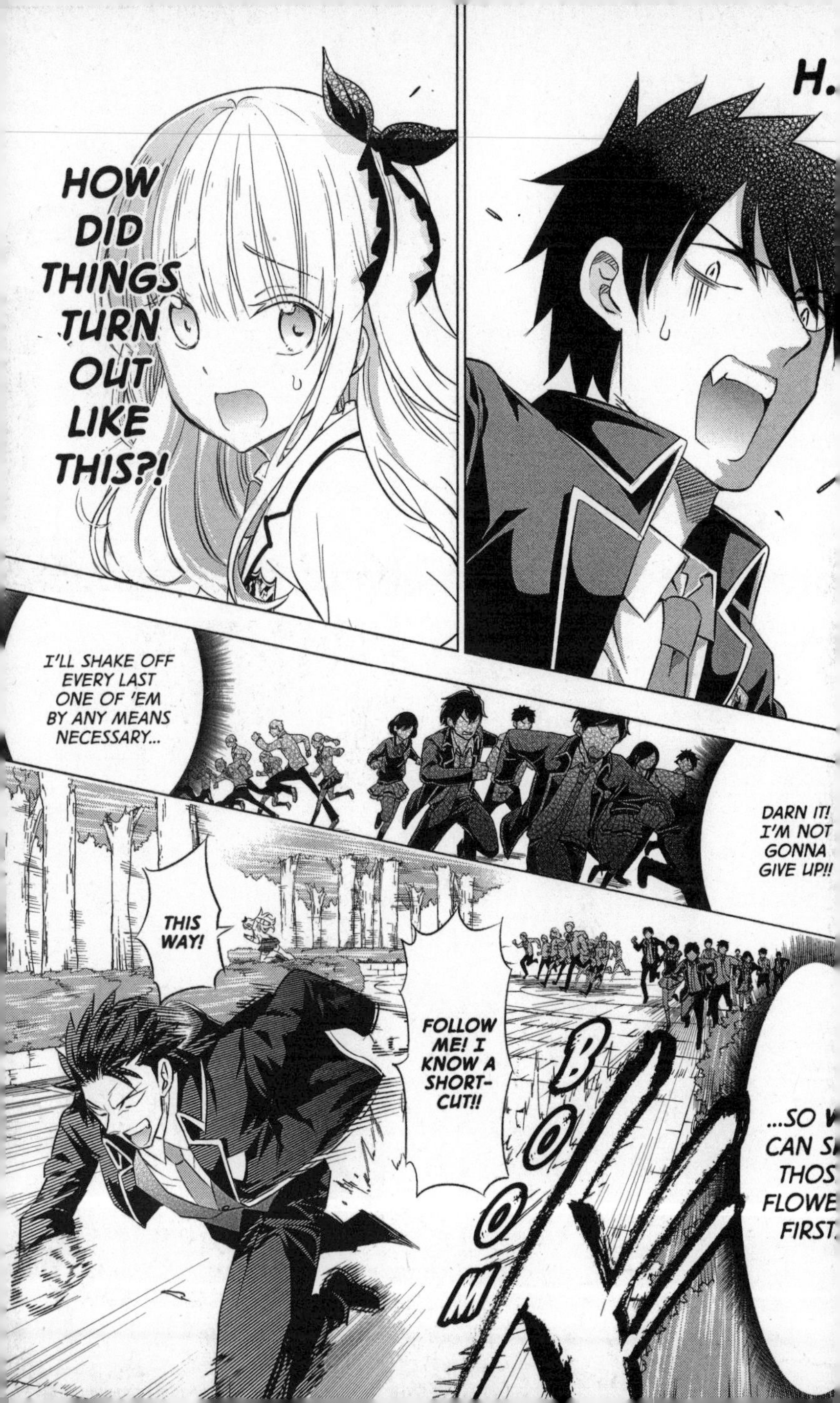
H..
HOW DID THINGS TURN OUT LIKE THIS?!
DARN IT! I'M NOT GONNA GIVE UP!!
I'LL SHAKE OFF EVERY LAST ONE OF 'EM BY ANY MEANS NECESSARY...
...SO W CAN S THOS FLOWE FIRST.
BOOOM
FOLLOW ME! I KNOW A SHORT-CUT!!
THIS WAY!

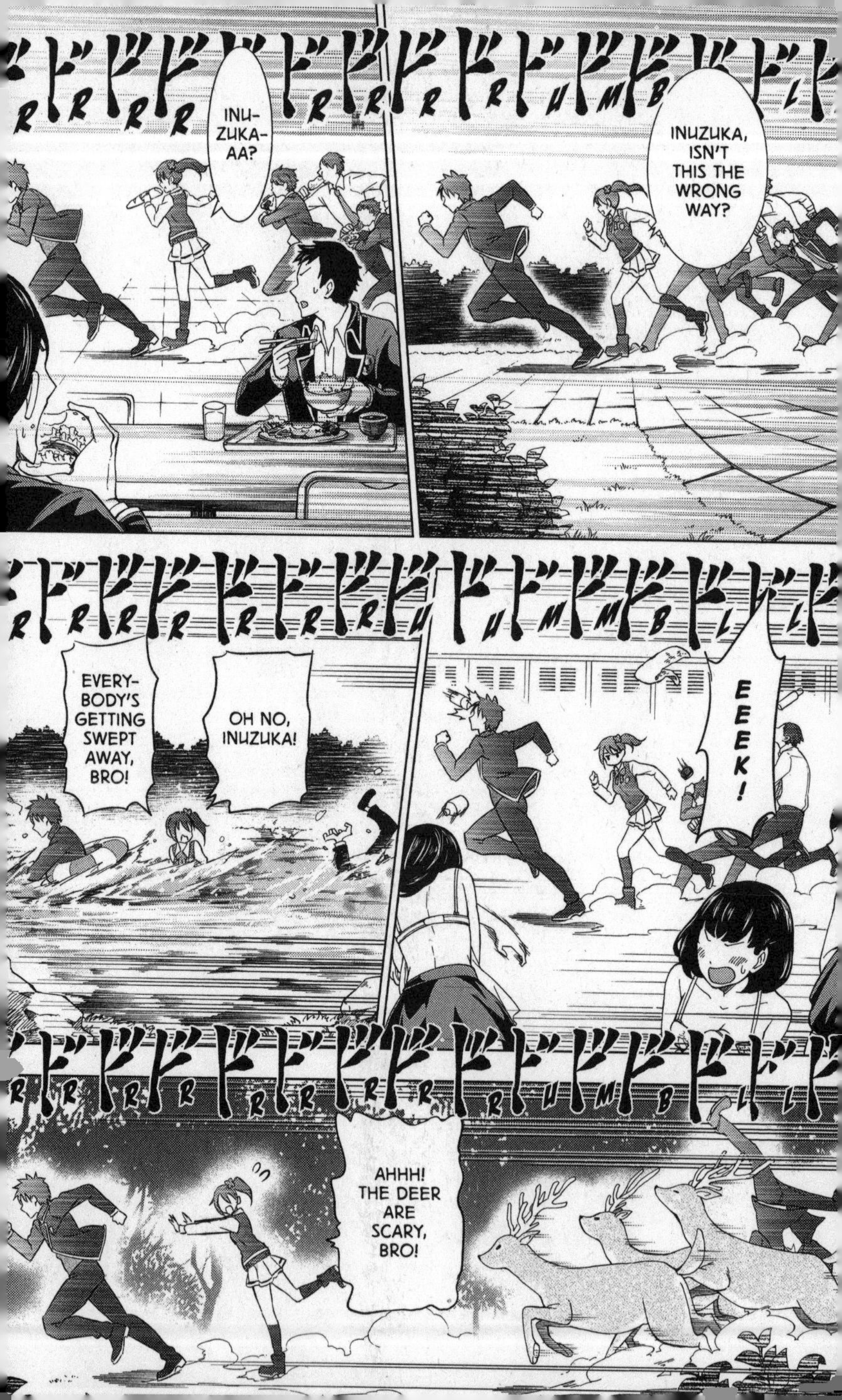
INUZUKA, ISN'T THIS THE WRONG WAY?
INU-ZUKA-AA?
EEEEK!
OH NO, INUZUKA!
EVERY-BODY'S GETTING SWEPT AWAY, BRO!
AHHH! THE DEER ARE SCARY, BRO!

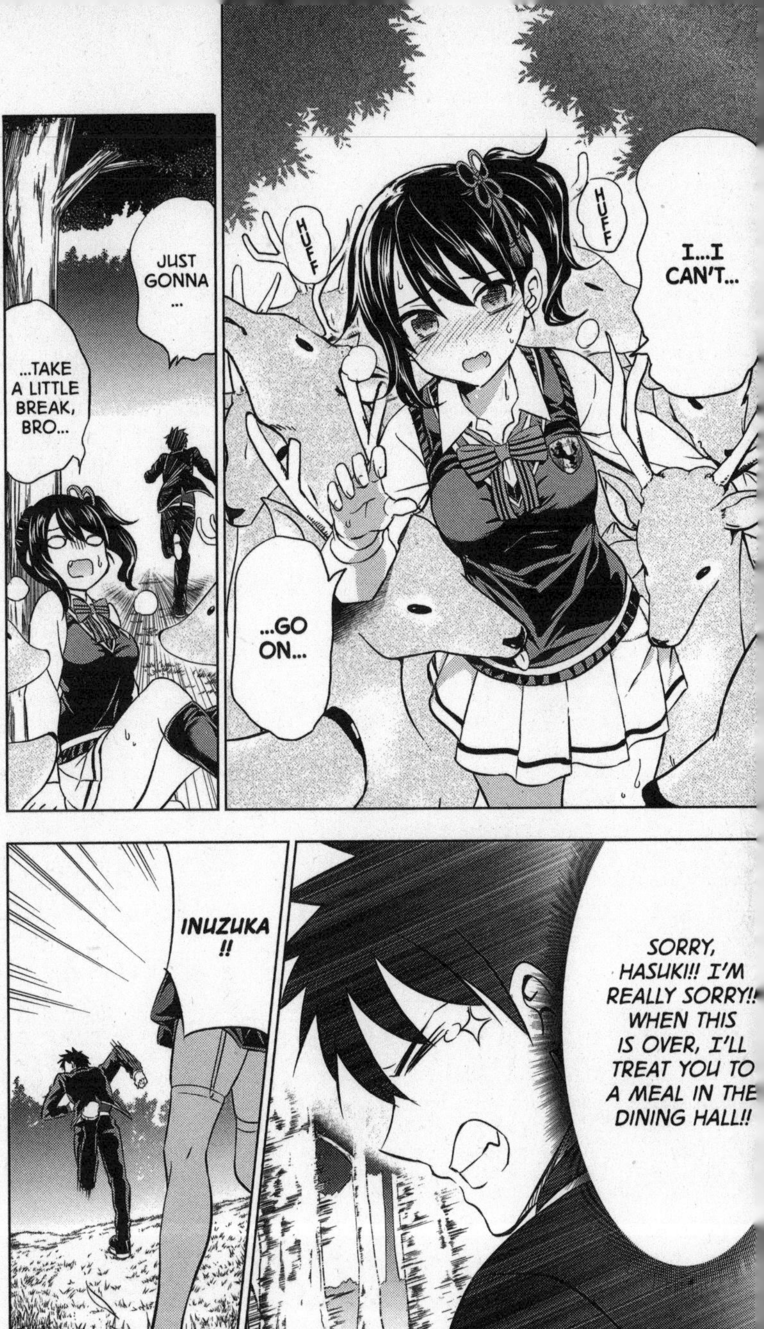
HUFF
HUFF
I...I CAN'T...
...GO ON...
JUST GONNA ...
...TAKE A LITTLE BREAK, BRO...
SORRY, HASUKI!! I'M REALLY SORRY!! WHEN THIS IS OVER, I'LL TREAT YOU TO A MEAL IN THE DINING HALL!!
INUZUKA !!

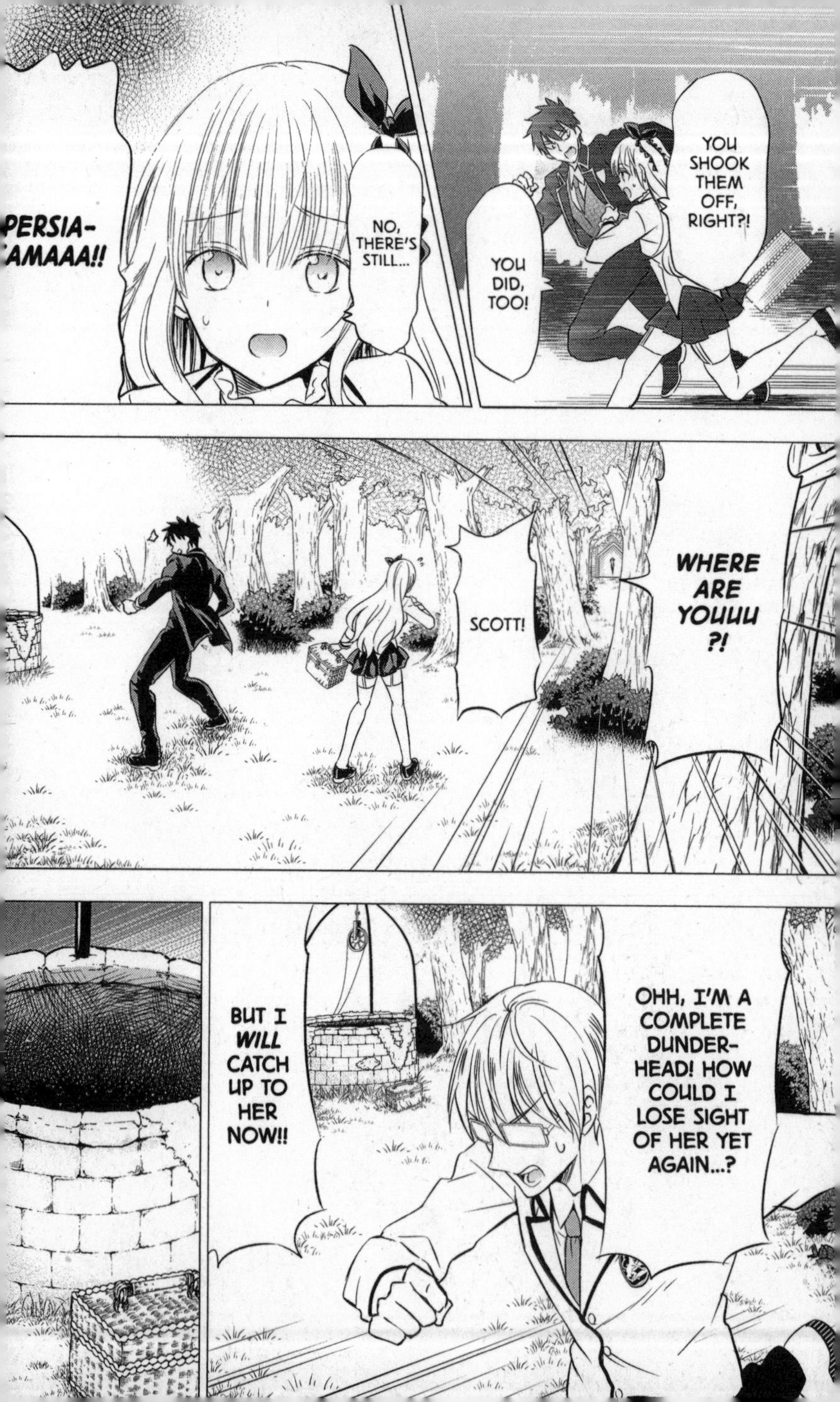
YOU SHOOK THEM OFF, RIGHT?!
YOU DID, TOO!
NO, THERE'S STILL...
PERSIA- AMAAA!!
WHERE ARE YOUUU?!
SCOTT!
OHH, I'M A COMPLETE DUNDER-HEAD! HOW COULD I LOSE SIGHT OF HER YET AGAIN...?
BUT I WILL CATCH UP TO HER NOW!!

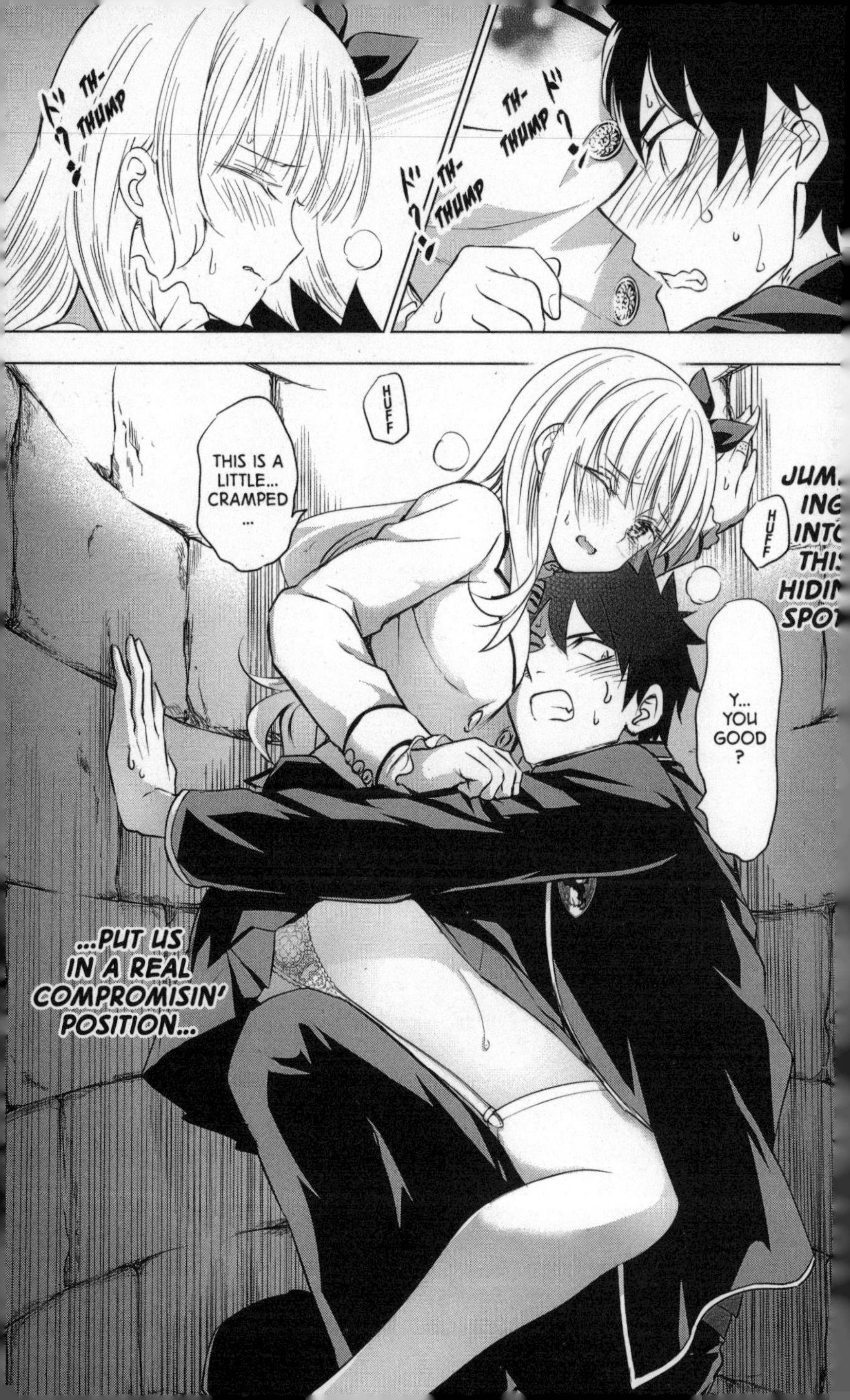
TH-THUMP
TH-THUMP
TH-THUMP
JUM ING INTO THIS HIDIN SPOT
HUFF
Y... YOU GOOD ?
HUFF
THIS IS A LITTLE... CRAMPED ...
...PUT US IN A REAL COMPROMISIN' POSITION...

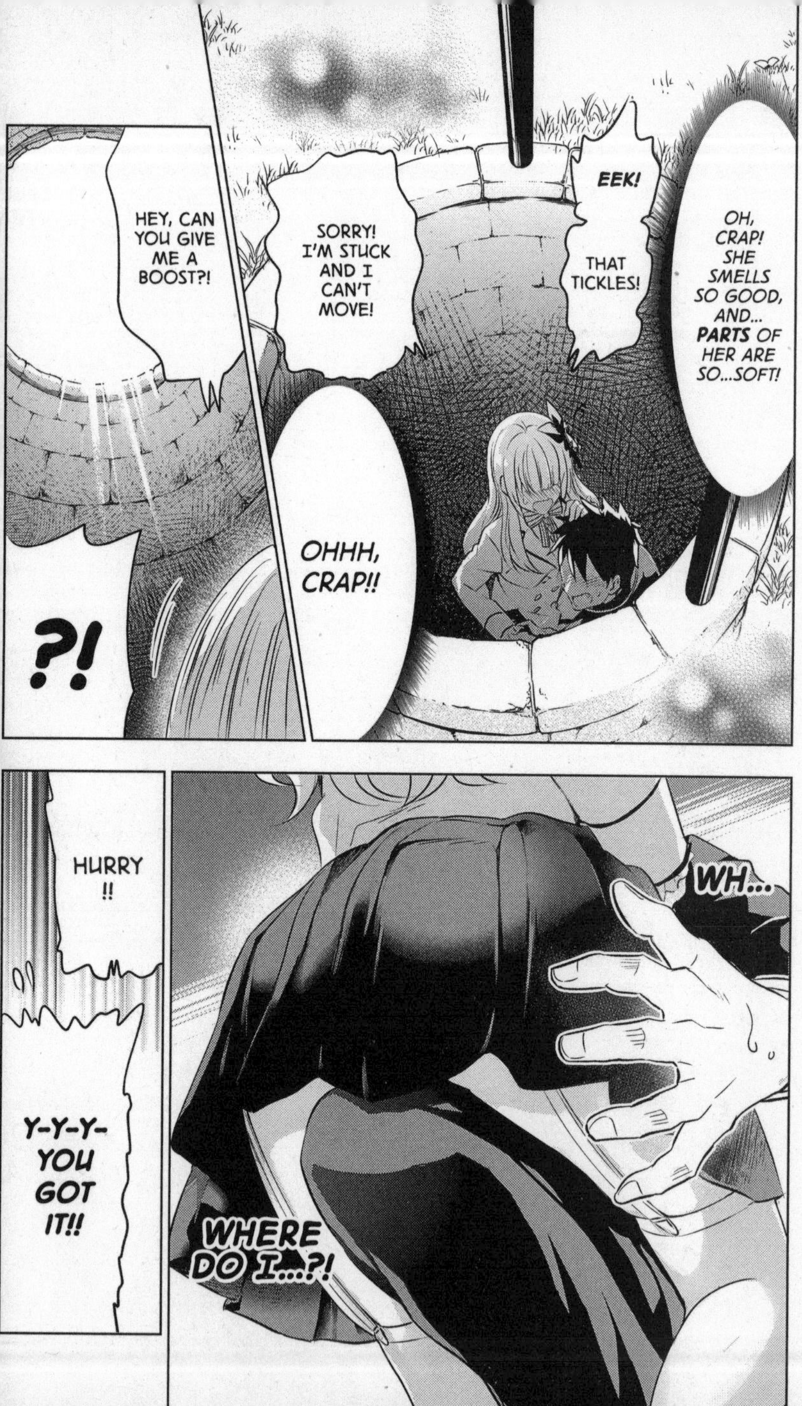
OH, CRAP! SHE SMELLS SO GOOD, AND... **PARTS** OF HER ARE SO...SOFT!
EEK!
THAT TICKLES!
SORRY! I'M STUCK AND I CAN'T MOVE!
OHHH, CRAP!!
HEY, CAN YOU GIVE ME A BOOST?!
?!
WH...
WHERE DO I...?!
HURRY!!
Y-Y-Y-YOU GOT IT!!

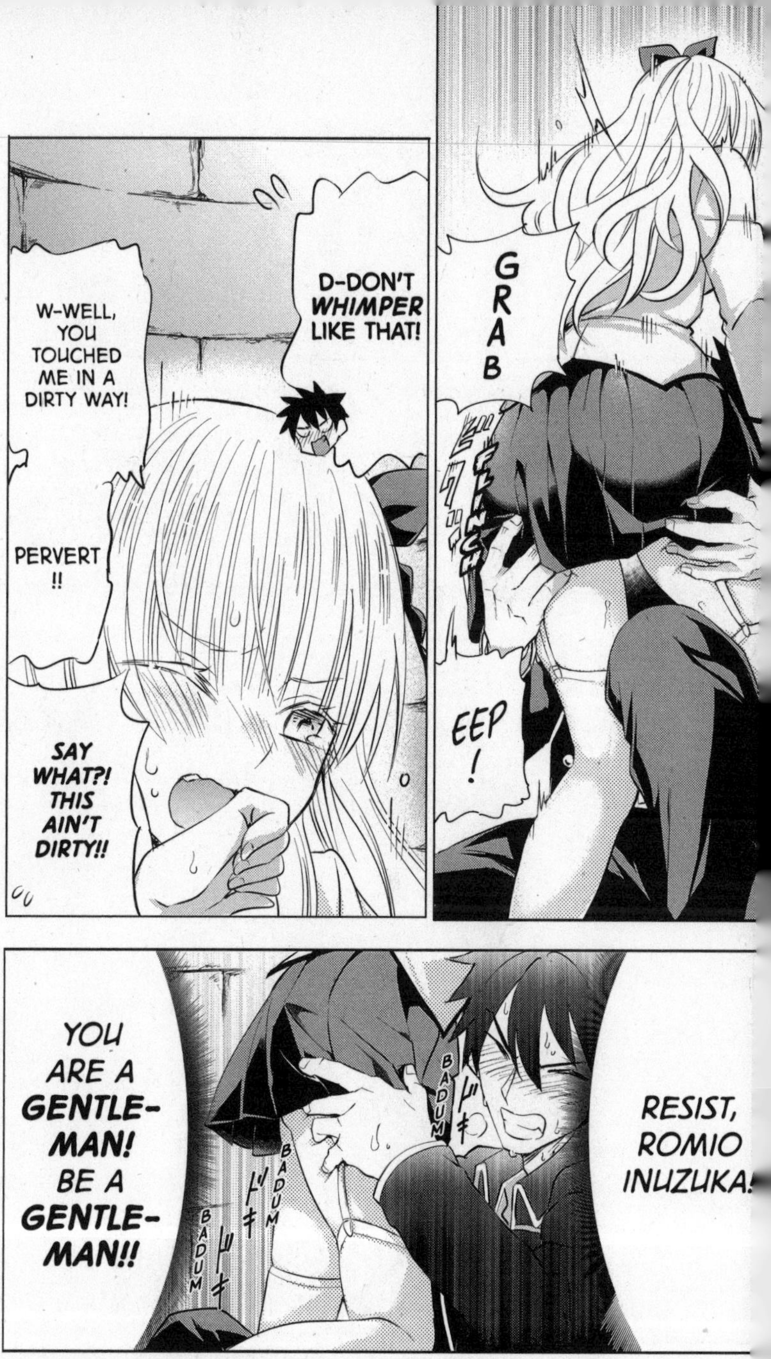
GRAB
FLINCH
EEP!
D-DON'T WHIMPER LIKE THAT!
W-WELL, YOU TOUCHED ME IN A DIRTY WAY!
PERVERT!!
SAY WHAT?! THIS AIN'T DIRTY!!
RESIST, ROMIO INUZUKA!
BADUM
BADUM
BADUM
YOU ARE A GENTLEMAN! BE A GENTLEMAN!!

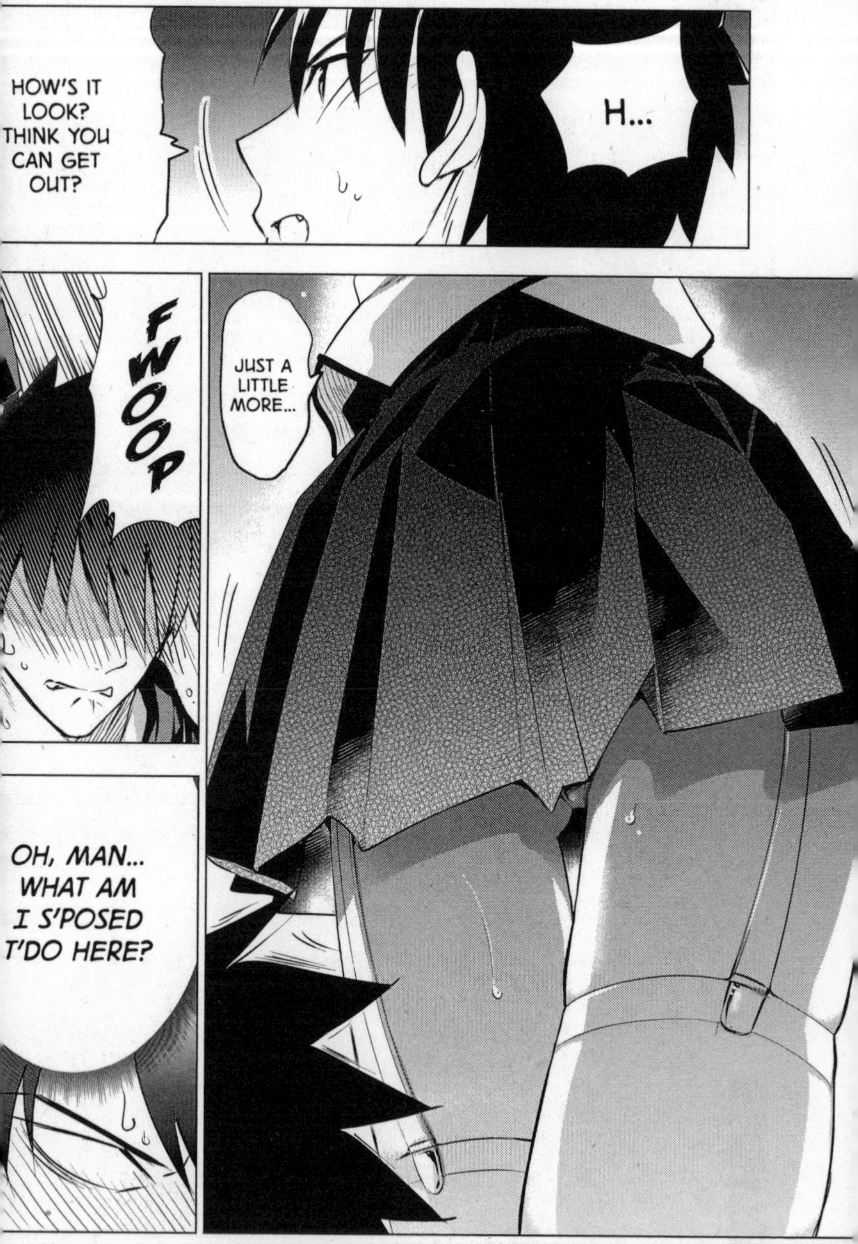
H...
HOW'S IT LOOK? THINK YOU CAN GET OUT?
JUST A LITTLE MORE...
FWOOP
OH, MAN... WHAT AM I S'POSED T'DO HERE?

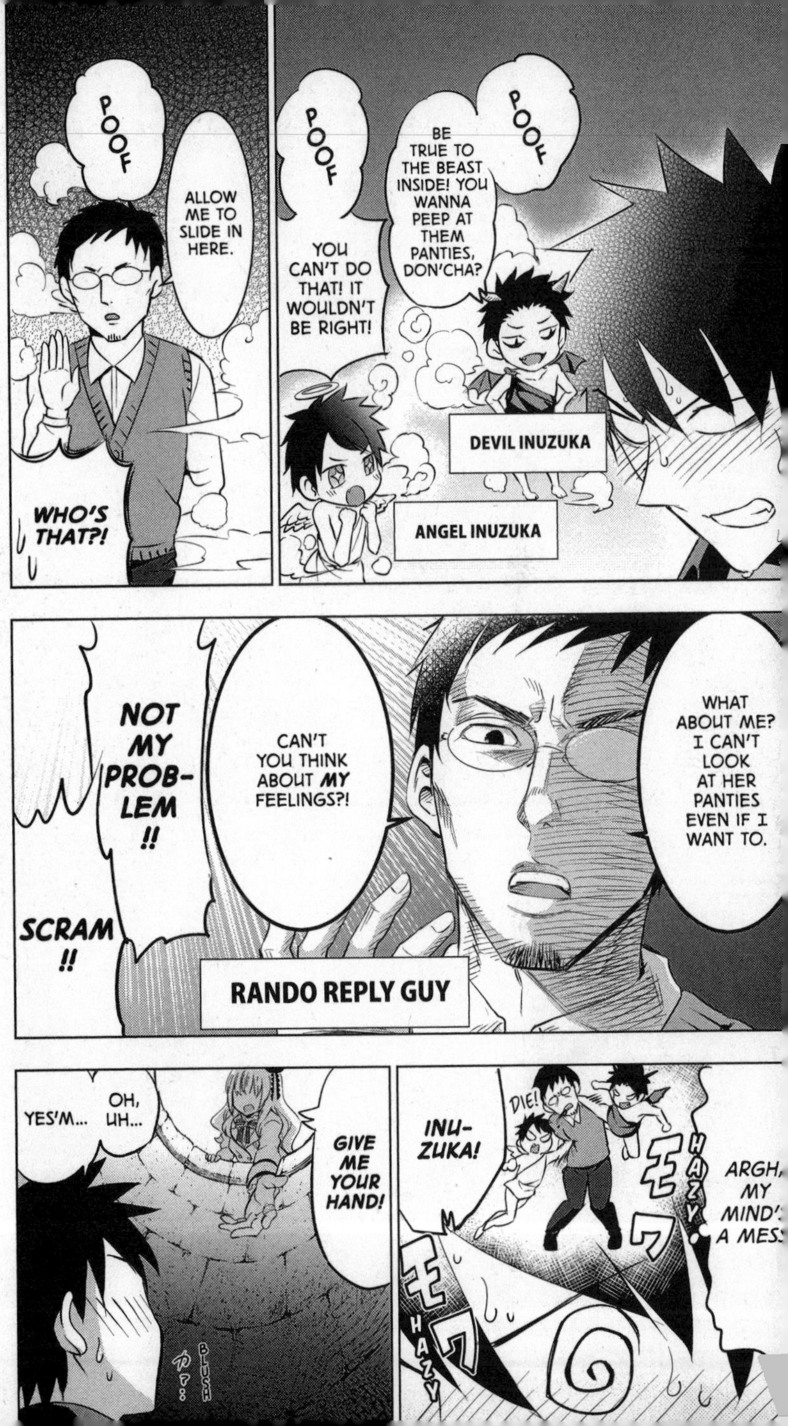
POOF
BE TRUE TO THE BEAST INSIDE! YOU WANNA PEEP AT THEM PANTIES, DON'CHA?
POOF
YOU CAN'T DO THAT! IT WOULDN'T BE RIGHT!
DEVIL INUZUKA
ANGEL INUZUKA
POOF
ALLOW ME TO SLIDE IN HERE.
WHO'S THAT?!
WHAT ABOUT ME? I CAN'T LOOK AT HER PANTIES EVEN IF I WANT TO.
CAN'T YOU THINK ABOUT MY FEELINGS?!
RANDO REPLY GUY
NOT MY PROB-LEM!!
SCRAM!!
ARGH MY MIND' A MES
HAZY
HAZY
DIE!
INU-ZUKA!
GIVE ME YOUR HAND!
OH, UH...
YES'M...
BLUSH

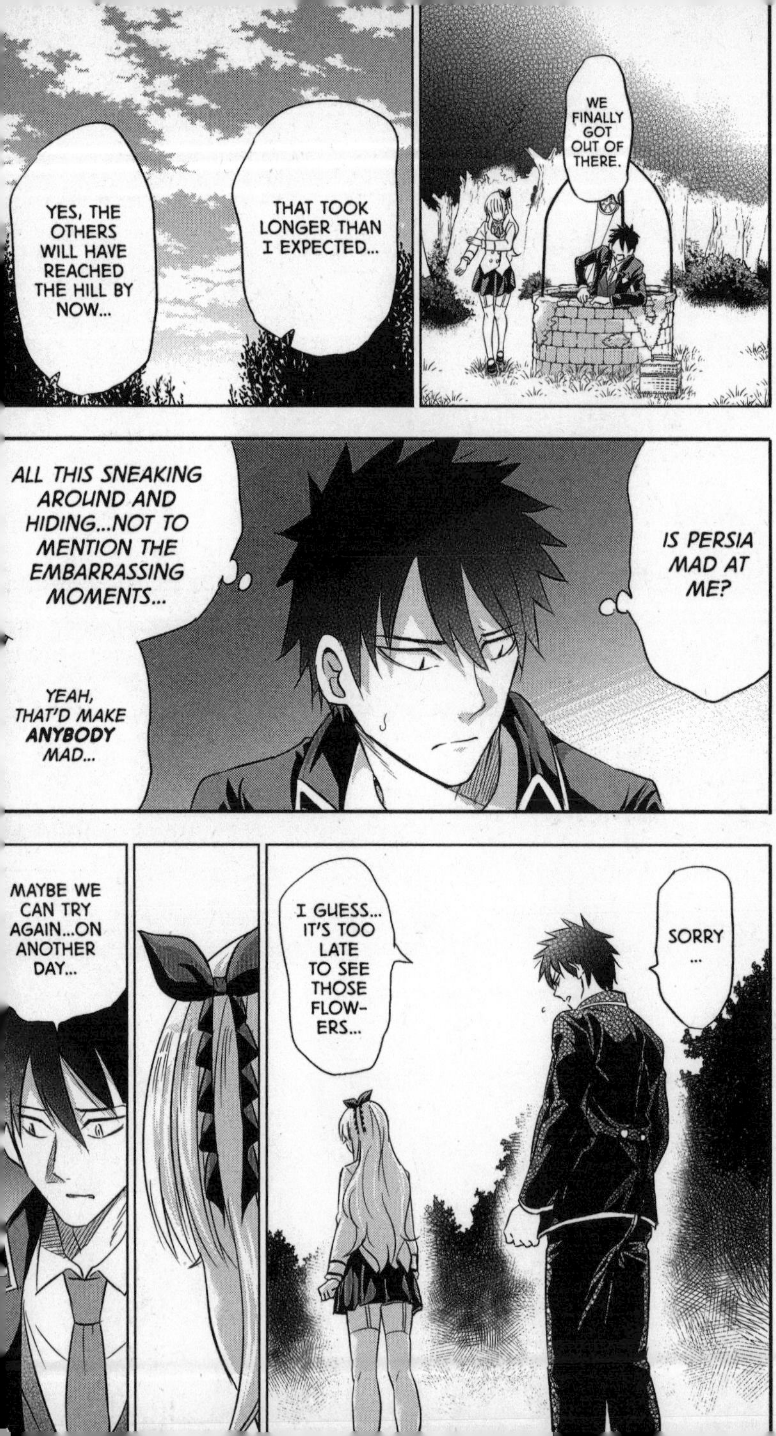
WE FINALLY GOT OUT OF THERE.
THAT TOOK LONGER THAN I EXPECTED...
YES, THE OTHERS WILL HAVE REACHED THE HILL BY NOW...
IS PERSIA MAD AT ME?
ALL THIS SNEAKING AROUND AND HIDING...NOT TO MENTION THE EMBARRASSING MOMENTS...
YEAH, THAT'D MAKE ANYBODY MAD...
SORRY ...
I GUESS... IT'S TOO LATE TO SEE THOSE FLOWERS...
MAYBE WE CAN TRY AGAIN...ON ANOTHER DAY...

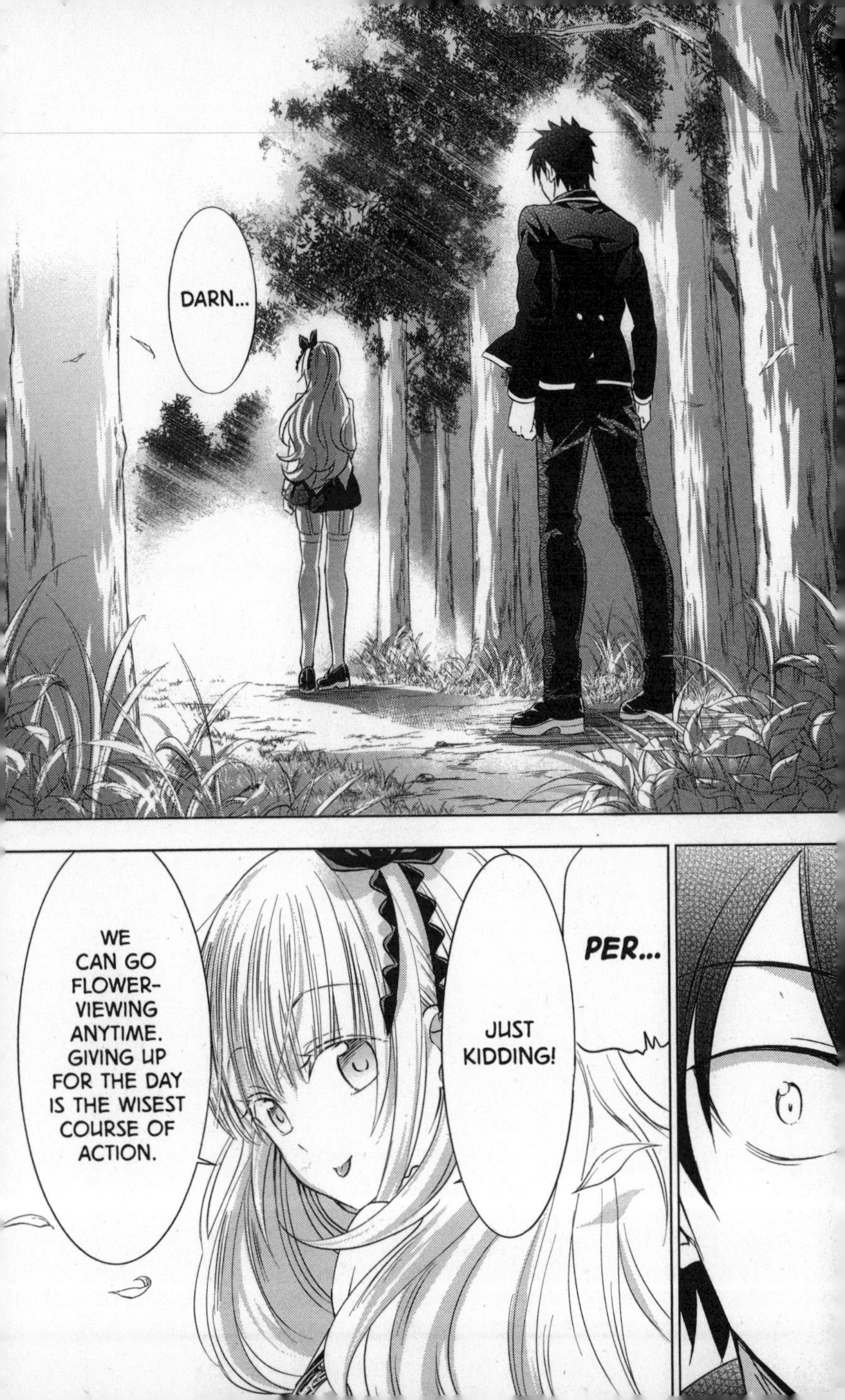
DARN...
PER...
JUST KIDDING!
WE CAN GO FLOWER-VIEWING ANYTIME. GIVING UP FOR THE DAY IS THE WISEST COURSE OF ACTION.

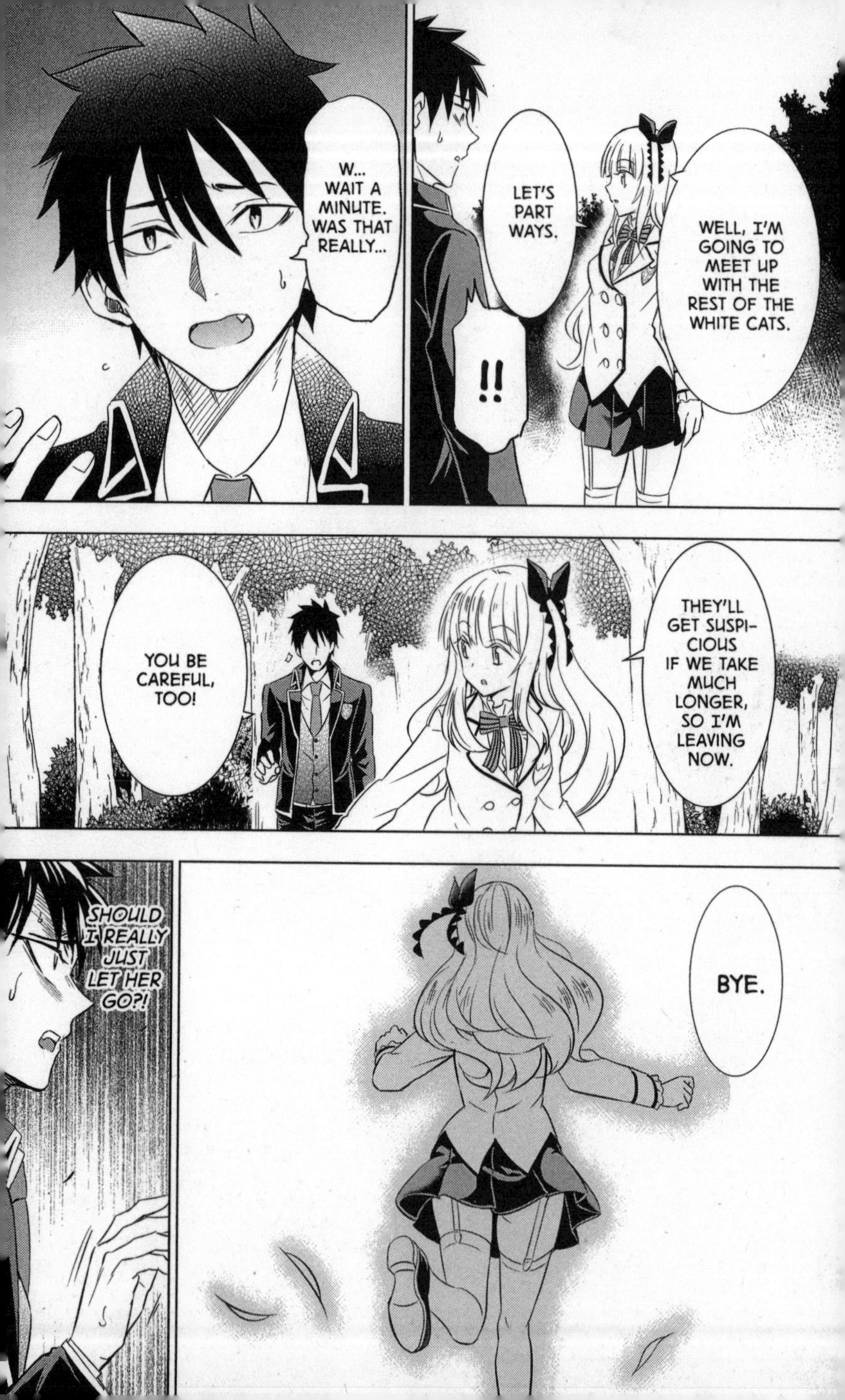
WELL, I'M GOING TO MEET UP WITH THE REST OF THE WHITE CATS.
LET'S PART WAYS.
!!
W... WAIT A MINUTE. WAS THAT REALLY...
THEY'LL GET SUSPI-CIOUS IF WE TAKE MUCH LONGER, SO I'M LEAVING NOW.
YOU BE CAREFUL, TOO!
BYE.
SHOULD I REALLY JUST LET HER GO?!

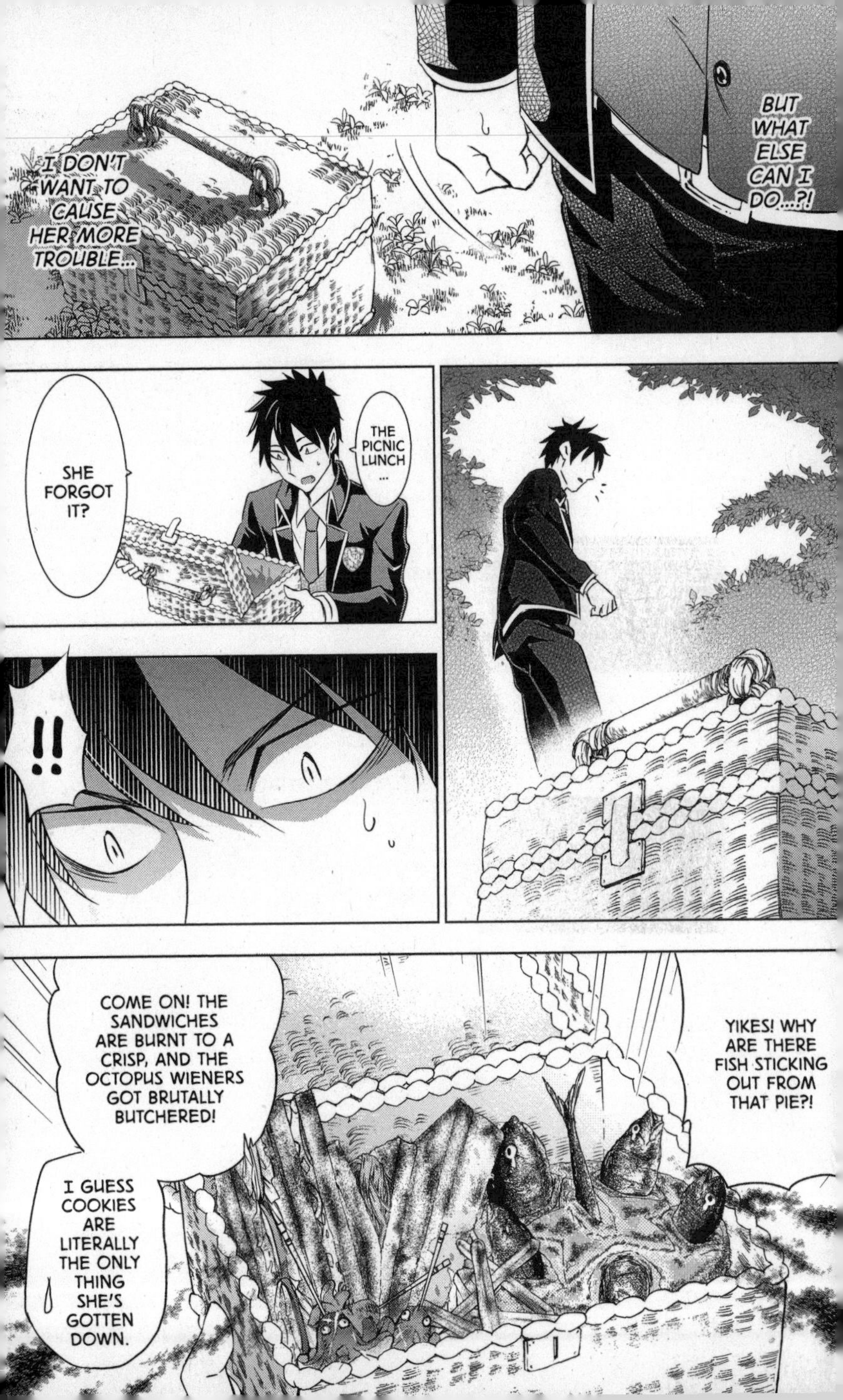
BUT WHAT ELSE CAN I DO...?!
I DON'T WANT TO CAUSE HER MORE TROUBLE...
THE PICNIC LUNCH ...
SHE FORGOT IT?
!!
YIKES! WHY ARE THERE FISH STICKING OUT FROM THAT PIE?!
COME ON! THE SANDWICHES ARE BURNT TO A CRISP, AND THE OCTOPUS WIENERS GOT BRUTALLY BUTCHERED!
I GUESS COOKIES ARE LITERALLY THE ONLY THING SHE'S GOTTEN DOWN.

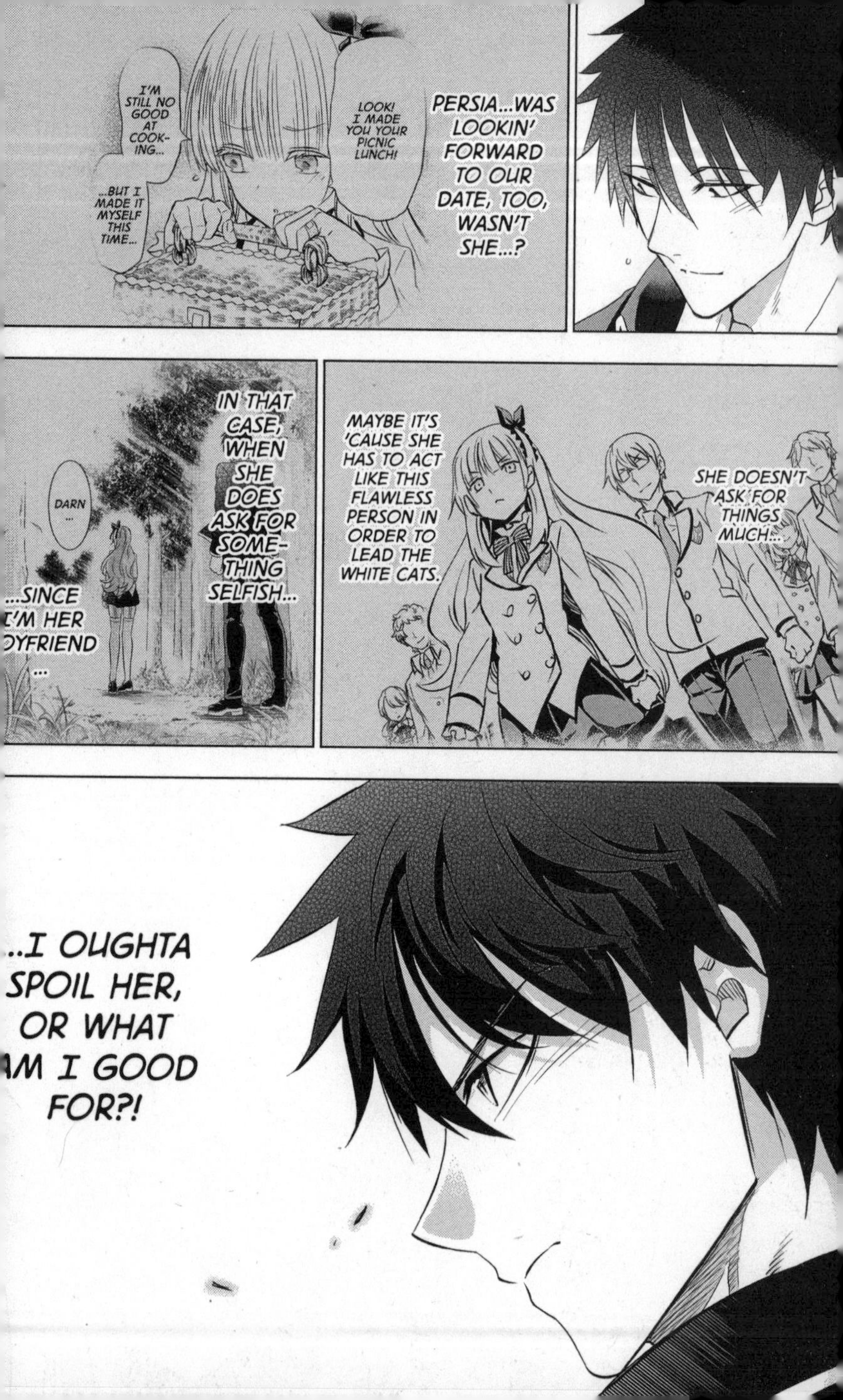

PERSIA...WAS LOOKIN' FORWARD TO OUR DATE, TOO, WASN'T SHE...?
LOOK! I MADE YOU YOUR PICNIC LUNCH!
I'M STILL NO GOOD AT COOK-ING...
...BUT I MADE IT MYSELF THIS TIME...
SHE DOESN'T ASK FOR THINGS MUCH...
MAYBE IT'S 'CAUSE SHE HAS TO ACT LIKE THIS FLAWLESS PERSON IN ORDER TO LEAD THE WHITE CATS.
IN THAT CASE, WHEN SHE DOES ASK FOR SOME-THING SELFISH...
DARN...
...SINCE I'M HER OYFRIEND...
...I OUGHTA SPOIL HER, OR WHAT M I GOOD FOR?!

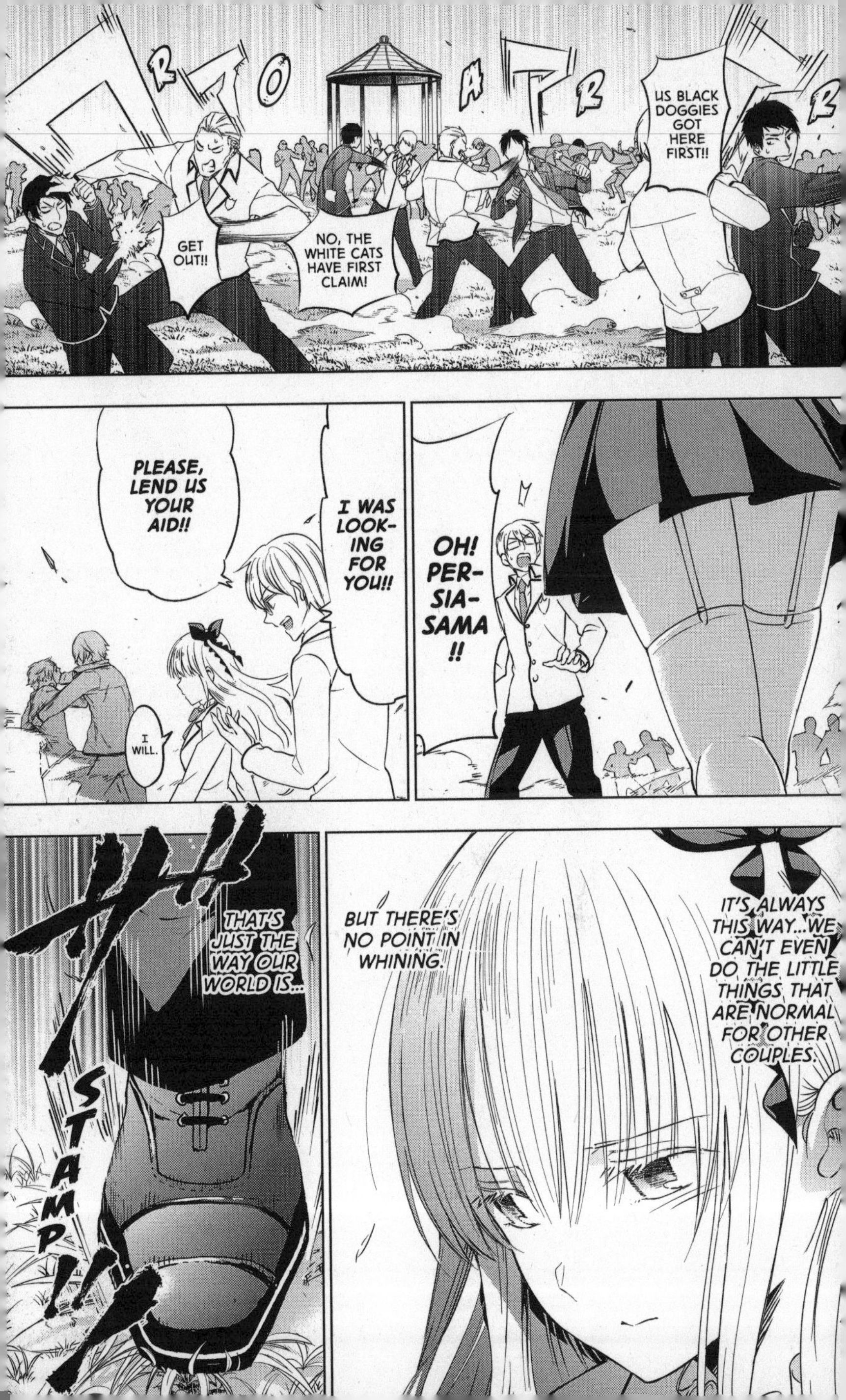
ROARR
US BLACK DOGGIES GOT HERE FIRST!!
NO, THE WHITE CATS HAVE FIRST CLAIM!
GET OUT!!
OH! PER-SIA-SAMA!!
I WAS LOOKING FOR YOU!!
PLEASE, LEND US YOUR AID!!
I WILL.
IT'S ALWAYS THIS WAY... WE CAN'T EVEN DO THE LITTLE THINGS THAT ARE NORMAL FOR OTHER COUPLES.
BUT THERE'S NO POINT IN WHINING.
THAT'S JUST THE WAY OUR WORLD IS...
STAMP!!

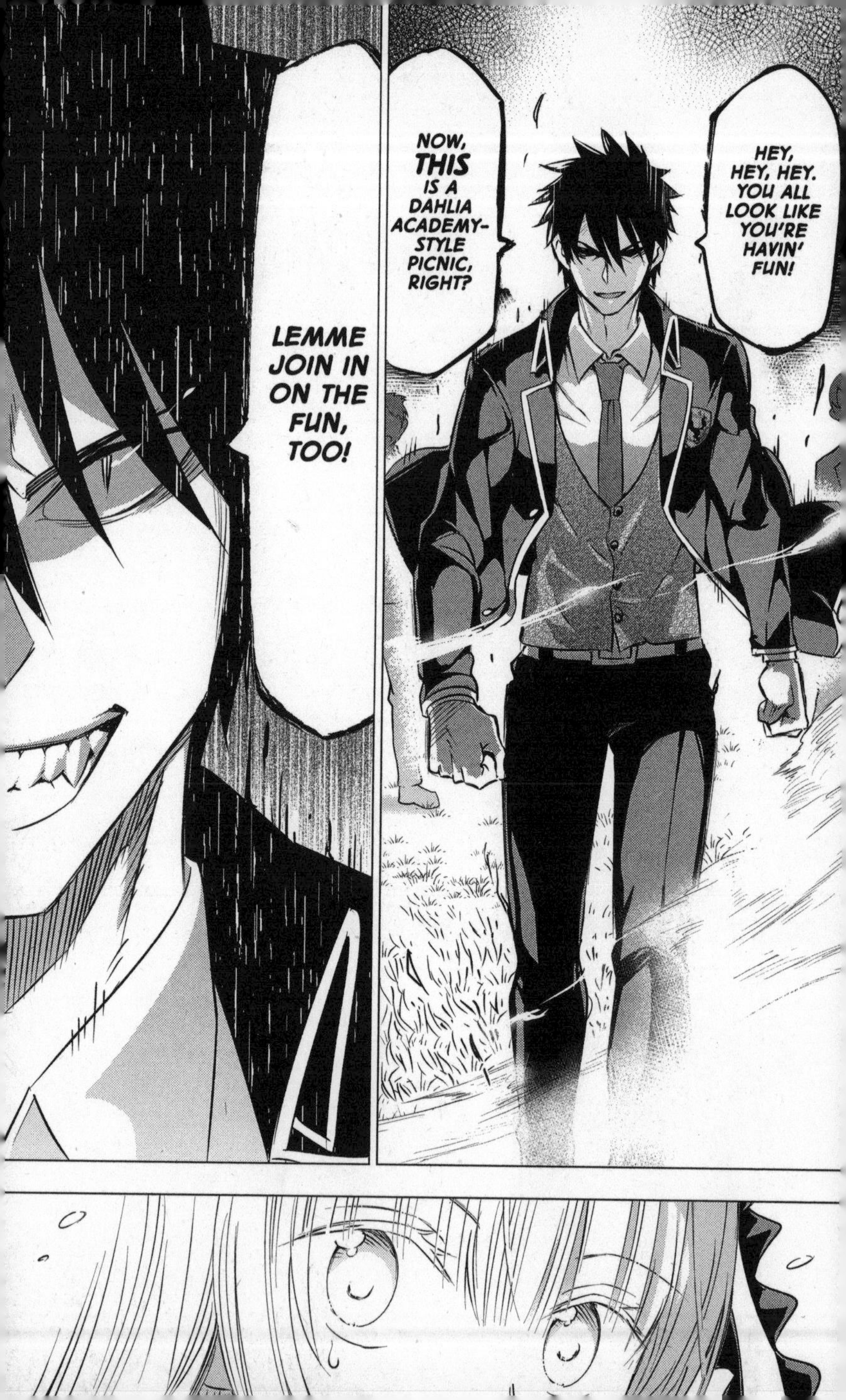
HEY, HEY, HEY. YOU ALL LOOK LIKE YOU'RE HAVIN' FUN!
NOW, THIS IS A DAHLIA ACADEMY-STYLE PICNIC, RIGHT?
LEMME JOIN IN ON THE FUN, TOO!

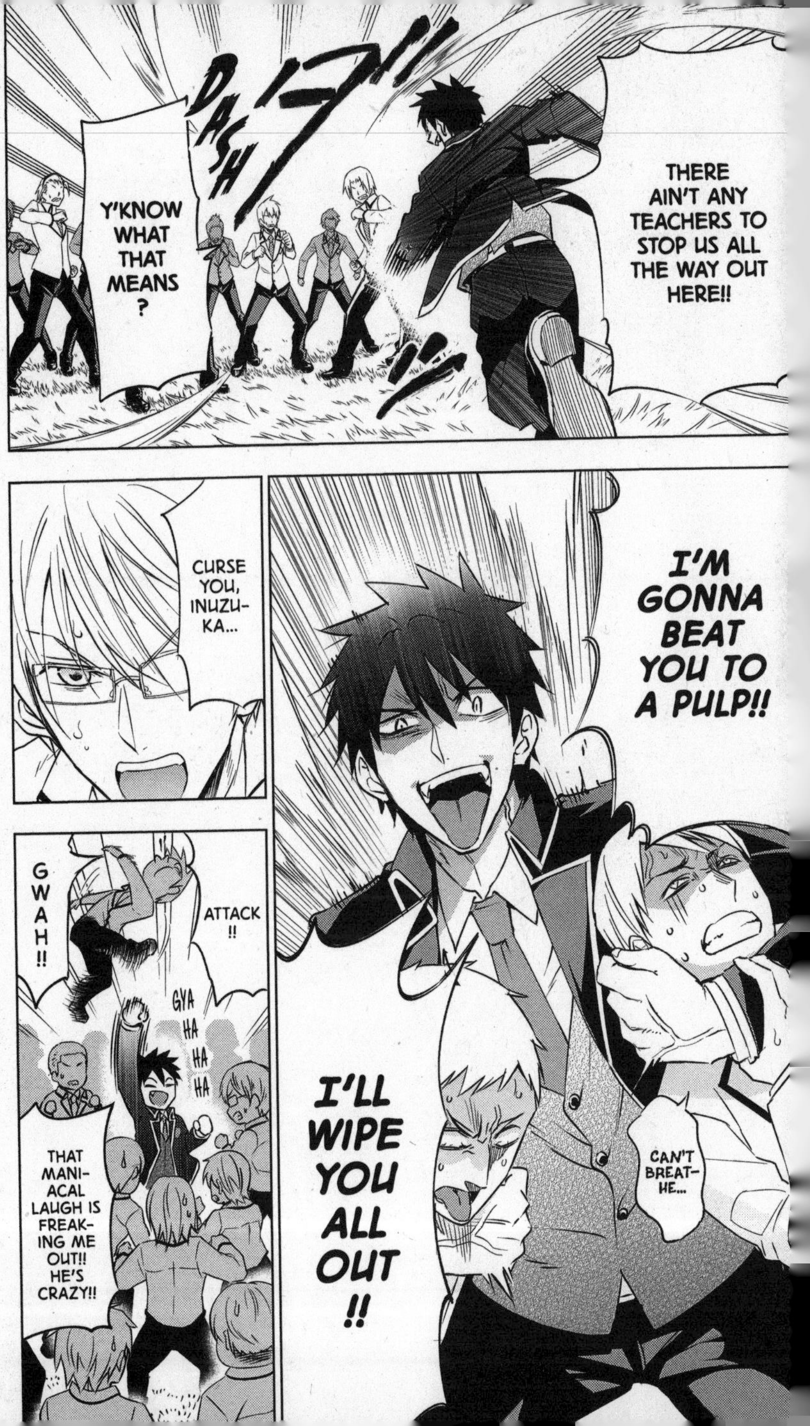
DASH
THERE AIN'T ANY TEACHERS TO STOP US ALL THE WAY OUT HERE!!
Y'KNOW WHAT THAT MEANS?
I'M GONNA BEAT YOU TO A PULP!!
CAN'T BREAT-HE...
I'LL WIPE YOU ALL OUT!!
CURSE YOU, INUZUKA...
ATTACK!!
GWAH!!
GYA HA HA HA
THAT MANIACAL LAUGH IS FREAKING ME OUT!! HE'S CRAZY!!

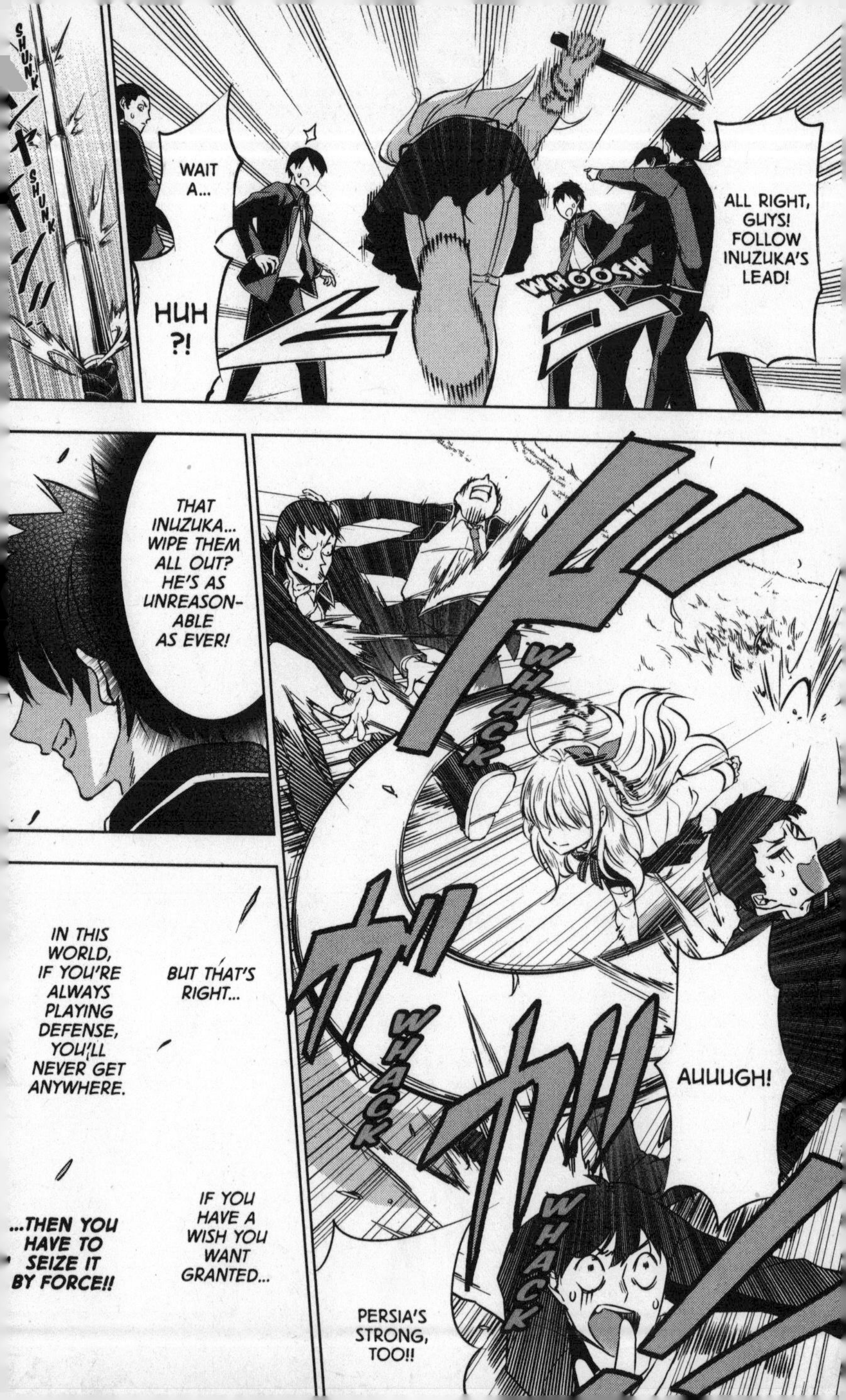
ALL RIGHT, GUYS! FOLLOW INUZUKA'S LEAD!
WHOOSH
WAIT A...
HUH ?!
SHUNK
SHUNK
WHACK
AUUUGH!
WHACK
WHACK
PERSIA'S STRONG, TOO!!
THAT INUZUKA... WIPE THEM ALL OUT? HE'S AS UNREASON-ABLE AS EVER!
BUT THAT'S RIGHT...
IN THIS WORLD, IF YOU'RE ALWAYS PLAYING DEFENSE, YOU'LL NEVER GET ANYWHERE.
IF YOU HAVE A WISH YOU WANT GRANTED...
...THEN YOU HAVE TO SEIZE IT BY FORCE!!

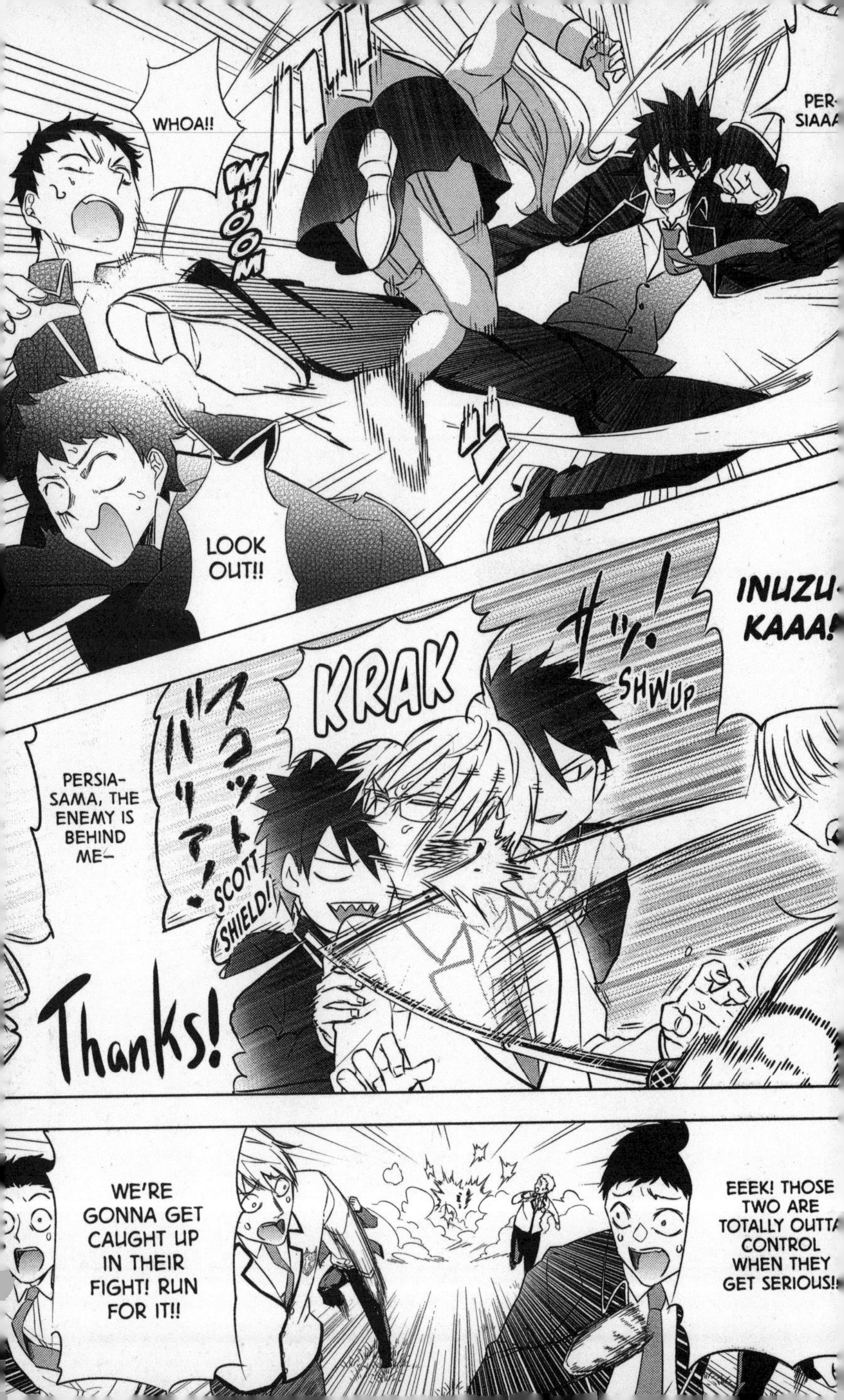
PER-SIAAA
WHOOM
WHOA!!
LOOK OUT!!
INUZU-KAAA!
サッ!
SHWUP
KRAK
スコットバリアー!
SCOTT SHIELD!
PERSIA-SAMA, THE ENEMY IS BEHIND ME–
Thanks!
EEEK! THOSE TWO ARE TOTALLY OUTTA CONTROL WHEN THEY GET SERIOUS!!
WE'RE GONNA GET CAUGHT UP IN THEIR FIGHT! RUN FOR IT!!

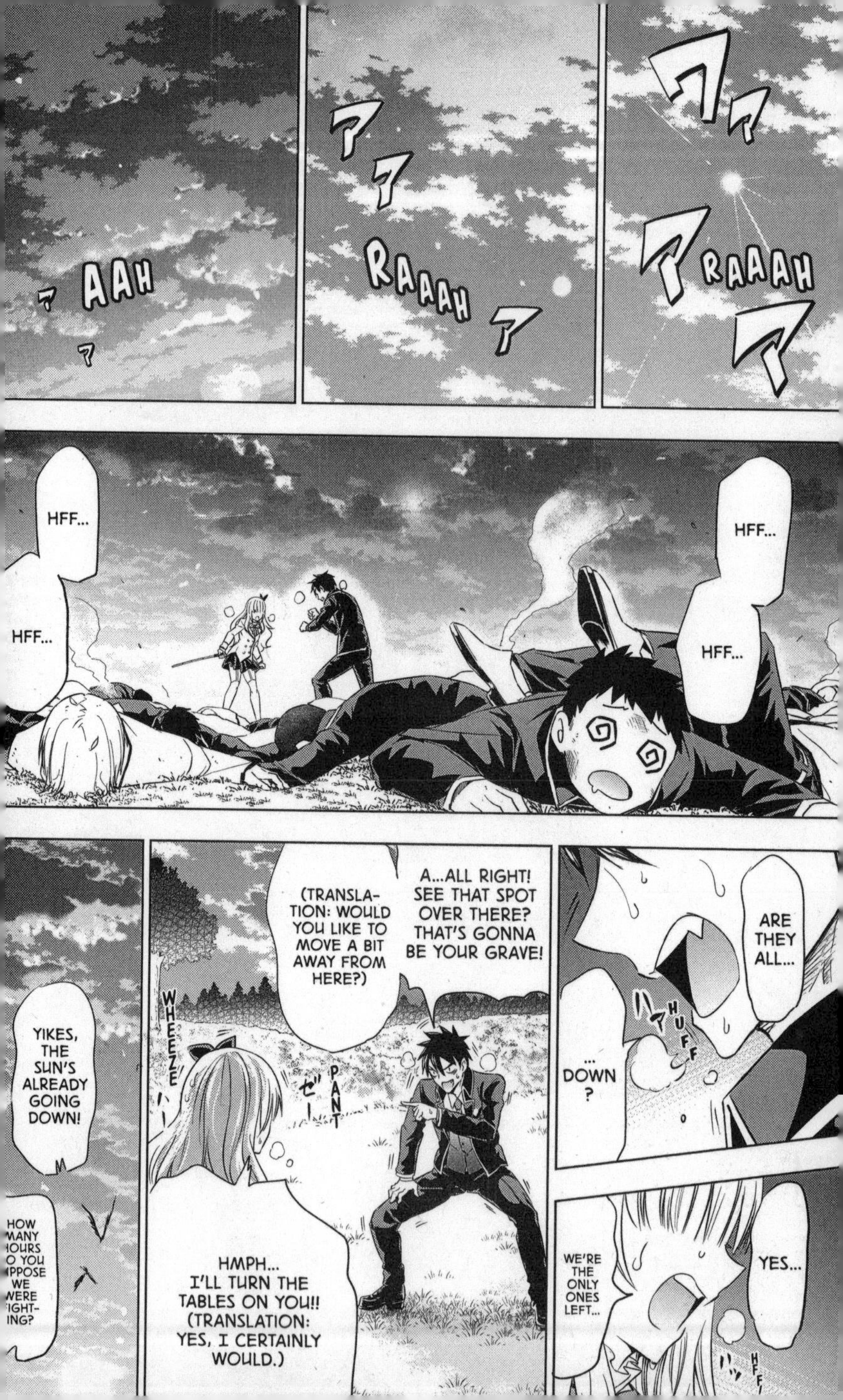
ワァ
ア
RAAAH
ア
ア
ア
RAAAH
ア
ア
AAH
ア
HFF...
HFF...
HFF...
HFF...
ARE THEY ALL...
ハァ HUFF
... DOWN ?
YES...
WE'RE THE ONLY ONES LEFT...
ハッ HFF
A...ALL RIGHT! SEE THAT SPOT OVER THERE? THAT'S GONNA BE YOUR GRAVE!
(TRANSLA-TION: WOULD YOU LIKE TO MOVE A BIT AWAY FROM HERE?)
ゼー PANT
ハー WHEEZE
HMPH... I'LL TURN THE TABLES ON YOU!! (TRANSLATION: YES, I CERTAINLY WOULD.)
YIKES, THE SUN'S ALREADY GOING DOWN!
HOW MANY HOURS O YOU PPOSE WE WERE FIGHT-ING?

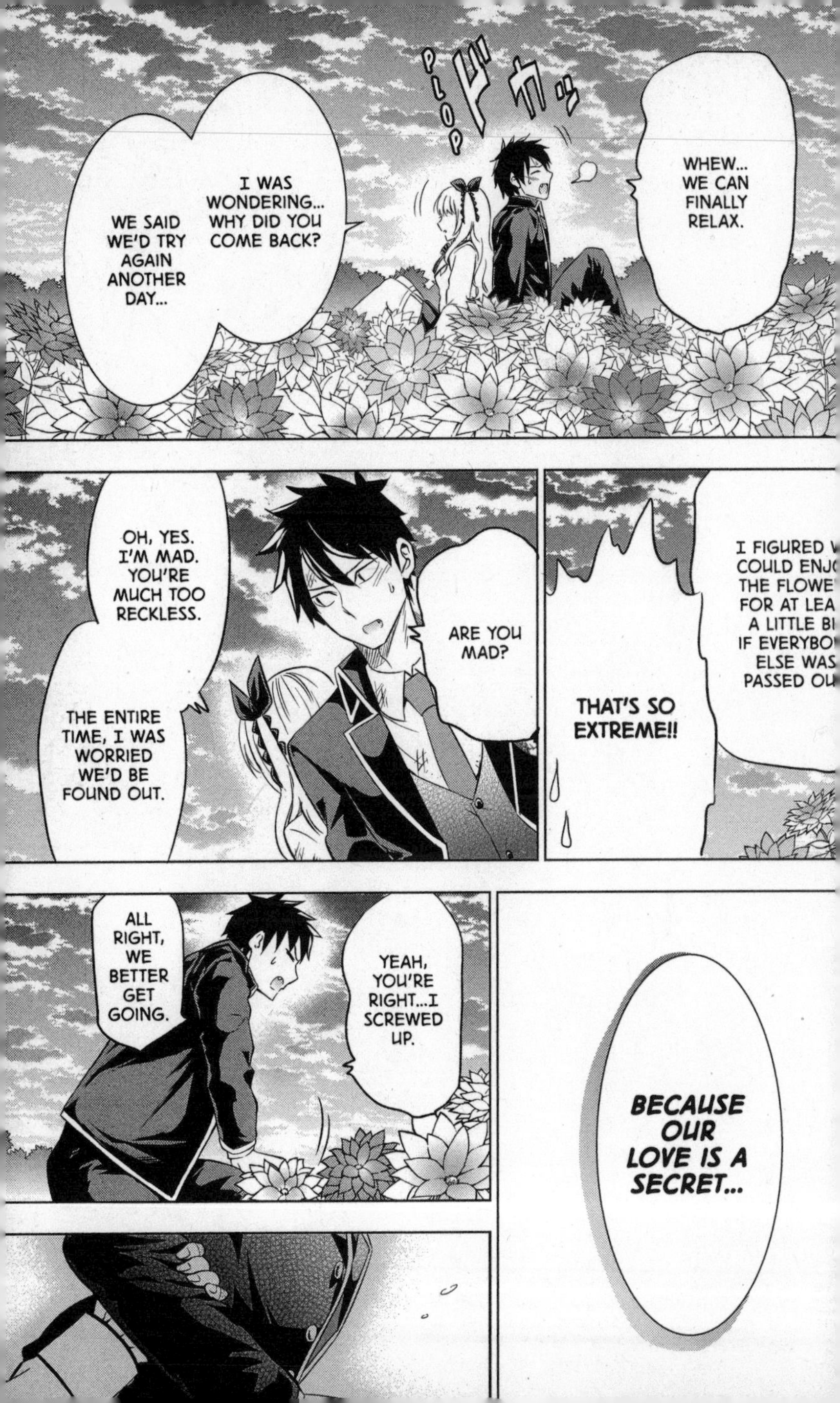
WHEW... WE CAN FINALLY RELAX.
PLOP
I WAS WONDERING... WHY DID YOU COME BACK?
WE SAID WE'D TRY AGAIN ANOTHER DAY...
I FIGURED COULD ENJ THE FLOWE FOR AT LEA A LITTLE BI IF EVERYBO ELSE WAS PASSED OU
THAT'S SO EXTREME!!
ARE YOU MAD?
OH, YES. I'M MAD. YOU'RE MUCH TOO RECKLESS.
THE ENTIRE TIME, I WAS WORRIED WE'D BE FOUND OUT.
BECAUSE OUR LOVE IS A SECRET...
YEAH, YOU'RE RIGHT...I SCREWED UP.
ALL RIGHT, WE BETTER GET GOING.

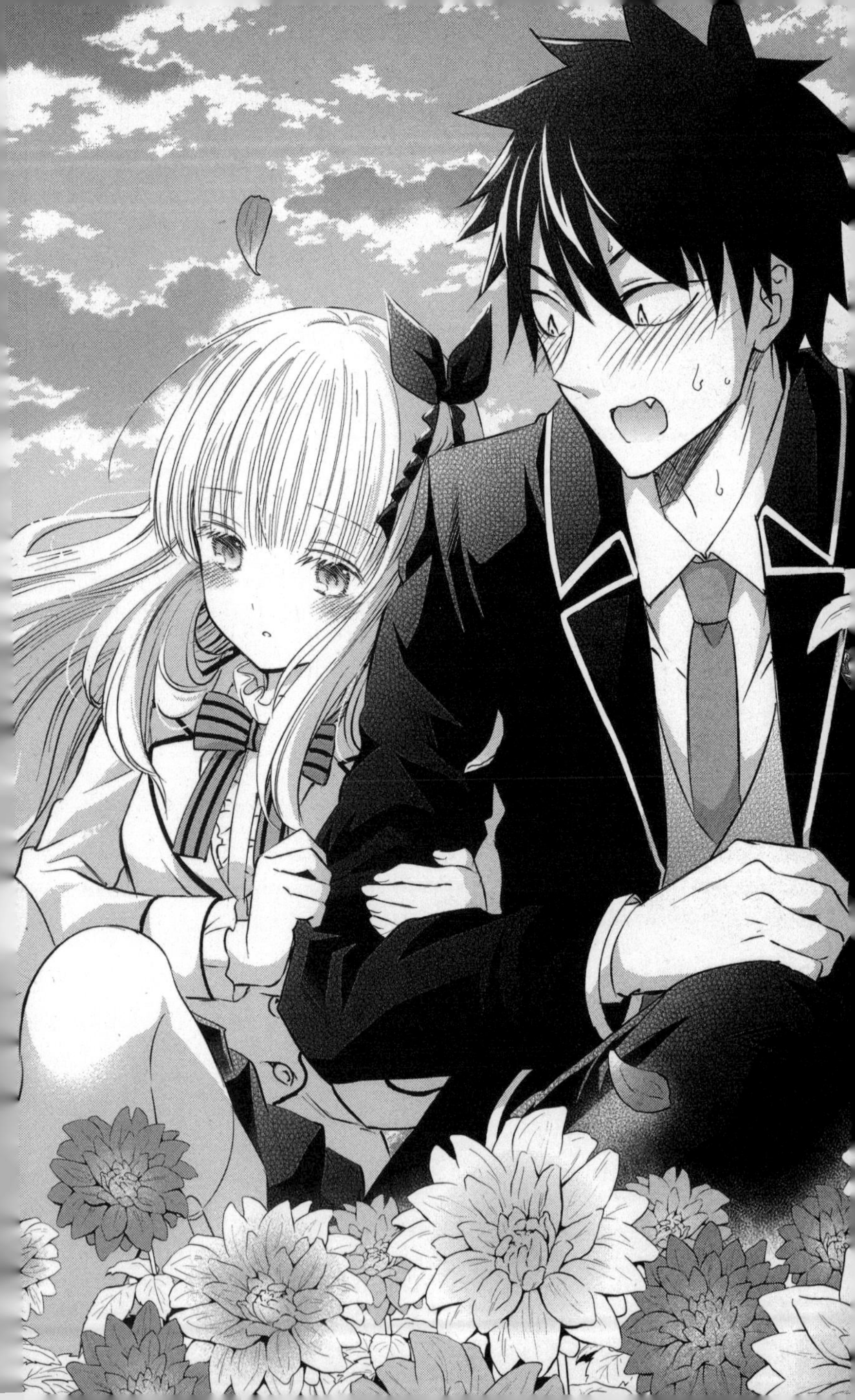

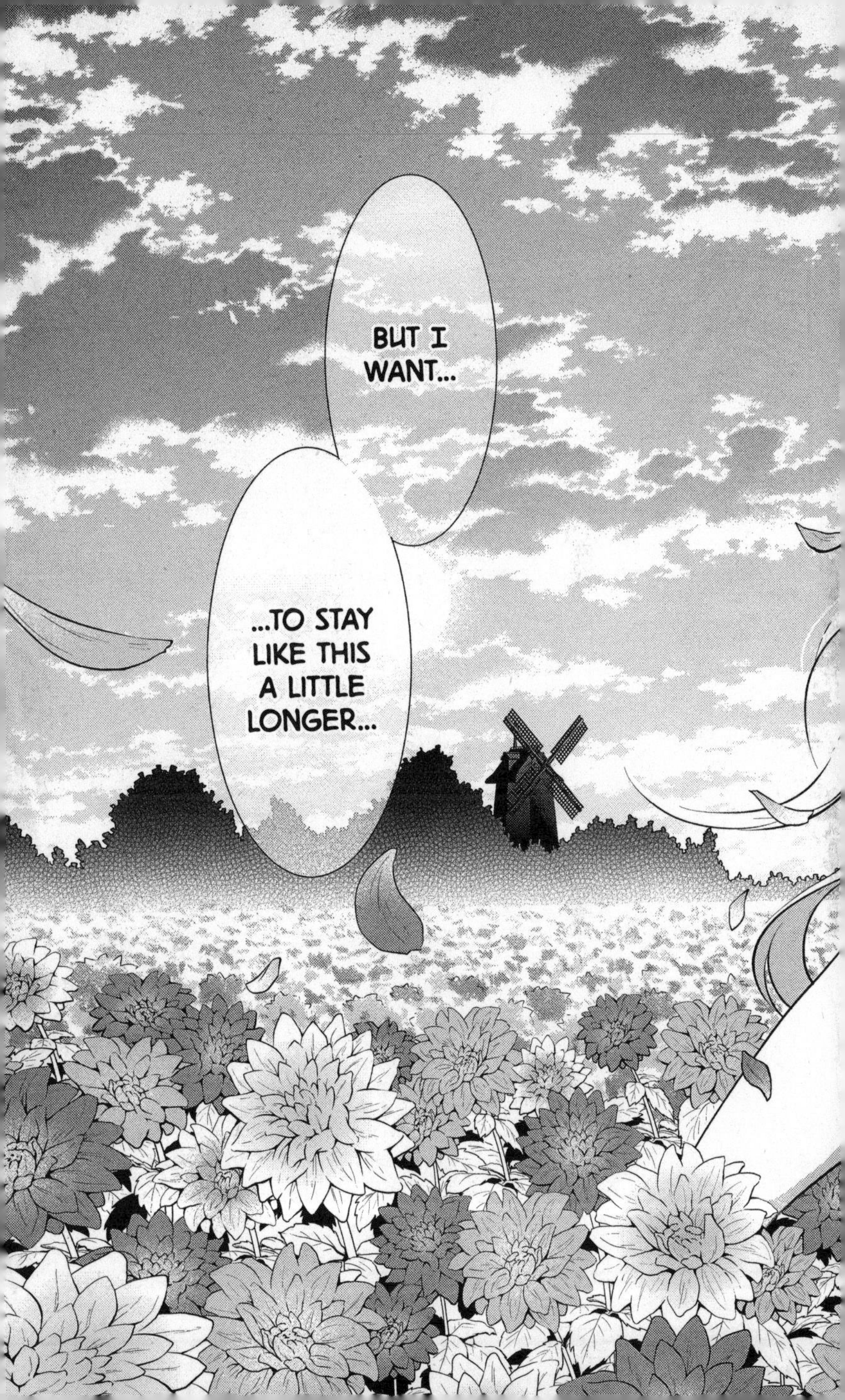
BUT I WANT...
...TO STAY LIKE THIS A LITTLE LONGER...

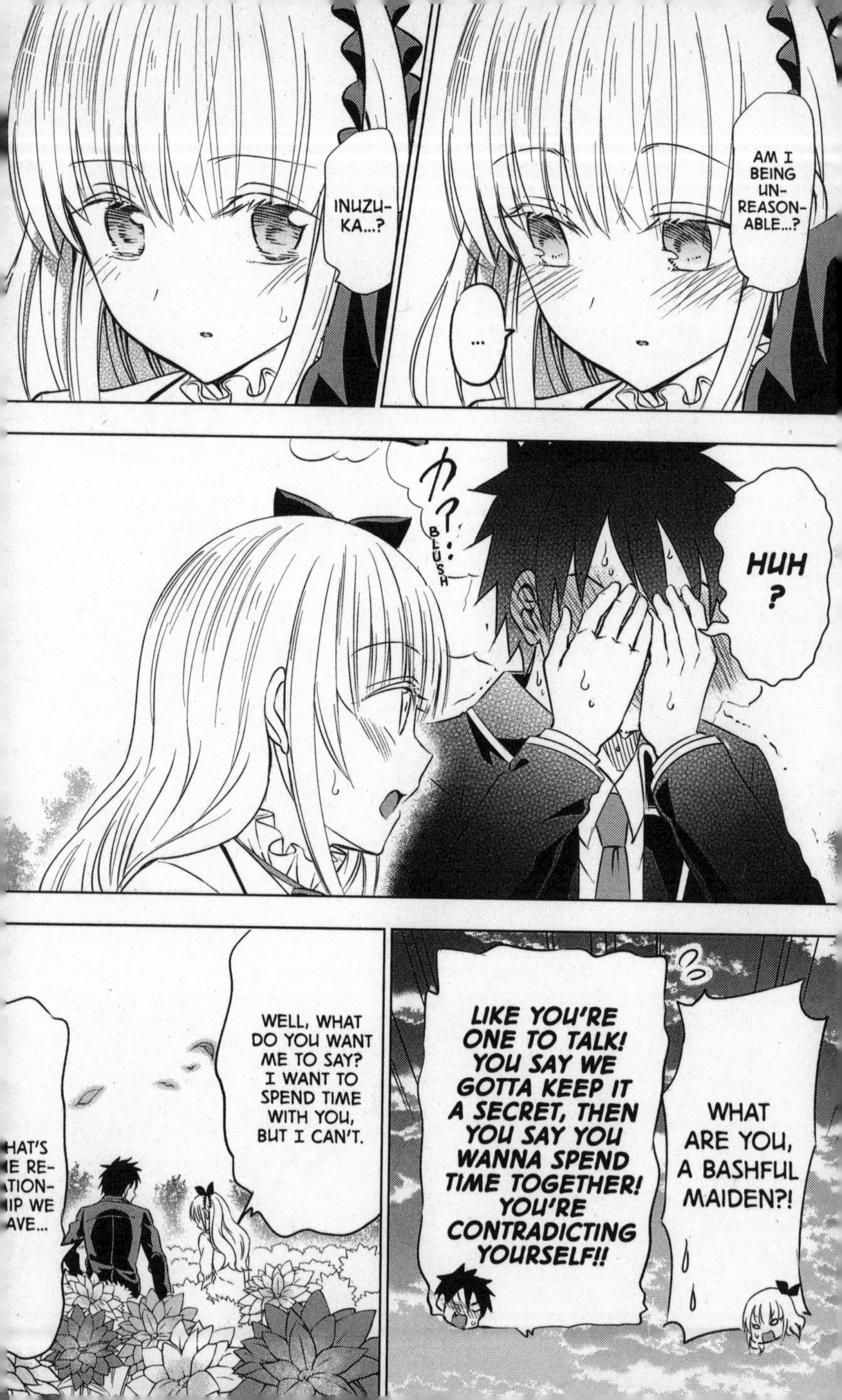

AM I BEING UN-REASONABLE...?
...
INUZUKA...?
BLUSH
HUH?
WHAT ARE YOU, A BASHFUL MAIDEN?!
LIKE YOU'RE ONE TO TALK! YOU SAY WE GOTTA KEEP IT A SECRET, THEN YOU SAY YOU WANNA SPEND TIME TOGETHER! YOU'RE CONTRADICTING YOURSELF!!
WELL, WHAT DO YOU WANT ME TO SAY? I WANT TO SPEND TIME WITH YOU, BUT I CAN'T.

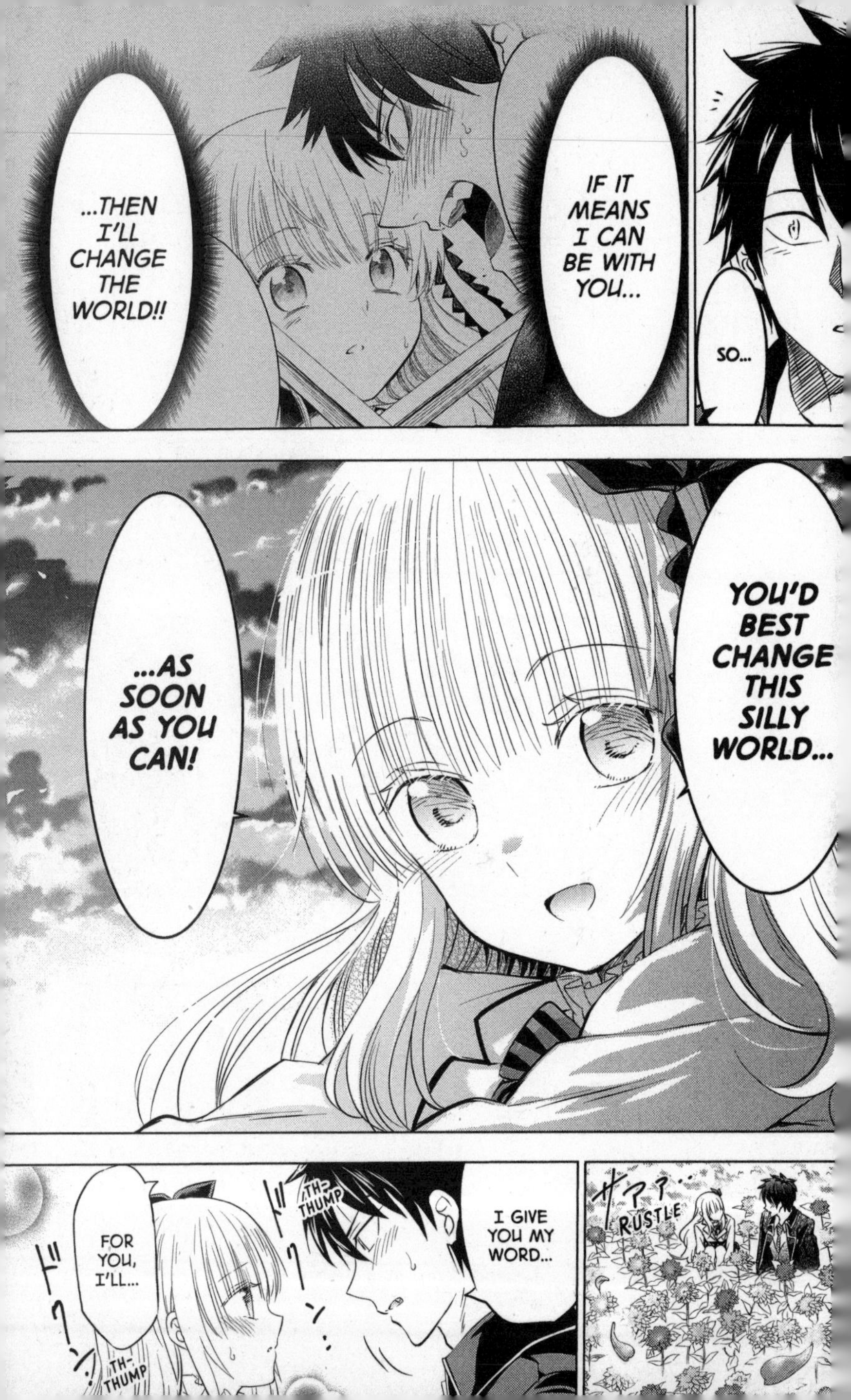
SO...
IF IT MEANS I CAN BE WITH YOU...
...THEN I'LL CHANGE THE WORLD!!
YOU'D BEST CHANGE THIS SILLY WORLD...
...AS SOON AS YOU CAN!
RUSTLE
I GIVE YOU MY WORD...
TH-THUMP
FOR YOU, I'LL...
TH-THUMP

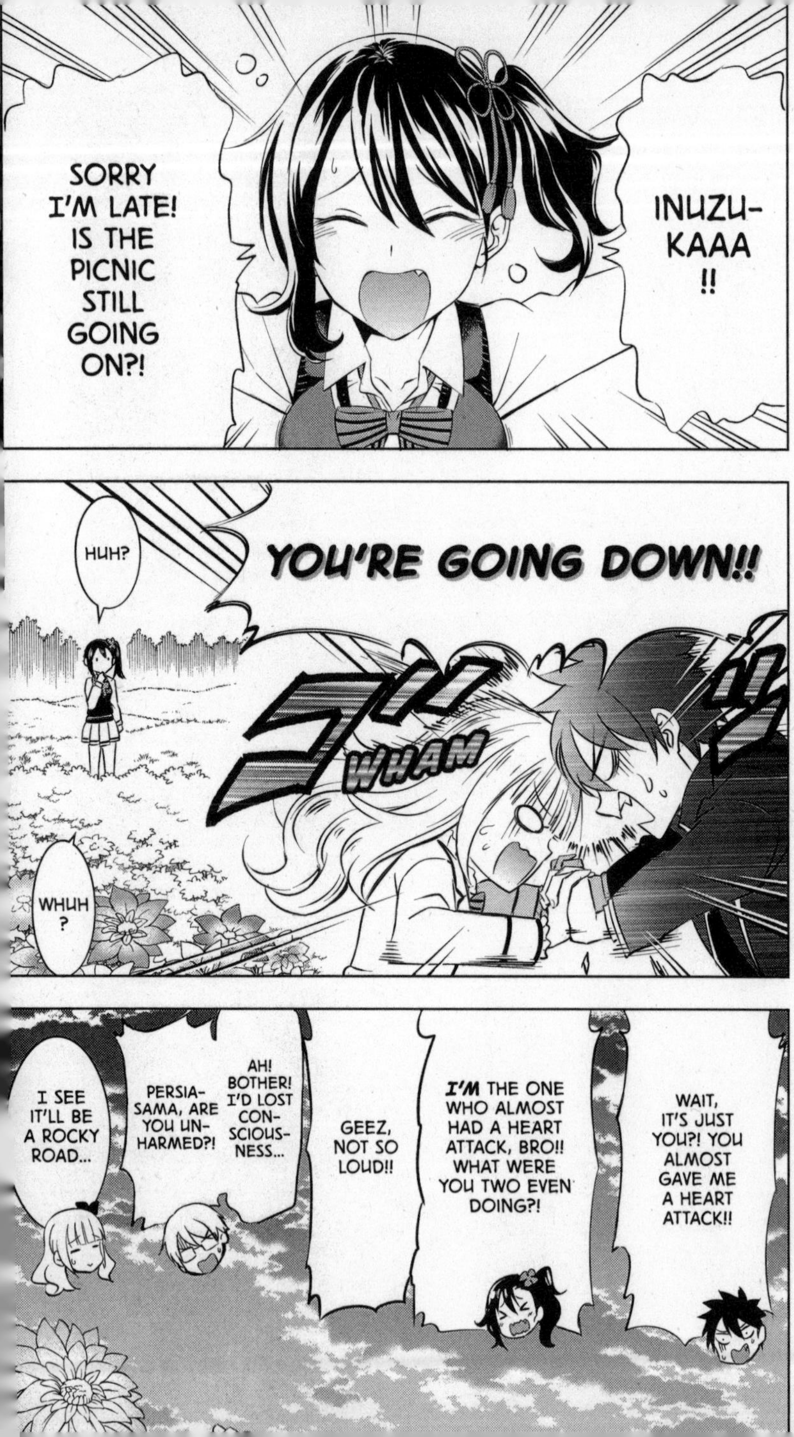
INUZU-KAAA!!
SORRY I'M LATE! IS THE PICNIC STILL GOING ON?!
YOU'RE GOING DOWN!!
WHAM
HUH?
WHUH?
WAIT, IT'S JUST YOU?! YOU ALMOST GAVE ME A HEART ATTACK!!
I'M THE ONE WHO ALMOST HAD A HEART ATTACK, BRO!! WHAT WERE YOU TWO EVEN DOING?!
GEEZ, NOT SO LOUD!!
AH! BOTHER! I'D LOST CONSCIOUSNESS...
PERSIA-SAMA, ARE YOU UNHARMED?!
I SEE IT'LL BE A ROCKY ROAD...

DAHLIA ACADEMY GUIDE #1: MAIN BUILDING

This building is used by all students, and houses staff rooms, large conference rooms, the historical archive, the student affairs office, the computer lab, etc.

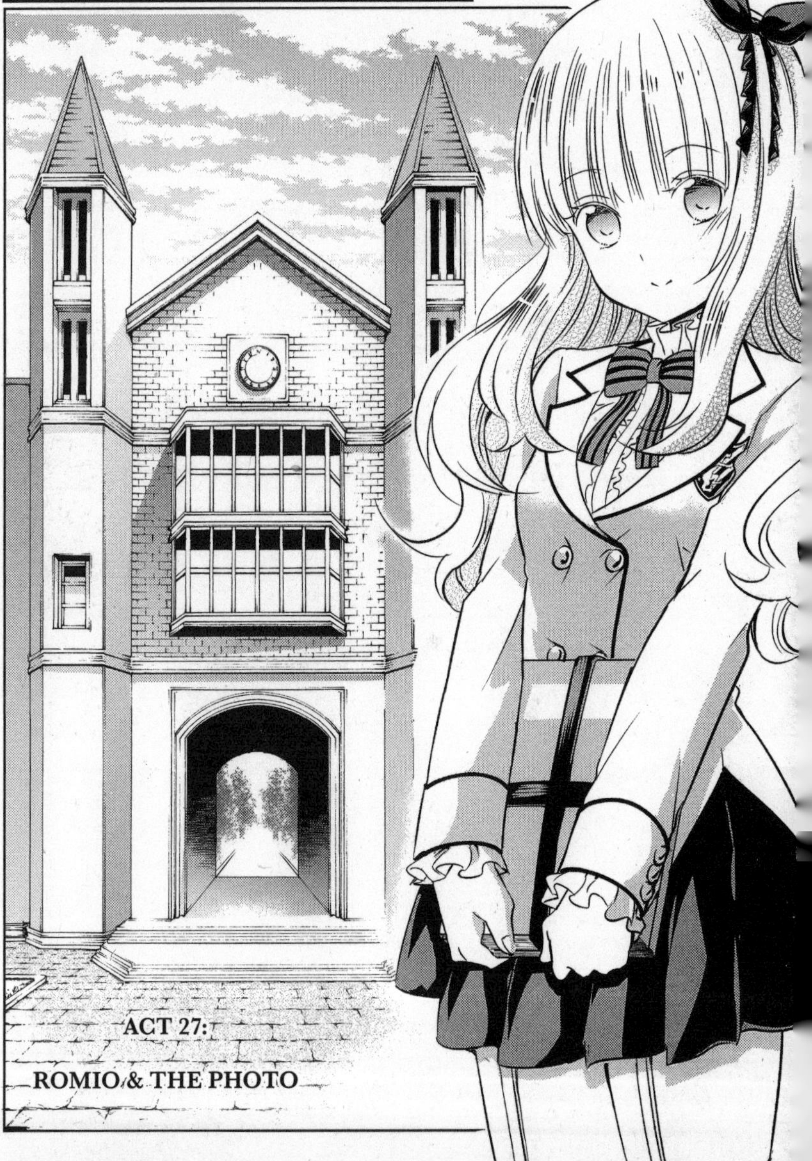
ACT 27:
ROMIO & THE PHOTO

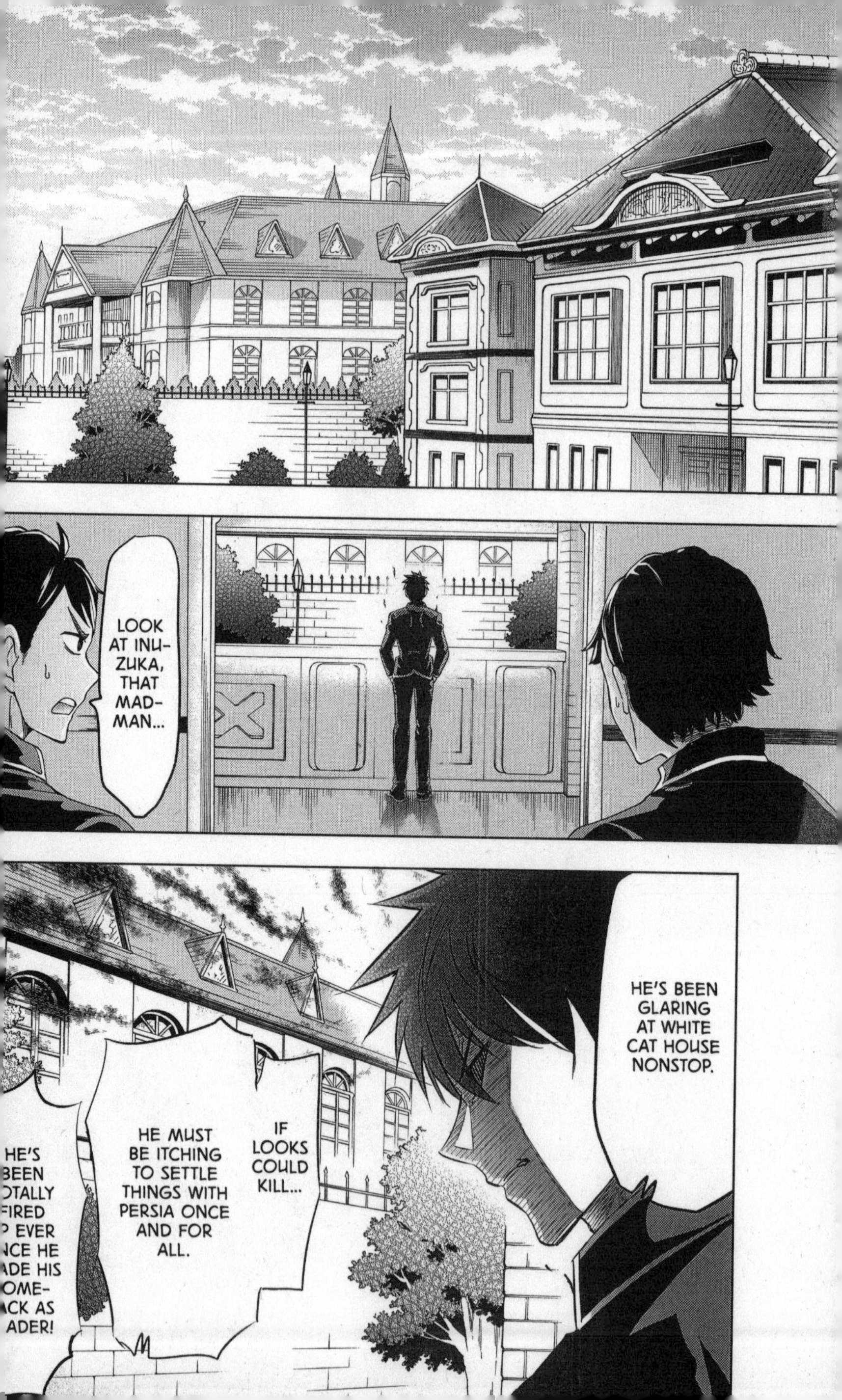
LOOK AT INUZUKA, THAT MADMAN...
HE'S BEEN GLARING AT WHITE CAT HOUSE NONSTOP.
IF LOOKS COULD KILL...
HE MUST BE ITCHING TO SETTLE THINGS WITH PERSIA ONCE AND FOR ALL.
HE'S BEEN OTALLY FIRED P EVER NCE HE ADE HIS OME- ACK AS ADER!

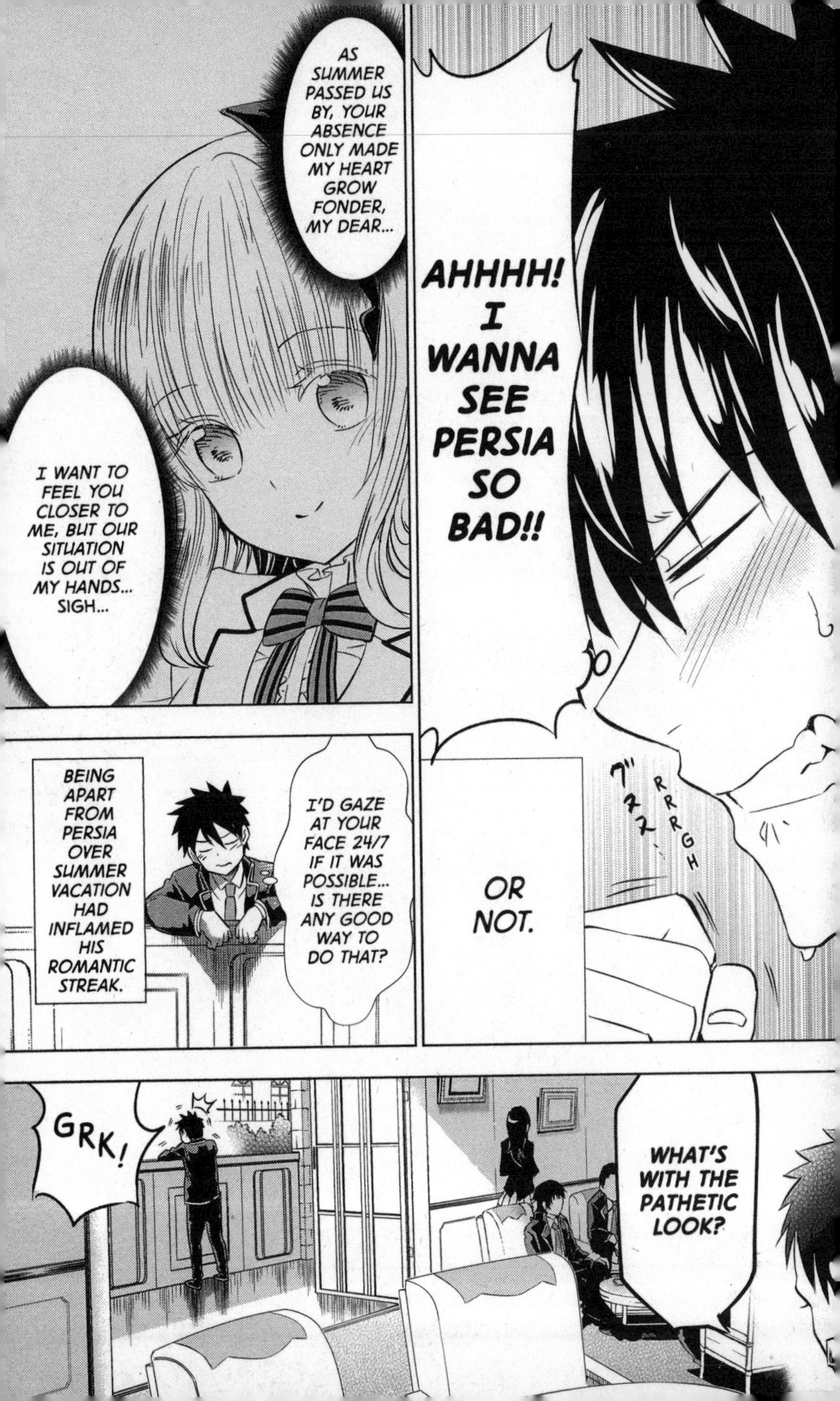
AHHHH! I WANNA SEE PERSIA SO BAD!!
RRRRGH
OR NOT.
AS SUMMER PASSED US BY, YOUR ABSENCE ONLY MADE MY HEART GROW FONDER, MY DEAR...
I WANT TO FEEL YOU CLOSER TO ME, BUT OUR SITUATION IS OUT OF MY HANDS... SIGH...
I'D GAZE AT YOUR FACE 24/7 IF IT WAS POSSIBLE... IS THERE ANY GOOD WAY TO DO THAT?
BEING APART FROM PERSIA OVER SUMMER VACATION HAD INFLAMED HIS ROMANTIC STREAK.
WHAT'S WITH THE PATHETIC LOOK?
GRK!

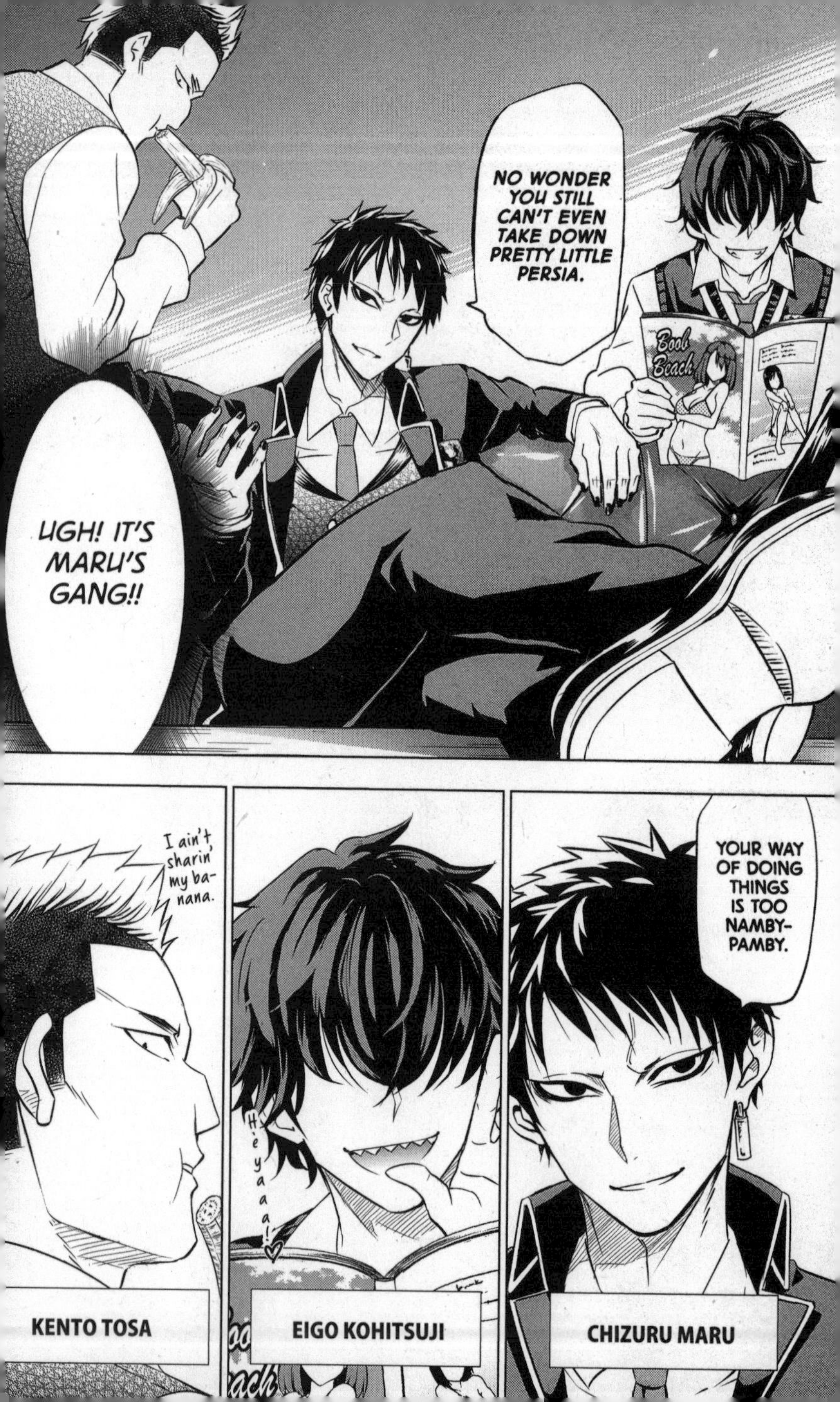
NO WONDER YOU STILL CAN'T EVEN TAKE DOWN PRETTY LITTLE PERSIA.
Boob Beach
UGH! IT'S MARU'S GANG!!
YOUR WAY OF DOING THINGS IS TOO NAMBY-PAMBY.
CHIZURU MARU
He yaaa!♥
EIGO KOHITSUJI
I ain't sharin' my ba-nana.
KENTO TOSA

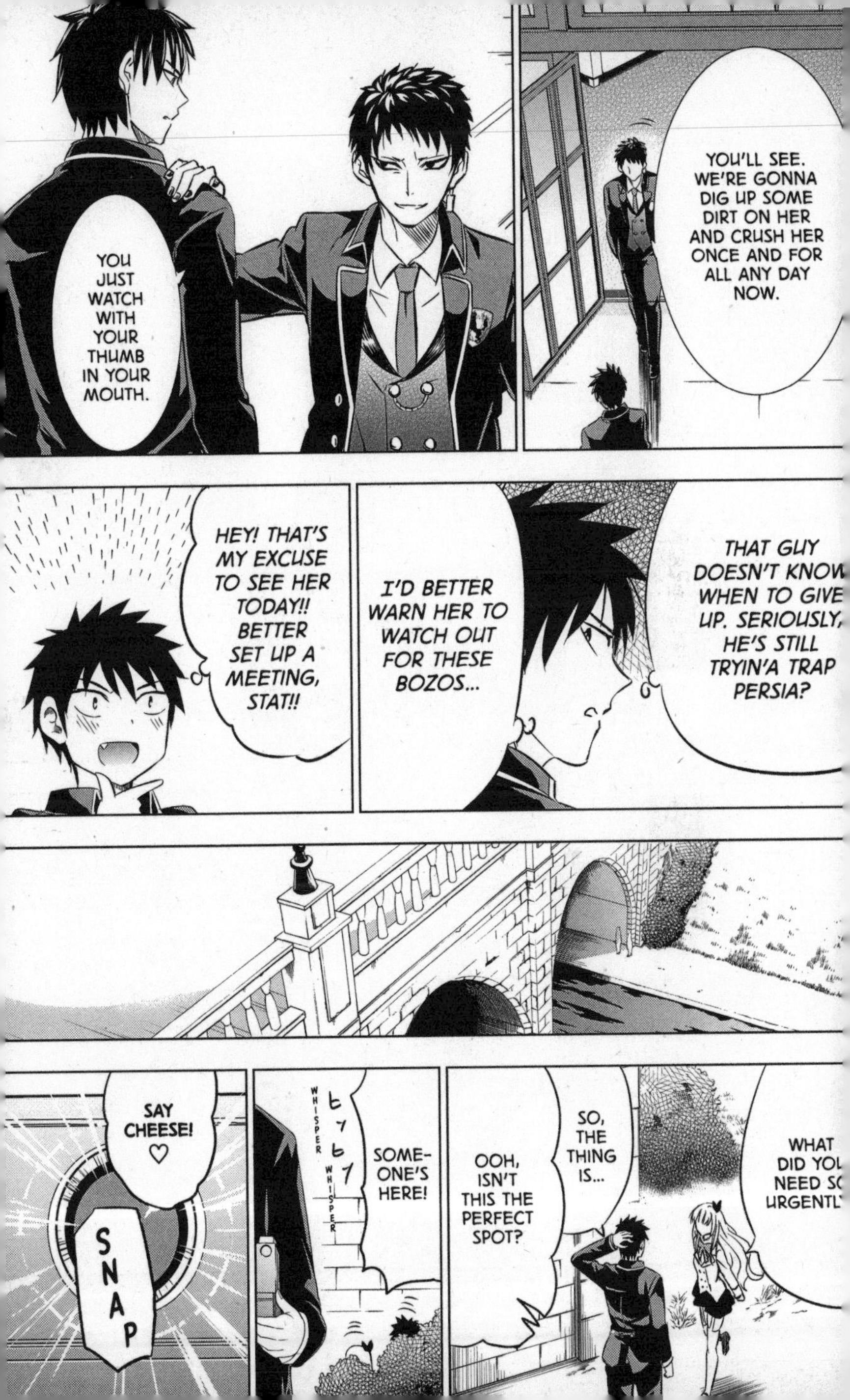
YOU'LL SEE. WE'RE GONNA DIG UP SOME DIRT ON HER AND CRUSH HER ONCE AND FOR ALL ANY DAY NOW.
YOU JUST WATCH WITH YOUR THUMB IN YOUR MOUTH.
THAT GUY DOESN'T KNOW WHEN TO GIVE UP. SERIOUSLY, HE'S STILL TRYIN'A TRAP PERSIA?
I'D BETTER WARN HER TO WATCH OUT FOR THESE BOZOS...
HEY! THAT'S MY EXCUSE TO SEE HER TODAY!! BETTER SET UP A MEETING, STAT!!
WHAT DID YOU NEED SO URGENTLY
SO, THE THING IS...
OOH, ISN'T THIS THE PERFECT SPOT?
SOME-ONE'S HERE!
ヒソヒソ
WHISPER WHISPER
SAY CHEESE! ♡
SNAP

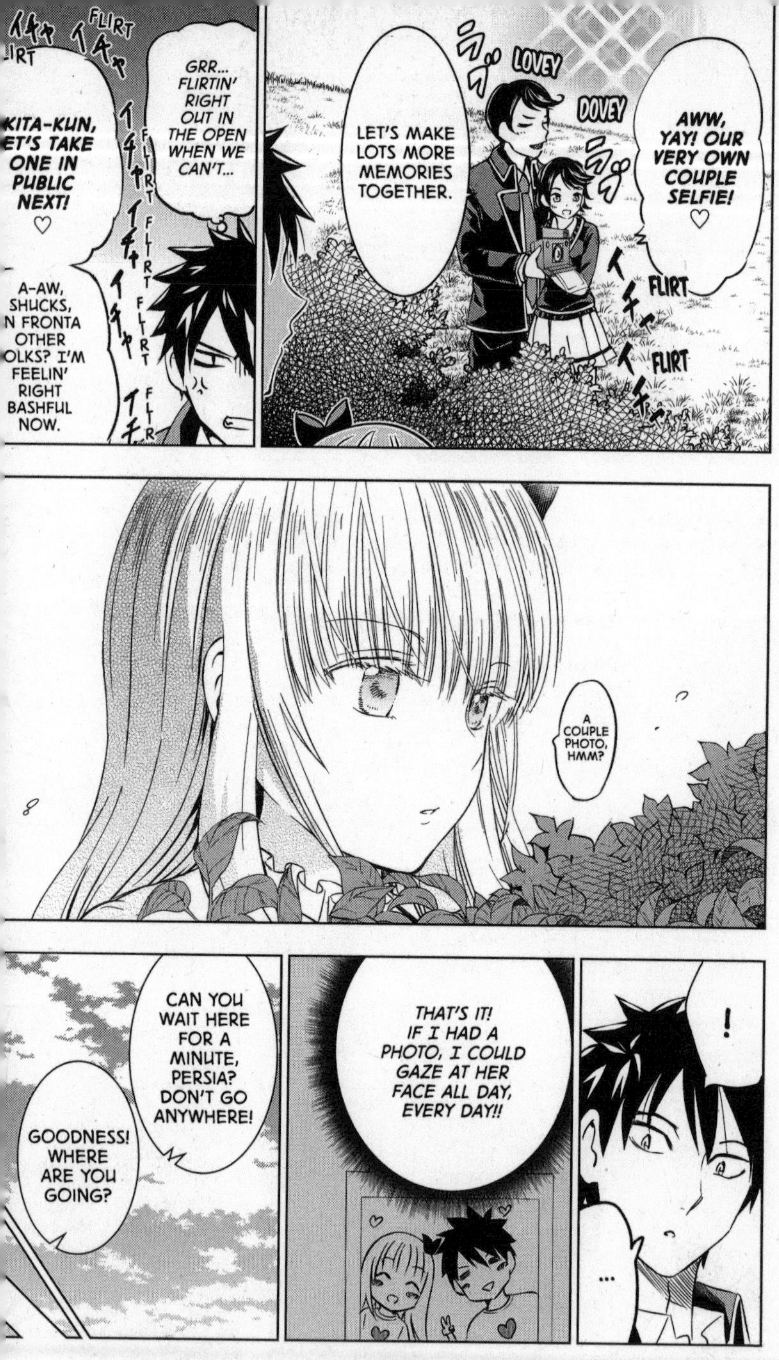

AWW, YAY! OUR VERY OWN COUPLE SELFIE! ♡
FLIRT
FLIRT
LOVEY
DOVEY
LET'S MAKE LOTS MORE MEMORIES TOGETHER.
FLIRT
GRR... FLIRTIN' RIGHT OUT IN THE OPEN WHEN WE CAN'T...
KITA-KUN, ET'S TAKE ONE IN PUBLIC NEXT! ♡
FLIRT FLIRT FLIRT FLIRT FLIRT
A-AW, SHUCKS, N FRONTA OTHER OLKS? I'M FEELIN' RIGHT BASHFUL NOW.
A COUPLE PHOTO, HMM?
!
...
THAT'S IT! IF I HAD A PHOTO, I COULD GAZE AT HER FACE ALL DAY, EVERY DAY!!
CAN YOU WAIT HERE FOR A MINUTE, PERSIA? DON'T GO ANYWHERE!
GOODNESS! WHERE ARE YOU GOING?

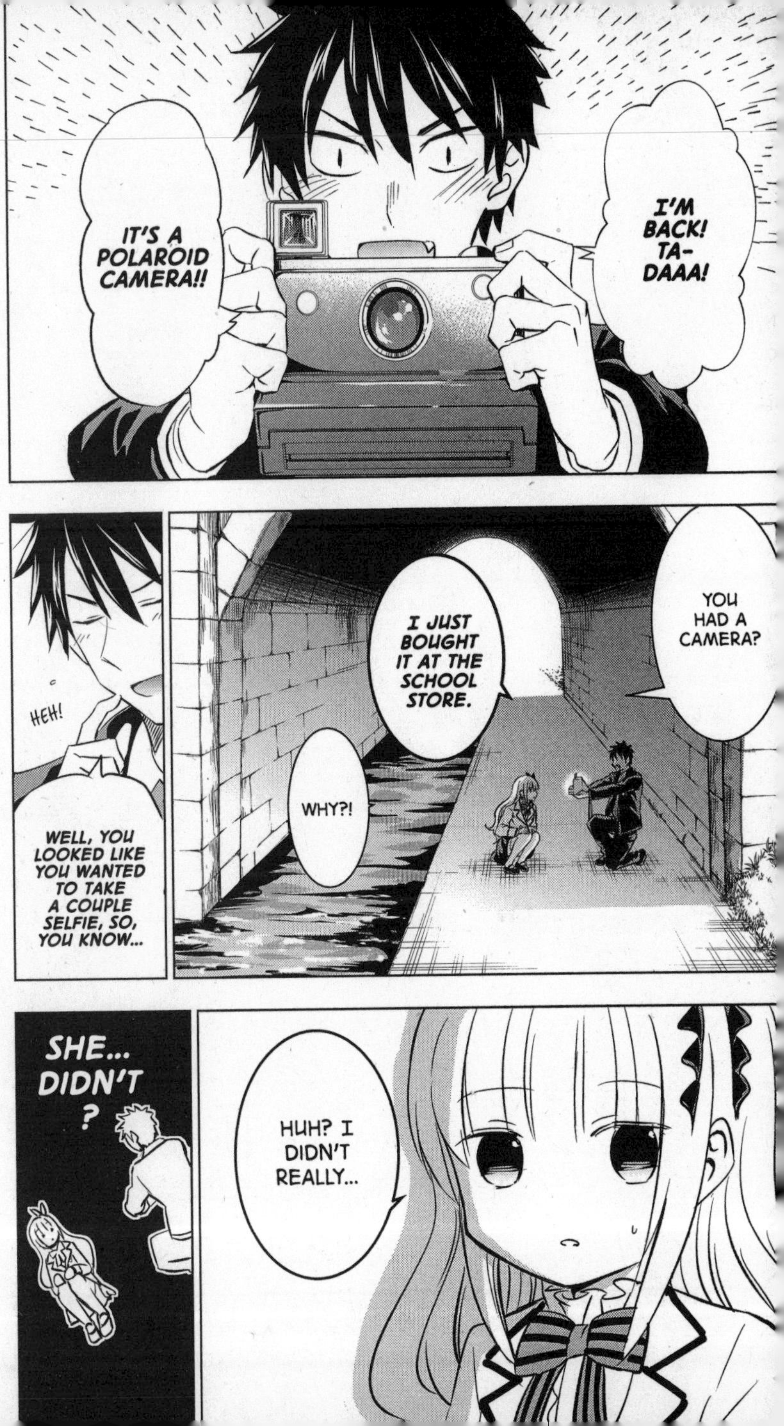
I'M BACK! TA-DAAA!
IT'S A POLAROID CAMERA!!
YOU HAD A CAMERA?
I JUST BOUGHT IT AT THE SCHOOL STORE.
WHY?!
HEH!
WELL, YOU LOOKED LIKE YOU WANTED TO TAKE A COUPLE SELFIE, SO, YOU KNOW...
HUH? I DIDN'T REALLY...
SHE... DIDN'T ?

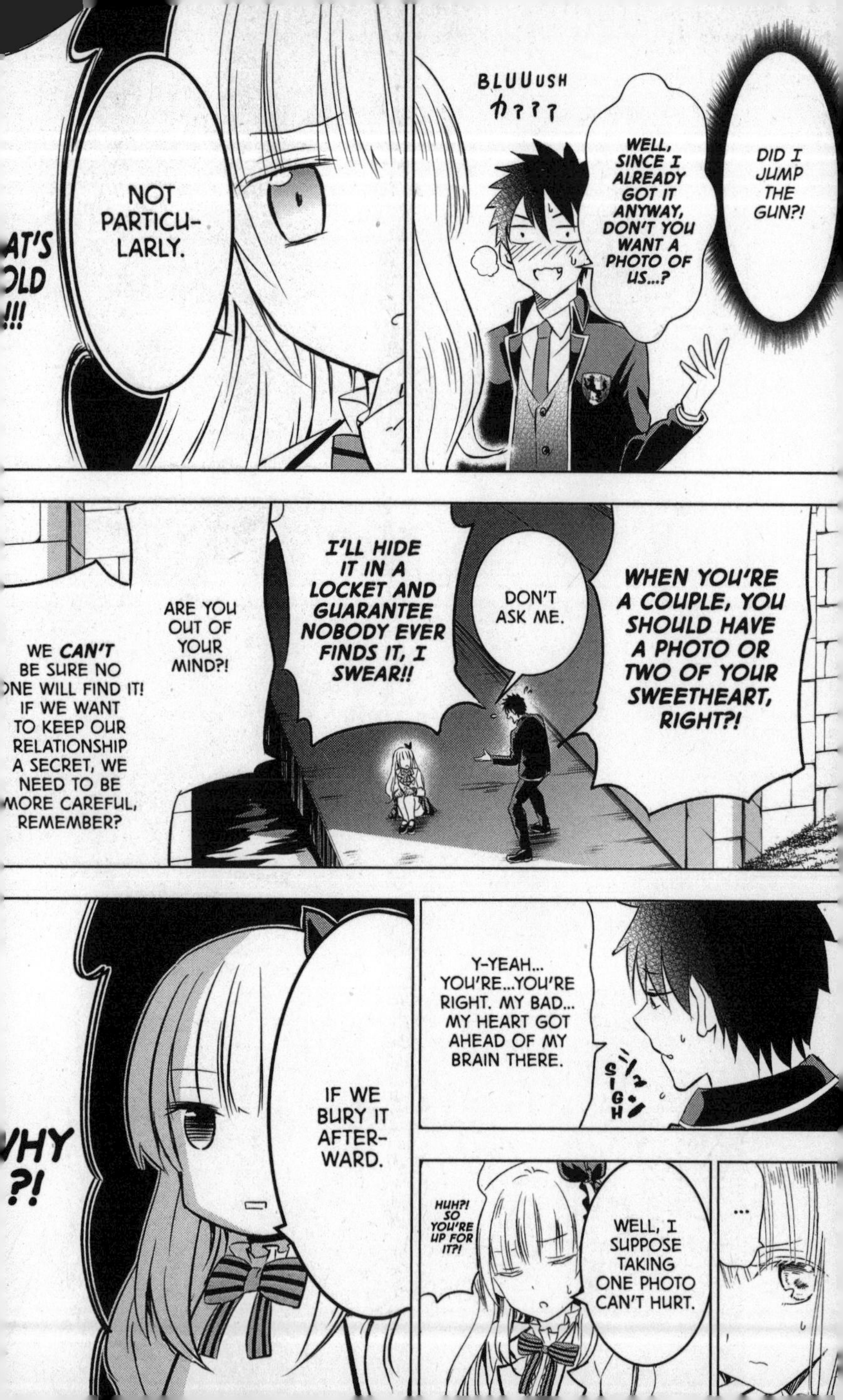
DID I JUMP THE GUN?!
BLUUUSH
WELL, SINCE I ALREADY GOT IT ANYWAY, DON'T YOU WANT A PHOTO OF US...?
NOT PARTICU-LARLY.
WHEN YOU'RE A COUPLE, YOU SHOULD HAVE A PHOTO OR TWO OF YOUR SWEETHEART, RIGHT?!
DON'T ASK ME.
I'LL HIDE IT IN A LOCKET AND GUARANTEE NOBODY EVER FINDS IT, I SWEAR!!
ARE YOU OUT OF YOUR MIND?!
WE CAN'T BE SURE NO ONE WILL FIND IT! IF WE WANT TO KEEP OUR RELATIONSHIP A SECRET, WE NEED TO BE MORE CAREFUL, REMEMBER?
Y-YEAH... YOU'RE...YOU'RE RIGHT. MY BAD... MY HEART GOT AHEAD OF MY BRAIN THERE.
SIGH
...
WELL, I SUPPOSE TAKING ONE PHOTO CAN'T HURT.
HUH?! SO YOU'RE UP FOR IT?!
IF WE BURY IT AFTER-WARD.

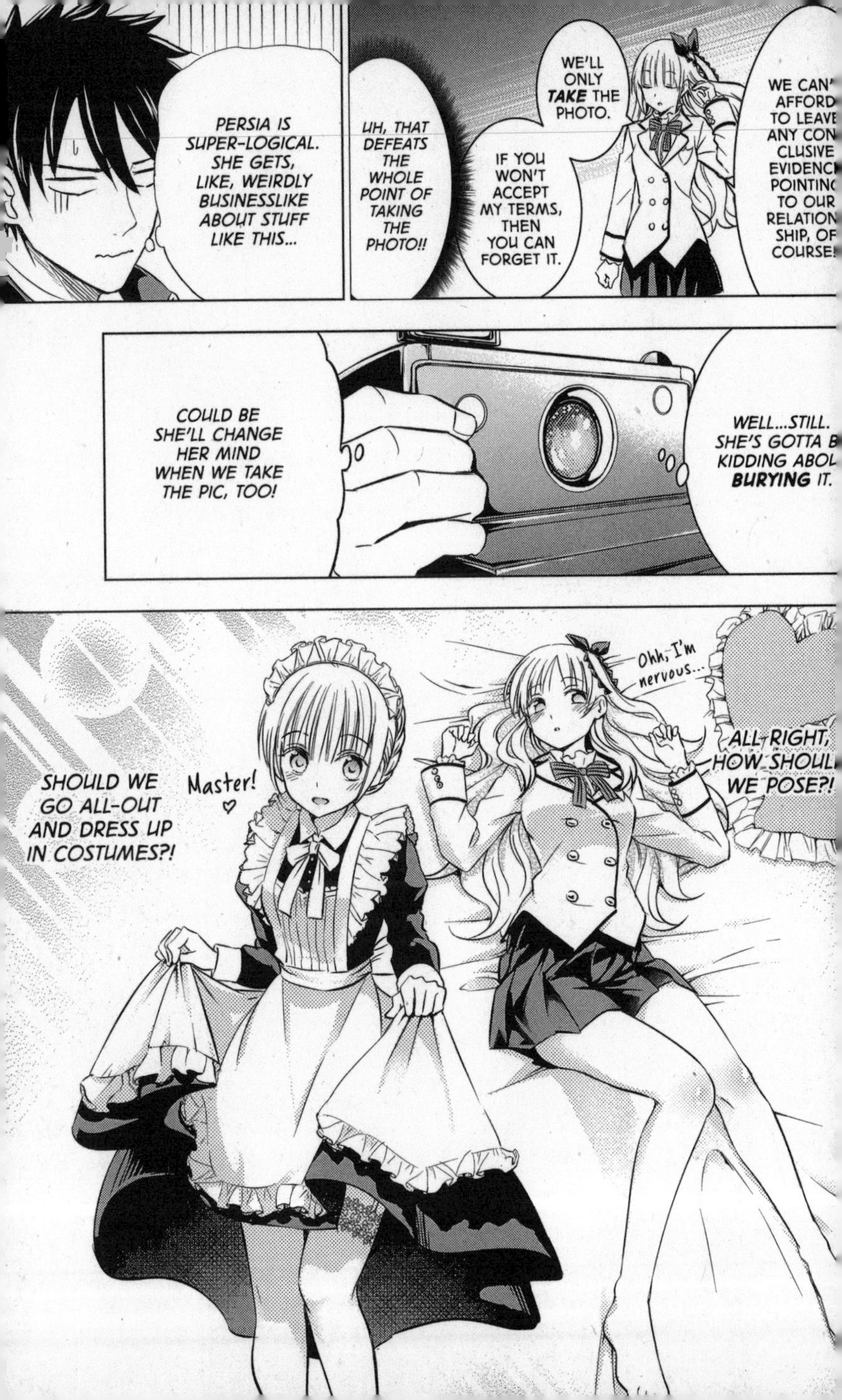

WE CAN' AFFORD TO LEAVE ANY CON CLUSIVE EVIDENC POINTIN TO OUR RELATION SHIP, OF COURSE!
WE'LL ONLY **TAKE** THE PHOTO.
IF YOU WON'T ACCEPT MY TERMS, THEN YOU CAN FORGET IT.
UH, THAT DEFEATS THE WHOLE POINT OF TAKING THE PHOTO!!
PERSIA IS SUPER-LOGICAL. SHE GETS, LIKE, WEIRDLY BUSINESSLIKE ABOUT STUFF LIKE THIS...
WELL...STILL. SHE'S GOTTA B KIDDING ABOU **BURYING** IT.
COULD BE SHE'LL CHANGE HER MIND WHEN WE TAKE THE PIC, TOO!
ALL RIGHT, HOW SHOUL WE POSE?!
Ohh, I'm nervous...
Master! ♡
SHOULD WE GO ALL-OUT AND DRESS UP IN COSTUMES?!

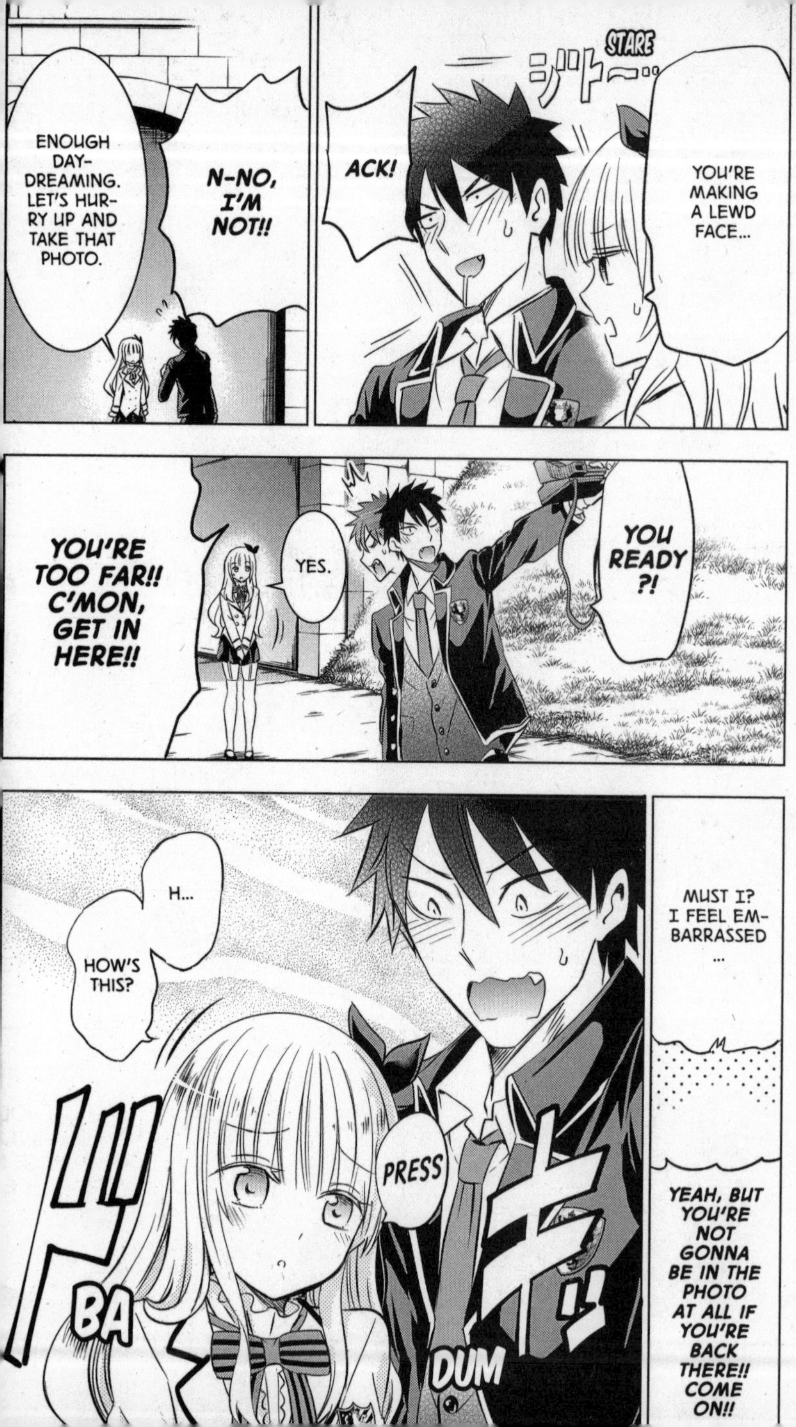

STARE
ジトー
YOU'RE MAKING A LEWD FACE...
ACK!
N-NO, I'M NOT!!
ENOUGH DAY-DREAMING. LET'S HUR-RY UP AND TAKE THAT PHOTO.
YOU READY?!
YES.
YOU'RE TOO FAR!! C'MON, GET IN HERE!!
MUST I? I FEEL EM-BARRASSED...
YEAH, BUT YOU'RE NOT GONNA BE IN THE PHOTO AT ALL IF YOU'RE BACK THERE!! COME ON!!
H...
HOW'S THIS?
PRESS
BA
DUM

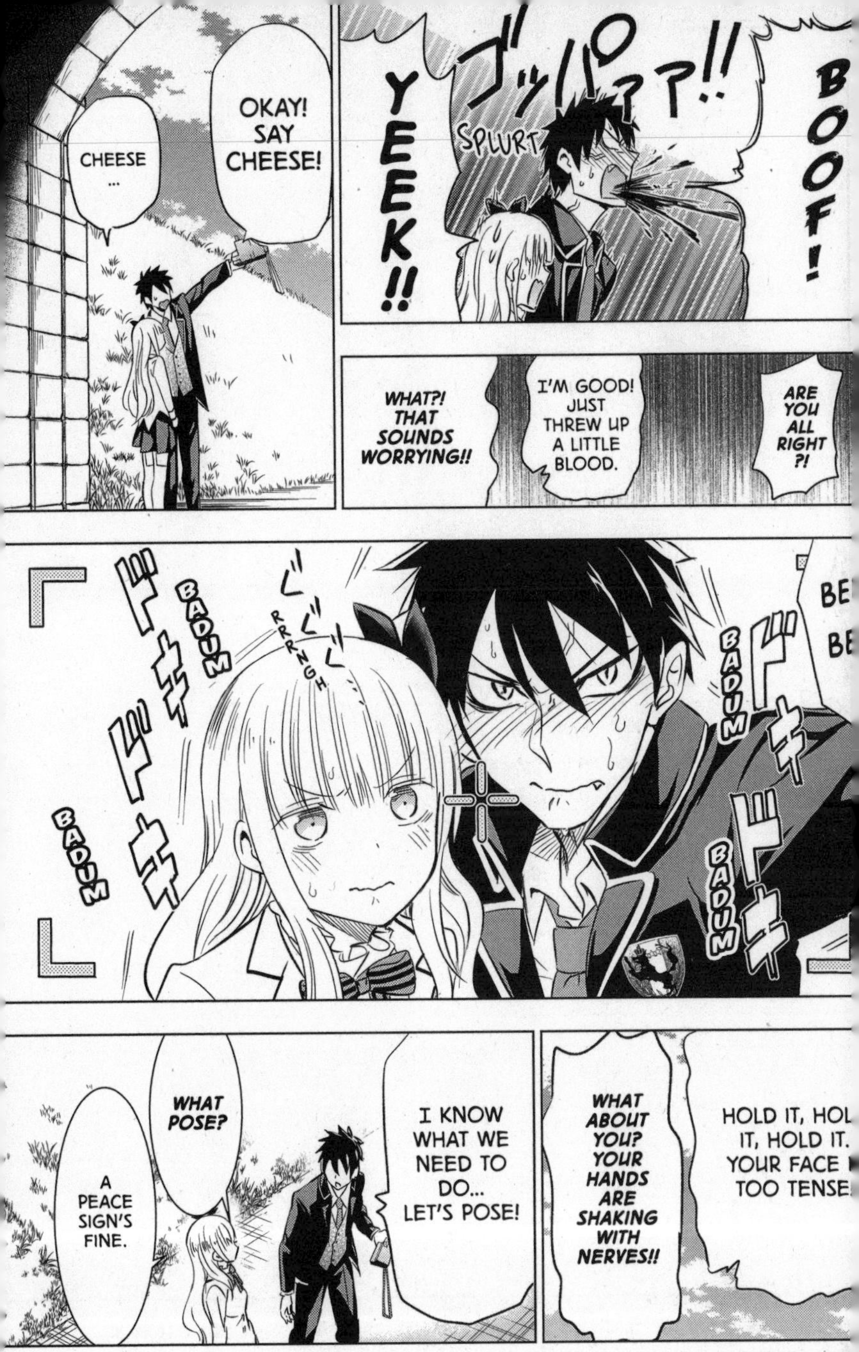
BOOOF!
ゴッパアア!!
SPLURT
YEEK!!
ARE YOU ALL RIGHT?!
I'M GOOD! JUST THREW UP A LITTLE BLOOD.
WHAT?! THAT SOUNDS WORRYING!!
OKAY! SAY CHEESE!
CHEESE ...
BE
BE
BADUM
ドキ
BADUM
ドキ
RRRNGH
BADUM
ドキ
BADUM
ドキ
HOLD IT, HOL
IT, HOLD IT.
YOUR FACE
TOO TENSE
WHAT ABOUT YOU? YOUR HANDS ARE SHAKING WITH NERVES!!
I KNOW WHAT WE NEED TO DO... LET'S POSE!
WHAT POSE?
A PEACE SIGN'S FINE.

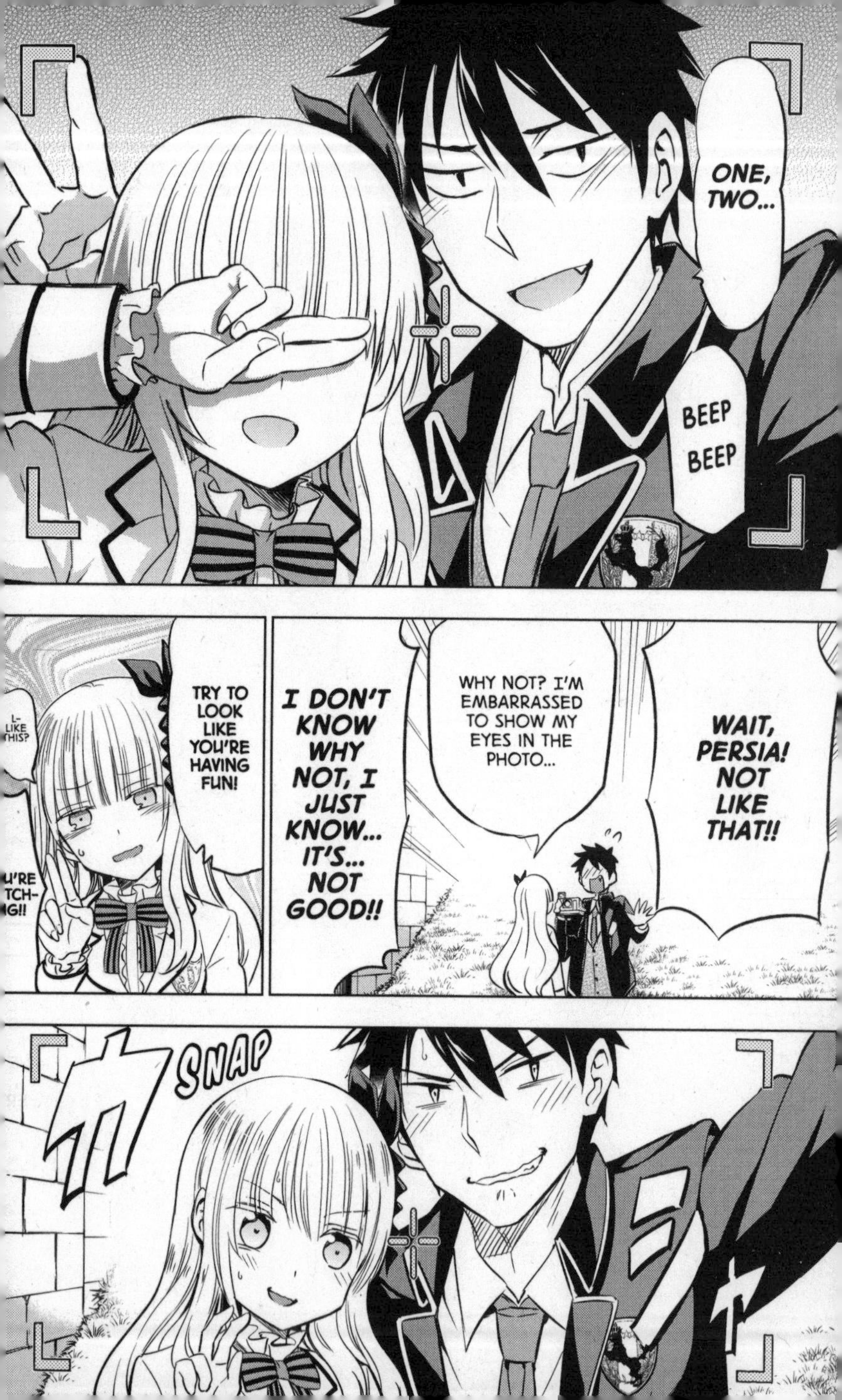
ONE, TWO...
BEEP BEEP
WAIT, PERSIA! NOT LIKE THAT!!
WHY NOT? I'M EMBARRASSED TO SHOW MY EYES IN THE PHOTO...
I DON'T KNOW WHY NOT, I JUST KNOW... IT'S... NOT GOOD!!
TRY TO LOOK LIKE YOU'RE HAVING FUN!
L-LIKE THIS?
SNAP

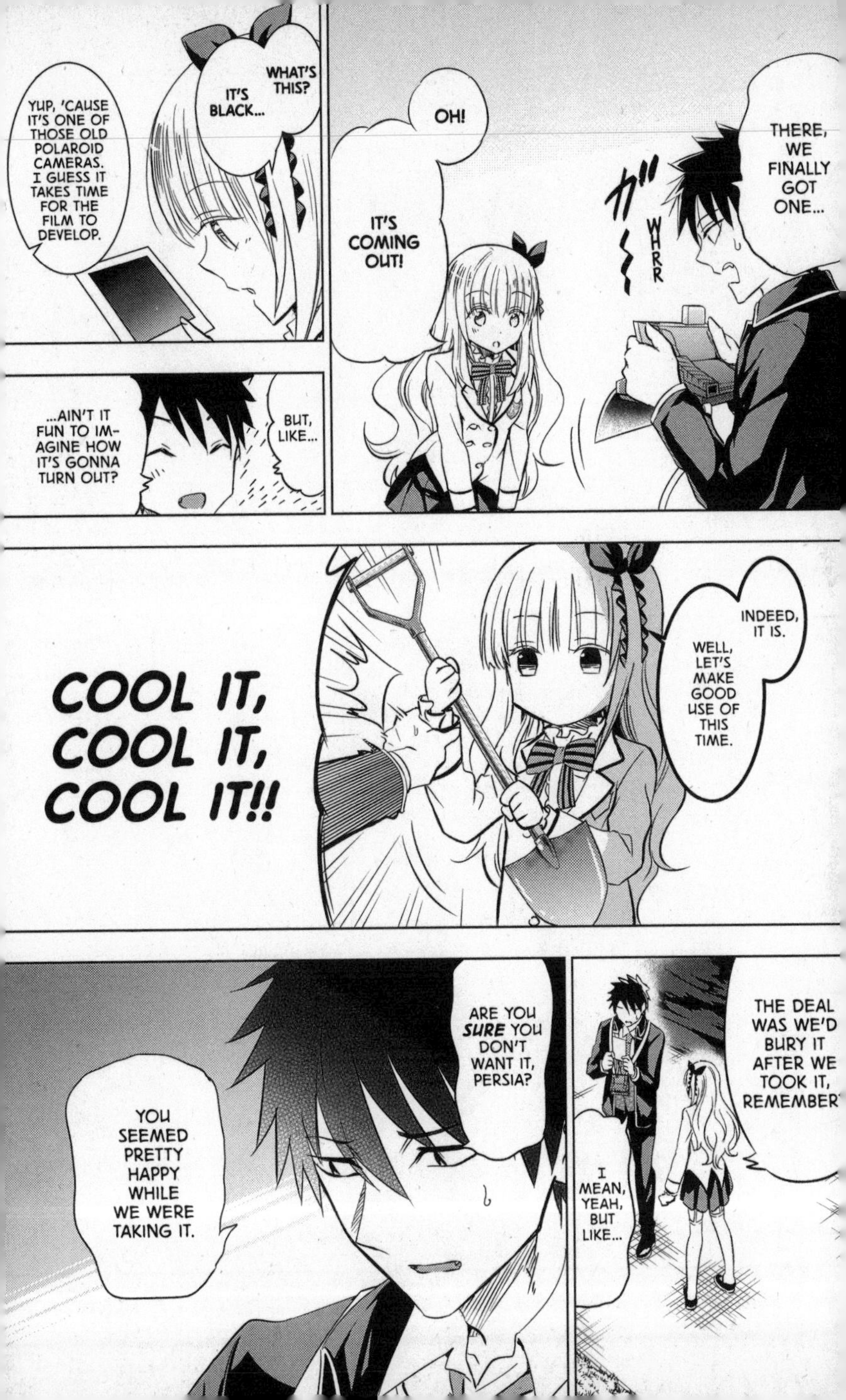
THERE, WE FINALLY GOT ONE...
WHRR
OH!
IT'S COMING OUT!
WHAT'S THIS? IT'S BLACK...
YUP, 'CAUSE IT'S ONE OF THOSE OLD POLAROID CAMERAS. I GUESS IT TAKES TIME FOR THE FILM TO DEVELOP.
BUT, LIKE...
...AIN'T IT FUN TO IMAGINE HOW IT'S GONNA TURN OUT?
INDEED, IT IS.
WELL, LET'S MAKE GOOD USE OF THIS TIME.
COOL IT, COOL IT, COOL IT!!
THE DEAL WAS WE'D BURY IT AFTER WE TOOK IT, REMEMBER
I MEAN, YEAH, BUT LIKE...
ARE YOU *SURE* YOU DON'T WANT IT, PERSIA?
YOU SEEMED PRETTY HAPPY WHILE WE WERE TAKING IT.

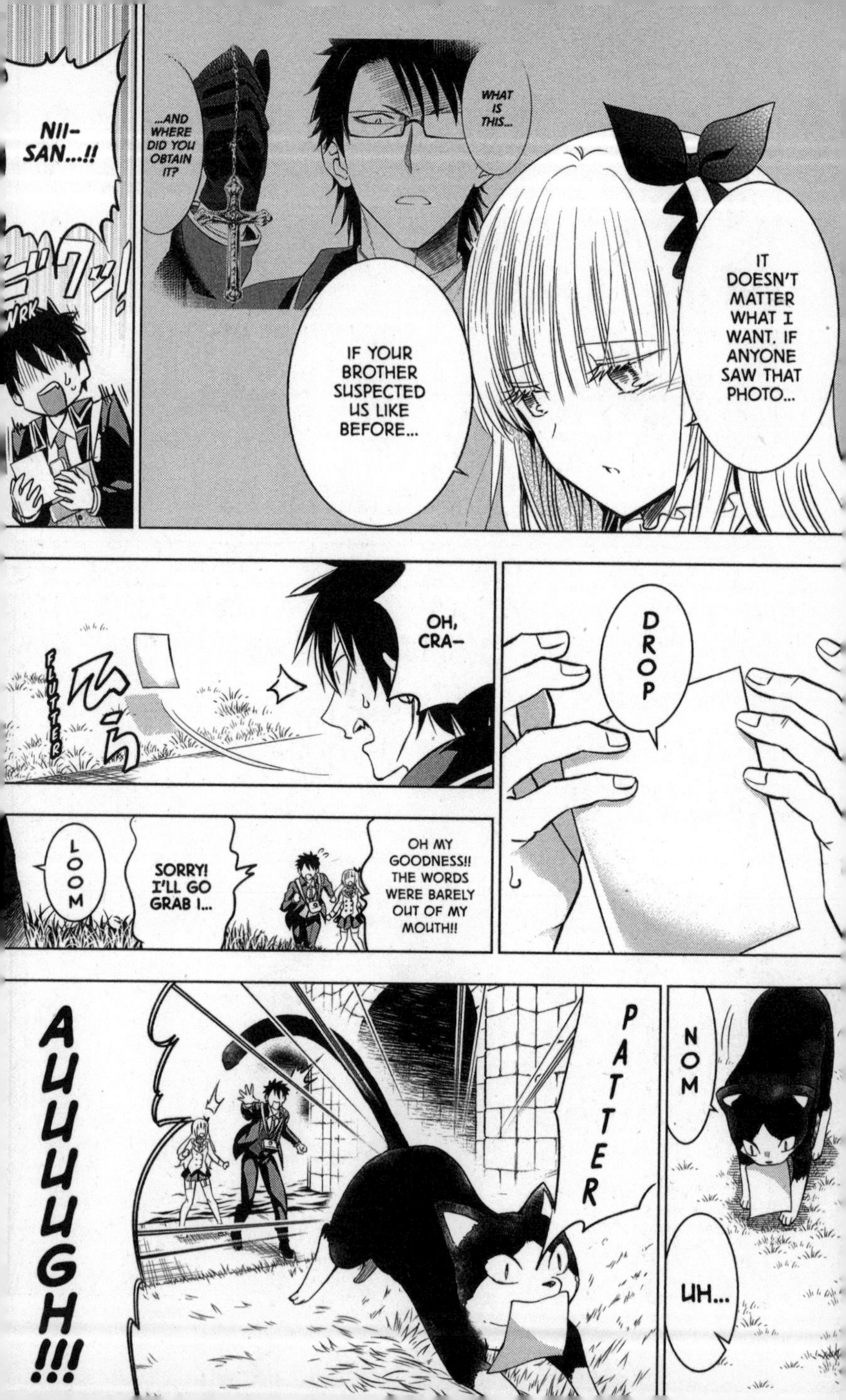
IT DOESN'T MATTER WHAT I WANT. IF ANYONE SAW THAT PHOTO...
IF YOUR BROTHER SUSPECTED US LIKE BEFORE...
WHAT IS THIS...
...AND WHERE DID YOU OBTAIN IT?
NII-SAN...!!
WRK
DROP
OH, CRA-
FLUTTER
OH MY GOODNESS!! THE WORDS WERE BARELY OUT OF MY MOUTH!!
SORRY! I'LL GO GRAB I...
LOOM
NOM
UH...
PATTER
AUUUUGH!!!

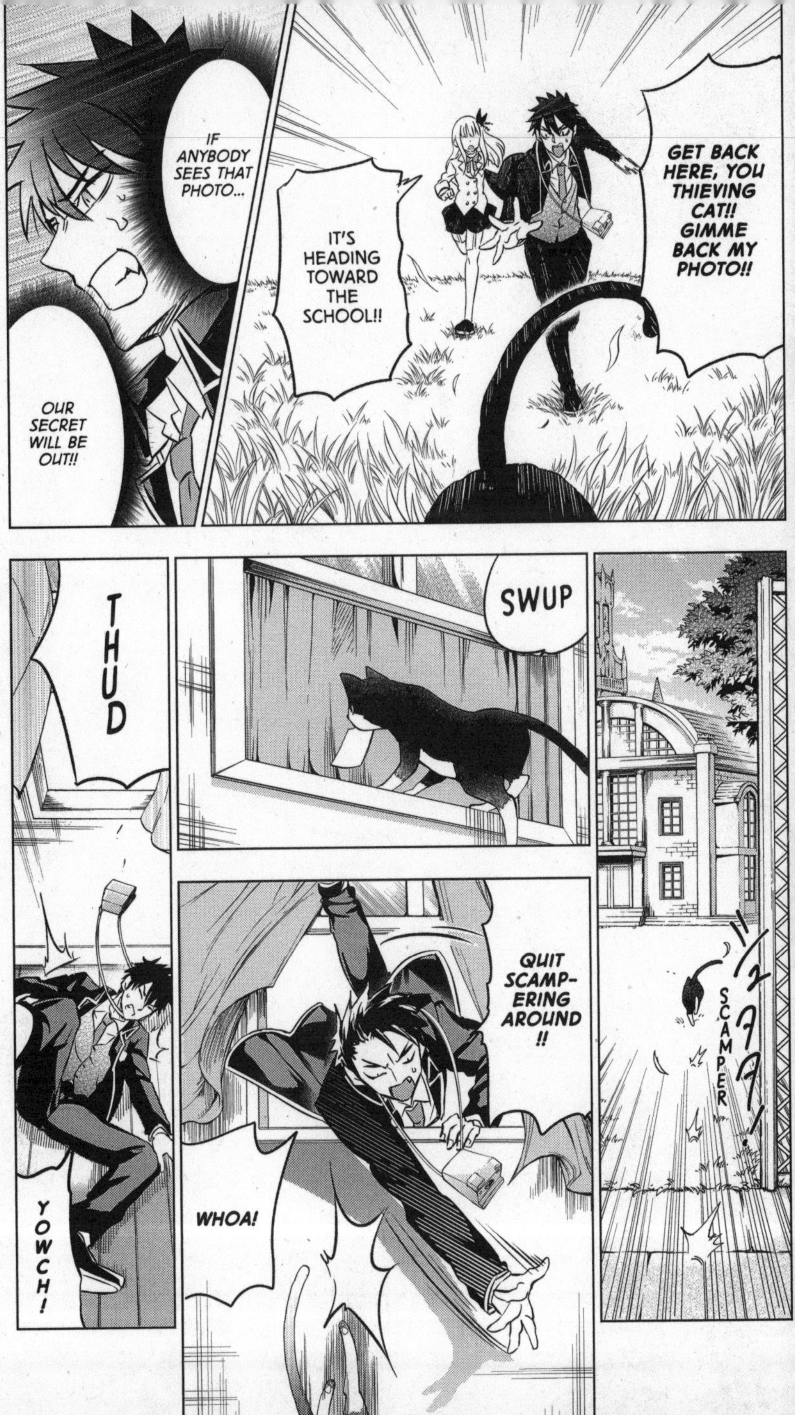

GET BACK HERE, YOU THIEVING CAT!! GIMME BACK MY PHOTO!!
IT'S HEADING TOWARD THE SCHOOL!!
IF ANYBODY SEES THAT PHOTO...
OUR SECRET WILL BE OUT!!
SCAMPER
SWUP
QUIT SCAMPERING AROUND!!
WHOA!
THUD
YOWCH!

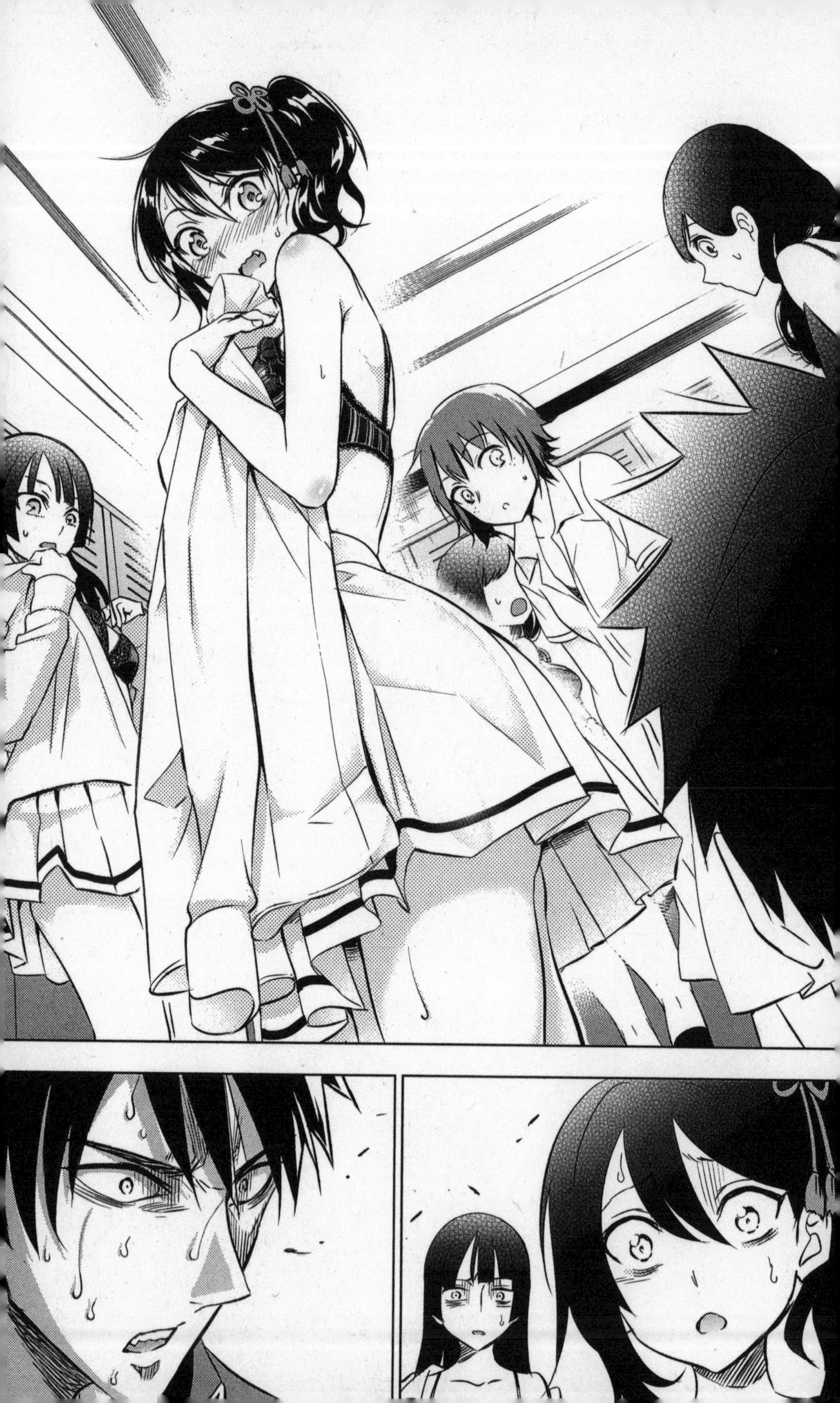

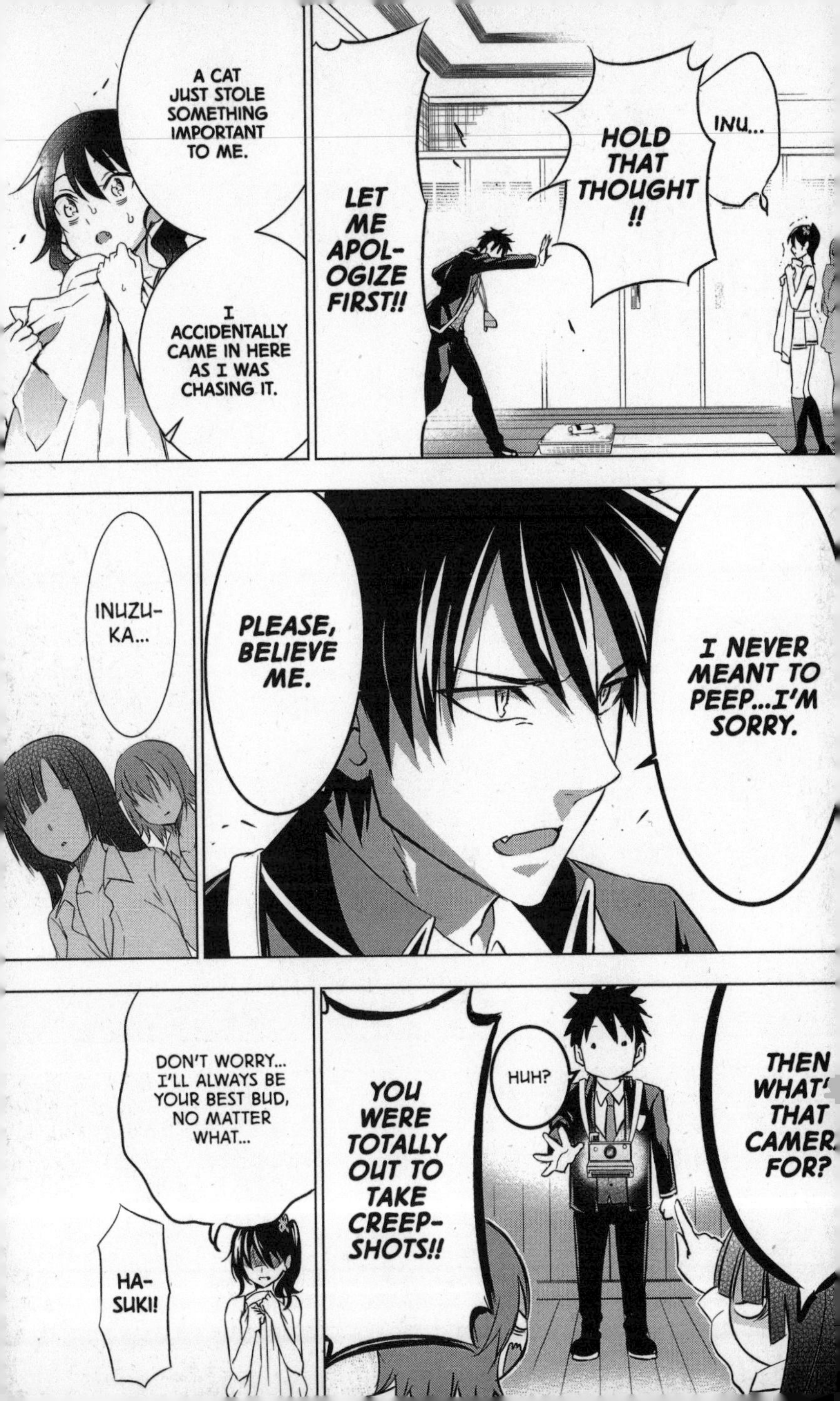
INU...
HOLD THAT THOUGHT!!
LET ME APOLOGIZE FIRST!!
A CAT JUST STOLE SOMETHING IMPORTANT TO ME.
I ACCIDENTALLY CAME IN HERE AS I WAS CHASING IT.
I NEVER MEANT TO PEEP...I'M SORRY.
PLEASE, BELIEVE ME.
INUZUKA...
THEN WHAT' THAT CAMER FOR?
HUH?
YOU WERE TOTALLY OUT TO TAKE CREEP-SHOTS!!
DON'T WORRY... I'LL ALWAYS BE YOUR BEST BUD, NO MATTER WHAT...
HA-SUKI!

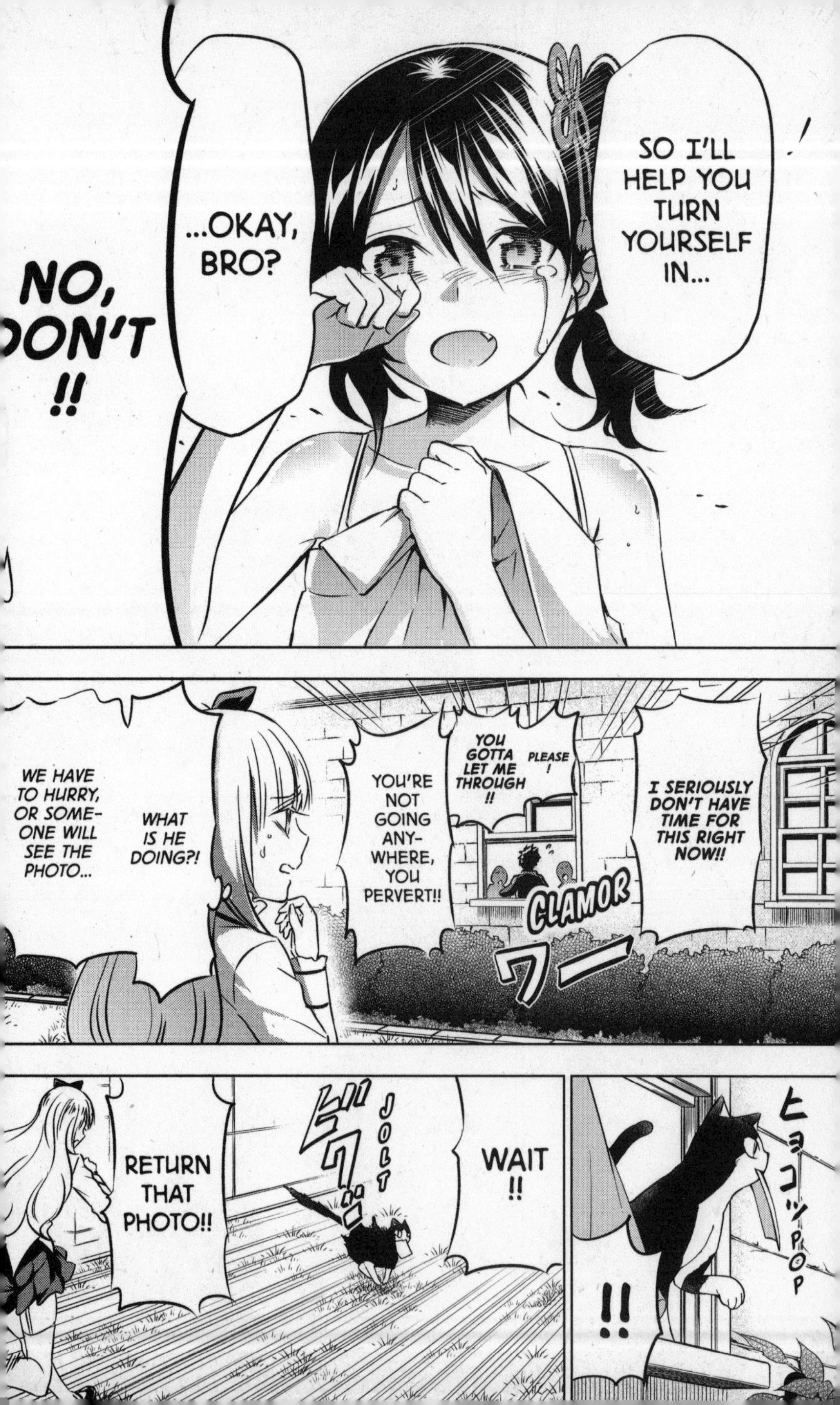
SO I'LL HELP YOU TURN YOURSELF IN...
...OKAY, BRO?
NO, DON'T !!
I SERIOUSLY DON'T HAVE TIME FOR THIS RIGHT NOW!!
PLEASE !
YOU GOTTA LET ME THROUGH !!
YOU'RE NOT GOING ANY-WHERE, YOU PERVERT!!
CLAMOR
ワー
WHAT IS HE DOING?!
WE HAVE TO HURRY, OR SOME-ONE WILL SEE THE PHOTO...
ヒョコッ
POP
!!
WAIT !!
ビクッ
JOLT
RETURN THAT PHOTO!!

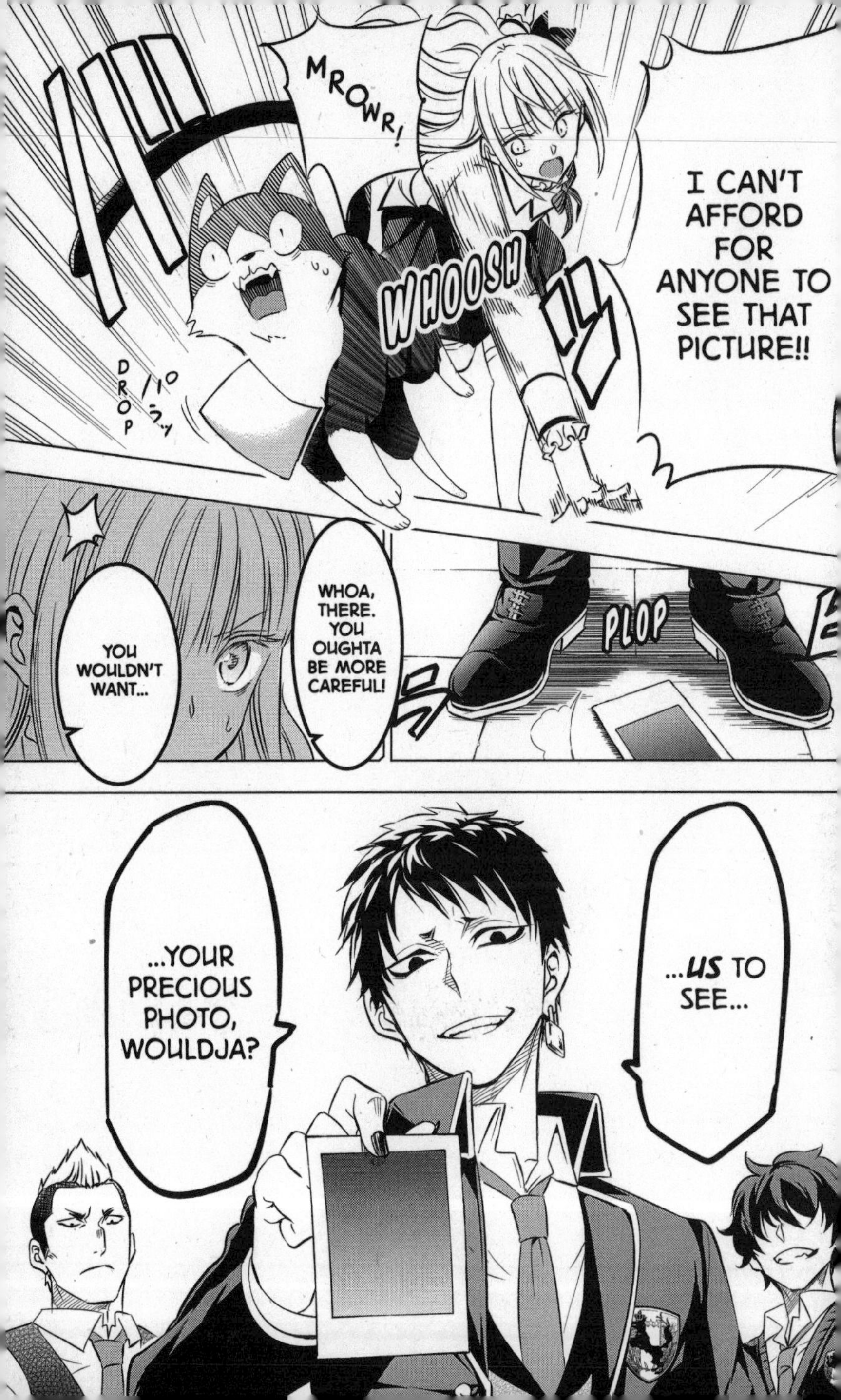
I CAN'T AFFORD FOR ANYONE TO SEE THAT PICTURE!!
MROWR!
WHOOSH
DROP
PLOP
WHOA, THERE. YOU OUGHTA BE MORE CAREFUL!
YOU WOULDN'T WANT...
...*US* TO SEE...
...YOUR PRECIOUS PHOTO, WOULDJA?

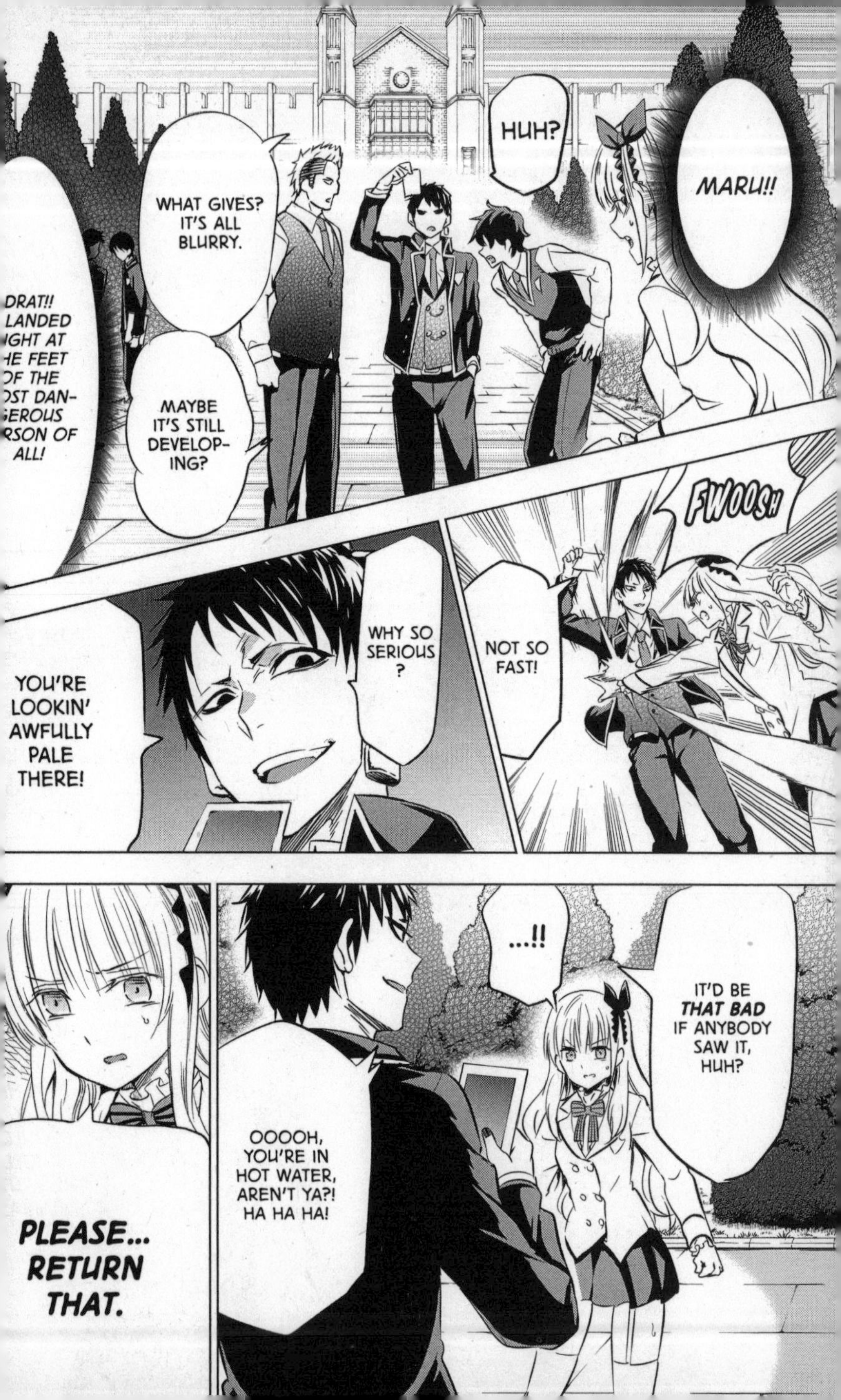
MARU!!
HUH?
WHAT GIVES? IT'S ALL BLURRY.
MAYBE IT'S STILL DEVELOP-ING?
DRAT!! LANDED IGHT AT HE FEET OF THE OST DAN-EROUS RSON OF ALL!
FWOOSH
NOT SO FAST!
WHY SO SERIOUS?
YOU'RE LOOKIN' AWFULLY PALE THERE!
IT'D BE *THAT BAD* IF ANYBODY SAW IT, HUH?
...!!
OOOOH, YOU'RE IN HOT WATER, AREN'T YA?! HA HA HA!
PLEASE... RETURN THAT.

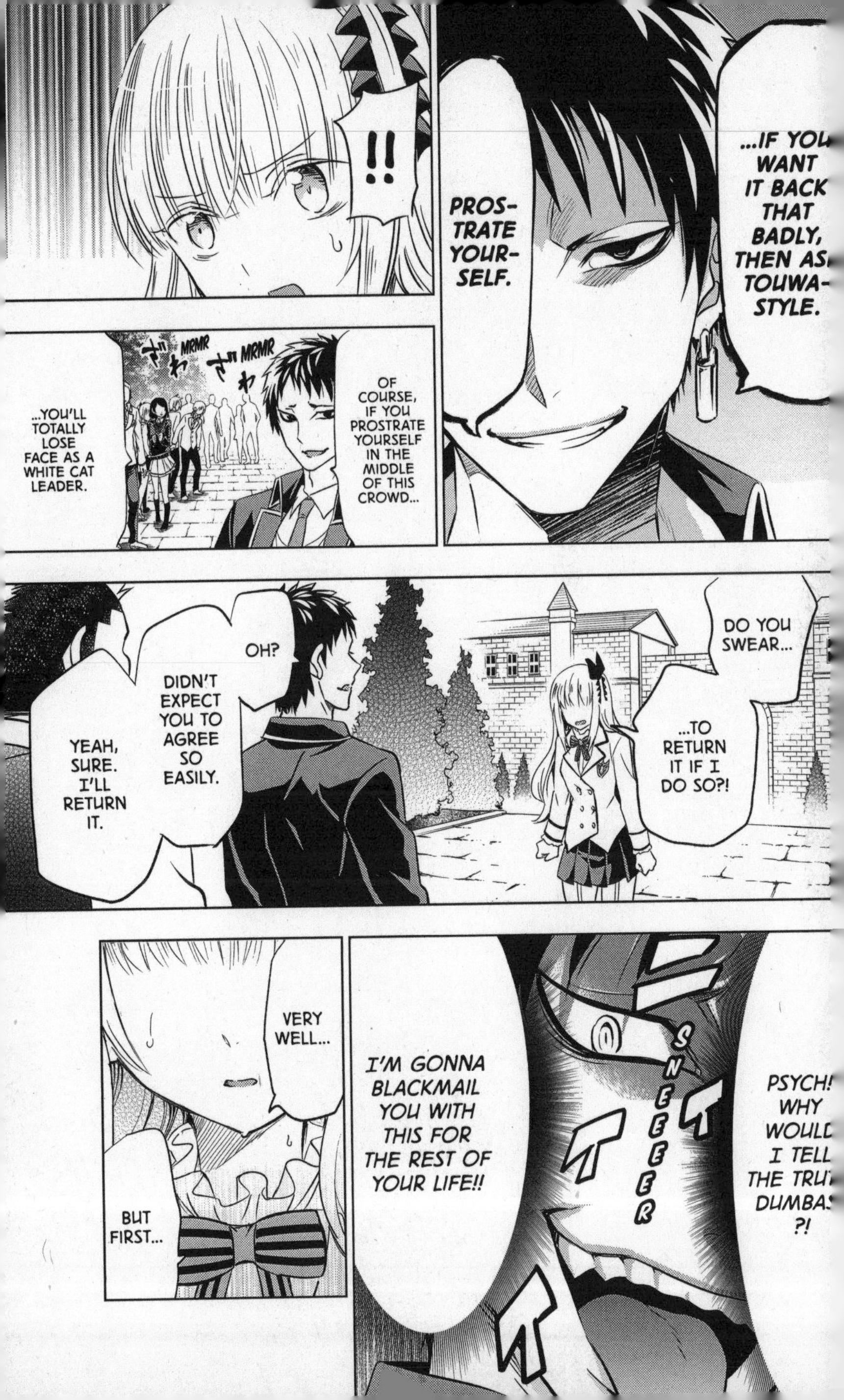
...IF YOU WANT IT BACK THAT BADLY, THEN AS TOUWA-STYLE.
PROS-TRATE YOUR-SELF.
!!
MRMR MRMR
OF COURSE, IF YOU PROSTRATE YOURSELF IN THE MIDDLE OF THIS CROWD...
...YOU'LL TOTALLY LOSE FACE AS A WHITE CAT LEADER.
DO YOU SWEAR...
...TO RETURN IT IF I DO SO?!
OH?
DIDN'T EXPECT YOU TO AGREE SO EASILY.
YEAH, SURE. I'LL RETURN IT.
PSYCH! WHY WOULD I TELL THE TRUT DUMBAS ?!
SNEEEER
I'M GONNA BLACKMAIL YOU WITH THIS FOR THE REST OF YOUR LIFE!!
VERY WELL...
BUT FIRST...

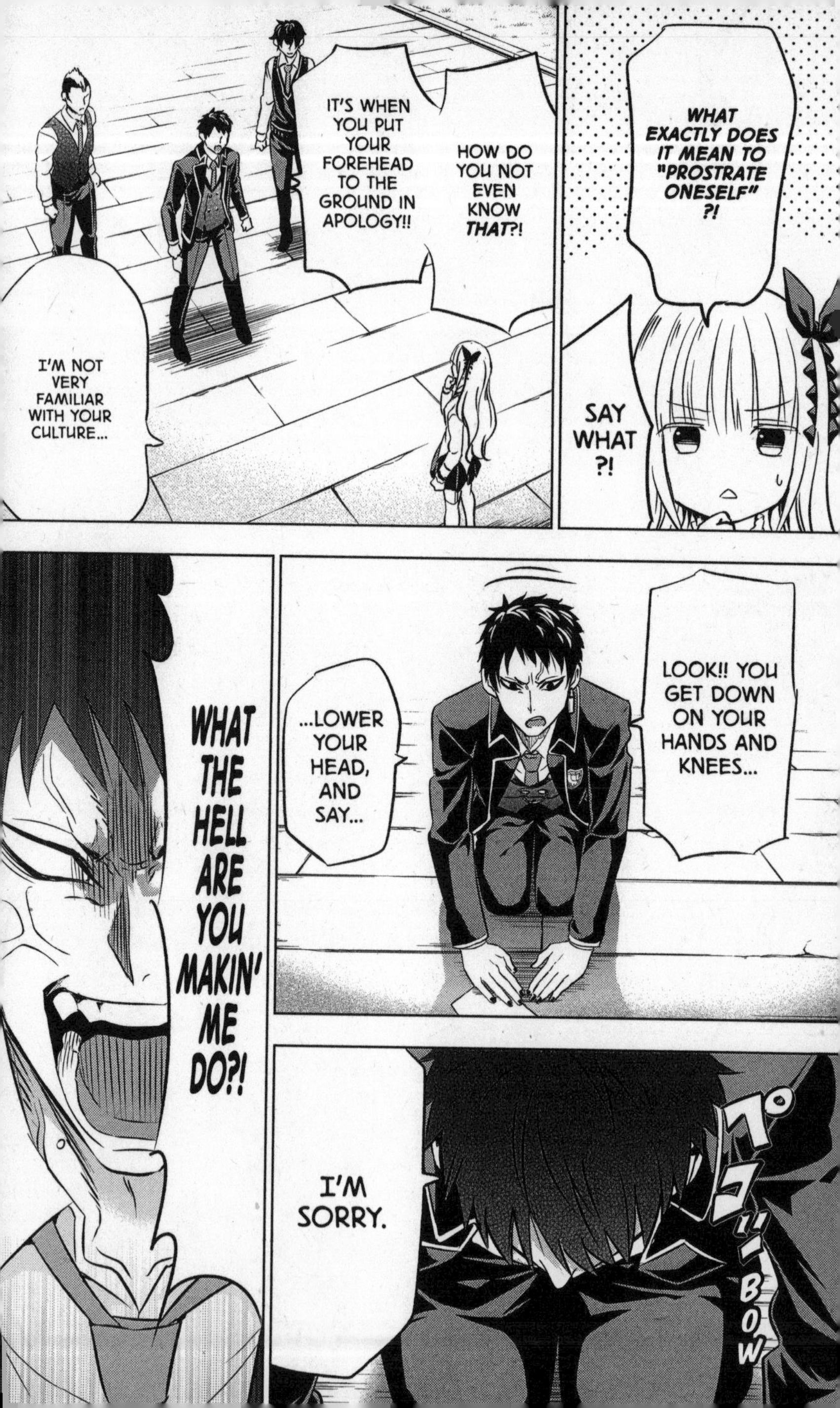
WHAT EXACTLY DOES IT MEAN TO "PROSTRATE ONESELF" ?!
SAY WHAT ?!
HOW DO YOU NOT EVEN KNOW *THAT*?!
IT'S WHEN YOU PUT YOUR FOREHEAD TO THE GROUND IN APOLOGY!!
I'M NOT VERY FAMILIAR WITH YOUR CULTURE...
LOOK!! YOU GET DOWN ON YOUR HANDS AND KNEES...
...LOWER YOUR HEAD, AND SAY...
I'M SORRY.
BOW
WHAT THE HELL ARE YOU MAKIN' ME DO?!

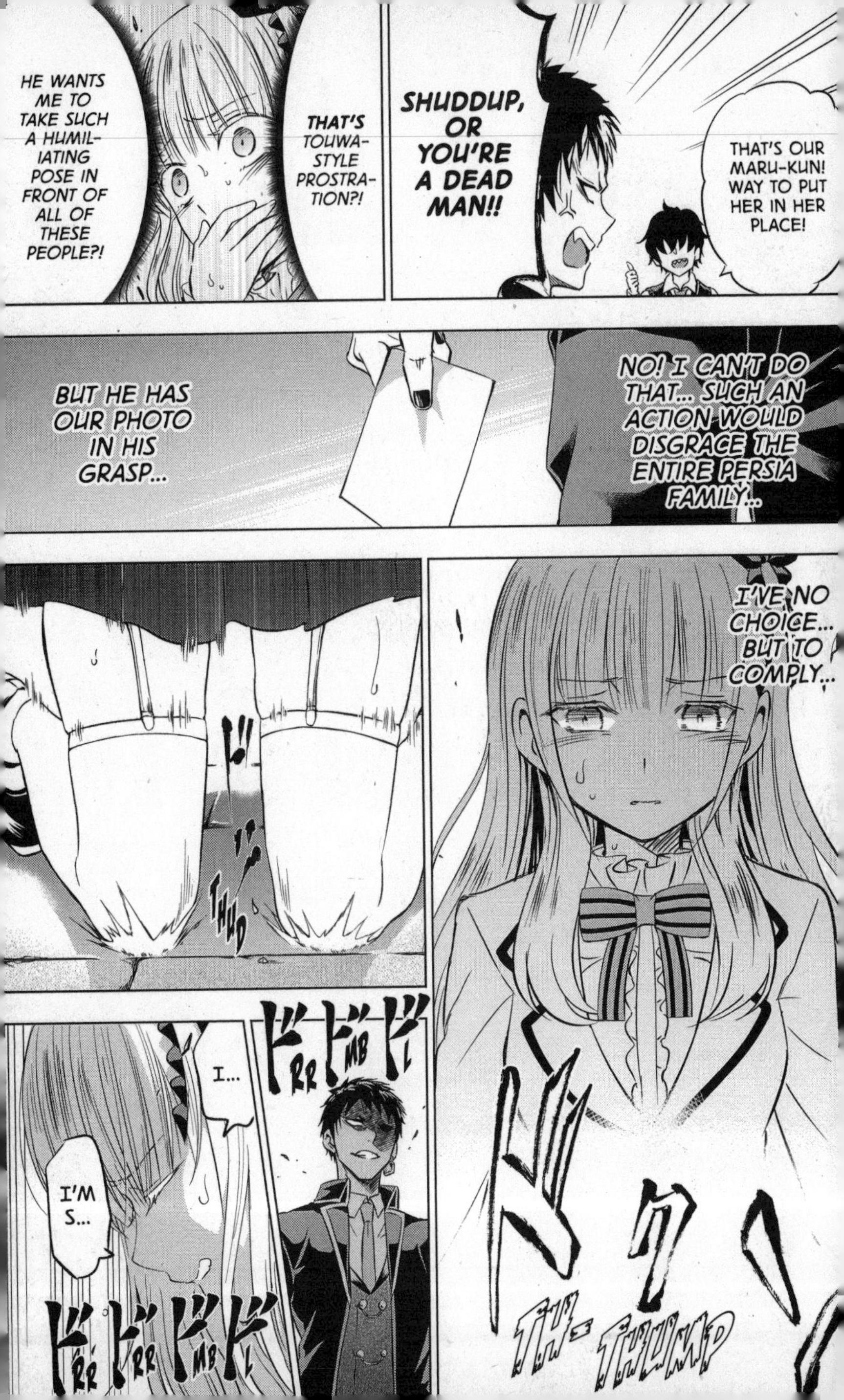
THAT'S OUR MARU-KUN! WAY TO PUT HER IN HER PLACE!
SHUDDUP, OR YOU'RE A DEAD MAN!!
THAT'S TOUWA-STYLE PROSTRATION?!
HE WANTS ME TO TAKE SUCH A HUMILIATING POSE IN FRONT OF ALL OF THESE PEOPLE?!
NO! I CAN'T DO THAT... SUCH AN ACTION WOULD DISGRACE THE ENTIRE PERSIA FAMILY...
BUT HE HAS OUR PHOTO IN HIS GRASP...
I'VE NO CHOICE... BUT TO COMPLY...
TH-THUMP
THUD
I...
I'M S...

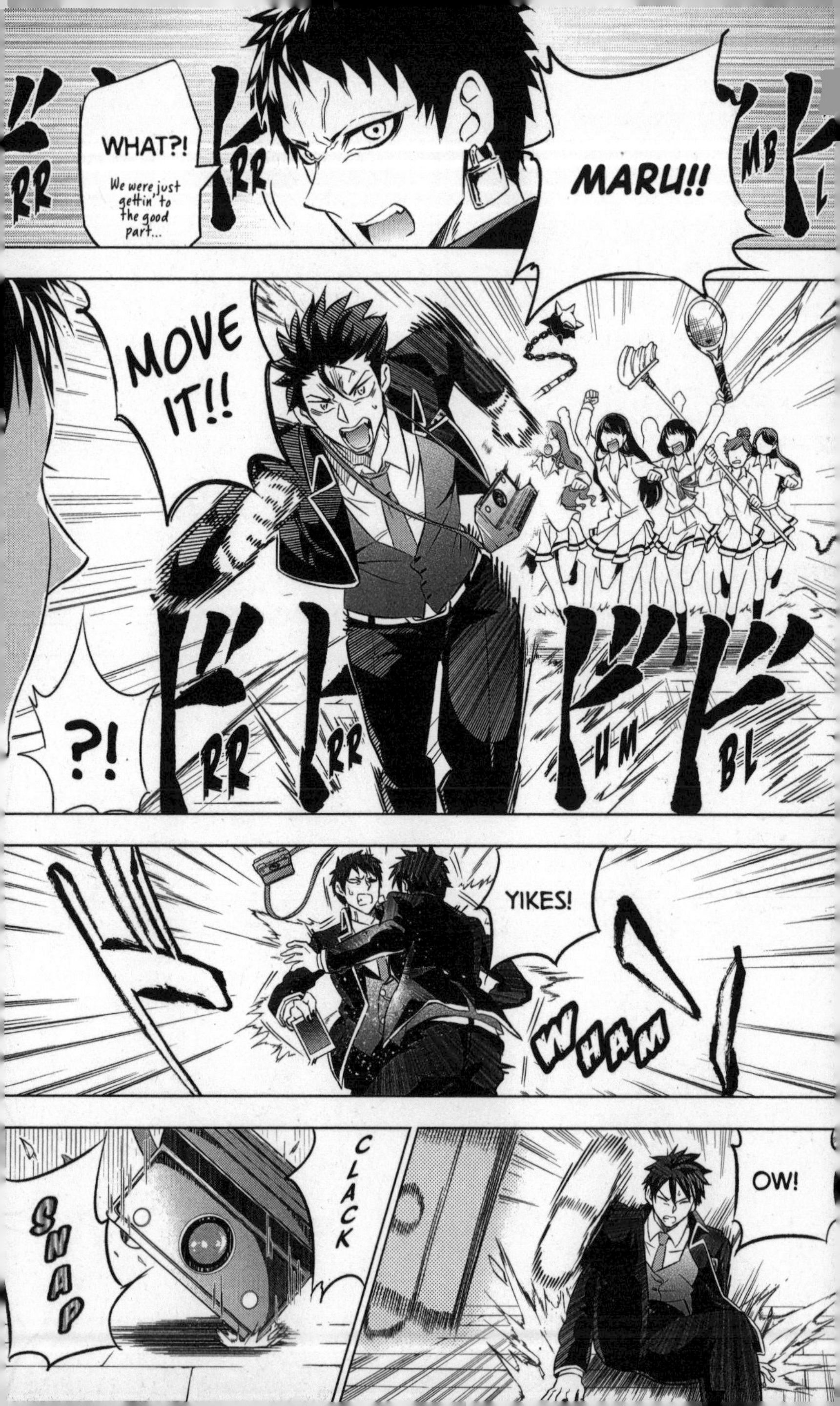
MB
L
MARU!!
RR
WHAT?!
We were just gettin' to the good part...
RR
MOVE IT!!
UM
BL
RR
RR
?!
YIKES!
WHAM
OW!
CLACK
SNAP

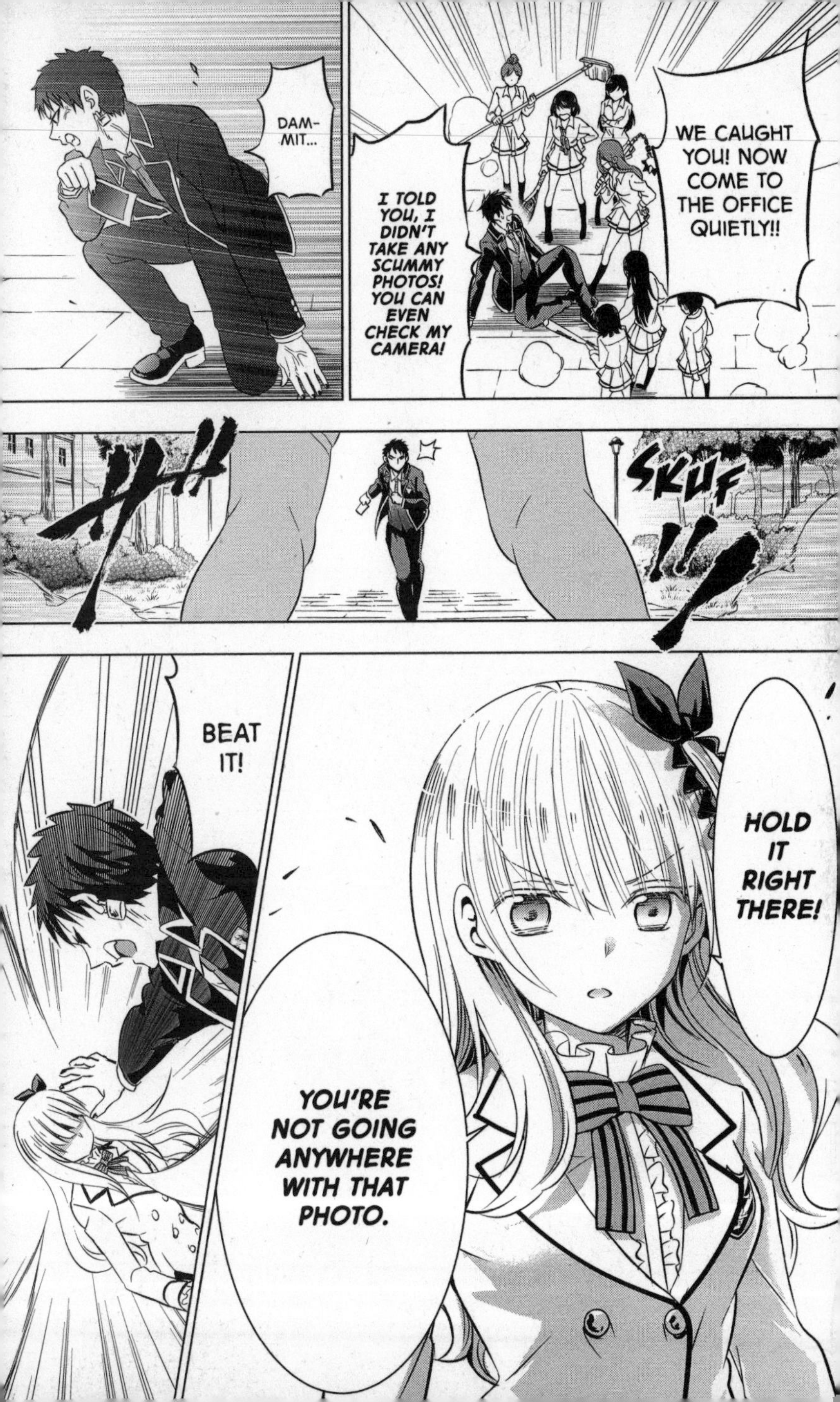
WE CAUGHT YOU! NOW COME TO THE OFFICE QUIETLY!!
I TOLD YOU, I DIDN'T TAKE ANY SCUMMY PHOTOS! YOU CAN EVEN CHECK MY CAMERA!
DAM-MIT...
SKUF
HOLD IT RIGHT THERE!
YOU'RE NOT GOING ANYWHERE WITH THAT PHOTO.
BEAT IT!

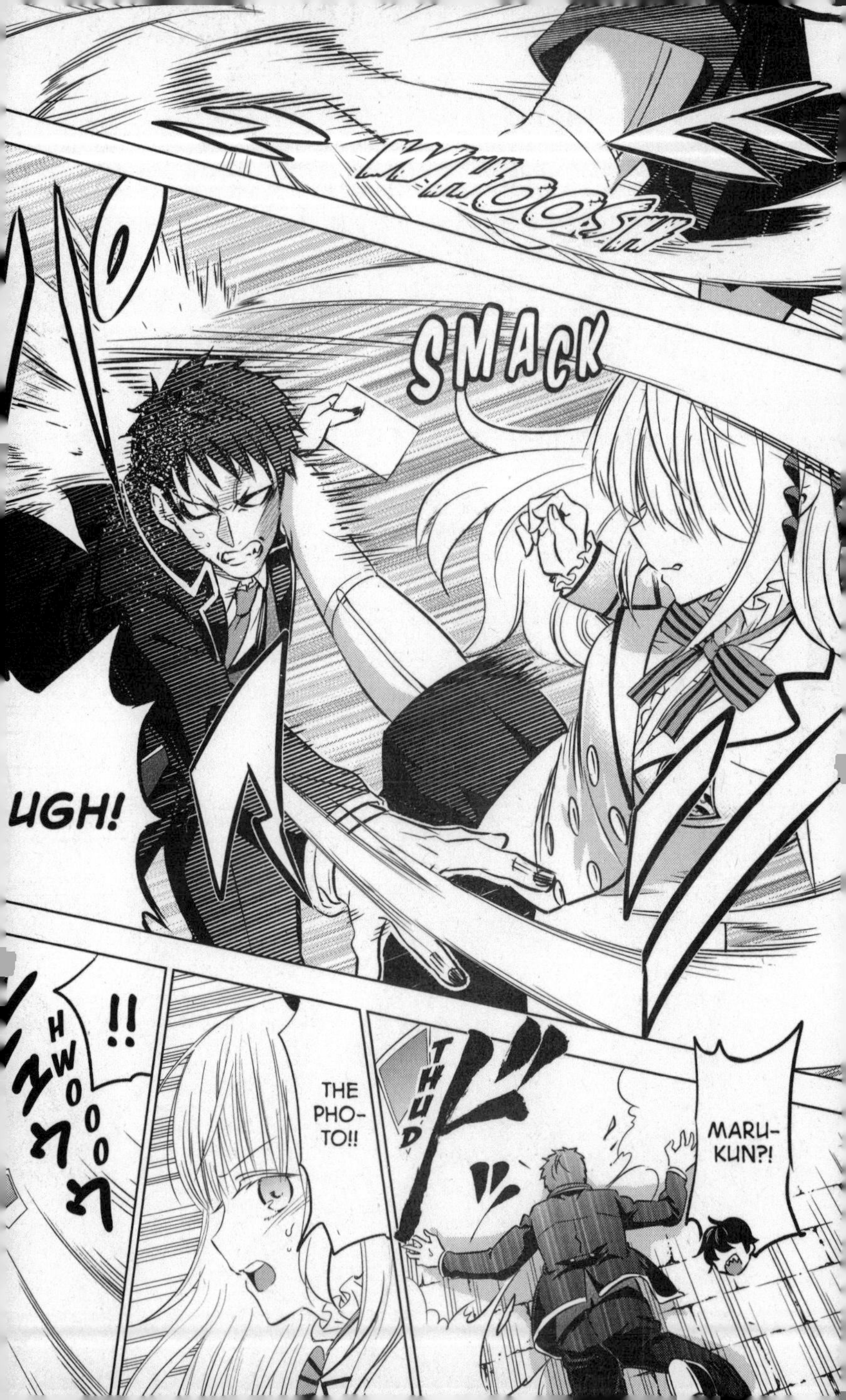
WHOOSH
SMACK
UGH!
MARU-KUN?!
THUD
THE PHO-TO!!
HWOOOO
!!

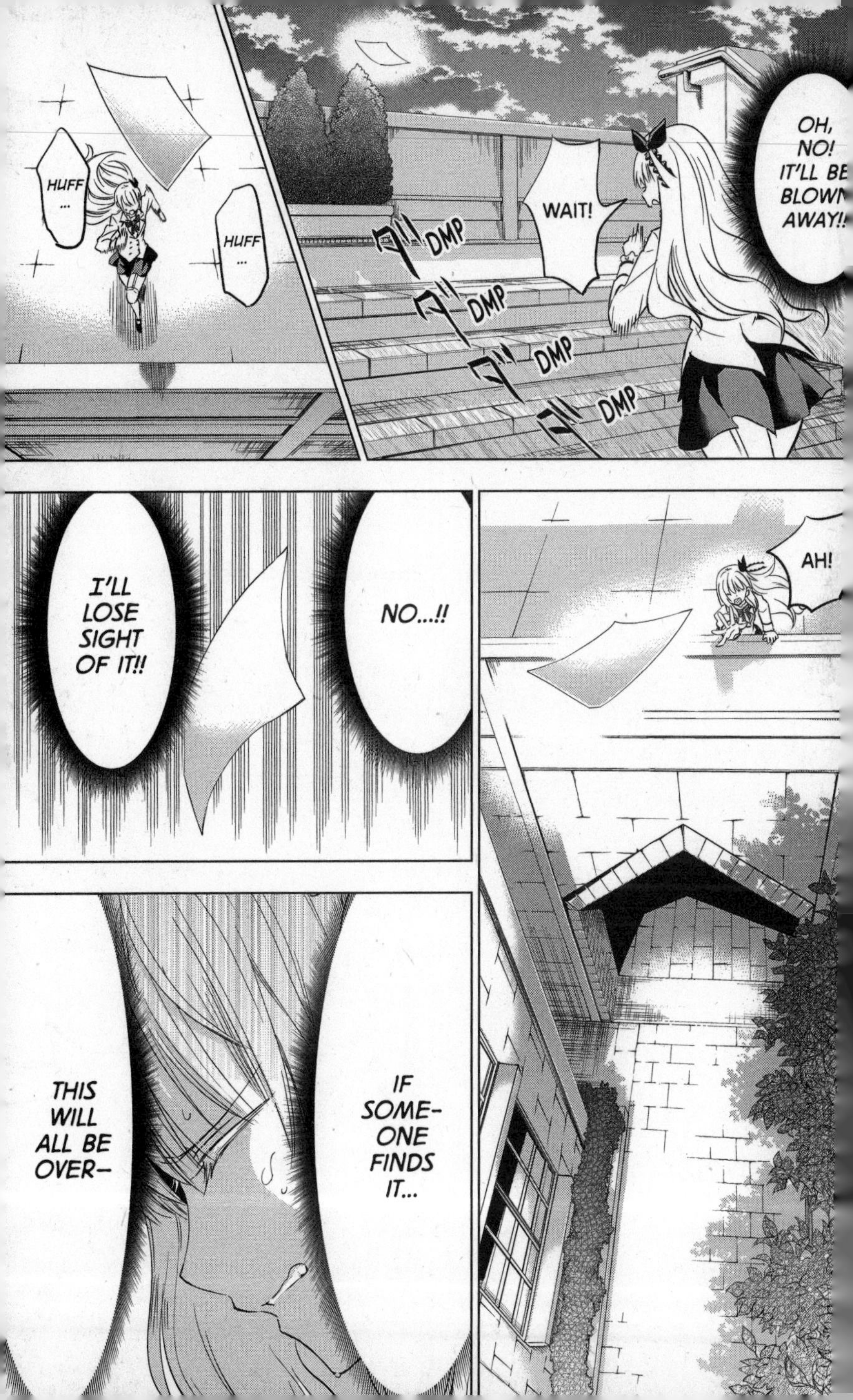
OH, NO! IT'LL BE BLOWN AWAY!!
WAIT!
DMP
DMP
DMP
DMP
HUFF...
HUFF...
AH!
NO...!!
I'LL LOSE SIGHT OF IT!!
IF SOME-ONE FINDS IT...
THIS WILL ALL BE OVER—

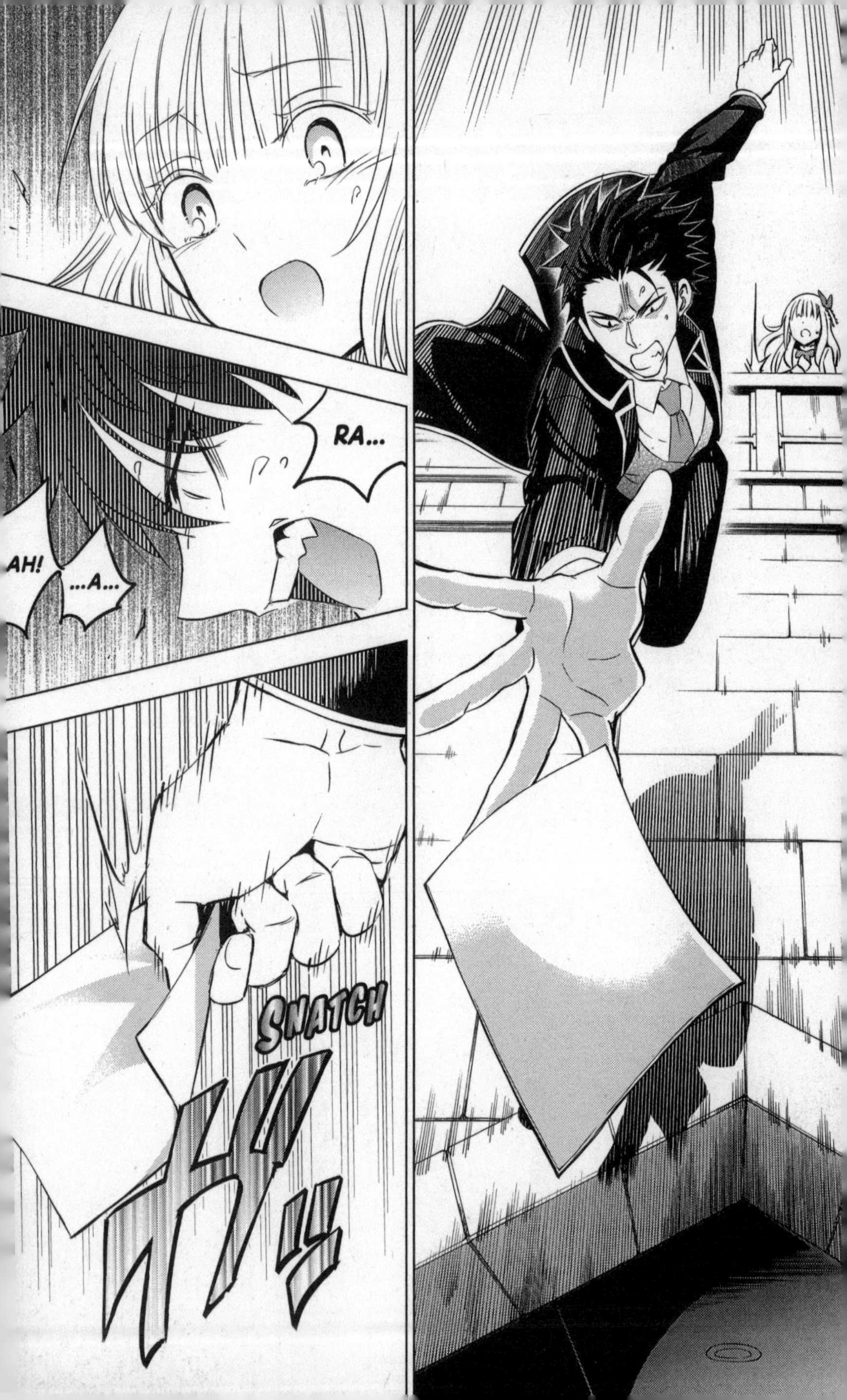
RA...
...A...
AH!
SNATCH

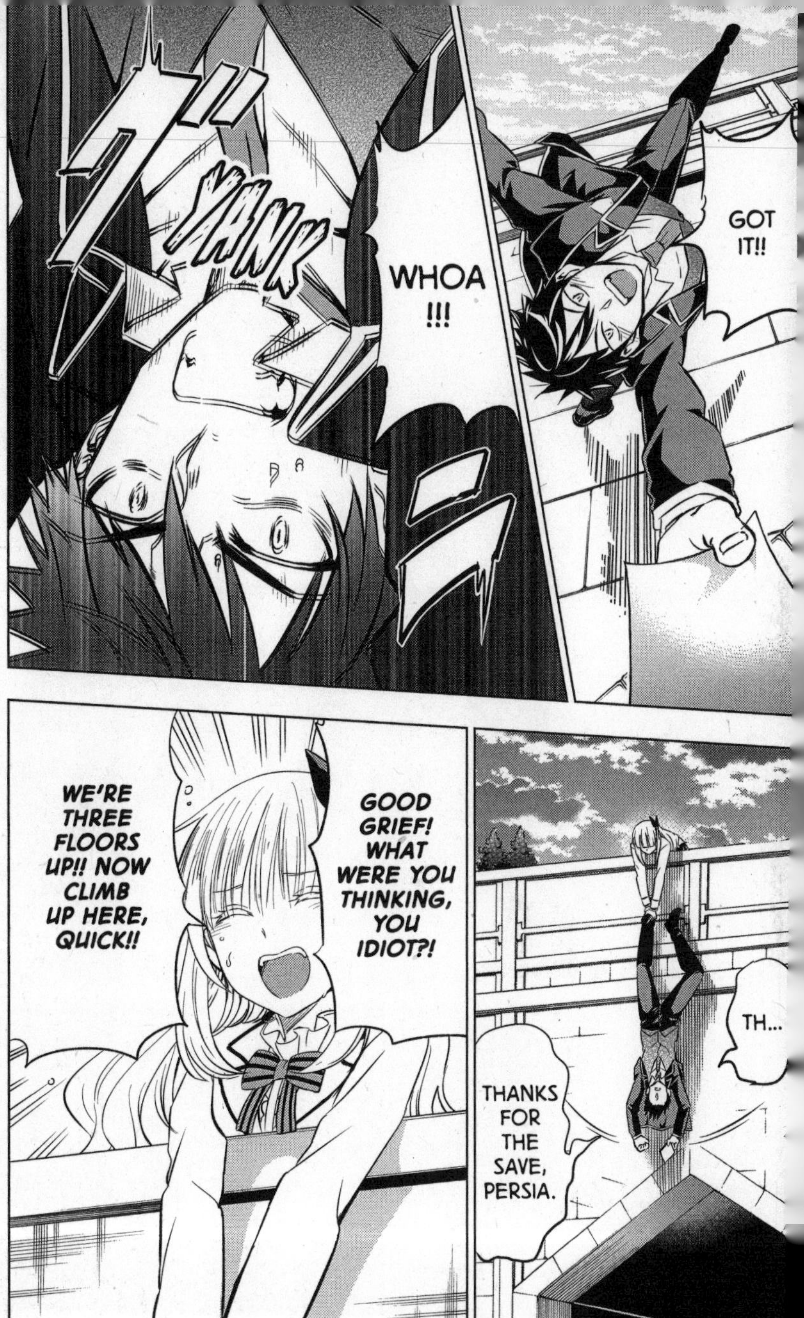
GOT IT!!
YANK
WHOA !!!
TH...
THANKS FOR THE SAVE, PERSIA.
GOOD GRIEF! WHAT WERE YOU THINKING, YOU IDIOT?!
WE'RE THREE FLOORS UP!! NOW CLIMB UP HERE, QUICK!!

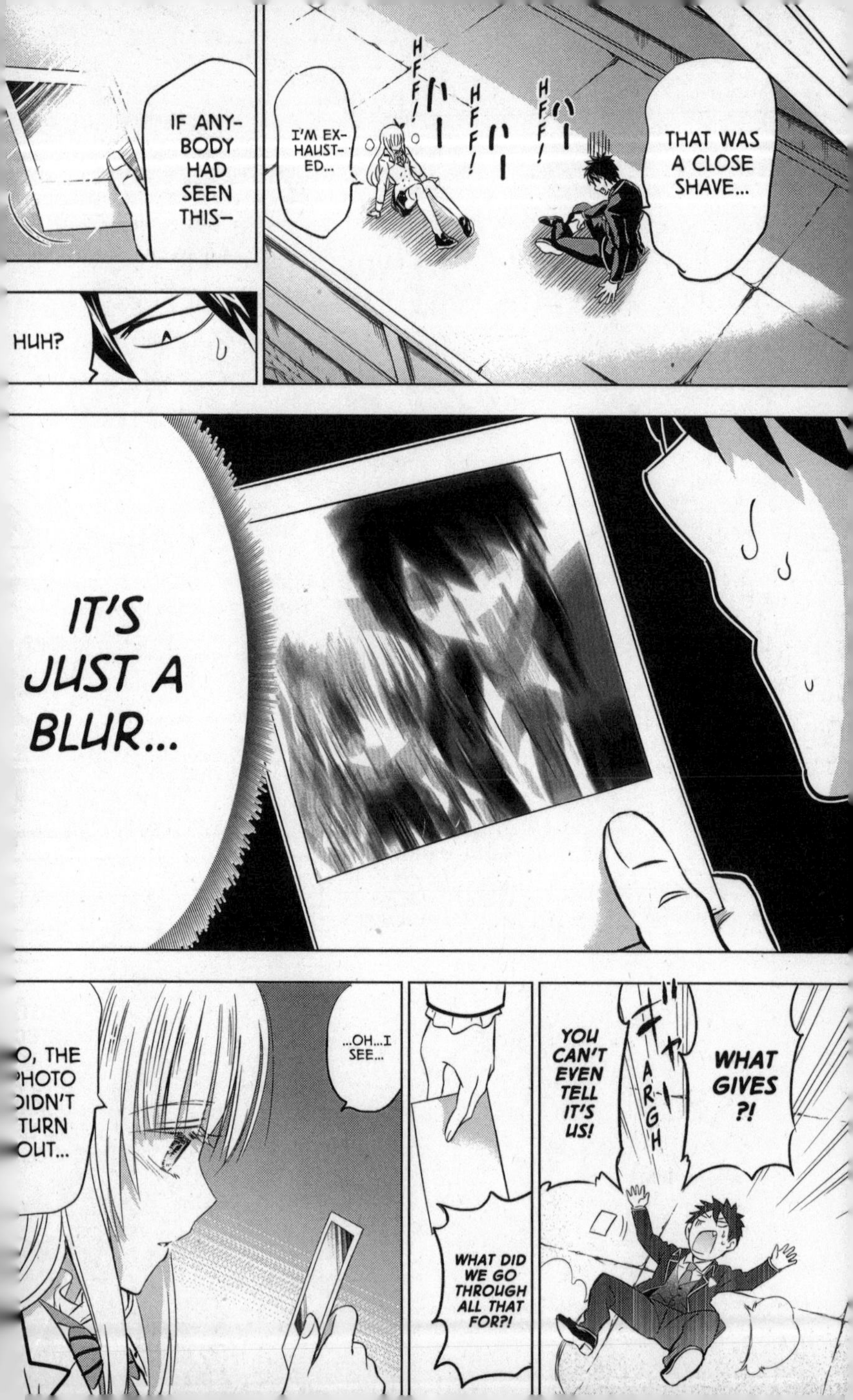
THAT WAS A CLOSE SHAVE...
HFF! HFF! HFF!
I'M EX-HAUSTED...
IF ANY-BODY HAD SEEN THIS—
HUH?
IT'S JUST A BLUR...
WHAT GIVES?!
ARGH
YOU CAN'T EVEN TELL IT'S US!
WHAT DID WE GO THROUGH ALL THAT FOR?!
...OH...I SEE...
O, THE PHOTO DIDN'T TURN OUT...

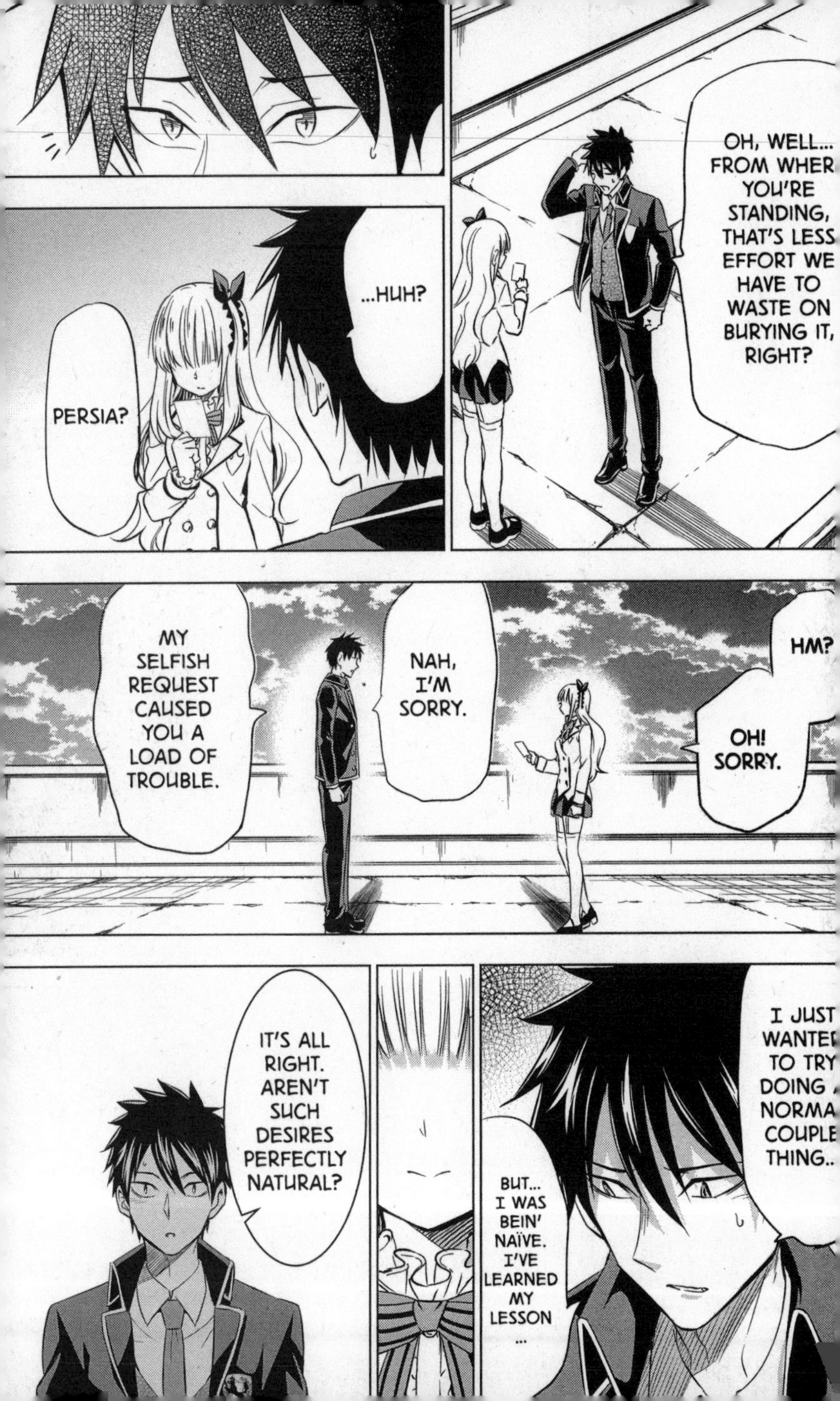
OH, WELL... FROM WHER YOU'RE STANDING, THAT'S LESS EFFORT WE HAVE TO WASTE ON BURYING IT, RIGHT?
...HUH?
PERSIA?
HM?
OH! SORRY.
NAH, I'M SORRY.
MY SELFISH REQUEST CAUSED YOU A LOAD OF TROUBLE.
I JUST WANTE TO TRY DOING NORMA COUPLE THING..
BUT... I WAS BEIN' NAÏVE. I'VE LEARNED MY LESSON ...
IT'S ALL RIGHT. AREN'T SUCH DESIRES PERFECTLY NATURAL?

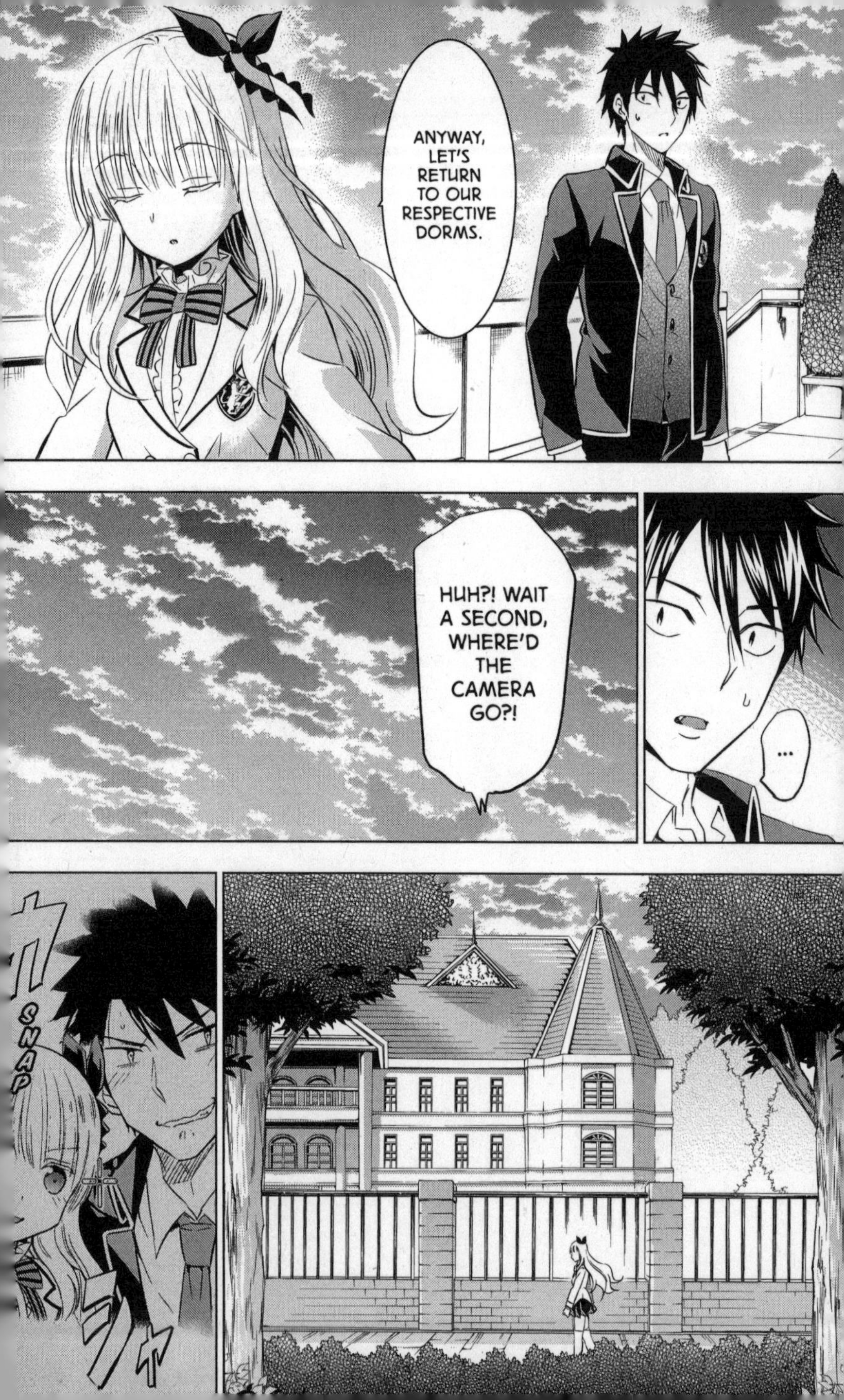
ANYWAY, LET'S RETURN TO OUR RESPECTIVE DORMS.
...
HUH?! WAIT A SECOND, WHERE'D THE CAMERA GO?!
SNAP

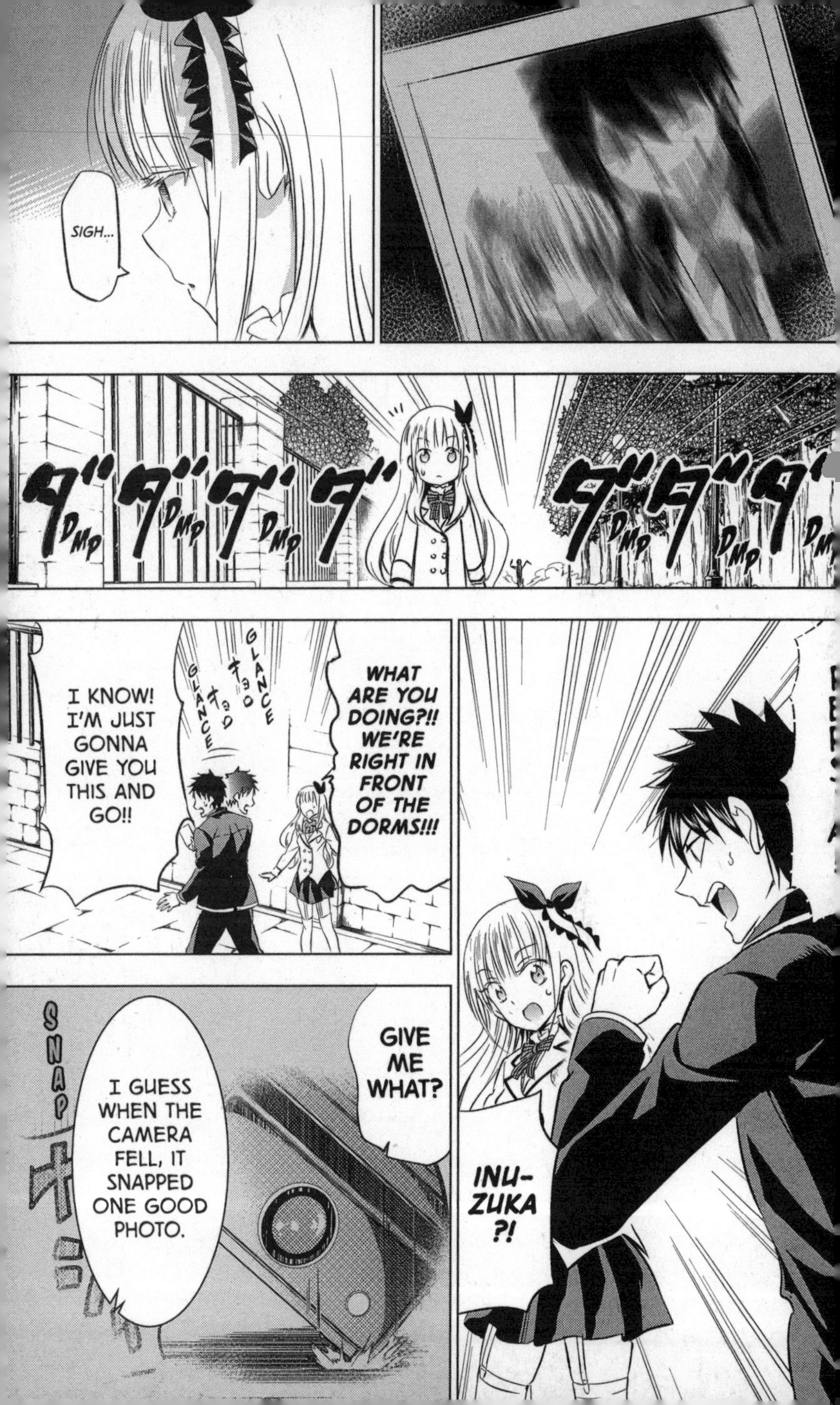
SIGH...
DMP DMP DMP
DMP DMP DMP
INU-ZUKA?!
WHAT ARE YOU DOING?!! WE'RE RIGHT IN FRONT OF THE DORMS!!!
GLANCE キョロ
GLANCE キョロ
I KNOW! I'M JUST GONNA GIVE YOU THIS AND GO!!
GIVE ME WHAT?
I GUESS WHEN THE CAMERA FELL, IT SNAPPED ONE GOOD PHOTO.
SNAP

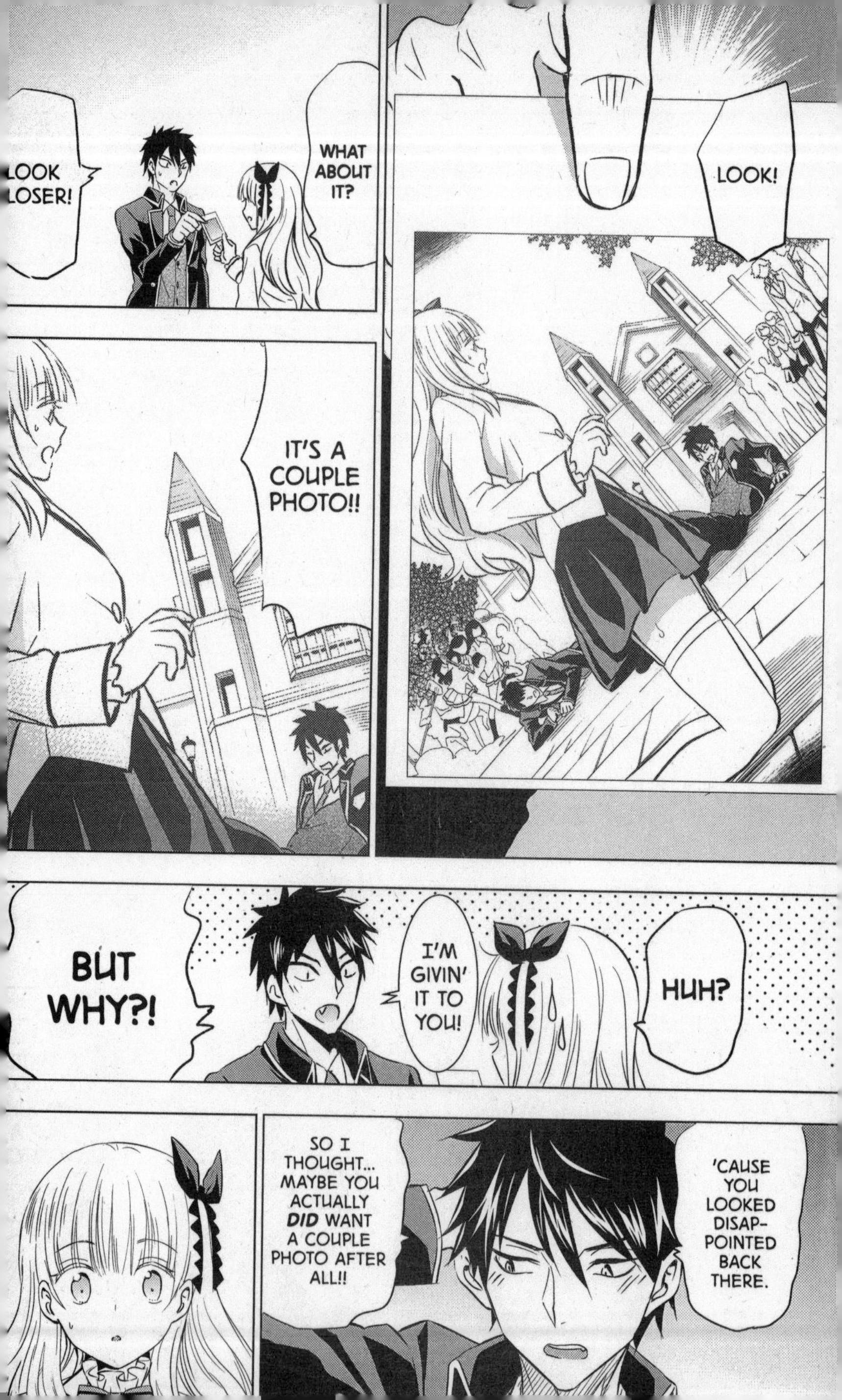

LOOK!
WHAT ABOUT IT?
LOOK LOSER!
IT'S A COUPLE PHOTO!!
HUH?
I'M GIVIN' IT TO YOU!
BUT WHY?!
'CAUSE YOU LOOKED DISAPPOINTED BACK THERE.
SO I THOUGHT... MAYBE YOU ACTUALLY *DID* WANT A COUPLE PHOTO AFTER ALL!!

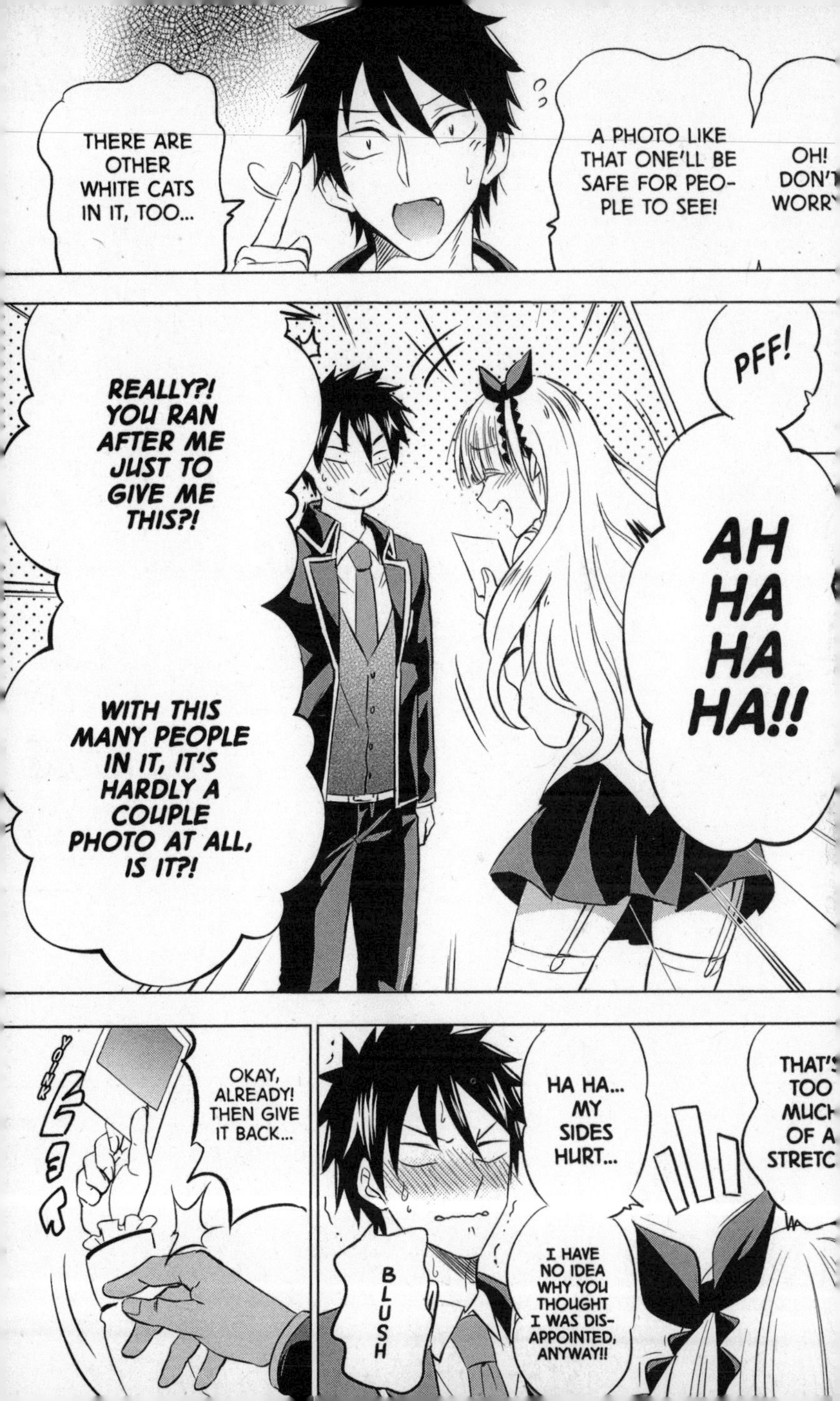
OH! DON'T WORRY
A PHOTO LIKE THAT ONE'LL BE SAFE FOR PEO-PLE TO SEE!
THERE ARE OTHER WHITE CATS IN IT, TOO...
PFF!
AH HA HA HA HA!!
REALLY?! YOU RAN AFTER ME JUST TO GIVE ME THIS?!
WITH THIS MANY PEOPLE IN IT, IT'S HARDLY A COUPLE PHOTO AT ALL, IS IT?!
THAT'S TOO MUCH OF A STRETCH
HA HA... MY SIDES HURT...
I HAVE NO IDEA WHY YOU THOUGHT I WAS DIS-APPOINTED, ANYWAY!!
BLUSH
OKAY, ALREADY! THEN GIVE IT BACK...
YOINK

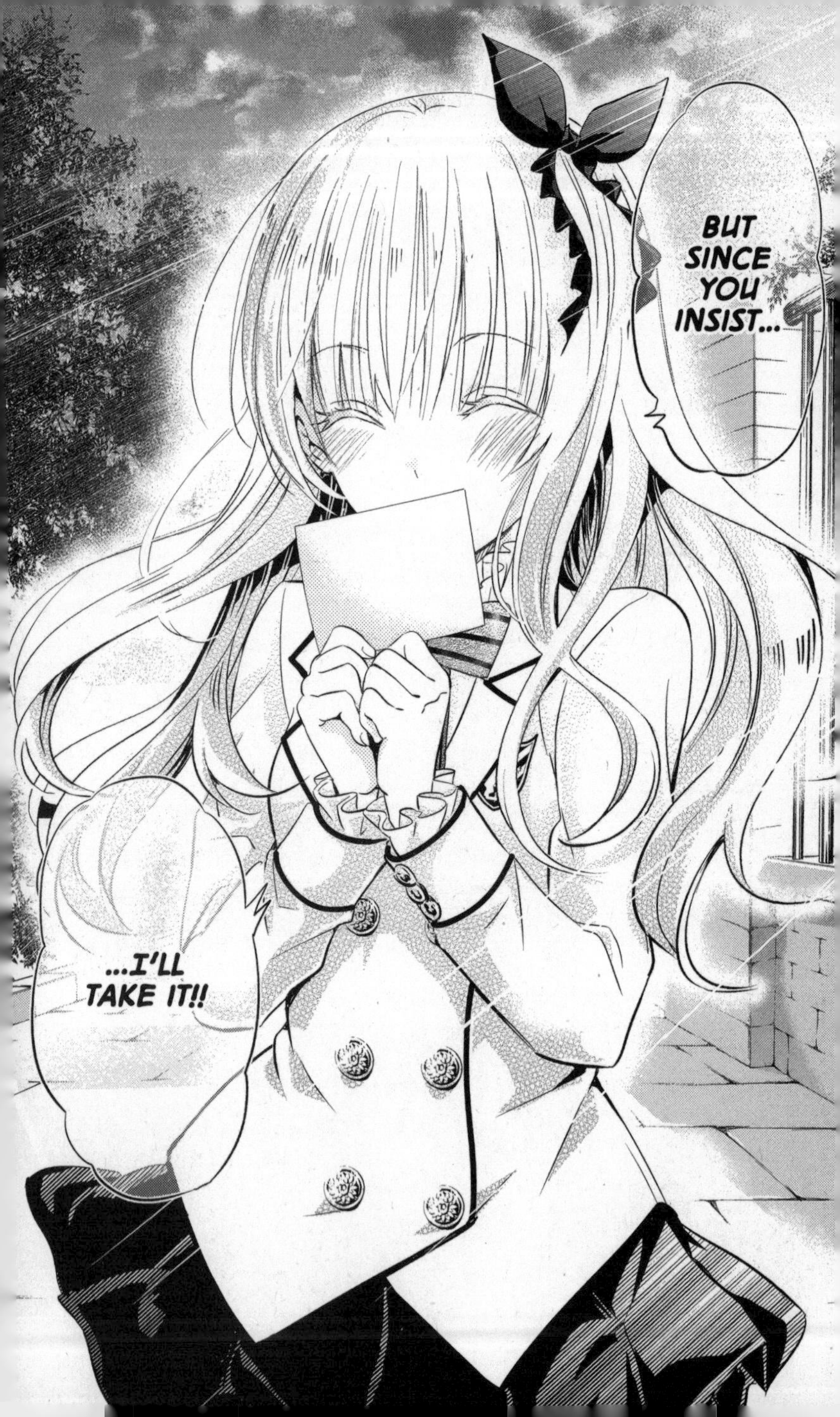
BUT SINCE YOU INSIST...
...I'LL TAKE IT!!

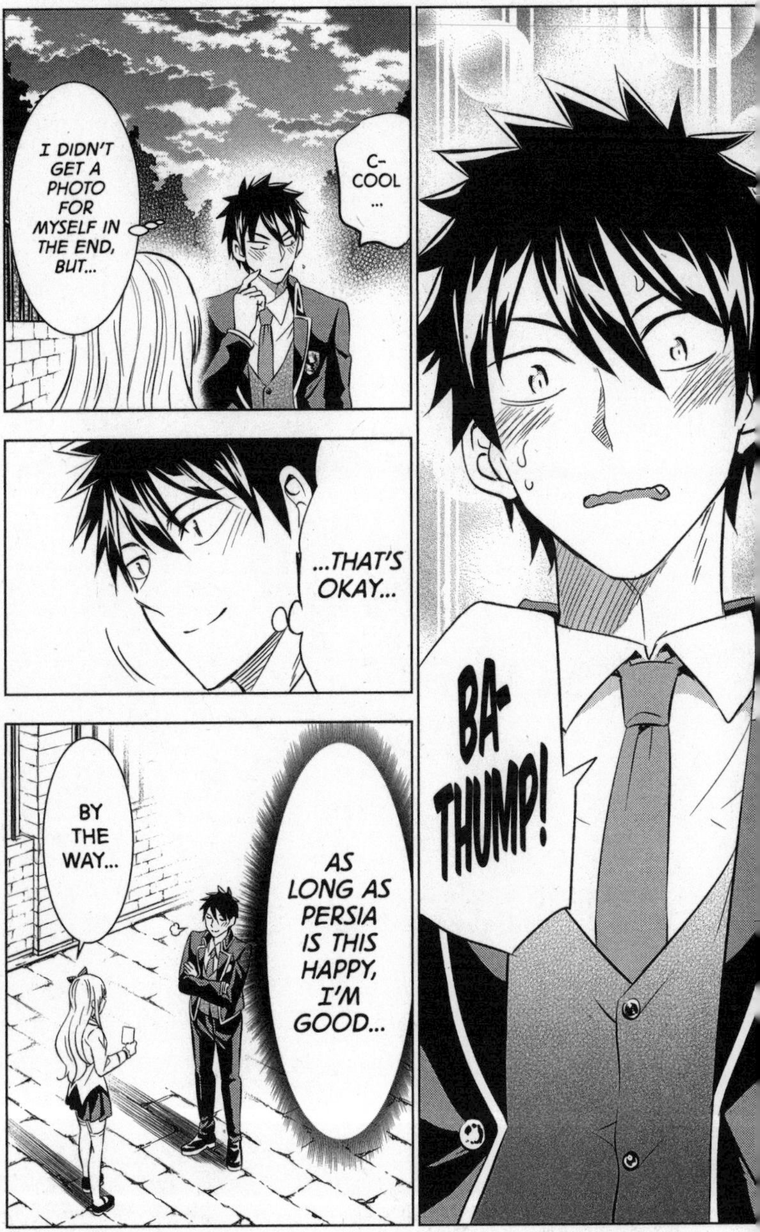
BA-THUMP!
C-COOL ...
I DIDN'T GET A PHOTO FOR MYSELF IN THE END, BUT...
...THAT'S OKAY...
AS LONG AS PERSIA IS THIS HAPPY, I'M GOOD...
BY THE WAY...

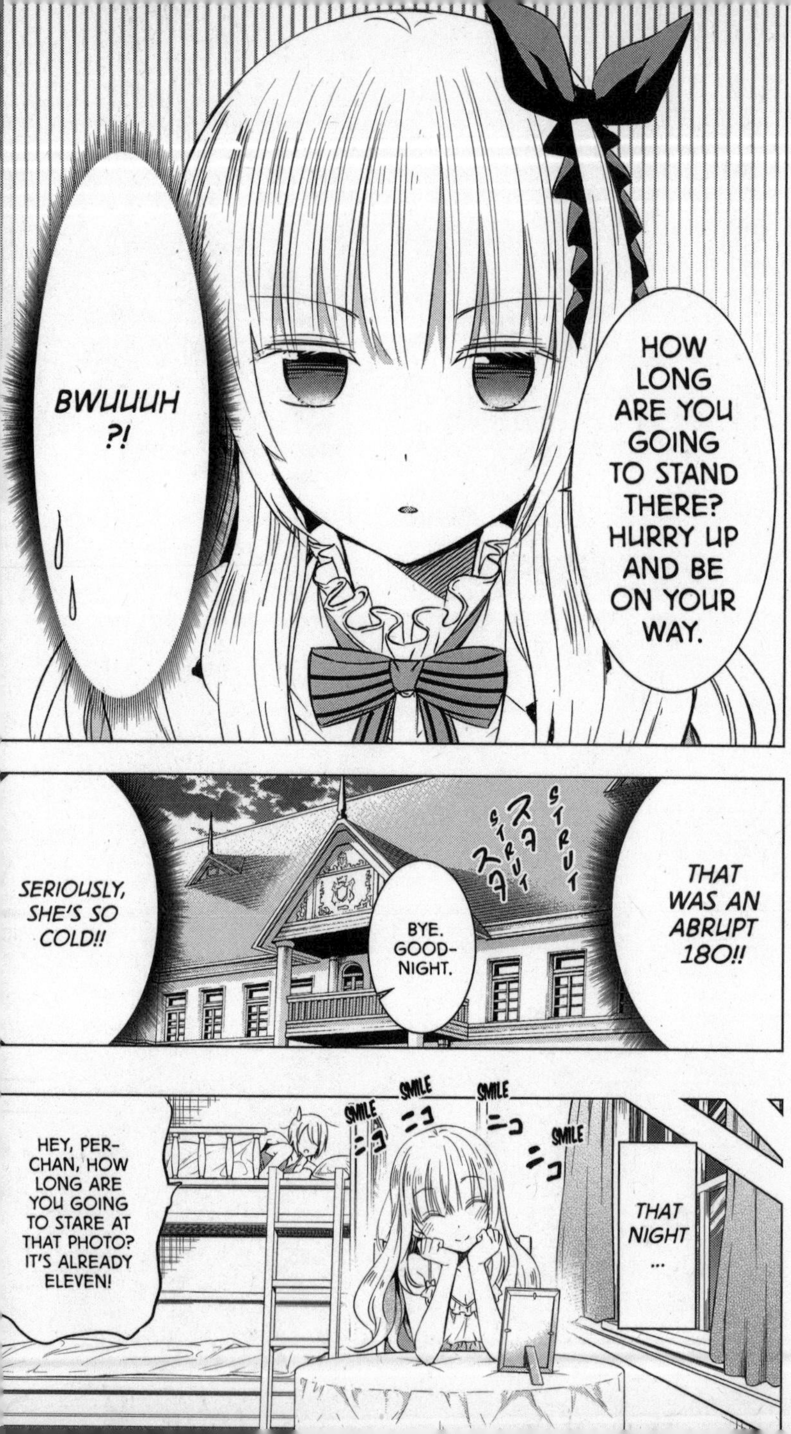
HOW LONG ARE YOU GOING TO STAND THERE? HURRY UP AND BE ON YOUR WAY.
BWUUUH ?!
THAT WAS AN ABRUPT 180!!
スタ スタ
STRUT STRUT
BYE. GOOD-NIGHT.
SERIOUSLY, SHE'S SO COLD!!
THAT NIGHT ...
ニコ ニコ ニコ ニコ
SMILE SMILE SMILE SMILE
HEY, PER-CHAN, HOW LONG ARE YOU GOING TO STARE AT THAT PHOTO? IT'S ALREADY ELEVEN!

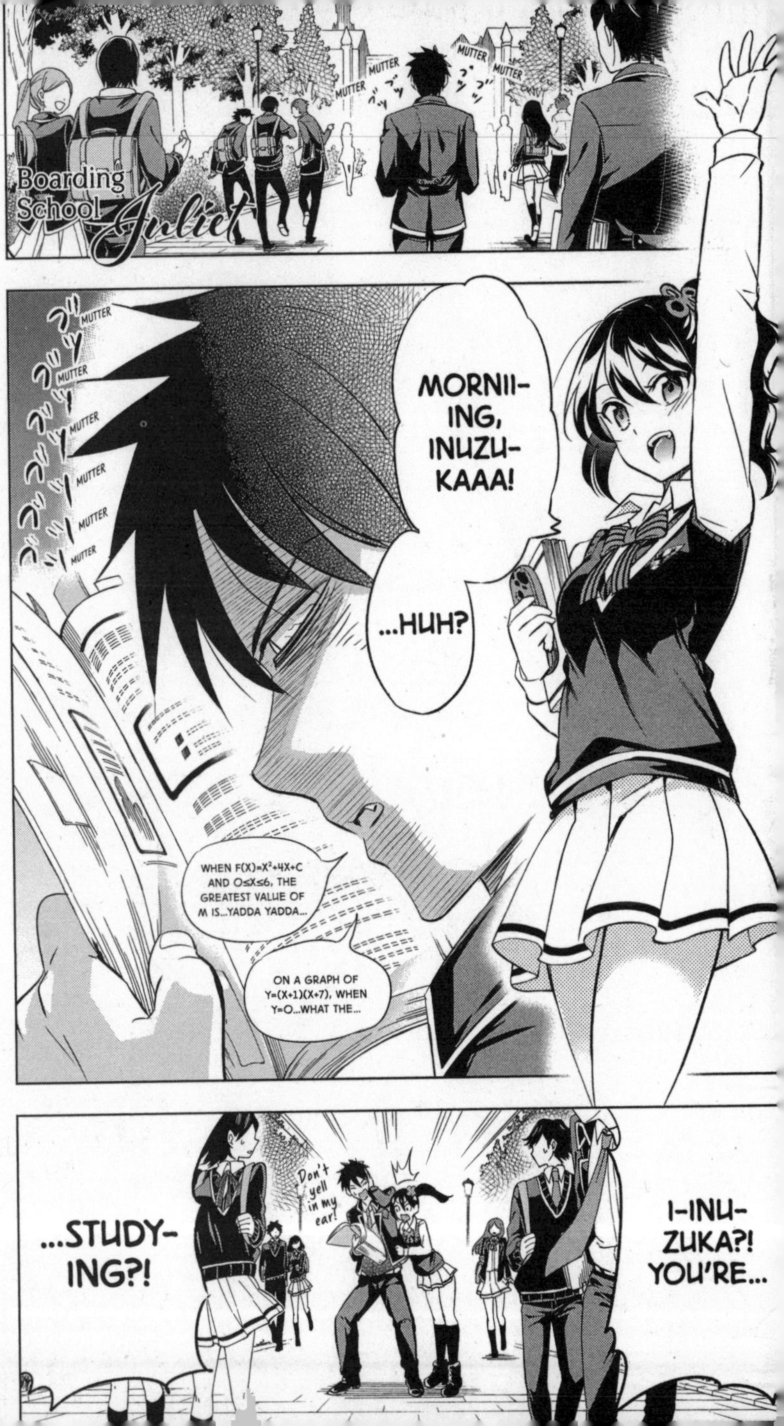
Boarding School Juliet
MUTTER
MUTTER
MUTTER
MUTTER
MUTTER
MUTTER
MUTTER
MUTTER
MUTTER
MUTTER
MUTTER
MORNIIING, INUZUKAAA!
...HUH?
WHEN $F(X)=X^2+4X+C$ AND $0 \le X \le 6$, THE GREATEST VALUE OF M IS...YADDA YADDA...
ON A GRAPH OF $Y=(X+1)(X+7)$, WHEN $Y=0$...WHAT THE...
I-INUZUKA?! YOU'RE...
Don't yell in my ear!
...STUDYING?!

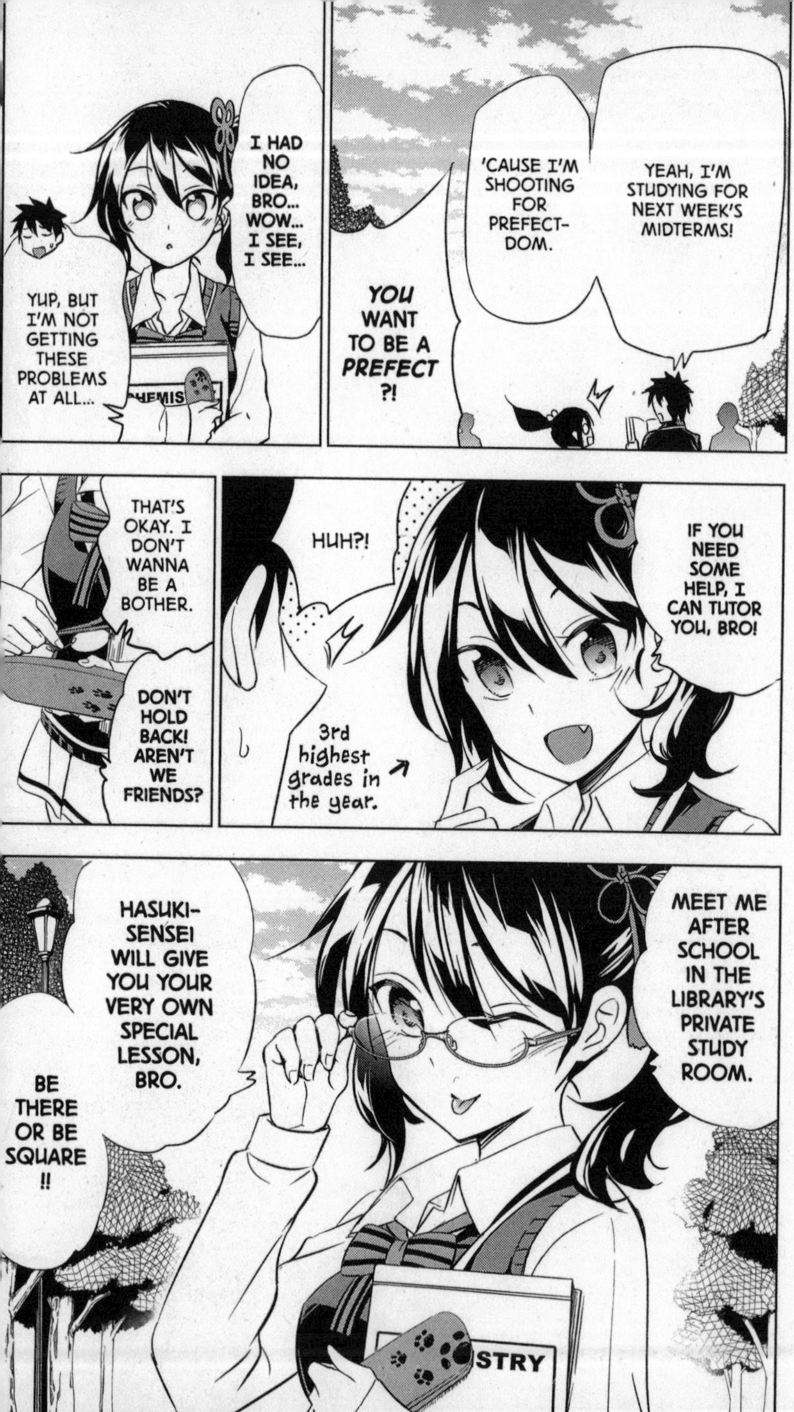
YEAH, I'M STUDYING FOR NEXT WEEK'S MIDTERMS!
'CAUSE I'M SHOOTING FOR PREFECT-DOM.
YOU WANT TO BE A *PREFECT*?!
I HAD NO IDEA, BRO... WOW... I SEE, I SEE...
YUP, BUT I'M NOT GETTING THESE PROBLEMS AT ALL...
IF YOU NEED SOME HELP, I CAN TUTOR YOU, BRO!
HUH?!
3rd highest grades in the year.
THAT'S OKAY. I DON'T WANNA BE A BOTHER.
DON'T HOLD BACK! AREN'T WE FRIENDS?
MEET ME AFTER SCHOOL IN THE LIBRARY'S PRIVATE STUDY ROOM.
HASUKI-SENSEI WILL GIVE YOU YOUR VERY OWN SPECIAL LESSON, BRO.
BE THERE OR BE SQUARE!!

DAHLIA ACADEMY GUIDE #2: BLACK DOGGY HOUSE

The dorm where Touwa's high school division students live. On the first floor: a reception hall, a lounge, large baths, traditional Touwanese-style rooms with *tatami* mat flooring, etc. Floors 2–4: general students' bedrooms, with two to three people per room.

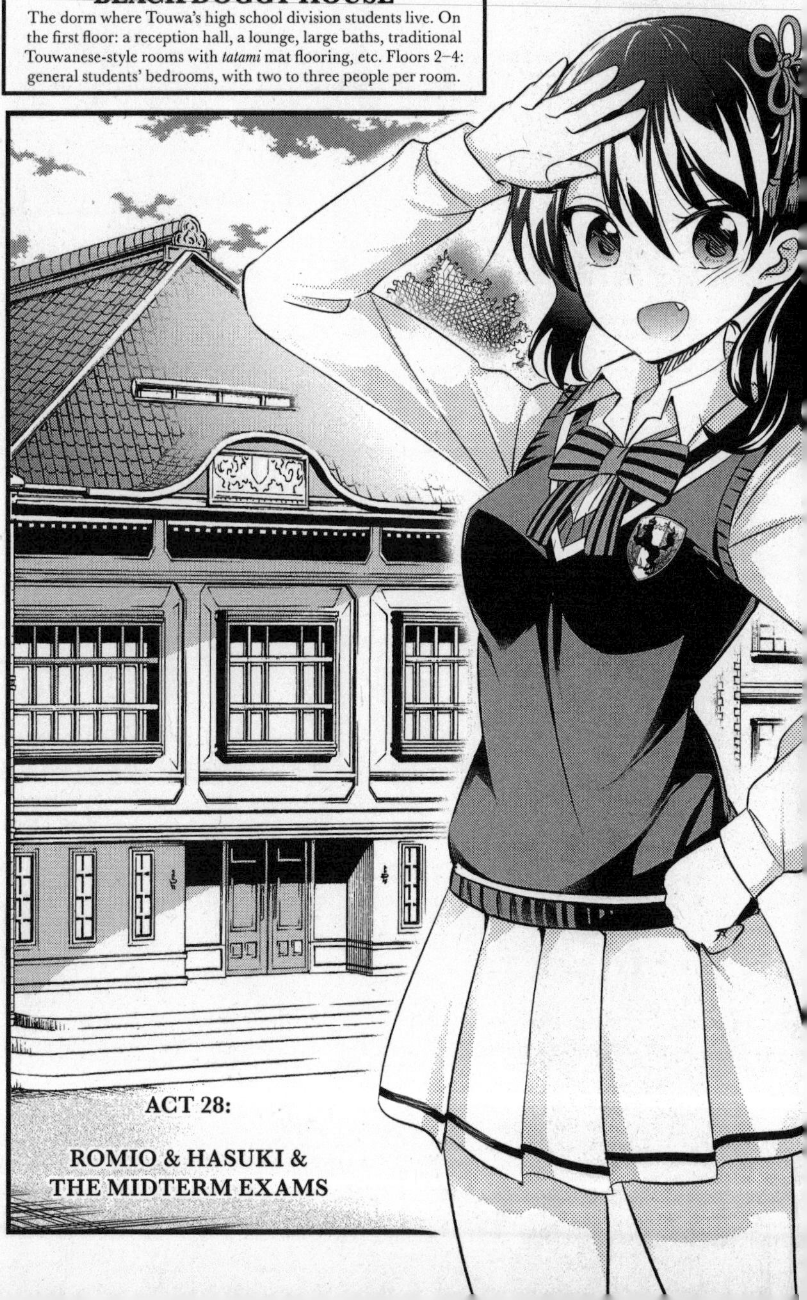

ACT 28:

ROMIO & HASUKI & THE MIDTERM EXAMS

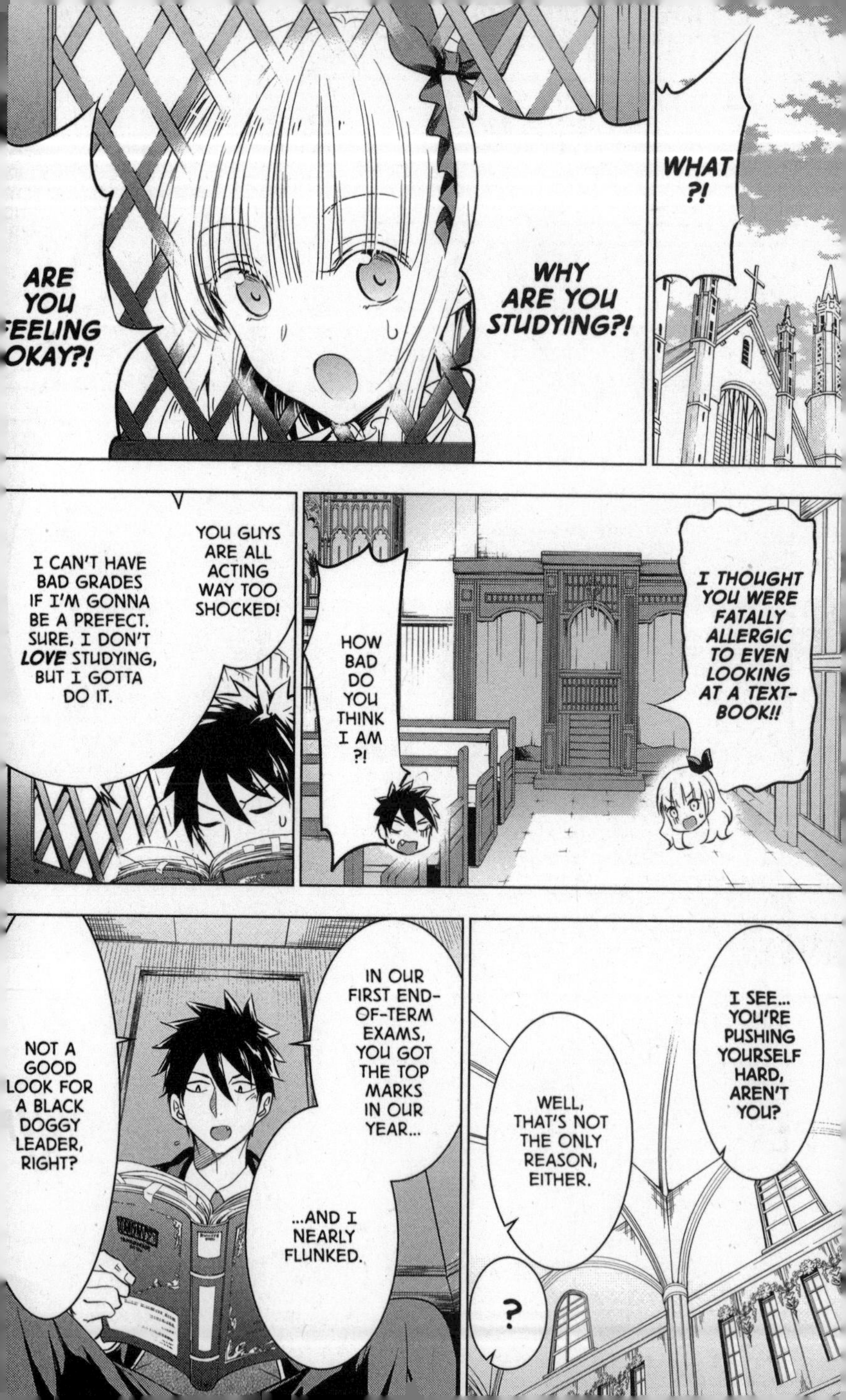
WHAT ?!
WHY ARE YOU STUDYING?!
ARE YOU FEELING OKAY?!
I THOUGHT YOU WERE FATALLY ALLERGIC TO EVEN LOOKING AT A TEXT-BOOK!!
HOW BAD DO YOU THINK I AM ?!
YOU GUYS ARE ALL ACTING WAY TOO SHOCKED!
I CAN'T HAVE BAD GRADES IF I'M GONNA BE A PREFECT. SURE, I DON'T *LOVE* STUDYING, BUT I GOTTA DO IT.
I SEE... YOU'RE PUSHING YOURSELF HARD, AREN'T YOU?
WELL, THAT'S NOT THE ONLY REASON, EITHER.
?
IN OUR FIRST END-OF-TERM EXAMS, YOU GOT THE TOP MARKS IN OUR YEAR...
...AND I NEARLY FLUNKED.
NOT A GOOD LOOK FOR A BLACK DOGGY LEADER, RIGHT?

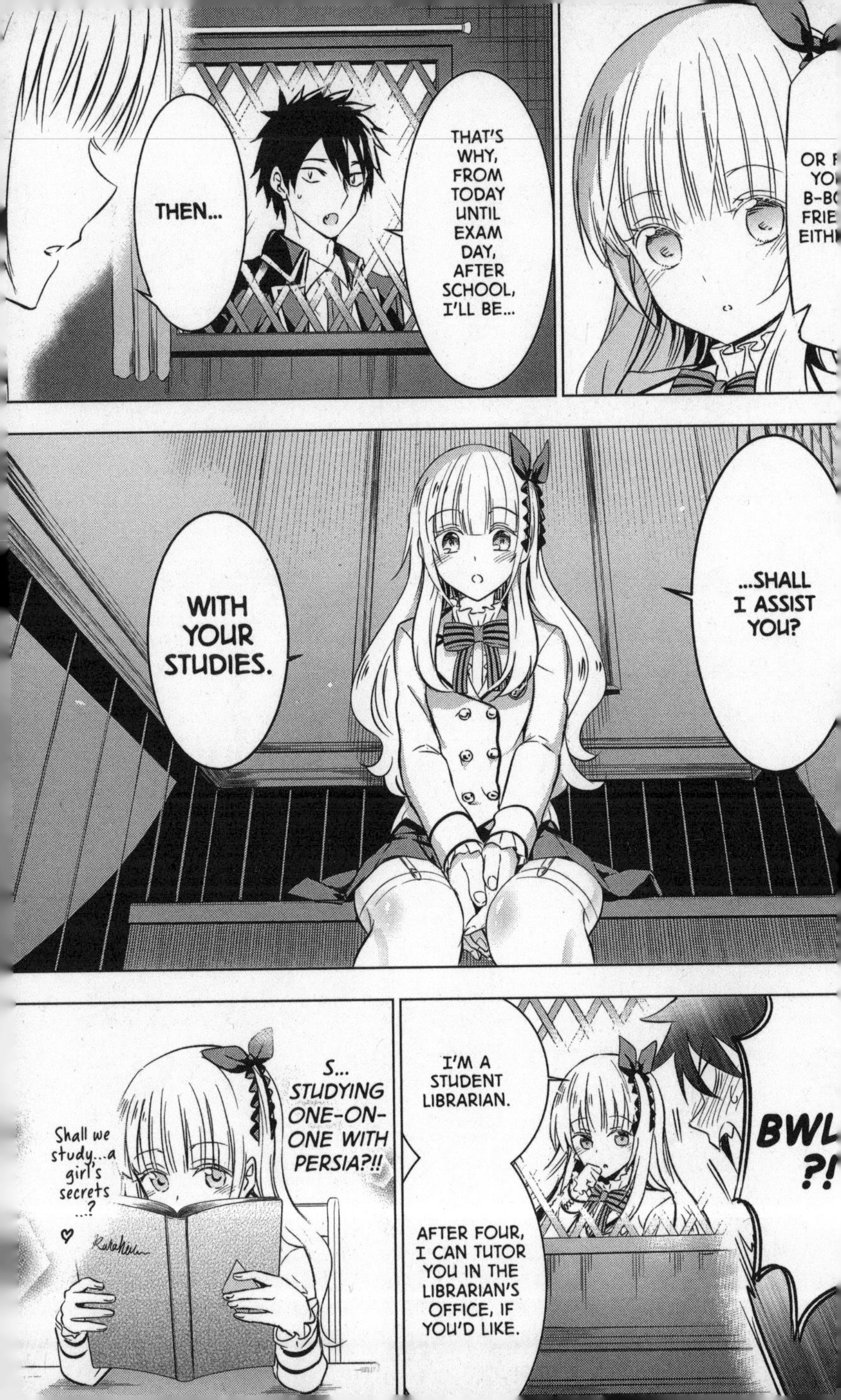
THAT'S WHY, FROM TODAY UNTIL EXAM DAY, AFTER SCHOOL, I'LL BE...
THEN...
...SHALL I ASSIST YOU?
WITH YOUR STUDIES.
I'M A STUDENT LIBRARIAN.
AFTER FOUR, I CAN TUTOR YOU IN THE LIBRARIAN'S OFFICE, IF YOU'D LIKE.
S... STUDYING ONE-ON-ONE WITH PERSIA?!!
Shall we study...a girl's secrets ...? ♡

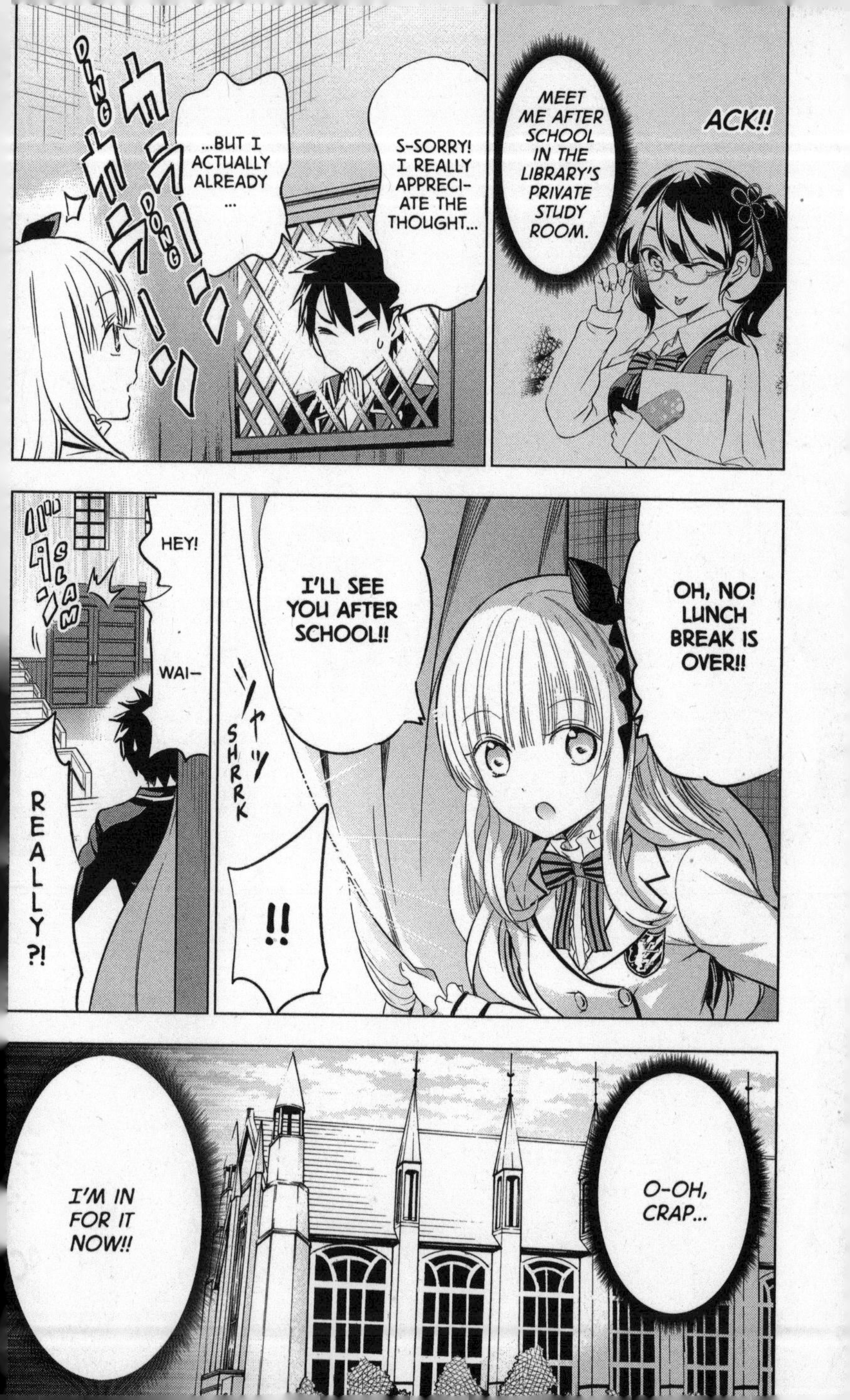
ACK!!
MEET ME AFTER SCHOOL IN THE LIBRARY'S PRIVATE STUDY ROOM.
S-SORRY! I REALLY APPRECIATE THE THOUGHT...
...BUT I ACTUALLY ALREADY ...
DING DONG
OH, NO! LUNCH BREAK IS OVER!!
I'LL SEE YOU AFTER SCHOOL!!
SHRRK
!!
HEY!
SLAM
WAI–
REALLY?!
O-OH, CRAP...
I'M IN FOR IT NOW!!

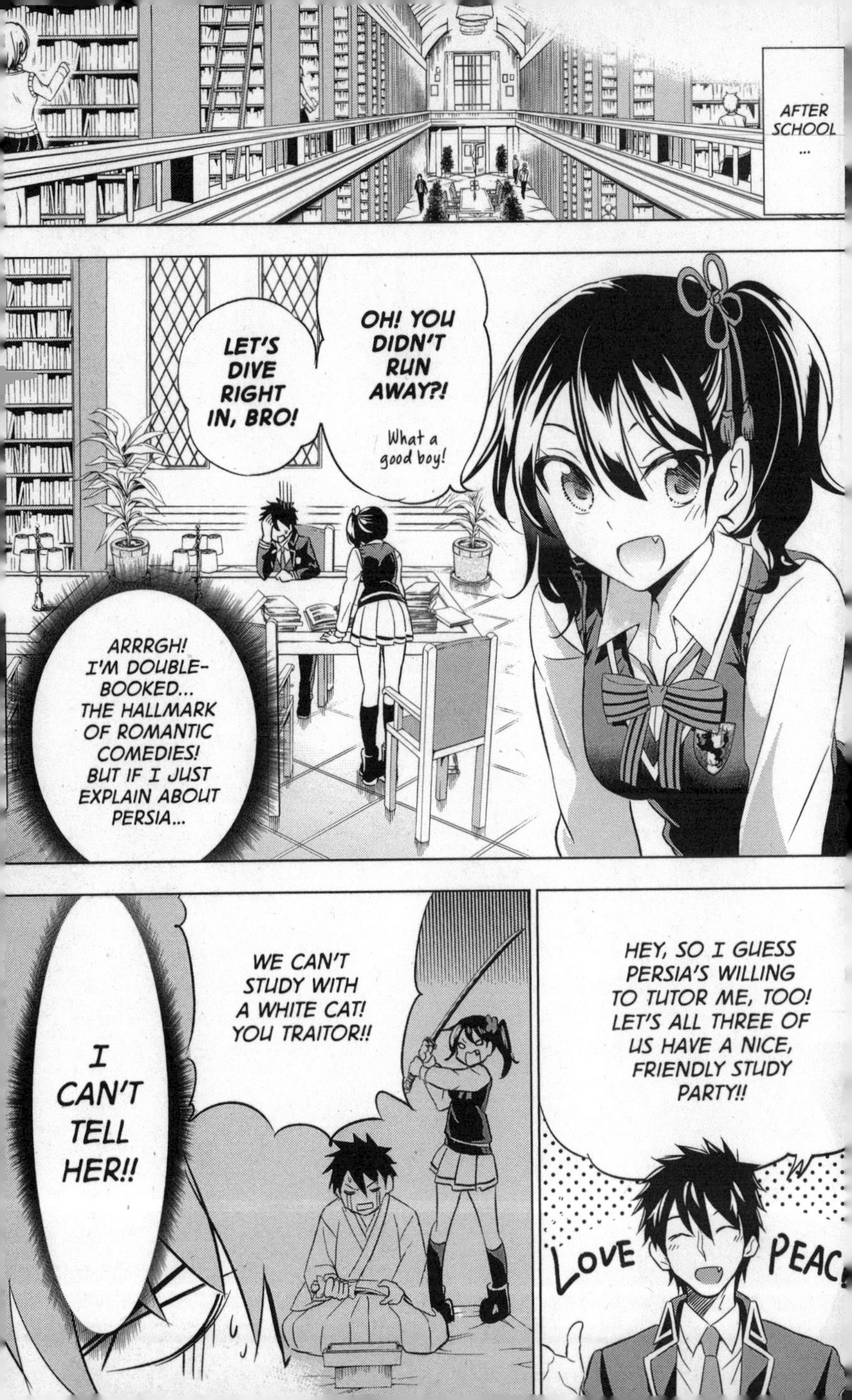
AFTER SCHOOL ...
OH! YOU DIDN'T RUN AWAY?!
What a good boy!
LET'S DIVE RIGHT IN, BRO!
ARRRGH! I'M DOUBLE-BOOKED... THE HALLMARK OF ROMANTIC COMEDIES! BUT IF I JUST EXPLAIN ABOUT PERSIA...
HEY, SO I GUESS PERSIA'S WILLING TO TUTOR ME, TOO! LET'S ALL THREE OF US HAVE A NICE, FRIENDLY STUDY PARTY!!
LOVE
PEAC
WE CAN'T STUDY WITH A WHITE CAT! YOU TRAITOR!!
I CAN'T TELL HER!!

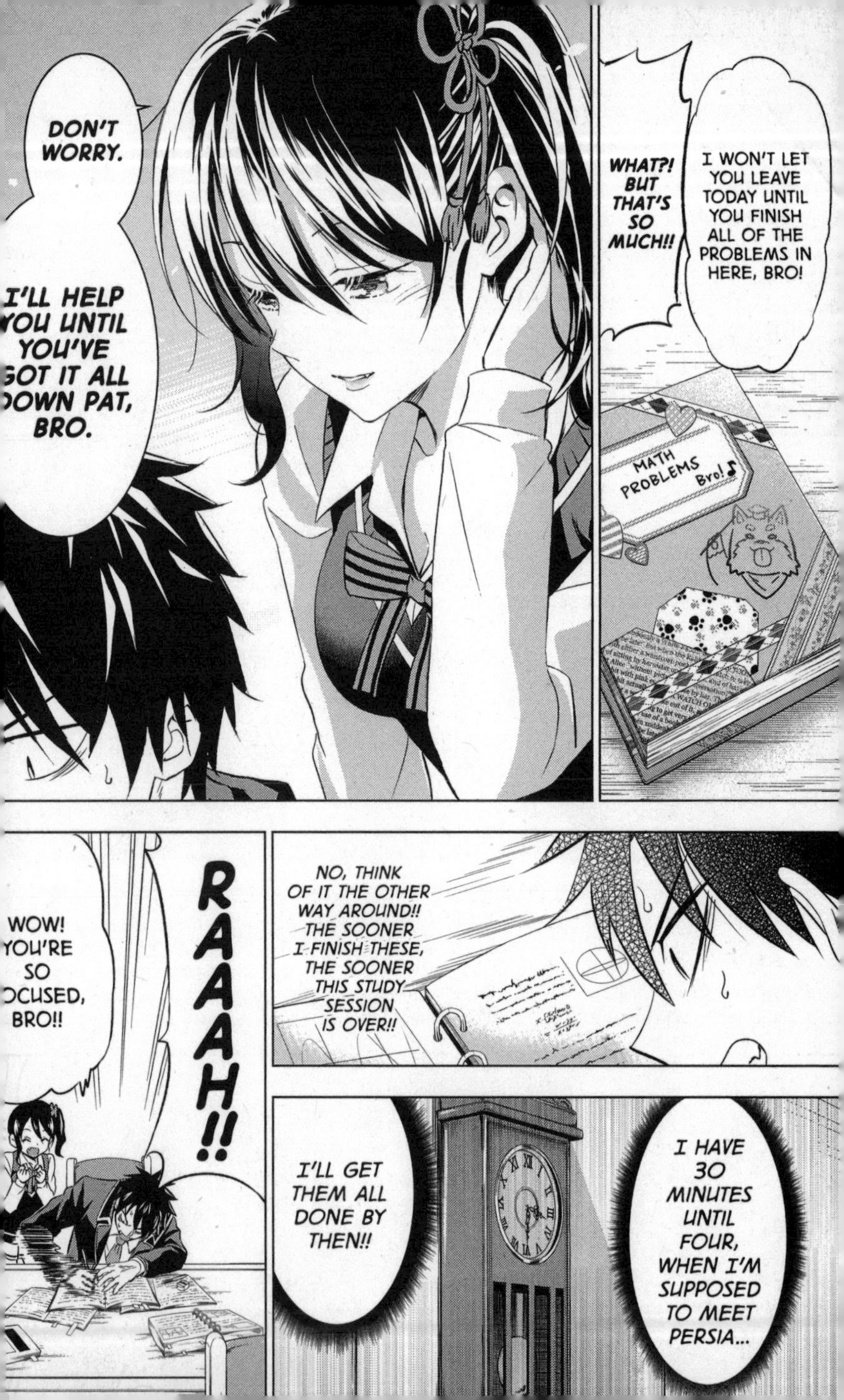
I WON'T LET YOU LEAVE TODAY UNTIL YOU FINISH ALL OF THE PROBLEMS IN HERE, BRO!
WHAT?! BUT THAT'S SO MUCH!!
MATH PROBLEMS Bro!♪
DON'T WORRY.
I'LL HELP YOU UNTIL YOU'VE GOT IT ALL DOWN PAT, BRO.
NO, THINK OF IT THE OTHER WAY AROUND!! THE SOONER I FINISH THESE, THE SOONER THIS STUDY SESSION IS OVER!!
I HAVE 30 MINUTES UNTIL FOUR, WHEN I'M SUPPOSED TO MEET PERSIA...
I'LL GET THEM ALL DONE BY THEN!!
RAAAAH!!
WOW! YOU'RE SO FOCUSED, BRO!!

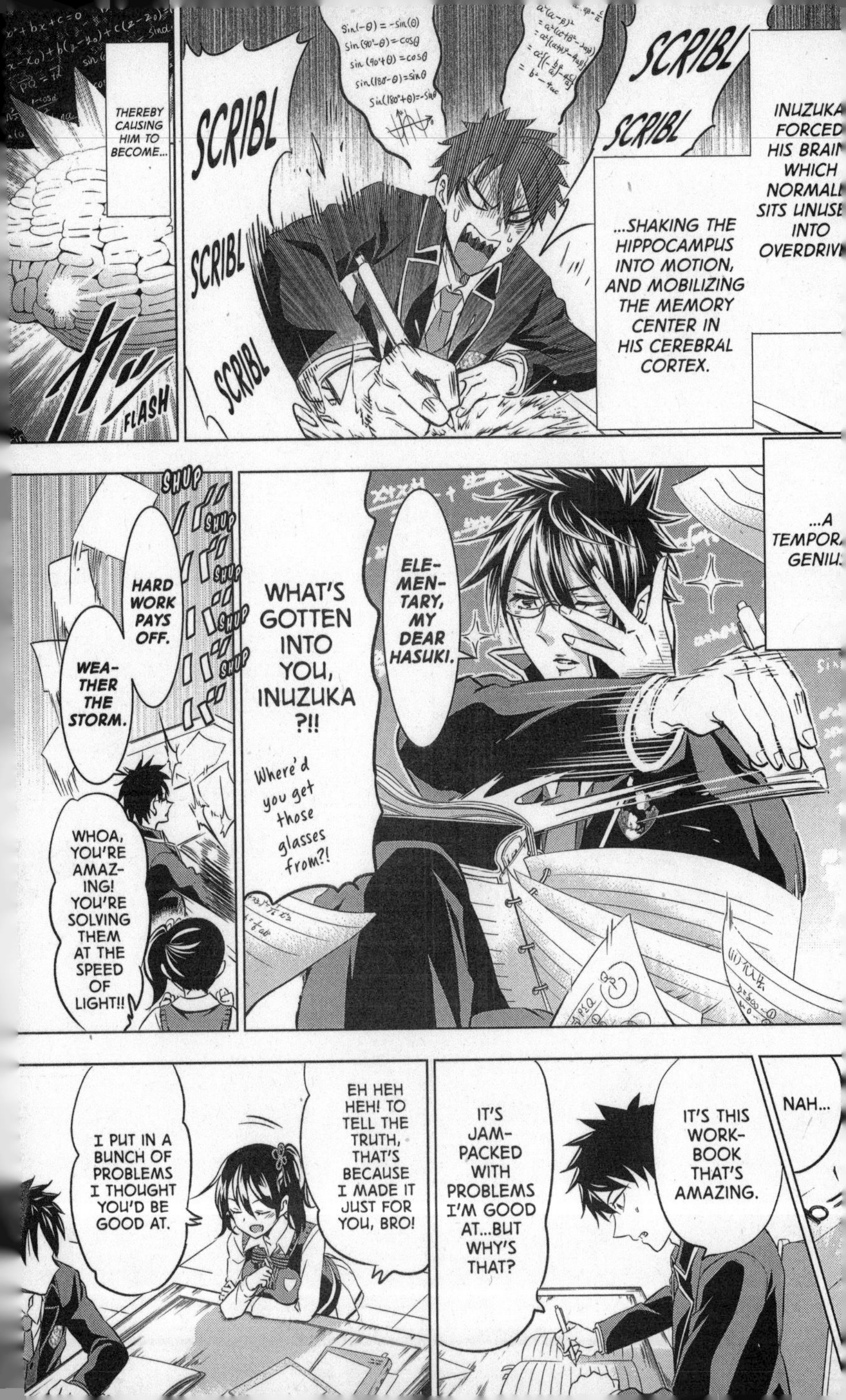
INUZUKA FORCED HIS BRAIN WHICH NORMALL SITS UNUSE INTO OVERDRIVE
SCRIBL SCRIBL
...SHAKING THE HIPPOCAMPUS INTO MOTION, AND MOBILIZING THE MEMORY CENTER IN HIS CEREBRAL CORTEX.
SCRIBL SCRIBL SCRIBL
THEREBY CAUSING HIM TO BECOME...
FLASH
...A TEMPORA GENIU
ELE-MEN-TARY, MY DEAR HASUKI.
WHAT'S GOTTEN INTO YOU, INUZUKA?!!
Where'd you get those glasses from?!
SHUP SHUP SHUP SHUP SHUP
HARD WORK PAYS OFF.
WEA-THER THE STORM.
WHOA, YOU'RE AMAZ-ING! YOU'RE SOLVING THEM AT THE SPEED OF LIGHT!!
NAH...
IT'S THIS WORK-BOOK THAT'S AMAZING.
IT'S JAM-PACKED WITH PROBLEMS I'M GOOD AT...BUT WHY'S THAT?
EH HEH HEH! TO TELL THE TRUTH, THAT'S BECAUSE I MADE IT JUST FOR YOU, BRO!
I PUT IN A BUNCH OF PROBLEMS I THOUGHT YOU'D BE GOOD AT.

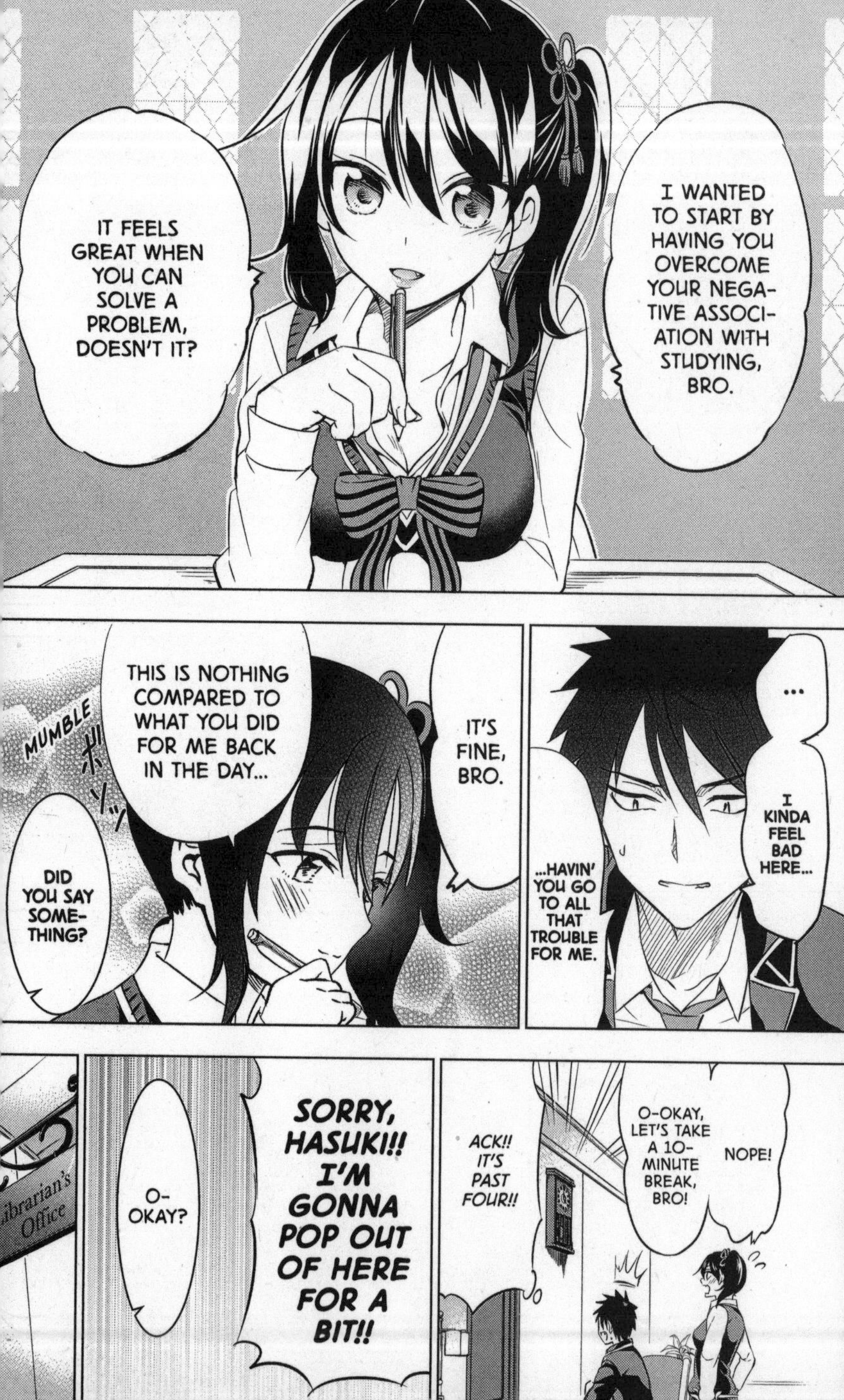
I WANTED TO START BY HAVING YOU OVERCOME YOUR NEGA-TIVE ASSOCI-ATION WITH STUDYING, BRO.
IT FEELS GREAT WHEN YOU CAN SOLVE A PROBLEM, DOESN'T IT?
...
I KINDA FEEL BAD HERE...
...HAVIN' YOU GO TO ALL THAT TROUBLE FOR ME.
IT'S FINE, BRO.
THIS IS NOTHING COMPARED TO WHAT YOU DID FOR ME BACK IN THE DAY...
MUMBLE
ボソッ
DID YOU SAY SOME-THING?
O-OKAY, LET'S TAKE A 10-MINUTE BREAK, BRO!
NOPE!
ACK!! IT'S PAST FOUR!!
SORRY, HASUKI!!! I'M GONNA POP OUT OF HERE FOR A BIT!!
O-OKAY?
Librarian's Office

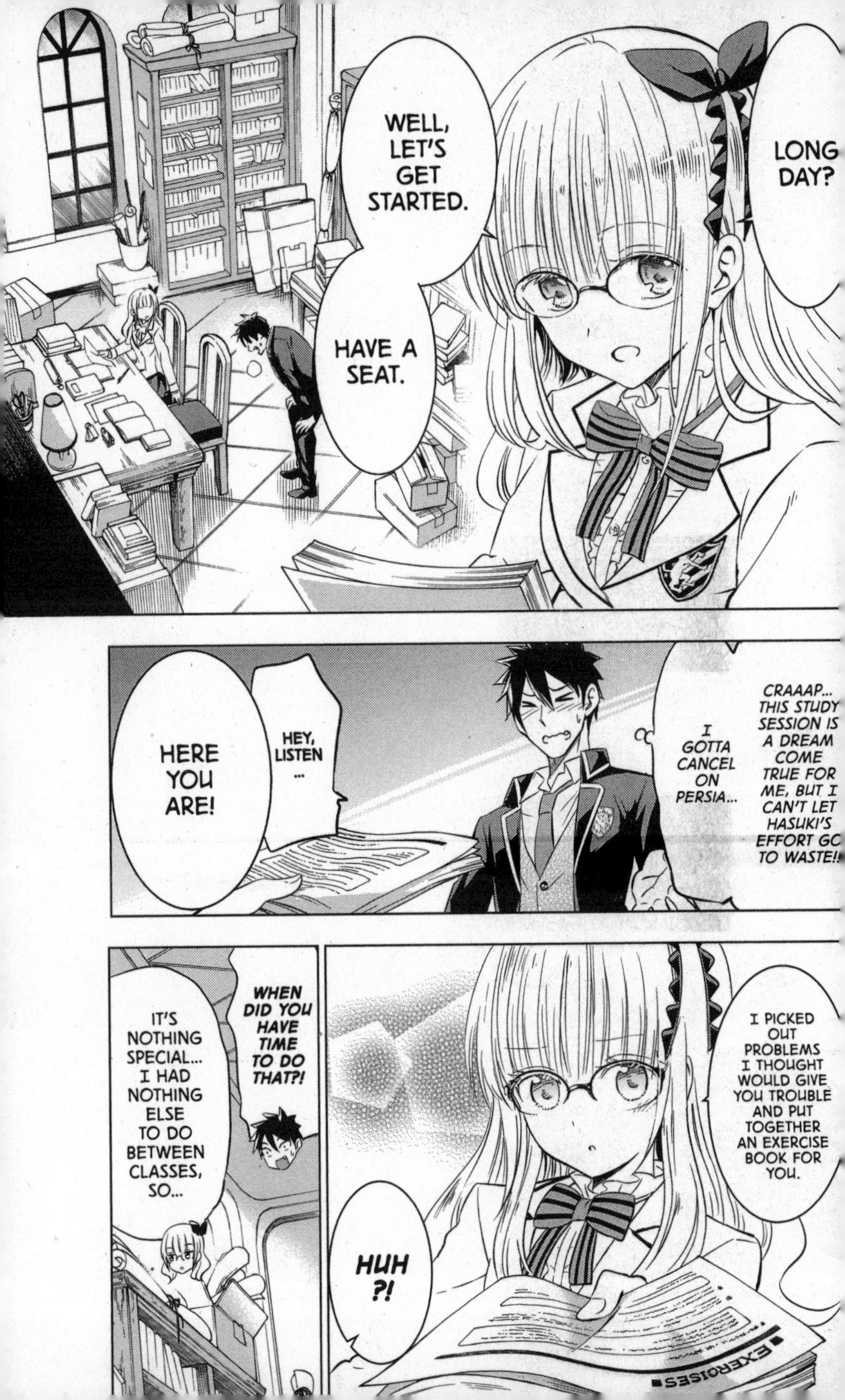
LONG DAY?
WELL, LET'S GET STARTED.
HAVE A SEAT.
CRAAAP... THIS STUDY SESSION IS A DREAM COME TRUE FOR ME, BUT I CAN'T LET HASUKI'S EFFORT GO TO WASTE!!
I GOTTA CANCEL ON PERSIA...
HEY, LISTEN ...
HERE YOU ARE!
I PICKED OUT PROBLEMS I THOUGHT WOULD GIVE YOU TROUBLE AND PUT TOGETHER AN EXERCISE BOOK FOR YOU.
HUH ?!
EXERCISES
WHEN DID YOU HAVE TIME TO DO THAT?!
IT'S NOTHING SPECIAL... I HAD NOTHING ELSE TO DO BETWEEN CLASSES, SO...

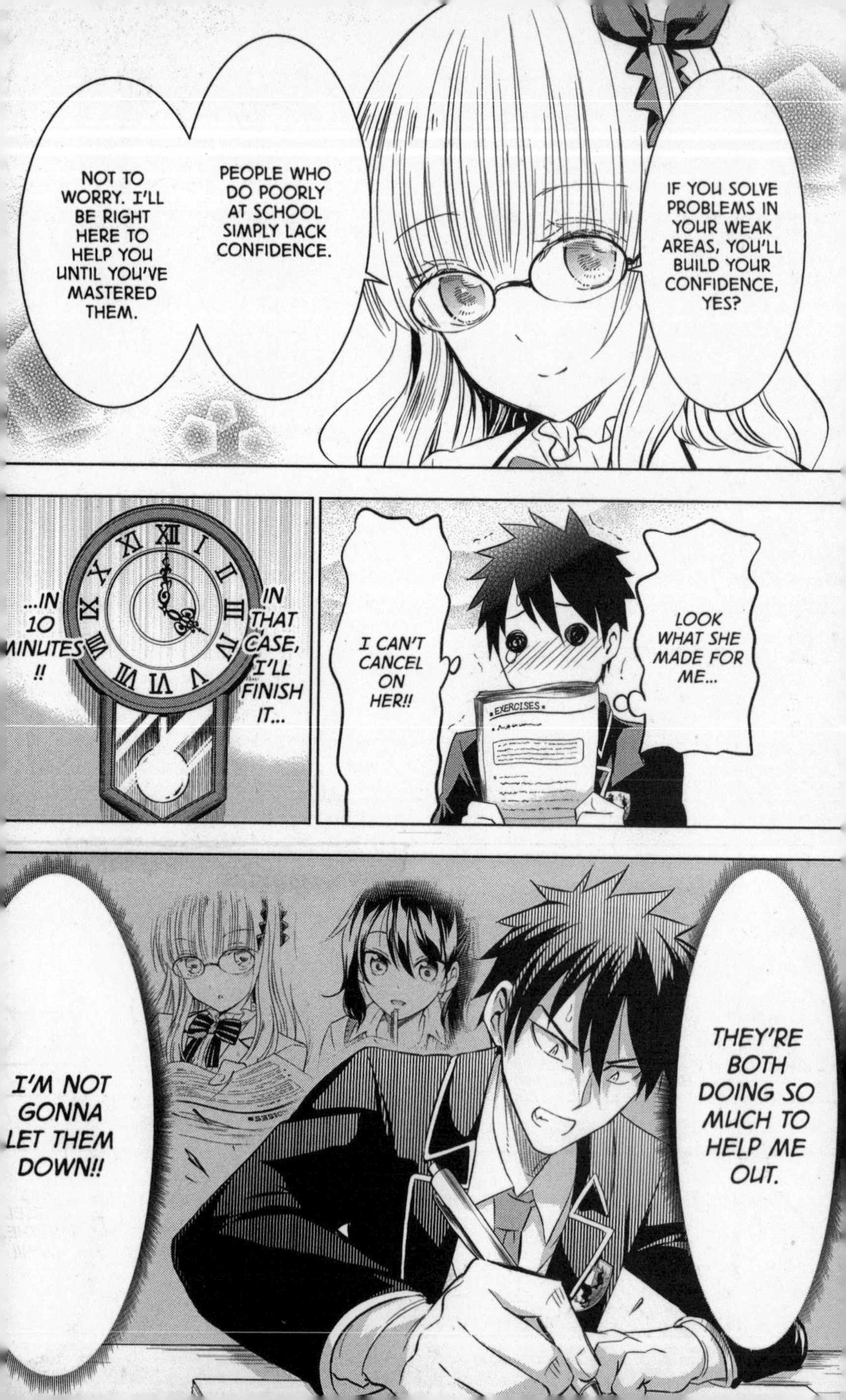
IF YOU SOLVE PROBLEMS IN YOUR WEAK AREAS, YOU'LL BUILD YOUR CONFIDENCE, YES?
PEOPLE WHO DO POORLY AT SCHOOL SIMPLY LACK CONFIDENCE.
NOT TO WORRY. I'LL BE RIGHT HERE TO HELP YOU UNTIL YOU'VE MASTERED THEM.
LOOK WHAT SHE MADE FOR ME...
EXERCISES
I CAN'T CANCEL ON HER!!
IN THAT CASE, I'LL FINISH IT...
...IN 10 MINUTES!!
THEY'RE BOTH DOING SO MUCH TO HELP ME OUT.
I'M NOT GONNA LET THEM DOWN!!

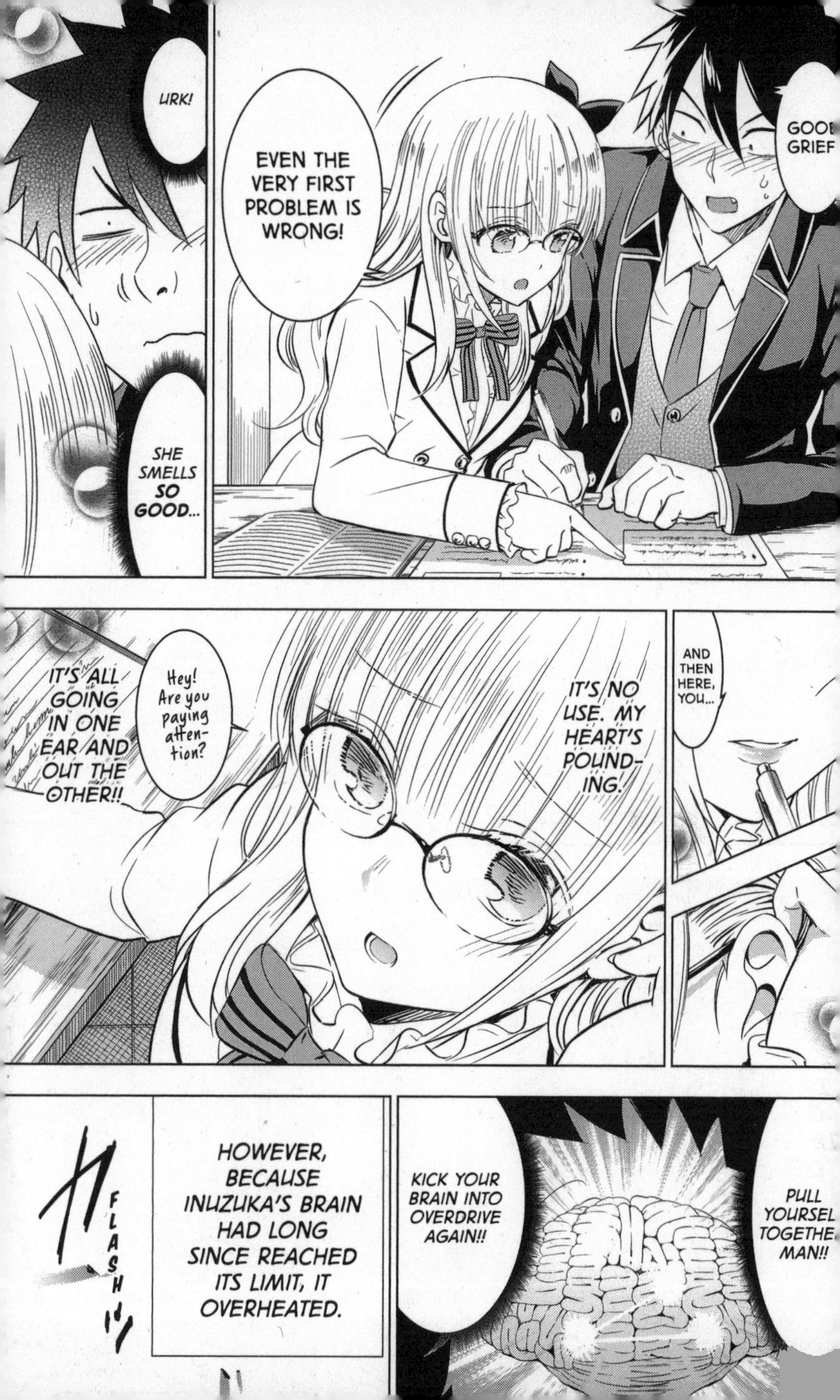
GOOD GRIEF
EVEN THE VERY FIRST PROBLEM IS WRONG!
URK!
SHE SMELLS SO GOOD...
AND THEN HERE, YOU...
IT'S NO USE. MY HEART'S POUNDING.
Hey! Are you paying attention?
IT'S ALL GOING IN ONE EAR AND OUT THE OTHER!!
PULL YOURSEL TOGETHE MAN!!
KICK YOUR BRAIN INTO OVERDRIVE AGAIN!!
HOWEVER, BECAUSE INUZUKA'S BRAIN HAD LONG SINCE REACHED ITS LIMIT, IT OVERHEATED.
FLASH

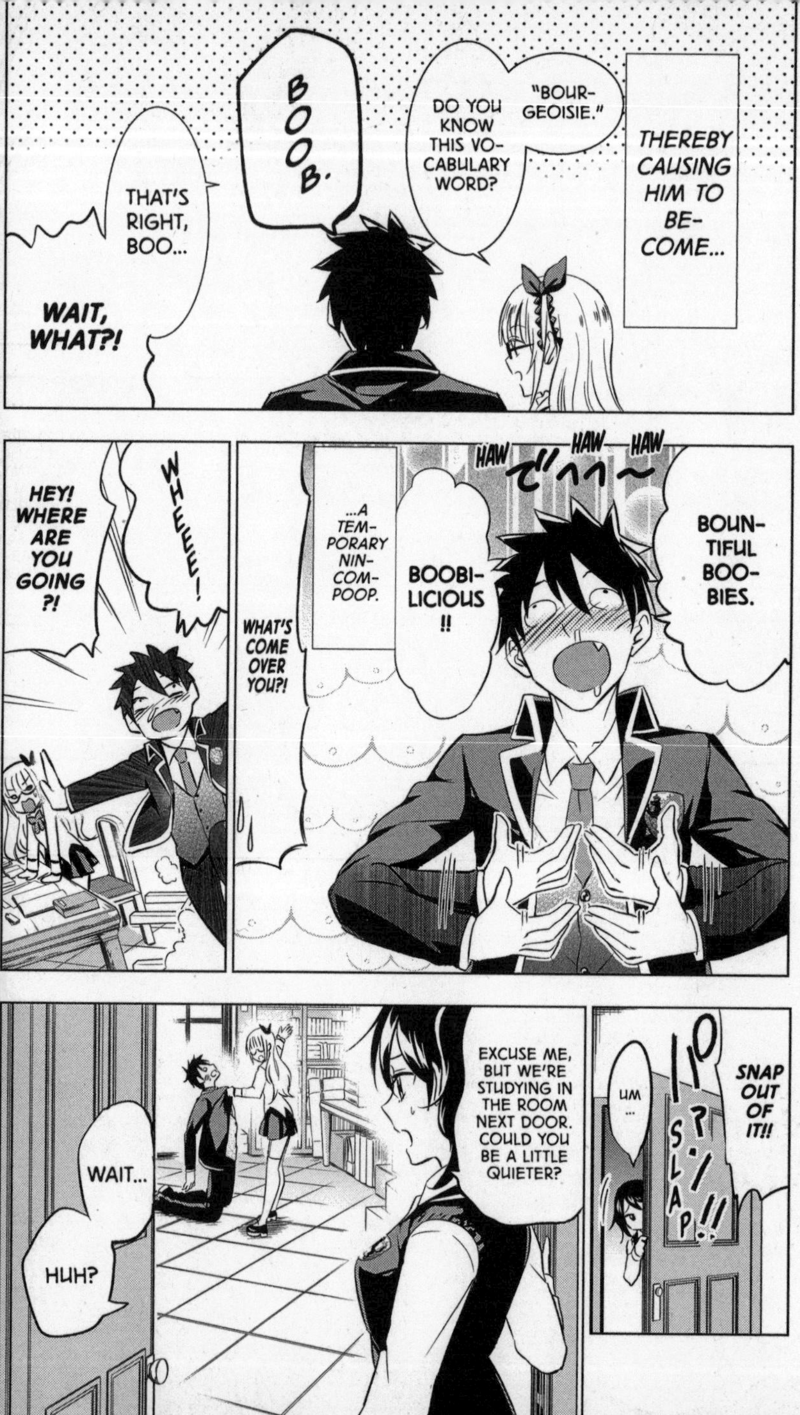
THEREBY CAUSING HIM TO BE-COME...
DO YOU KNOW THIS VO-CABULARY WORD? "BOUR-GEOISIE."
BOOB.
THAT'S RIGHT, BOO...
WAIT, WHAT?!
HAW HAW HAW
...A TEM-PORARY NIN-COM-POOP.
BOUN-TIFUL BOO-BIES.
BOOBI-LICIOUS !!
WHAT'S COME OVER YOU?!
WHEEEE!
HEY! WHERE ARE YOU GOING ?!
SNAP OUT OF IT!!
SLAP
?!
UM ...
EXCUSE ME, BUT WE'RE STUDYING IN THE ROOM NEXT DOOR. COULD YOU BE A LITTLE QUIETER?
WAIT...
HUH?

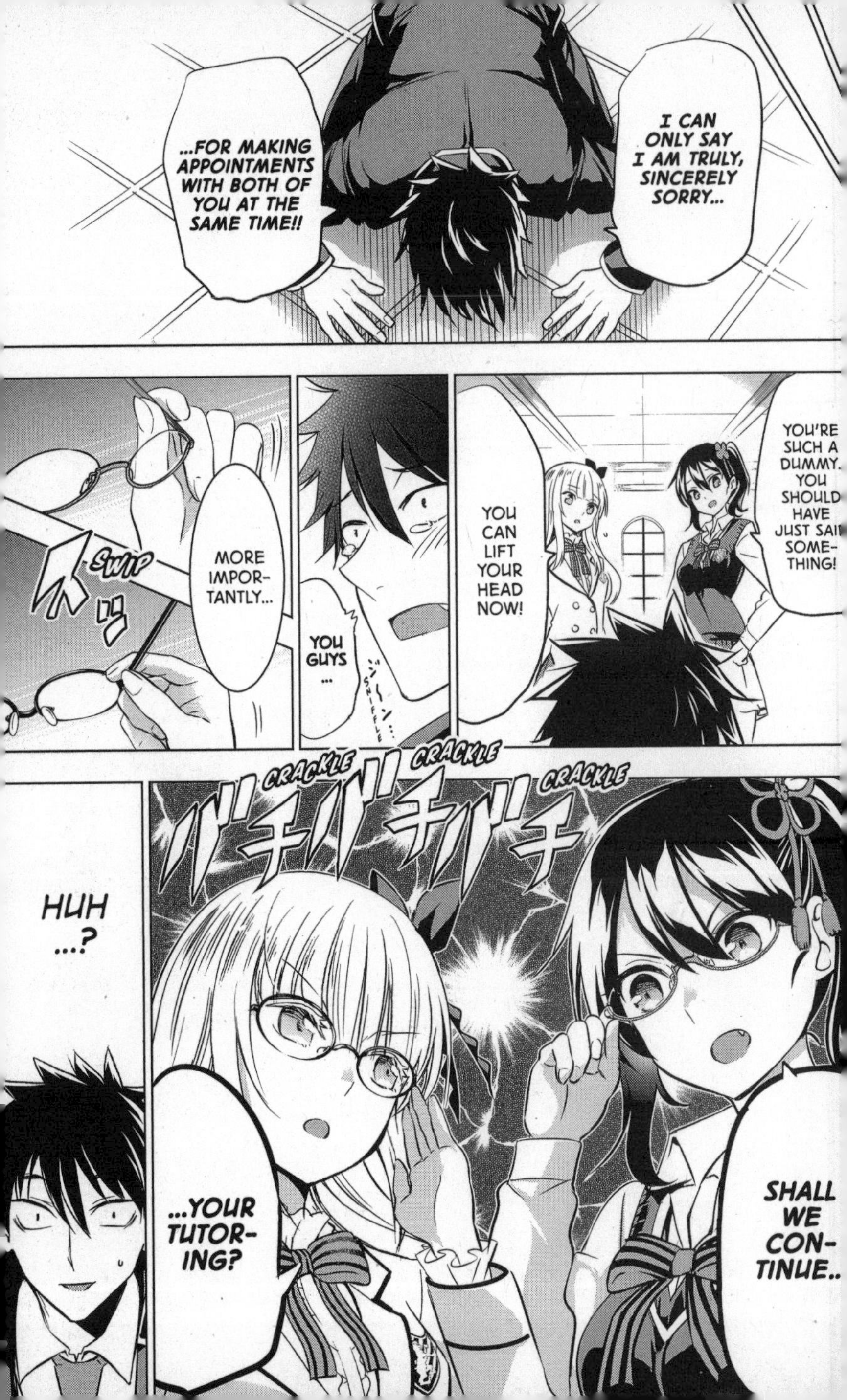
I CAN ONLY SAY I AM TRULY, SINCERELY SORRY...
...FOR MAKING APPOINTMENTS WITH BOTH OF YOU AT THE SAME TIME!!
YOU'RE SUCH A DUMMY. YOU SHOULD HAVE JUST SAI SOME-THING!
YOU CAN LIFT YOUR HEAD NOW!
YOU GUYS ...
SNIFFLE
MORE IMPOR-TANTLY...
SWIP
CRACKLE CRACKLE CRACKLE
SHALL WE CON-TINUE..
...YOUR TUTOR-ING?
HUH ...?

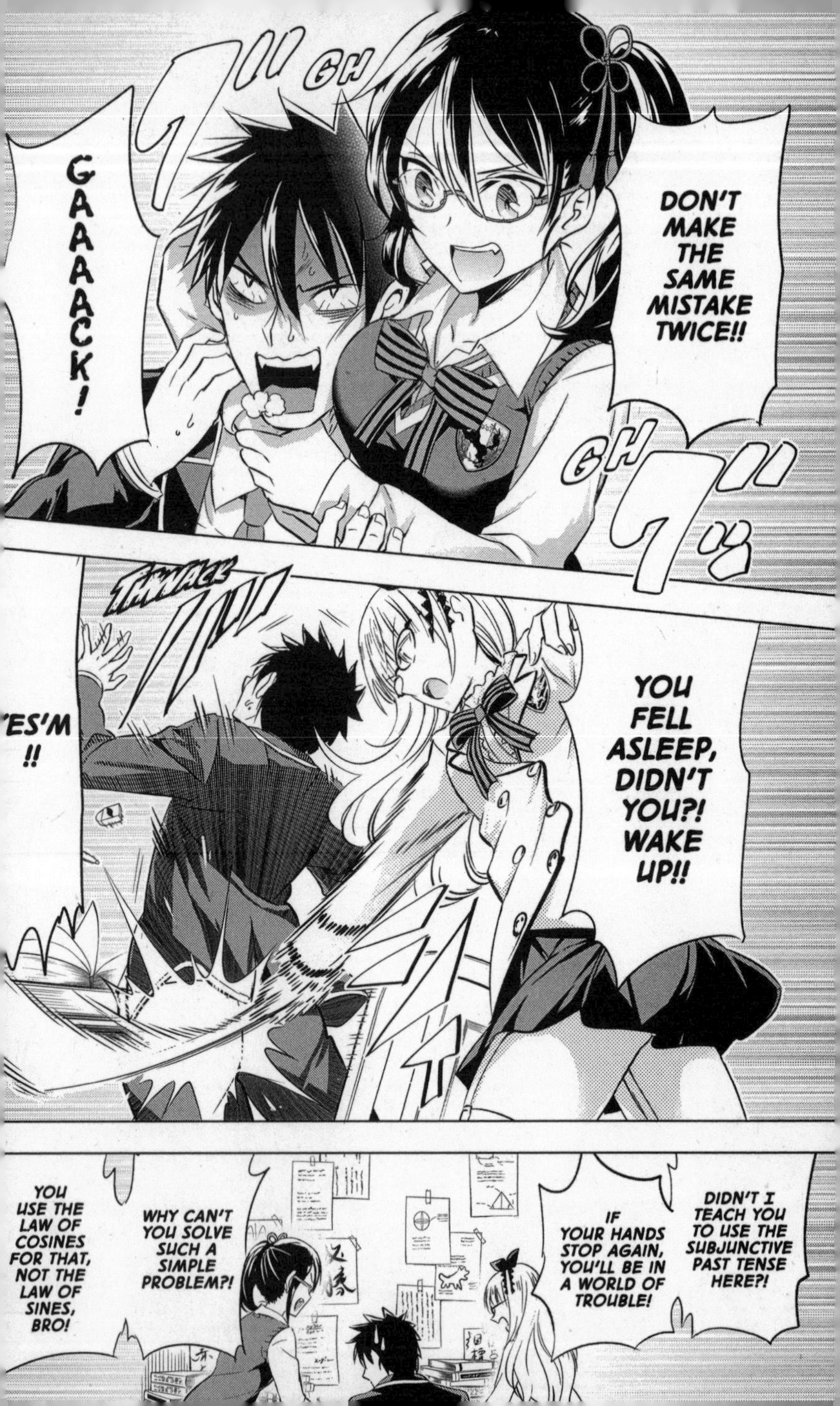

GH
DON'T MAKE THE SAME MISTAKE TWICE!!
GAAAACK!
GH
YOU FELL ASLEEP, DIDN'T YOU?! WAKE UP!!
THWACK
ES'M !!
DIDN'T I TEACH YOU TO USE THE SUBJUNCTIVE PAST TENSE HERE?!
IF YOUR HANDS STOP AGAIN, YOU'LL BE IN A WORLD OF TROUBLE!
WHY CAN'T YOU SOLVE SUCH A SIMPLE PROBLEM?!
YOU USE THE LAW OF COSINES FOR THAT, NOT THE LAW OF SINES, BRO!

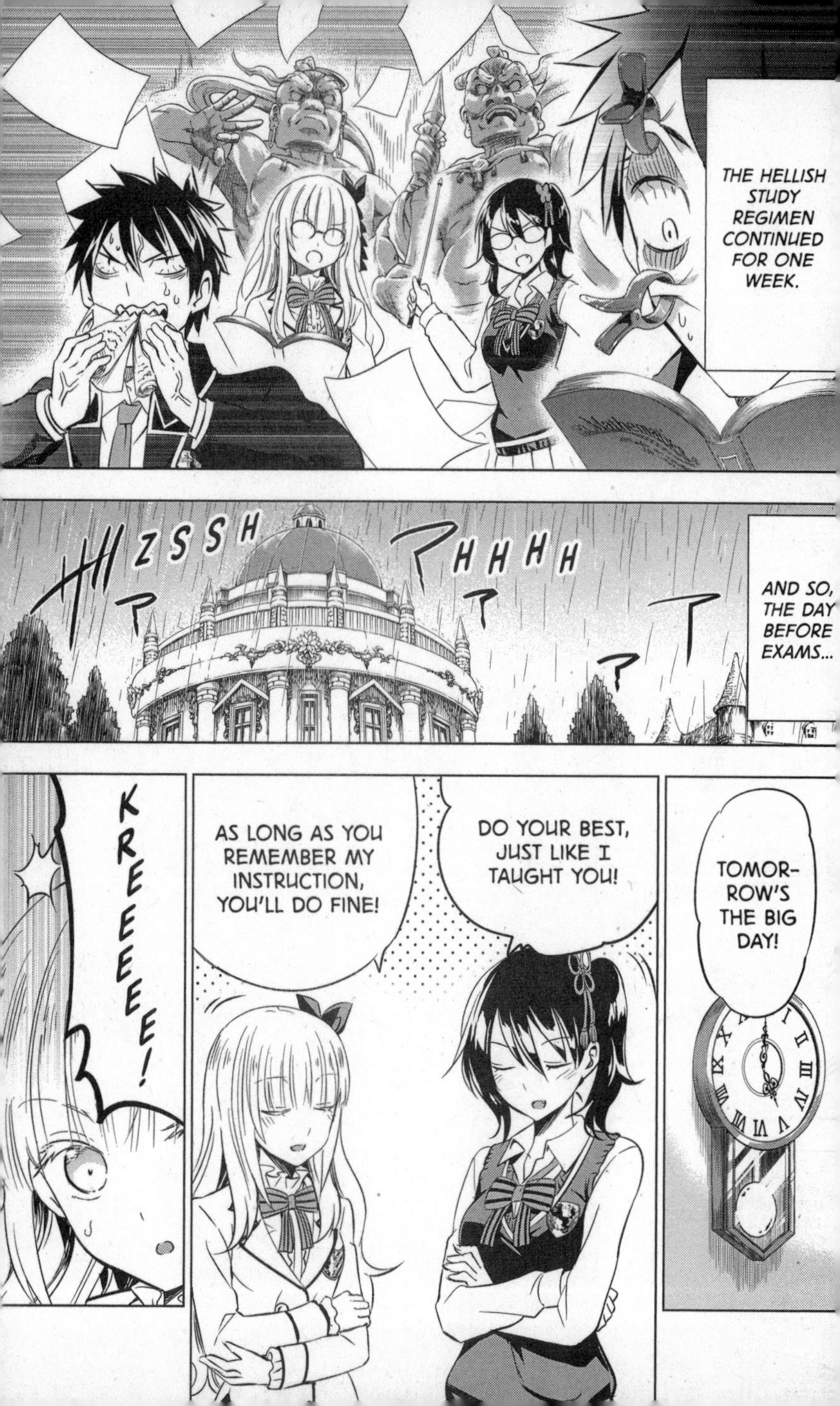
THE HELLISH STUDY REGIMEN CONTINUED FOR ONE WEEK.
AND SO, THE DAY BEFORE EXAMS...
ZSSH
HHHH
TOMOR-ROW'S THE BIG DAY!
DO YOUR BEST, JUST LIKE I TAUGHT YOU!
AS LONG AS YOU REMEMBER MY INSTRUCTION, YOU'LL DO FINE!
KREEEEEE!

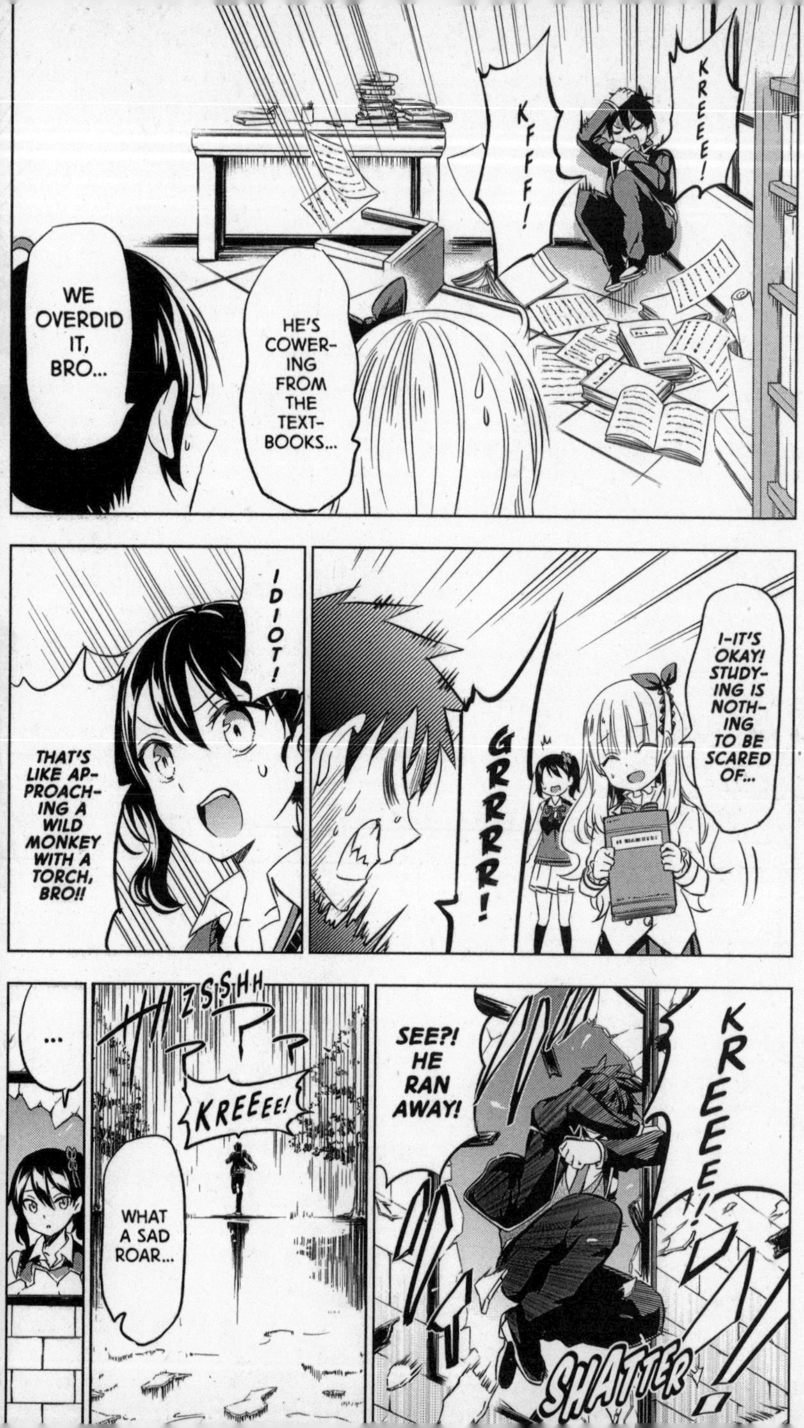
KREEE!
KFFF!
HE'S COWER-ING FROM THE TEXT-BOOKS...
WE OVERDID IT, BRO...
I-IT'S OKAY! STUDYING IS NOTHING TO BE SCARED OF...
GRRRRR!
IDIOT!
THAT'S LIKE AP-PROACHING A WILD MONKEY WITH A TORCH, BRO!!
KREEEE!
SEE?! HE RAN AWAY!
SHATTER
HZSSHH
KREEEE!
WHAT A SAD ROAR...
...

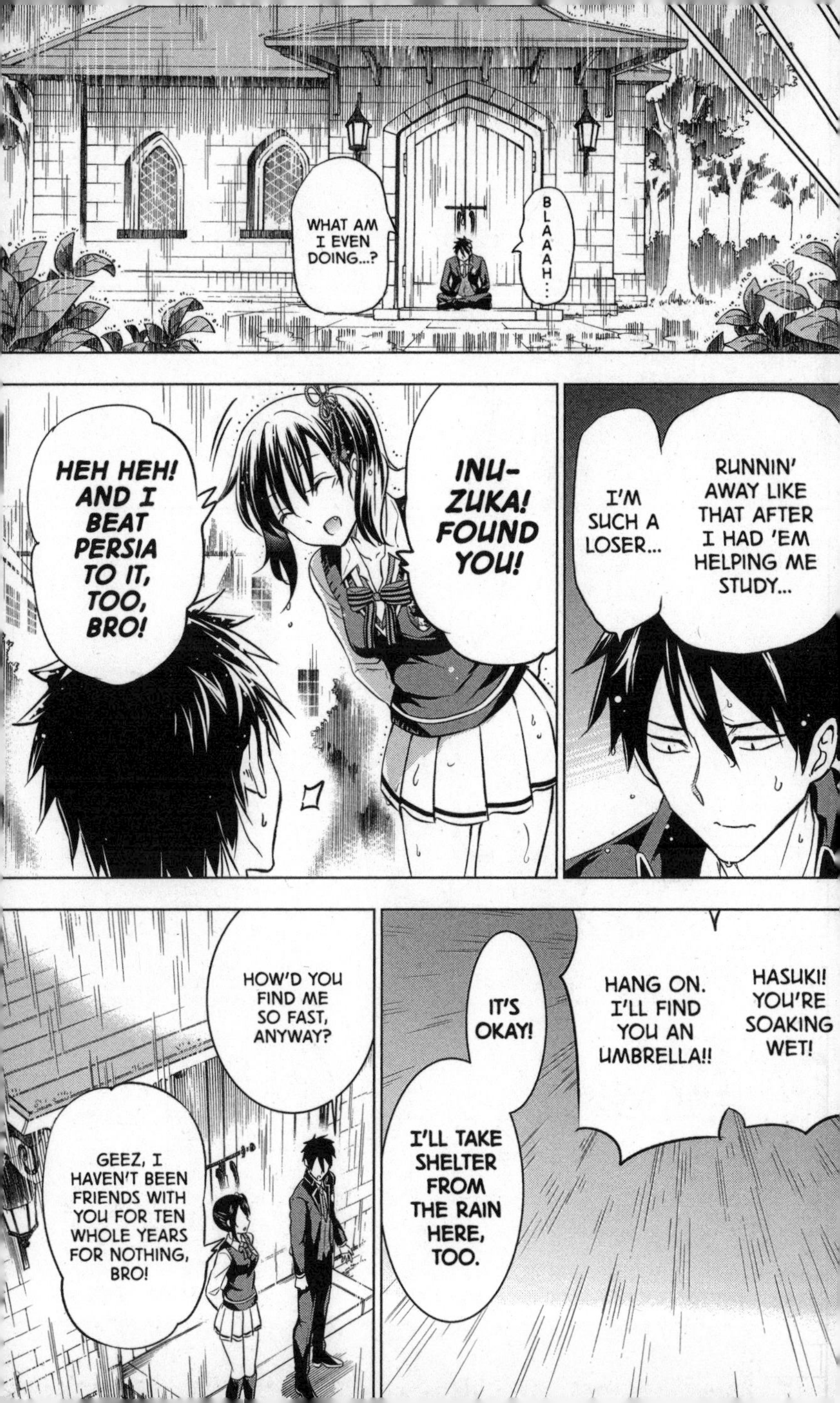
BLAAAH...
WHAT AM I EVEN DOING...?
RUNNIN' AWAY LIKE THAT AFTER I HAD 'EM HELPING ME STUDY...
I'M SUCH A LOSER...
INU-ZUKA! FOUND YOU!
HEH HEH! AND I BEAT PERSIA TO IT, TOO, BRO!
HASUKI! YOU'RE SOAKING WET!
HANG ON. I'LL FIND YOU AN UMBRELLA!!
IT'S OKAY!
I'LL TAKE SHELTER FROM THE RAIN HERE, TOO.
HOW'D YOU FIND ME SO FAST, ANYWAY?
GEEZ, I HAVEN'T BEEN FRIENDS WITH YOU FOR TEN WHOLE YEARS FOR NOTHING, BRO!

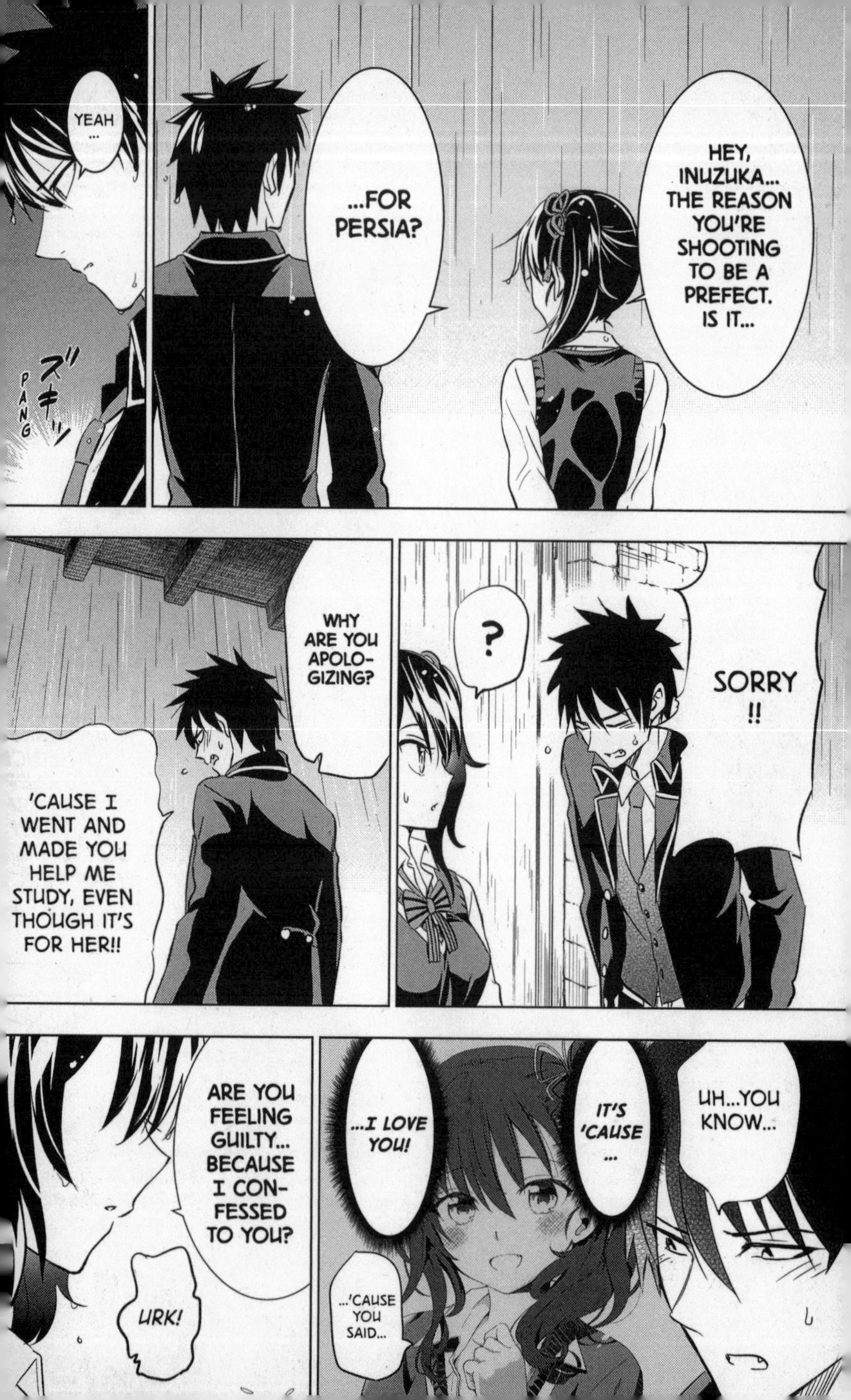
HEY, INUZUKA... THE REASON YOU'RE SHOOTING TO BE A PREFECT. IS IT...
...FOR PERSIA?
YEAH ...
ズキッ
PANG
SORRY !!
?
WHY ARE YOU APOLO-GIZING?
'CAUSE I WENT AND MADE YOU HELP ME STUDY, EVEN THOUGH IT'S FOR HER!!
UH...YOU KNOW...
IT'S 'CAUSE ...
...I LOVE YOU!
...'CAUSE YOU SAID...
ARE YOU FEELING GUILTY... BECAUSE I CON-FESSED TO YOU?
URK!

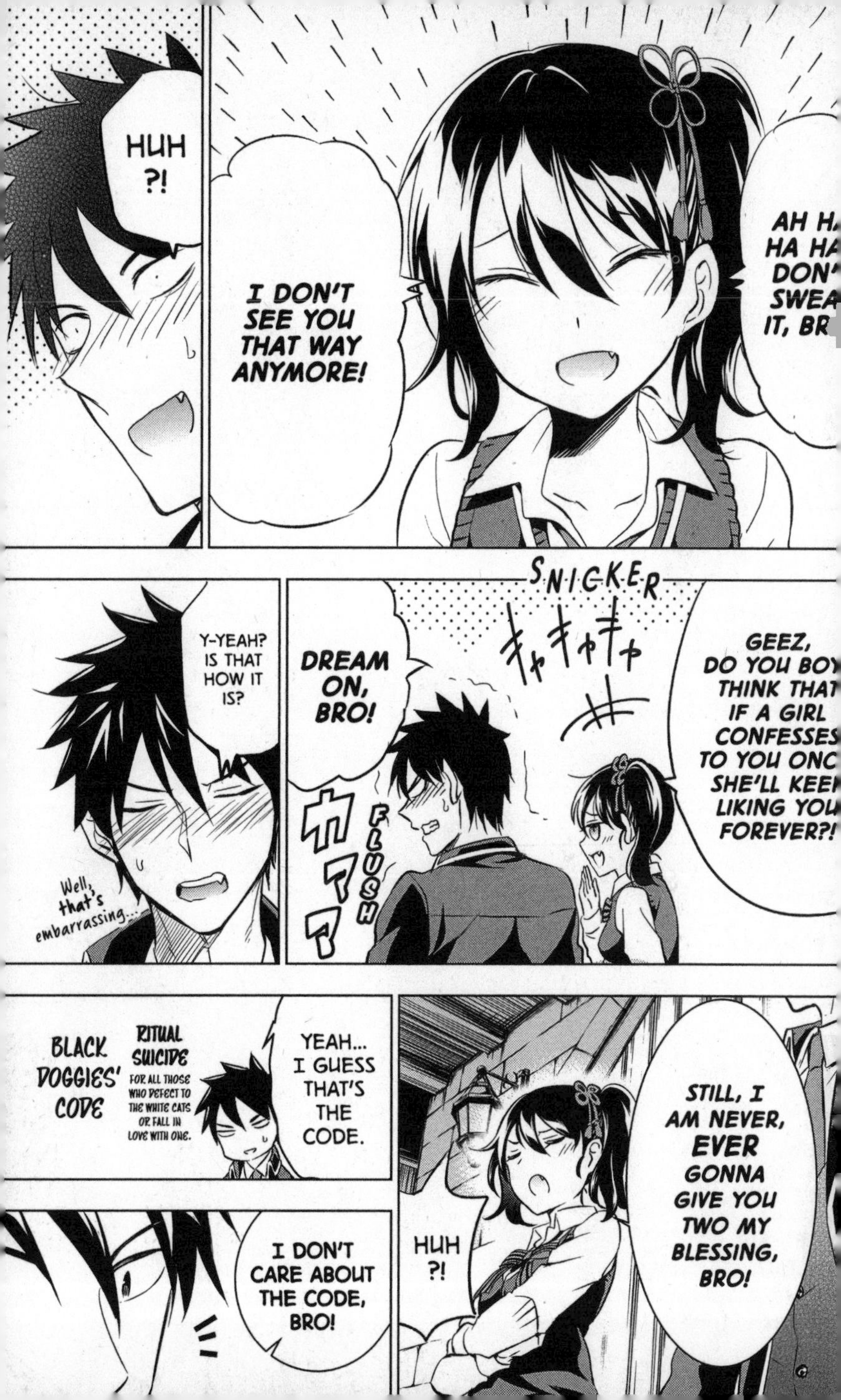
AH H
HA HA
DON'
SWEA
IT, BR
I DON'T SEE YOU THAT WAY ANYMORE!
HUH ?!
GEEZ, DO YOU BOY THINK THAT IF A GIRL CONFESSES TO YOU ONC SHE'LL KEE LIKING YOU FOREVER?!
SNICKER
キャキャキャ
DREAM ON, BRO!
FLUSH
カァァァ
Y-YEAH? IS THAT HOW IT IS?
Well, that's embarrassing...
STILL, I AM NEVER, EVER GONNA GIVE YOU TWO MY BLESSING, BRO!
HUH ?!
YEAH... I GUESS THAT'S THE CODE.
BLACK DOGGIES' CODE
RITUAL SUICIDE FOR ALL THOSE WHO DEFECT TO THE WHITE CATS OR FALL IN LOVE WITH ONE.
I DON'T CARE ABOUT THE CODE, BRO!

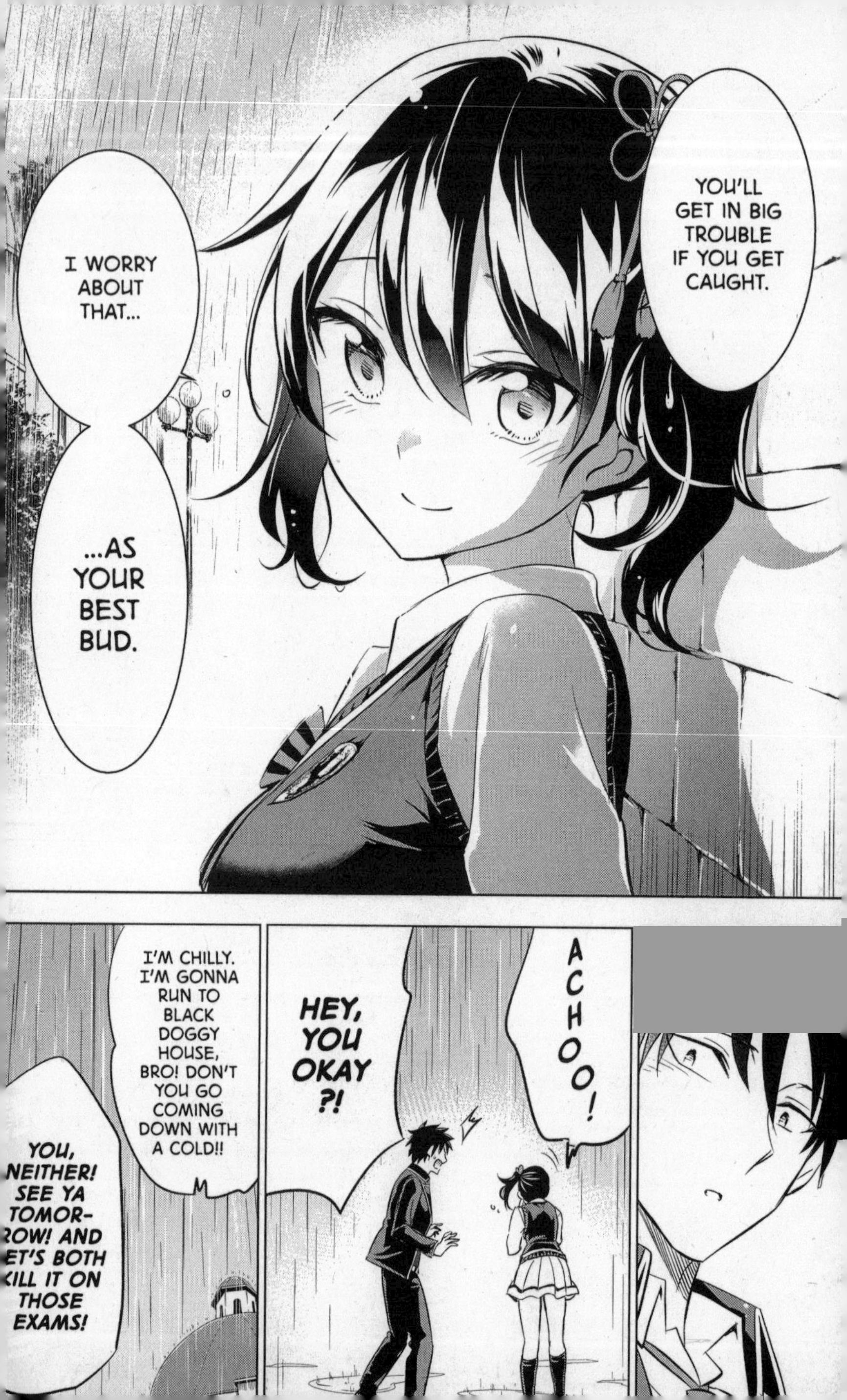
YOU'LL GET IN BIG TROUBLE IF YOU GET CAUGHT.
I WORRY ABOUT THAT...
...AS YOUR BEST BUD.
ACHOO!
HEY, YOU OKAY?!
I'M CHILLY. I'M GONNA RUN TO BLACK DOGGY HOUSE, BRO! DON'T YOU GO COMING DOWN WITH A COLD!!
YOU, NEITHER! SEE YA TOMOR-ROW! AND ET'S BOTH ILL IT ON THOSE EXAMS!

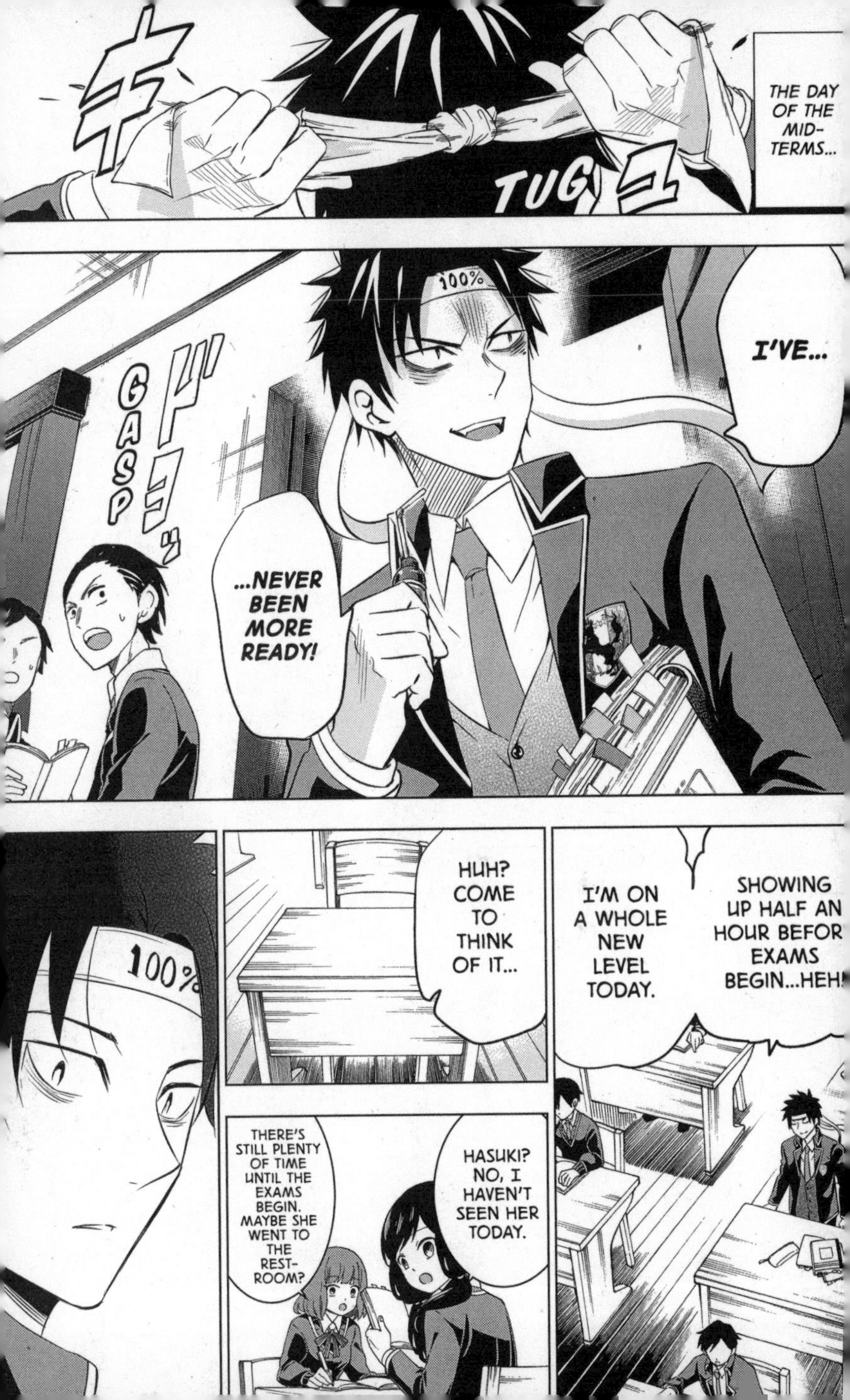
THE DAY OF THE MID-TERMS...
TUG
I'VE...
100%
...NEVER BEEN MORE READY!
GASP
SHOWING UP HALF AN HOUR BEFOR EXAMS BEGIN...HEH!
I'M ON A WHOLE NEW LEVEL TODAY.
HUH? COME TO THINK OF IT...
HASUKI? NO, I HAVEN'T SEEN HER TODAY.
THERE'S STILL PLENTY OF TIME UNTIL THE EXAMS BEGIN. MAYBE SHE WENT TO THE REST-ROOM?
100%

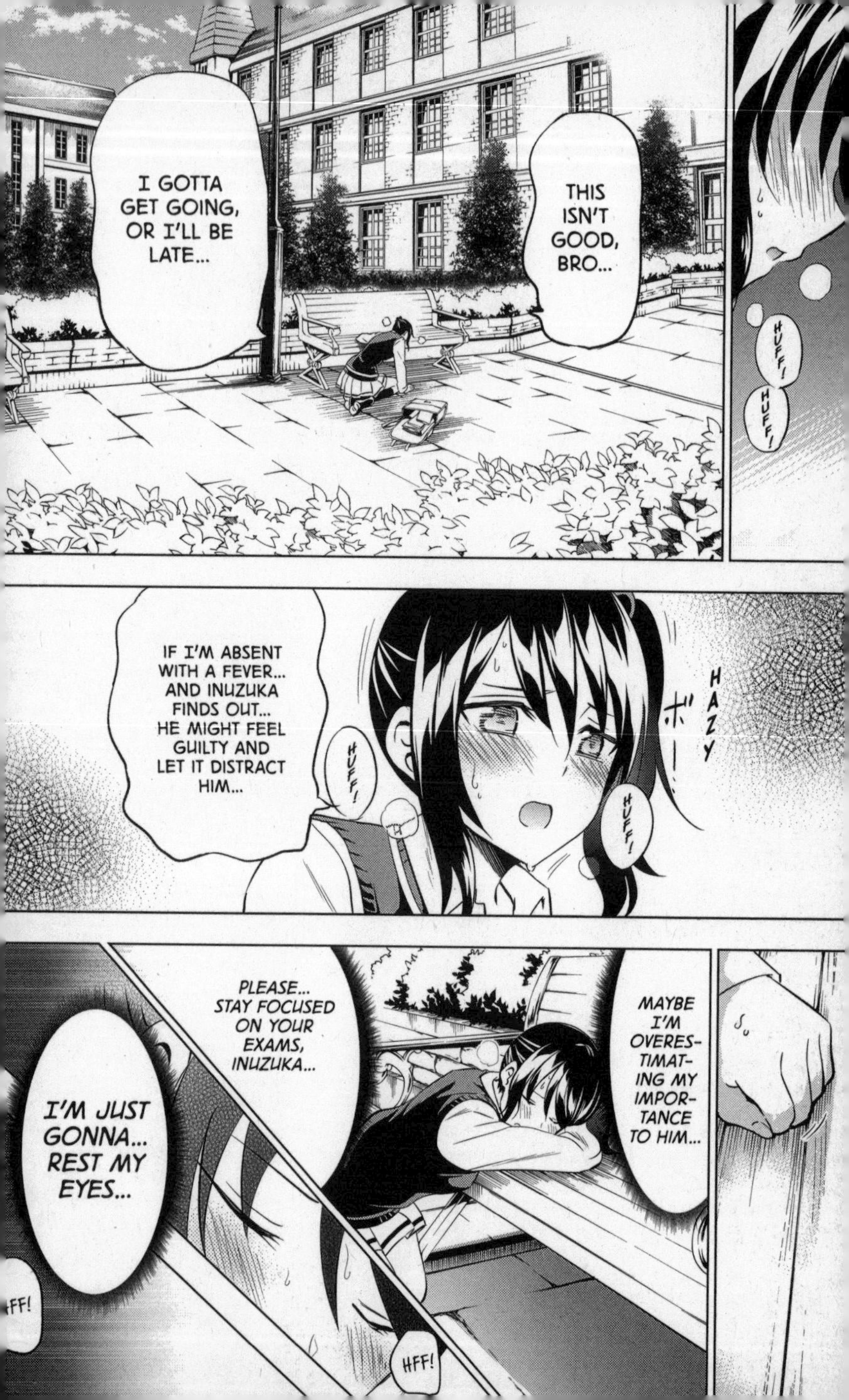
HUFF! HUFF!
THIS ISN'T GOOD, BRO...
I GOTTA GET GOING, OR I'LL BE LATE...
HAZY
HUFF!
IF I'M ABSENT WITH A FEVER... AND INUZUKA FINDS OUT... HE MIGHT FEEL GUILTY AND LET IT DISTRACT HIM...
HUFF!
MAYBE I'M OVERES-TIMAT-ING MY IMPOR-TANCE TO HIM...
PLEASE... STAY FOCUSED ON YOUR EXAMS, INUZUKA...
I'M JUST GONNA... REST MY EYES...
HFF!

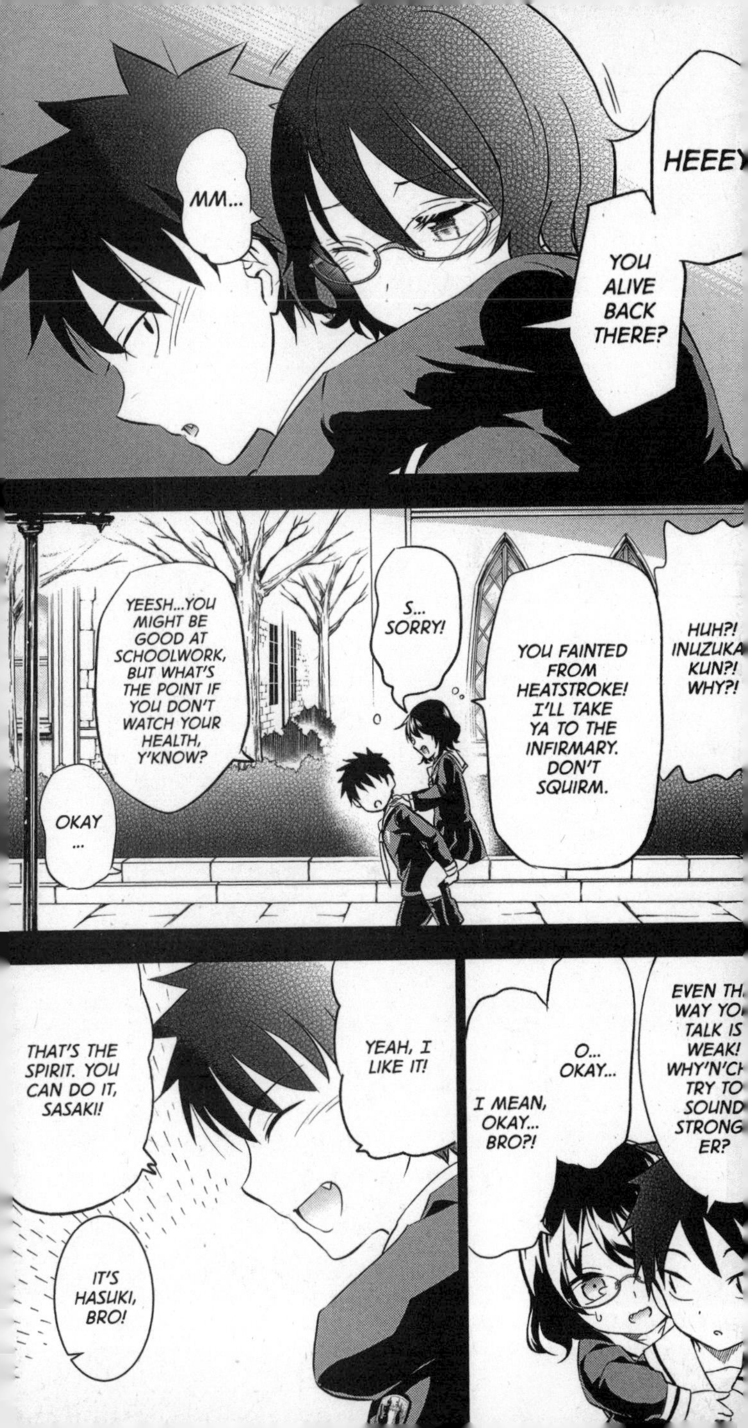
HEEEY
YOU ALIVE BACK THERE?
MM...
HUH?! INUZUKA KUN?! WHY?!
YOU FAINTED FROM HEATSTROKE! I'LL TAKE YA TO THE INFIRMARY. DON'T SQUIRM.
S... SORRY!
YEESH...YOU MIGHT BE GOOD AT SCHOOLWORK, BUT WHAT'S THE POINT IF YOU DON'T WATCH YOUR HEALTH, Y'KNOW?
OKAY ...
EVEN TH WAY YO TALK IS WEAK! WHY'N'C TRY TO SOUND STRONGER?
O... OKAY...
I MEAN, OKAY... BRO?!
YEAH, I LIKE IT!
THAT'S THE SPIRIT. YOU CAN DO IT, SASAKI!
IT'S HASUKI, BRO!

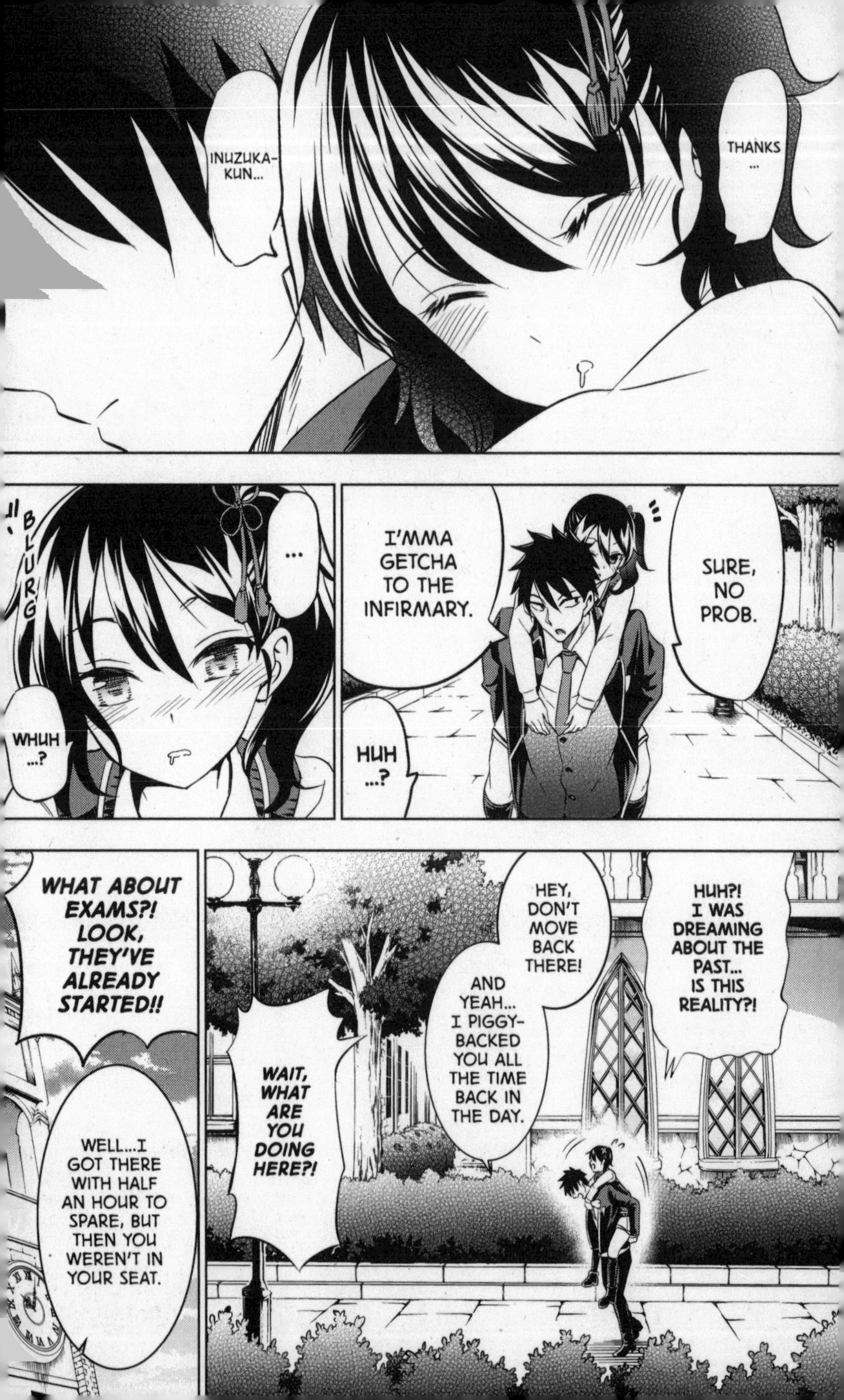
THANKS...
INUZUKA-KUN...
SURE, NO PROB.
I'MMA GETCHA TO THE INFIRMARY.
HUH...?
...
BLURG!!
WHUH...?
HUH?! I WAS DREAMING ABOUT THE PAST... IS THIS REALITY?!
HEY, DON'T MOVE BACK THERE!
AND YEAH... I PIGGY-BACKED YOU ALL THE TIME BACK IN THE DAY.
WAIT, WHAT ARE YOU DOING HERE?!
WHAT ABOUT EXAMS?! LOOK, THEY'VE ALREADY STARTED!!
WELL...I GOT THERE WITH HALF AN HOUR TO SPARE, BUT THEN YOU WEREN'T IN YOUR SEAT.

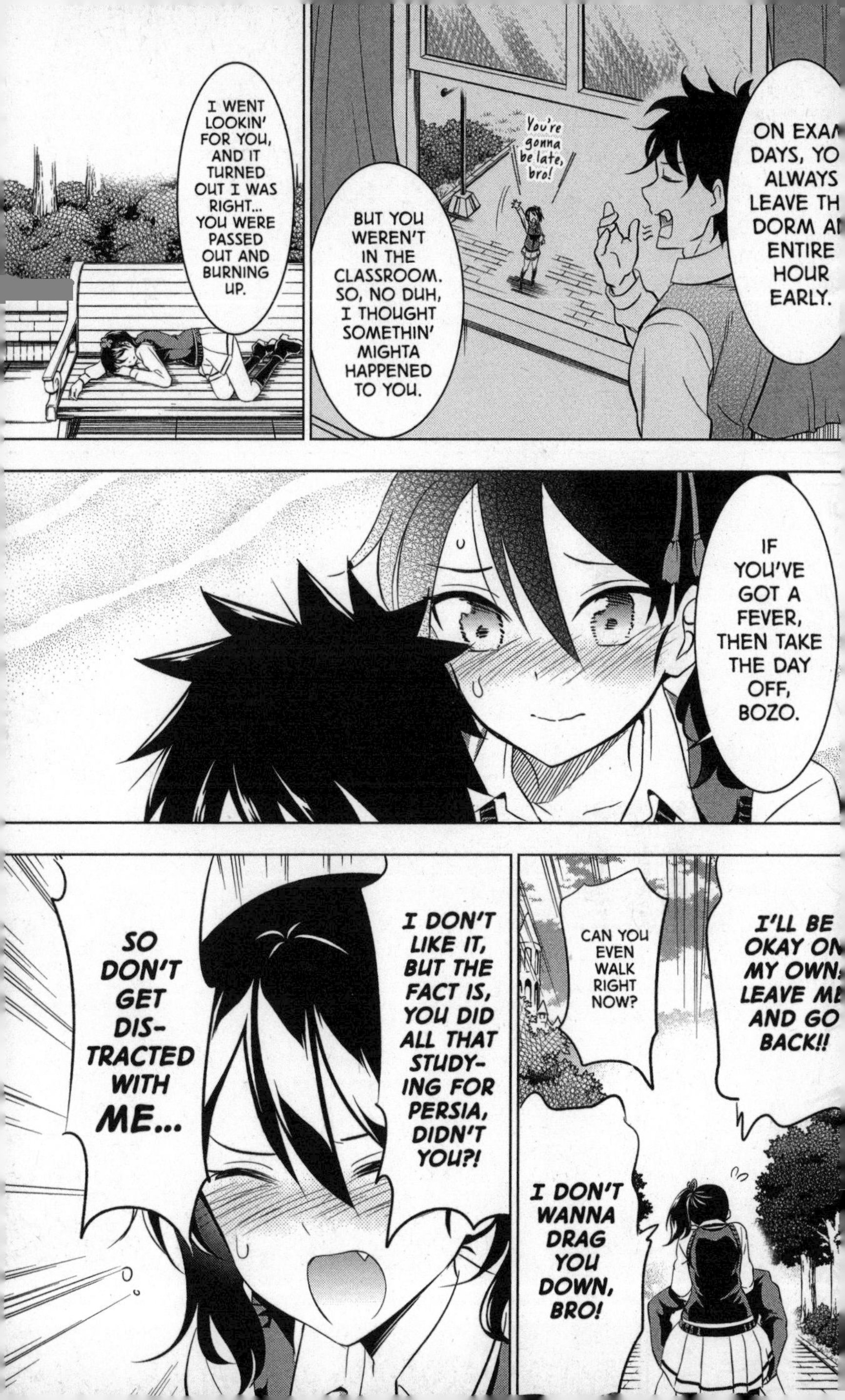
ON EXA DAYS, YO ALWAYS LEAVE TH DORM A ENTIRE HOUR EARLY.
You're gonna be late, bro!
BUT YOU WEREN'T IN THE CLASSROOM. SO, NO DUH, I THOUGHT SOMETHIN' MIGHTA HAPPENED TO YOU.
I WENT LOOKIN' FOR YOU, AND IT TURNED OUT I WAS RIGHT... YOU WERE PASSED OUT AND BURNING UP.
IF YOU'VE GOT A FEVER, THEN TAKE THE DAY OFF, BOZO.
I'LL BE OKAY O MY OWN LEAVE M AND GO BACK!!
CAN YOU EVEN WALK RIGHT NOW?
I DON'T WANNA DRAG YOU DOWN, BRO!
I DON'T LIKE IT, BUT THE FACT IS, YOU DID ALL THAT STUDY-ING FOR PERSIA, DIDN'T YOU?!
SO DON'T GET DIS-TRACTED WITH ME...

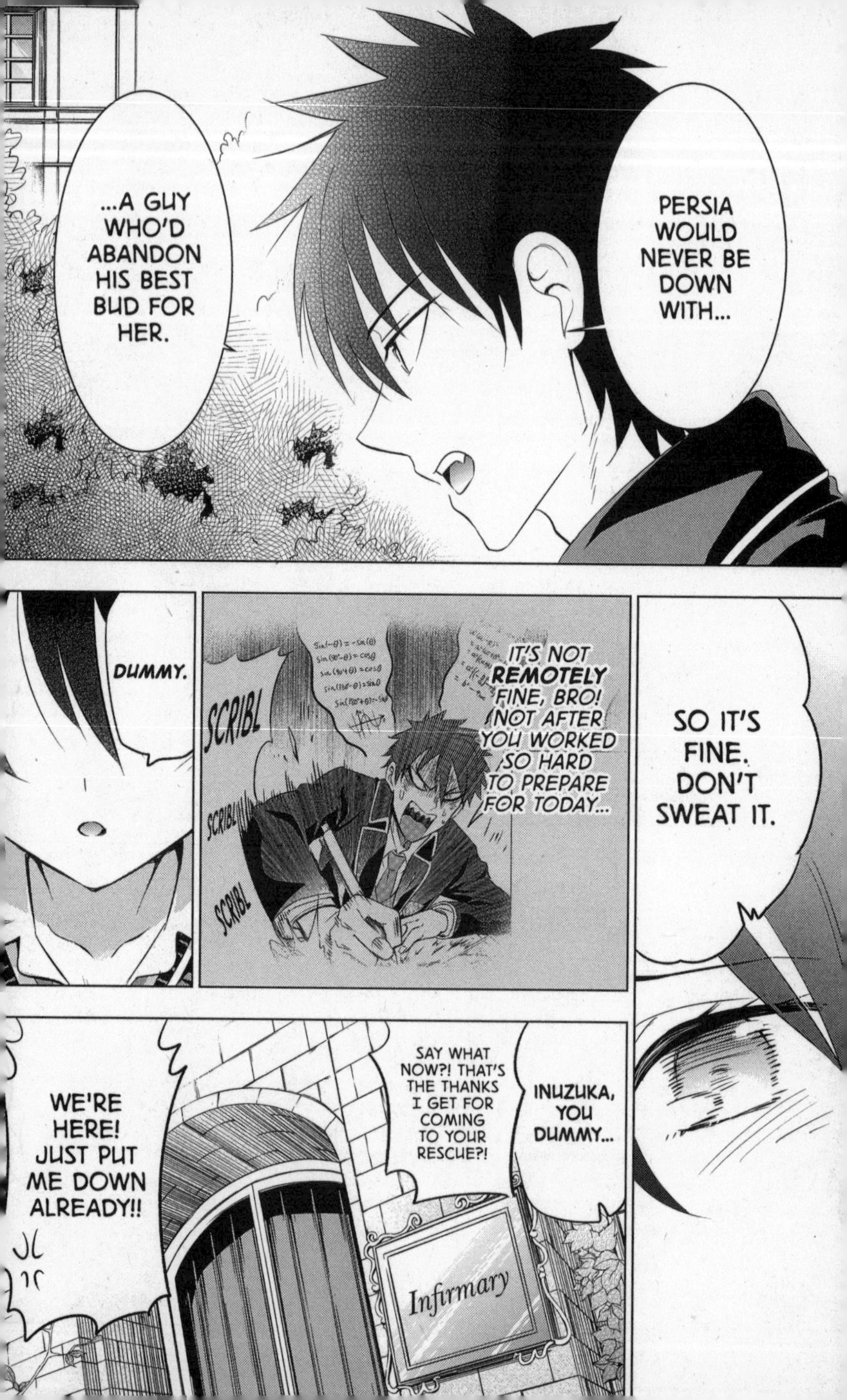
PERSIA WOULD NEVER BE DOWN WITH...
...A GUY WHO'D ABANDON HIS BEST BUD FOR HER.
SO IT'S FINE. DON'T SWEAT IT.
IT'S NOT REMOTELY FINE, BRO! NOT AFTER YOU WORKED SO HARD TO PREPARE FOR TODAY...
SCRIBL
SCRIBL
SCRIBL
DUMMY.
INUZUKA, YOU DUMMY...
SAY WHAT NOW?! THAT'S THE THANKS I GET FOR COMING TO YOUR RESCUE?!
WE'RE HERE! JUST PUT ME DOWN ALREADY!!
Infirmary

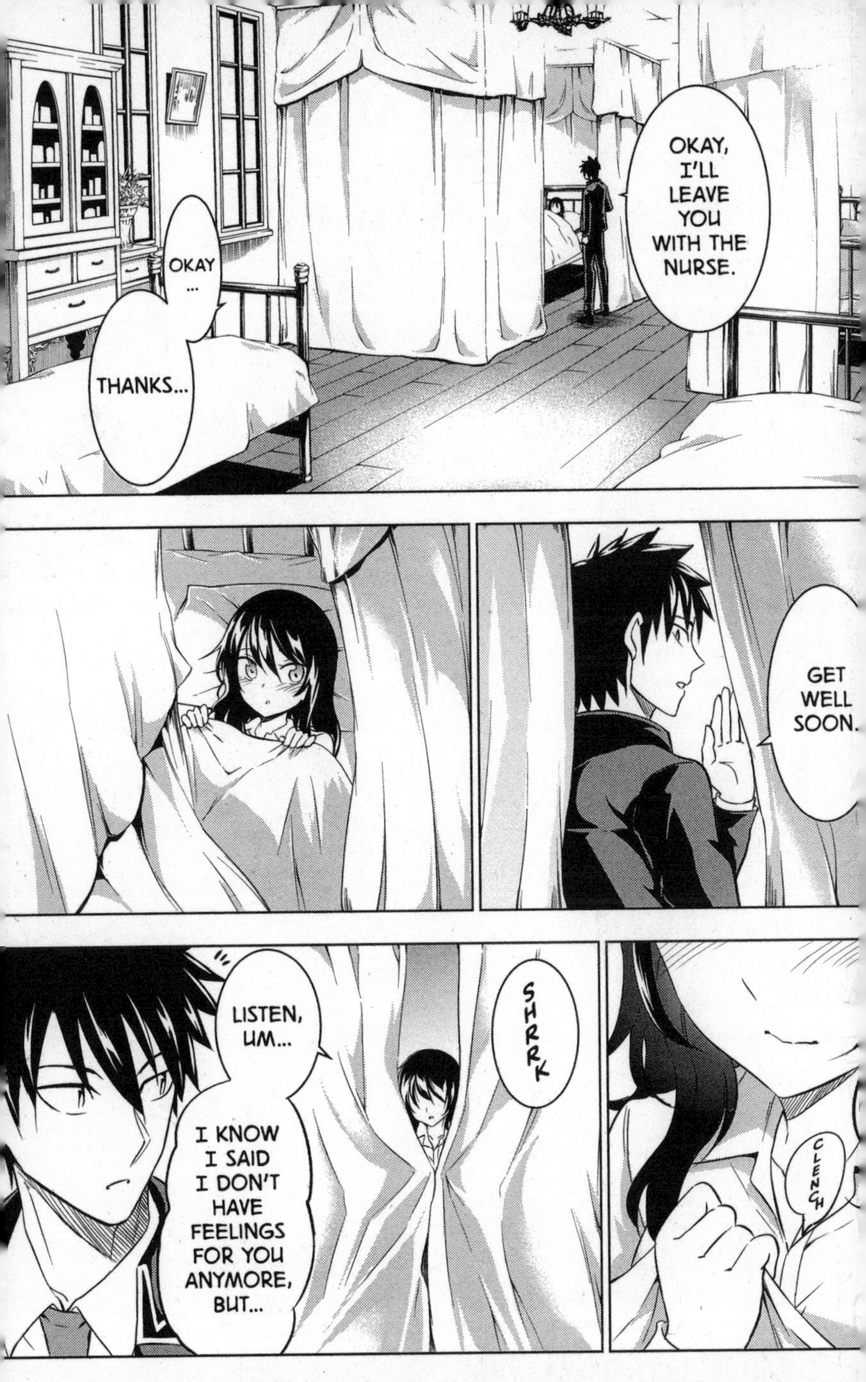
OKAY, I'LL LEAVE YOU WITH THE NURSE.
OKAY ...
THANKS...
GET WELL SOON.
CLENCH
SHRRK
LISTEN, UM...
I KNOW I SAID I DON'T HAVE FEELINGS FOR YOU ANYMORE, BUT...

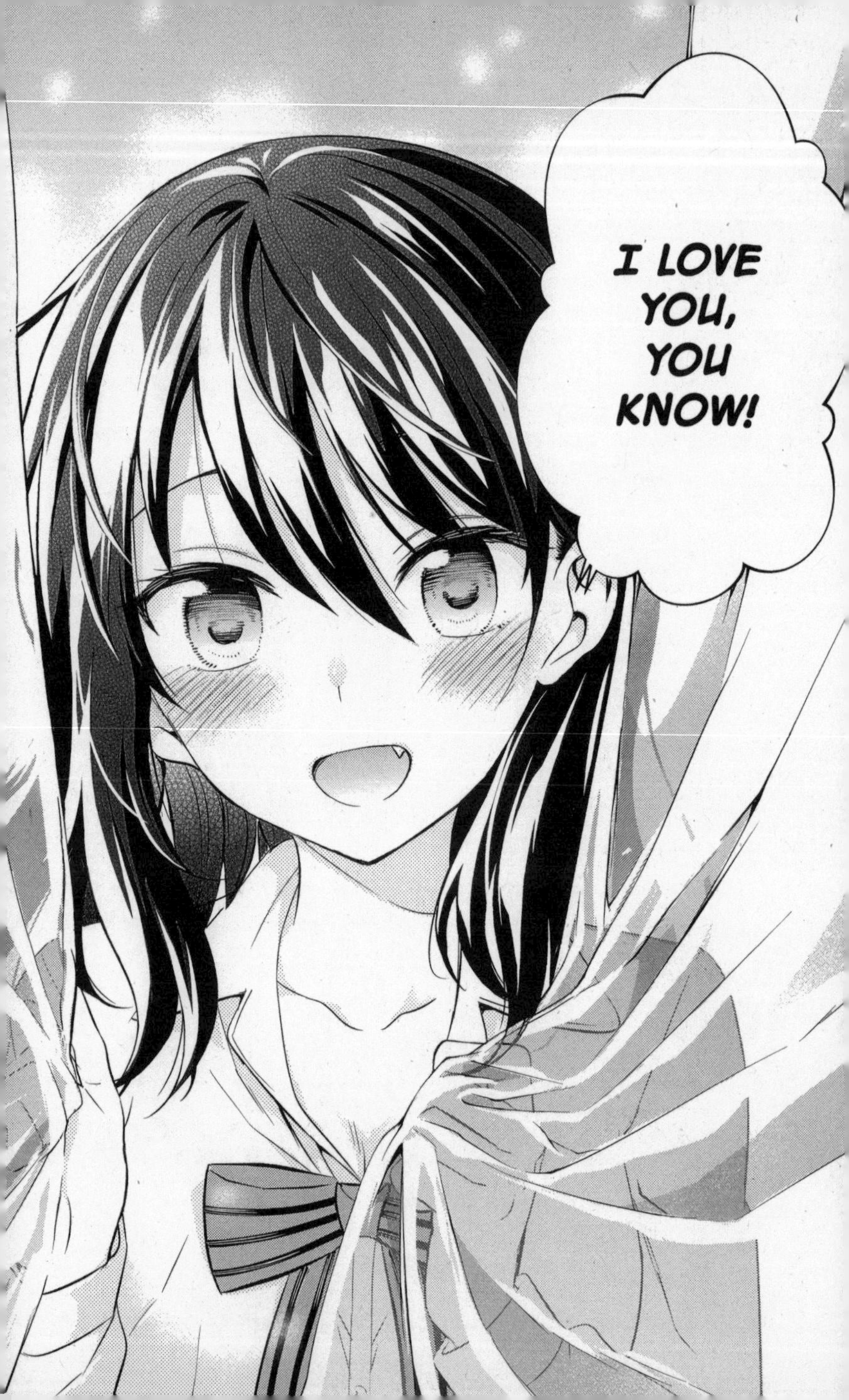
I LOVE YOU, YOU KNOW!

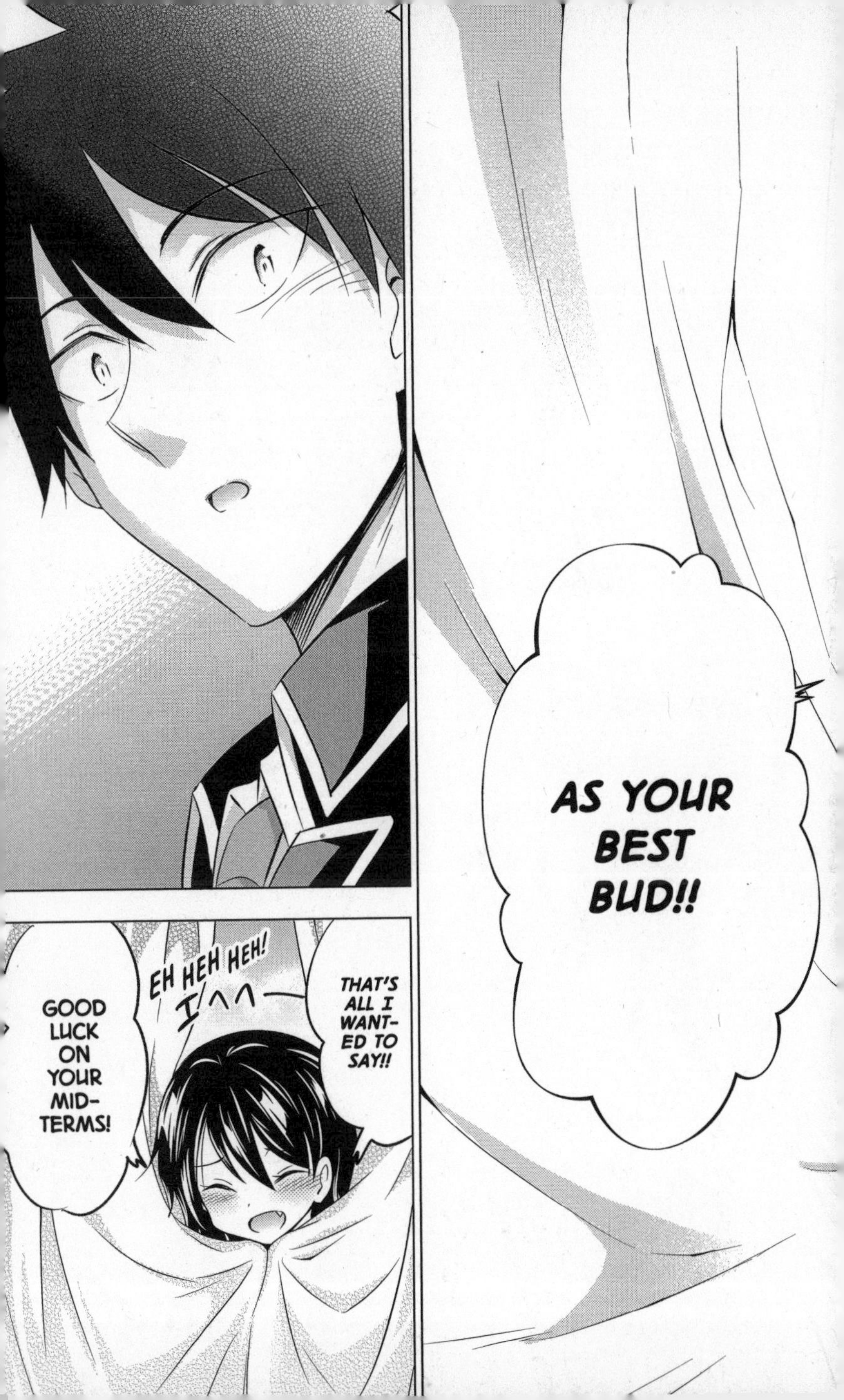
AS YOUR BEST BUD!!
THAT'S ALL I WANTED TO SAY!!
EH HEH HEH!
GOOD LUCK ON YOUR MIDTERMS!

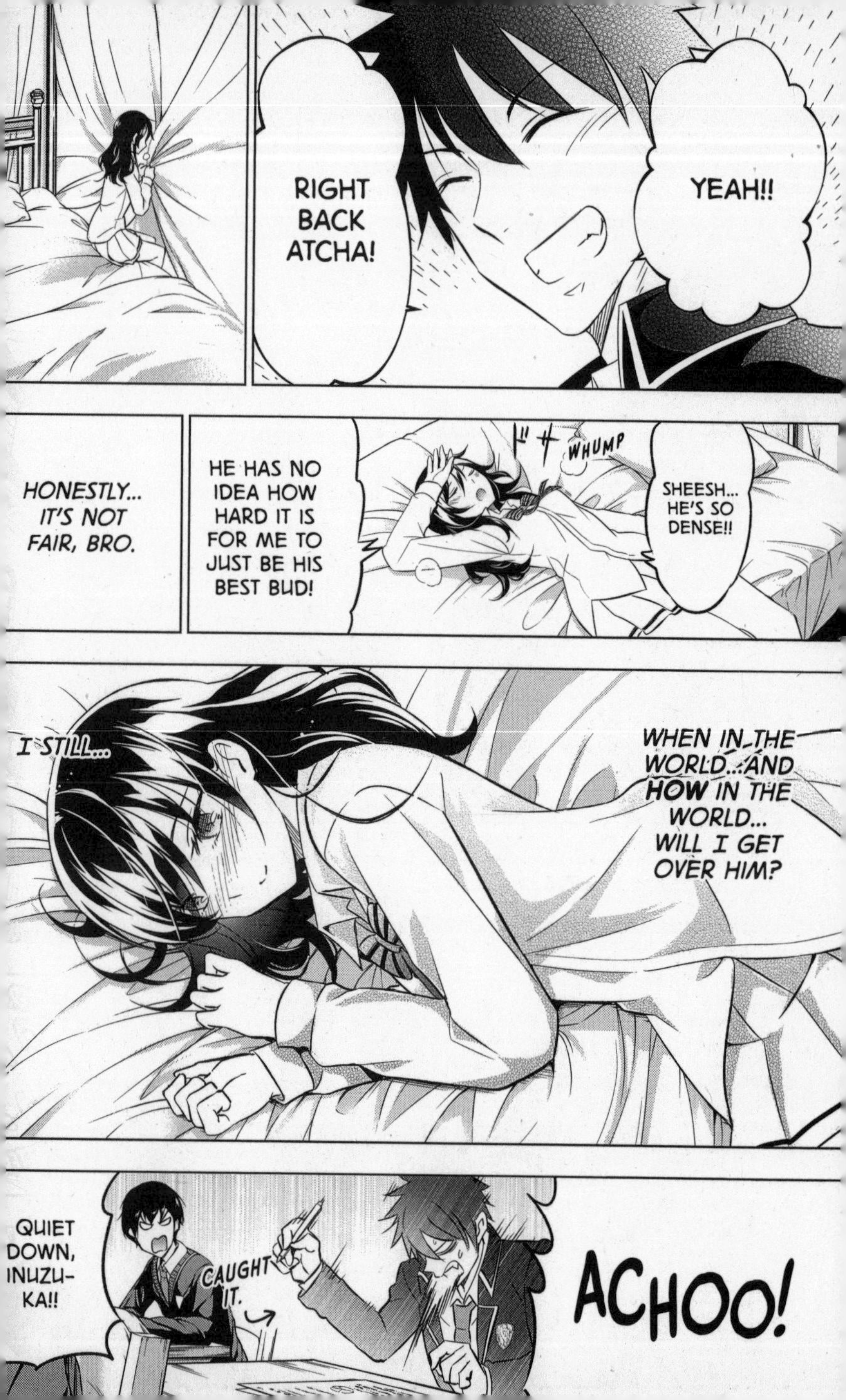
YEAH!!
RIGHT BACK ATCHA!
SHEESH... HE'S SO DENSE!!
ドサ
WHUMP
HE HAS NO IDEA HOW HARD IT IS FOR ME TO JUST BE HIS BEST BUD!
HONESTLY... IT'S NOT FAIR, BRO.
WHEN IN THE WORLD... AND HOW IN THE WORLD... WILL I GET OVER HIM?
I STILL...
ACHOO!
CAUGHT IT.
QUIET DOWN, INUZUKA!!

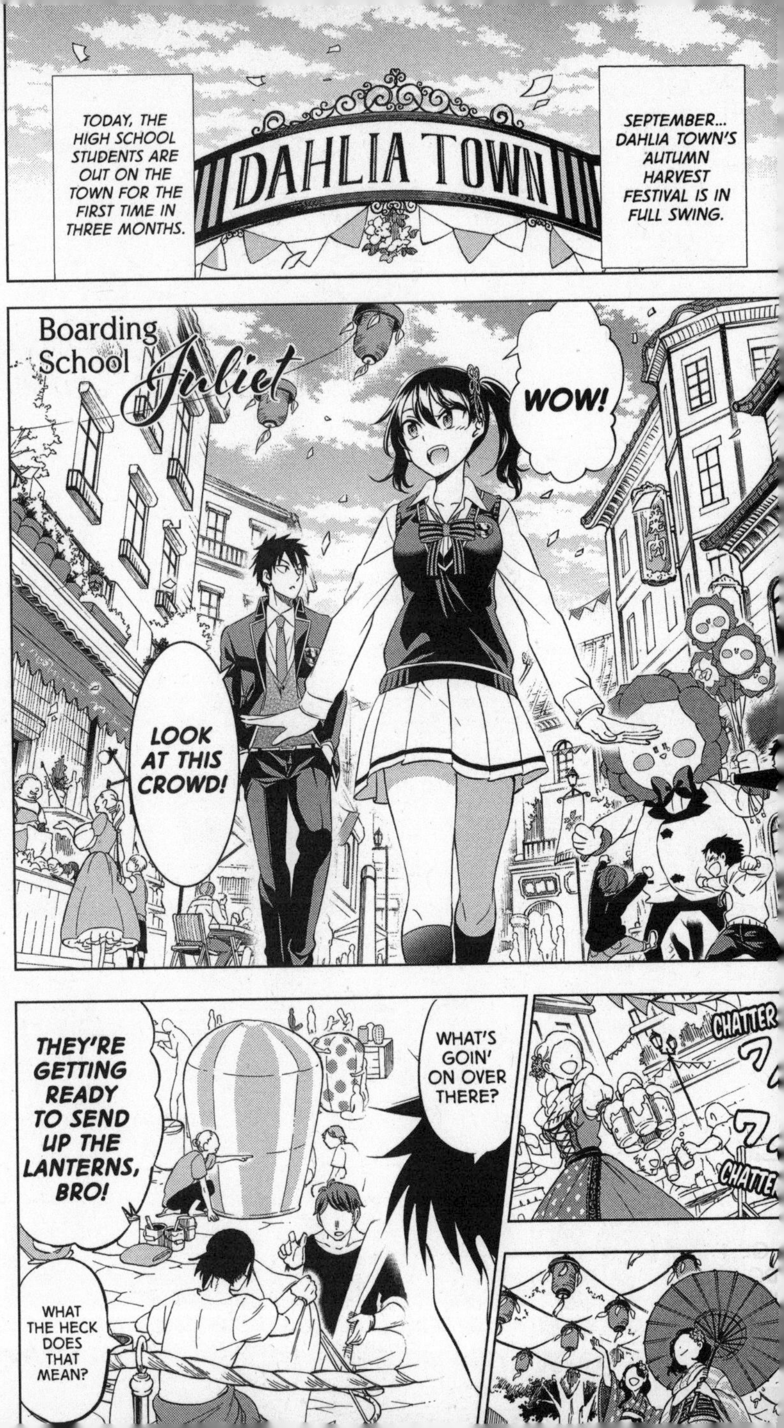
SEPTEMBER... DAHLIA TOWN'S AUTUMN HARVEST FESTIVAL IS IN FULL SWING.
DAHLIA TOWN
TODAY, THE HIGH SCHOOL STUDENTS ARE OUT ON THE TOWN FOR THE FIRST TIME IN THREE MONTHS.
Boarding School Juliet
WOW!
LOOK AT THIS CROWD!
CHATTER
CHATTER
WHAT'S GOIN' ON OVER THERE?
THEY'RE GETTING READY TO SEND UP THE LANTERNS, BRO!
WHAT THE HECK DOES THAT MEAN?

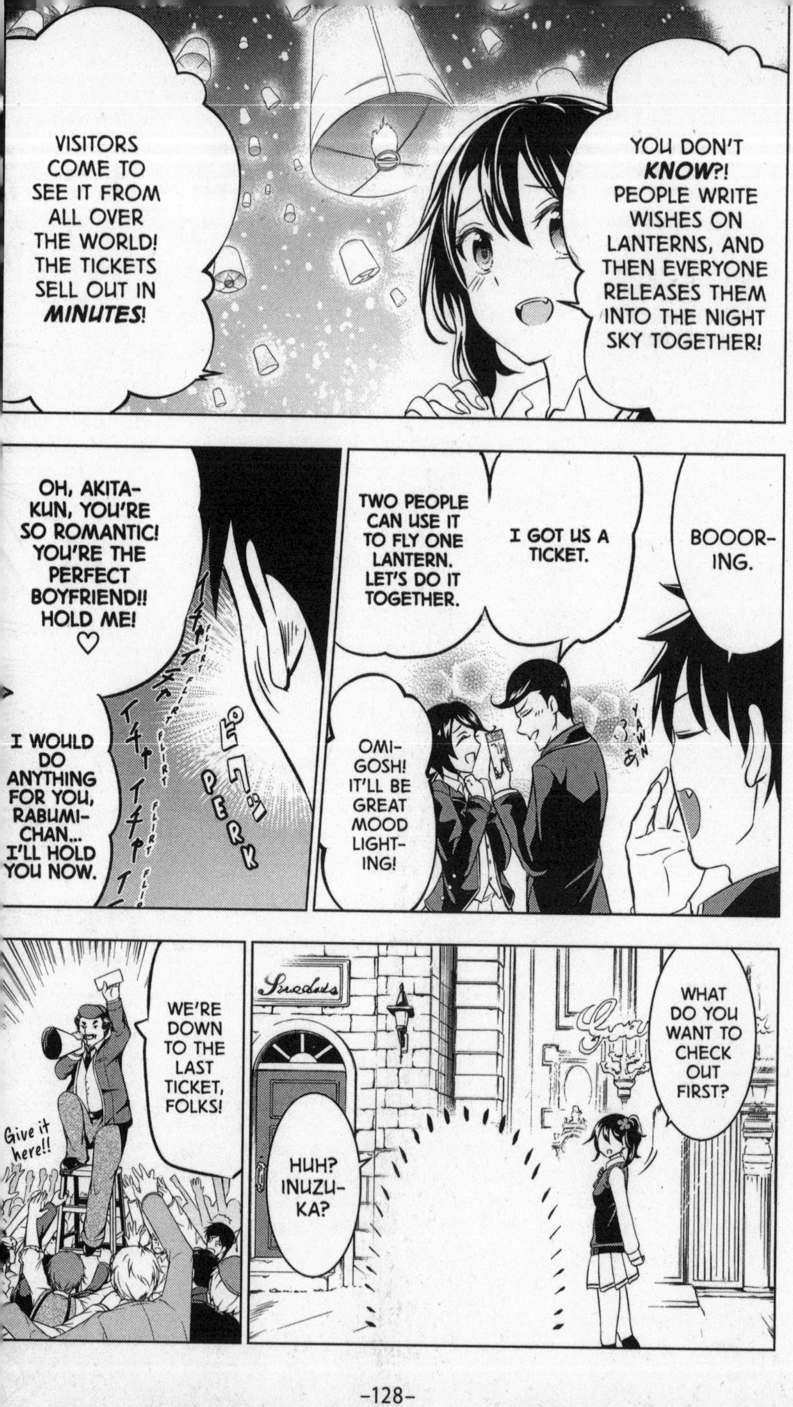
YOU DON'T KNOW?! PEOPLE WRITE WISHES ON LANTERNS, AND THEN EVERYONE RELEASES THEM INTO THE NIGHT SKY TOGETHER!
VISITORS COME TO SEE IT FROM ALL OVER THE WORLD! THE TICKETS SELL OUT IN MINUTES!
BOOOR-ING.
YAWN
I GOT US A TICKET.
TWO PEOPLE CAN USE IT TO FLY ONE LANTERN. LET'S DO IT TOGETHER.
OMI-GOSH! IT'LL BE GREAT MOOD LIGHT-ING!
OH, AKITA-KUN, YOU'RE SO ROMANTIC! YOU'RE THE PERFECT BOYFRIEND!! HOLD ME! ♡
PERK
FLIRT FLIRT FLIRT FLIRT
I WOULD DO ANYTHING FOR YOU, RABUMI-CHAN... I'LL HOLD YOU NOW.
WHAT DO YOU WANT TO CHECK OUT FIRST?
HUH? INUZU-KA?
WE'RE DOWN TO THE LAST TICKET, FOLKS!
Give it here!!

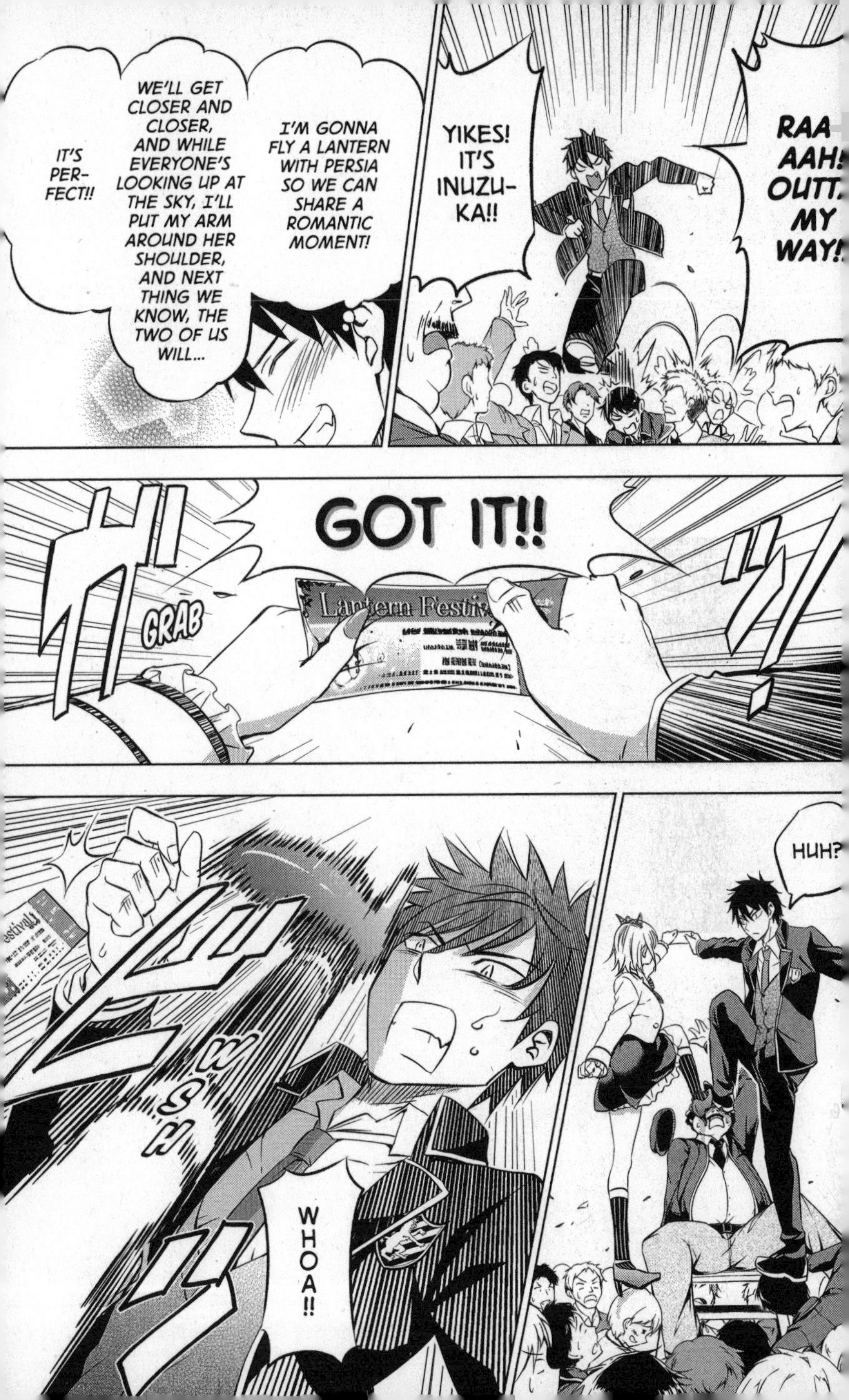
RAA AAH! OUTTA MY WAY!!
YIKES! IT'S INUZU-KA!!
I'M GONNA FLY A LANTERN WITH PERSIA SO WE CAN SHARE A ROMANTIC MOMENT!
WE'LL GET CLOSER AND CLOSER, AND WHILE EVERYONE'S LOOKING UP AT THE SKY, I'LL PUT MY ARM AROUND HER SHOULDER, AND NEXT THING WE KNOW, THE TWO OF US WILL...
IT'S PER-FECT!!
GOT IT!!
GRAB
Lantern Festiv
HUH?
WHSH
WHOA!!

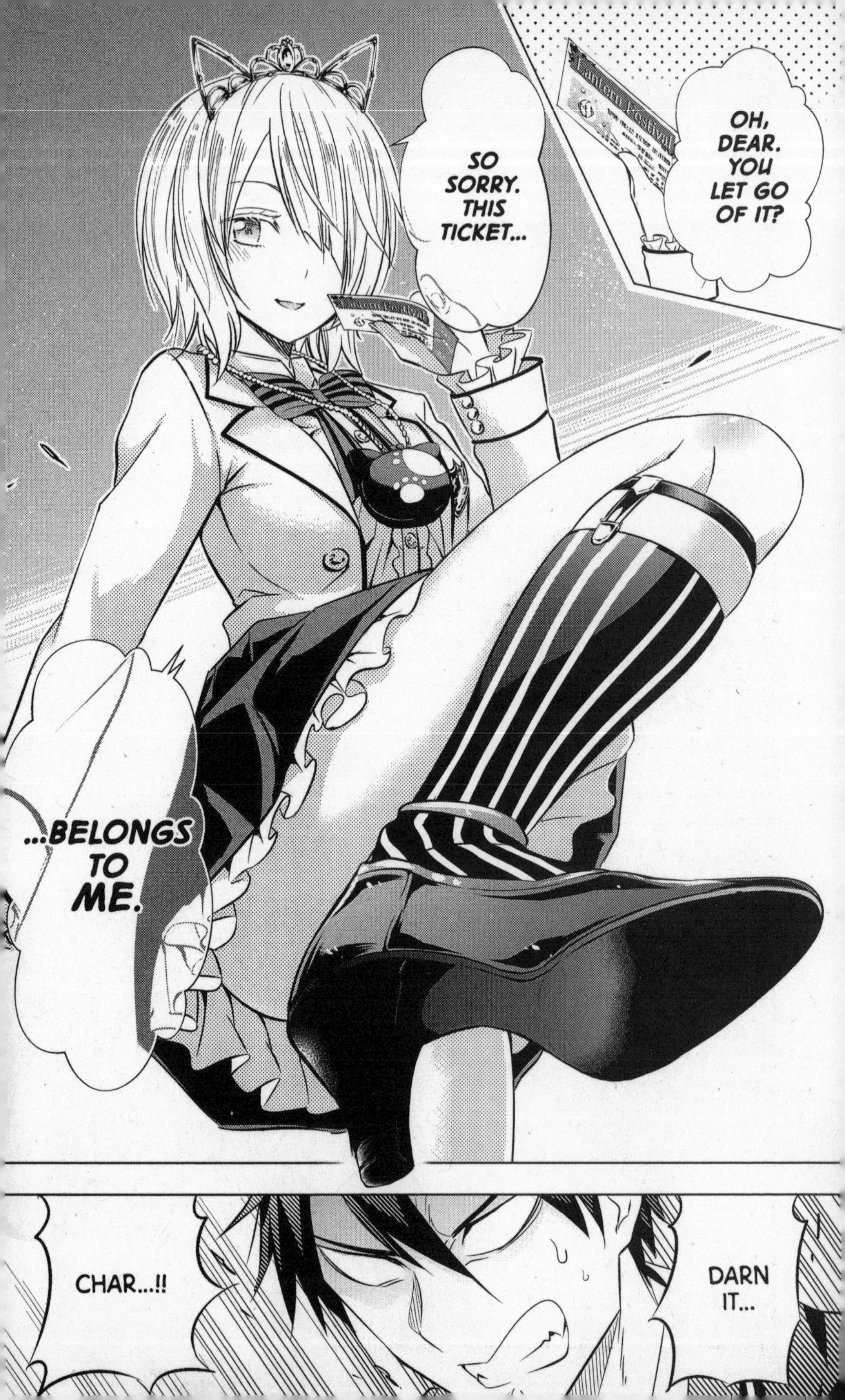
Lantern Festival
OH, DEAR. YOU LET GO OF IT?
SO SORRY. THIS TICKET...
...BELONGS TO ME.
DARN IT...
CHAR...!!

DAHLIA ACADEMY GUIDE #3: WHITE CAT HOUSE

The dorm for the Principality of West's high school division students. Floor 1: an open-air café, showers, a records room exhibiting weapons and armor, etc. There's no communal bath, but there is a very spacious sauna room attached to the showers. Floor 2 and above are the same as Black Doggy House's.

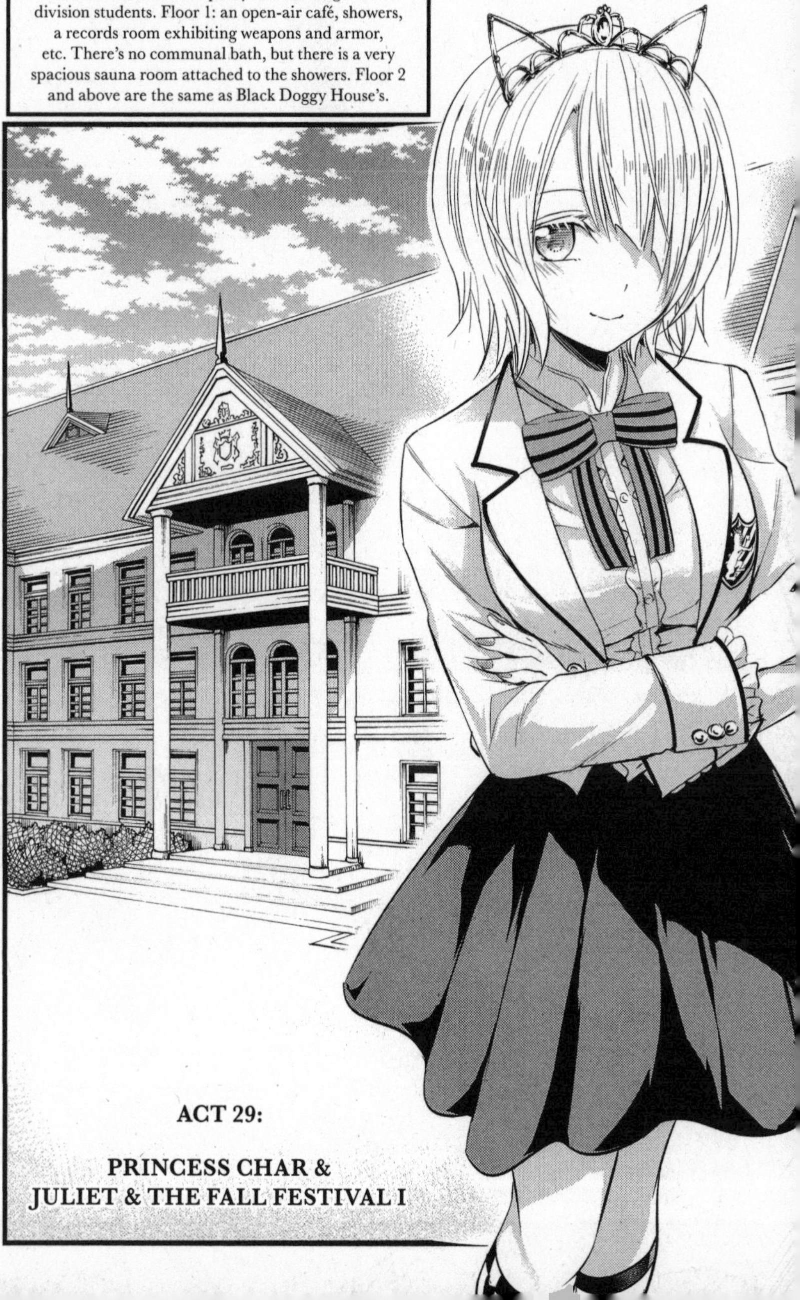
ACT 29:
PRINCESS CHAR & JULIET & THE FALL FESTIVAL I

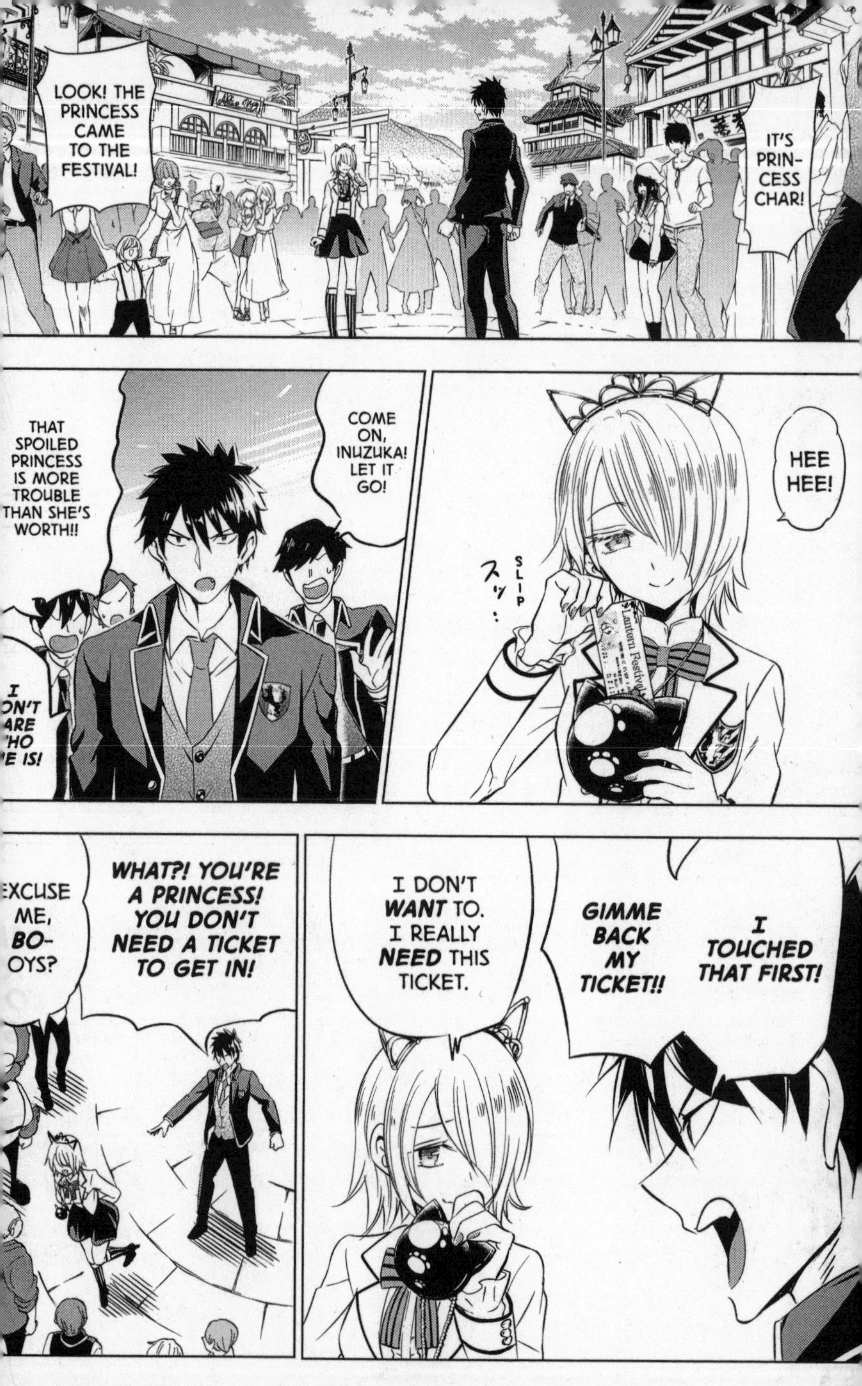
IT'S PRIN-CESS CHAR!
LOOK! THE PRINCESS CAME TO THE FESTIVAL!
HEE HEE!
SLIP
スッ
COME ON, INUZUKA! LET IT GO!
THAT SPOILED PRINCESS IS MORE TROUBLE THAN SHE'S WORTH!!
I TOUCHED THAT FIRST!
GIMME BACK MY TICKET!!
I DON'T *WANT* TO. I REALLY *NEED* THIS TICKET.
WHAT?! YOU'RE A PRINCESS! YOU DON'T NEED A TICKET TO GET IN!
EXCUSE ME, *BO-*OYS?

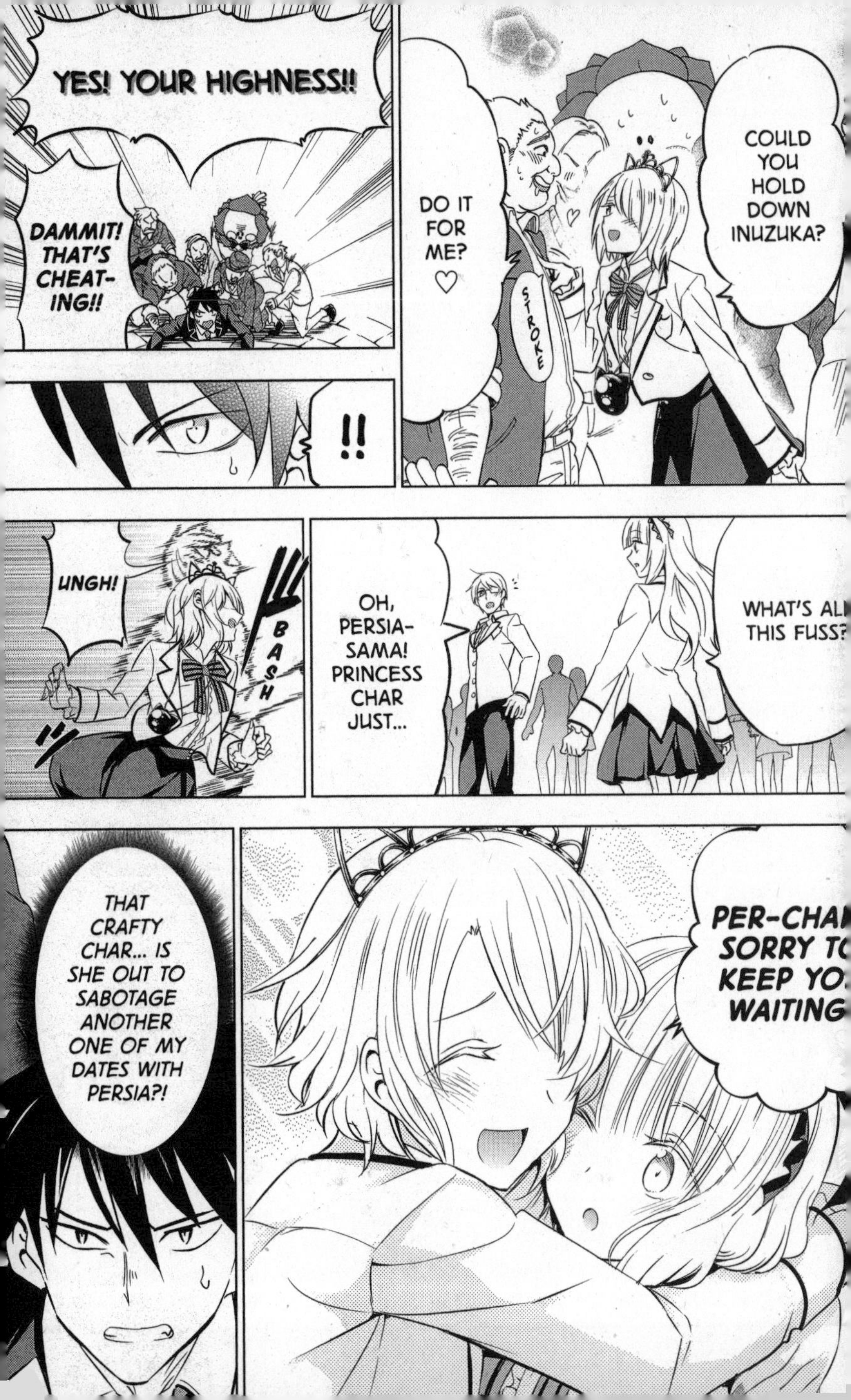
COULD YOU HOLD DOWN INUZUKA?
DO IT FOR ME? ♡
STROKE
YES! YOUR HIGHNESS!!
DAMMIT! THAT'S CHEATING!!
!!
WHAT'S AL THIS FUSS?
OH, PERSIA-SAMA! PRINCESS CHAR JUST...
UNGH!
BASH
PER-CHA SORRY TO KEEP YO WAITING
THAT CRAFTY CHAR... IS SHE OUT TO SABOTAGE ANOTHER ONE OF MY DATES WITH PERSIA?!

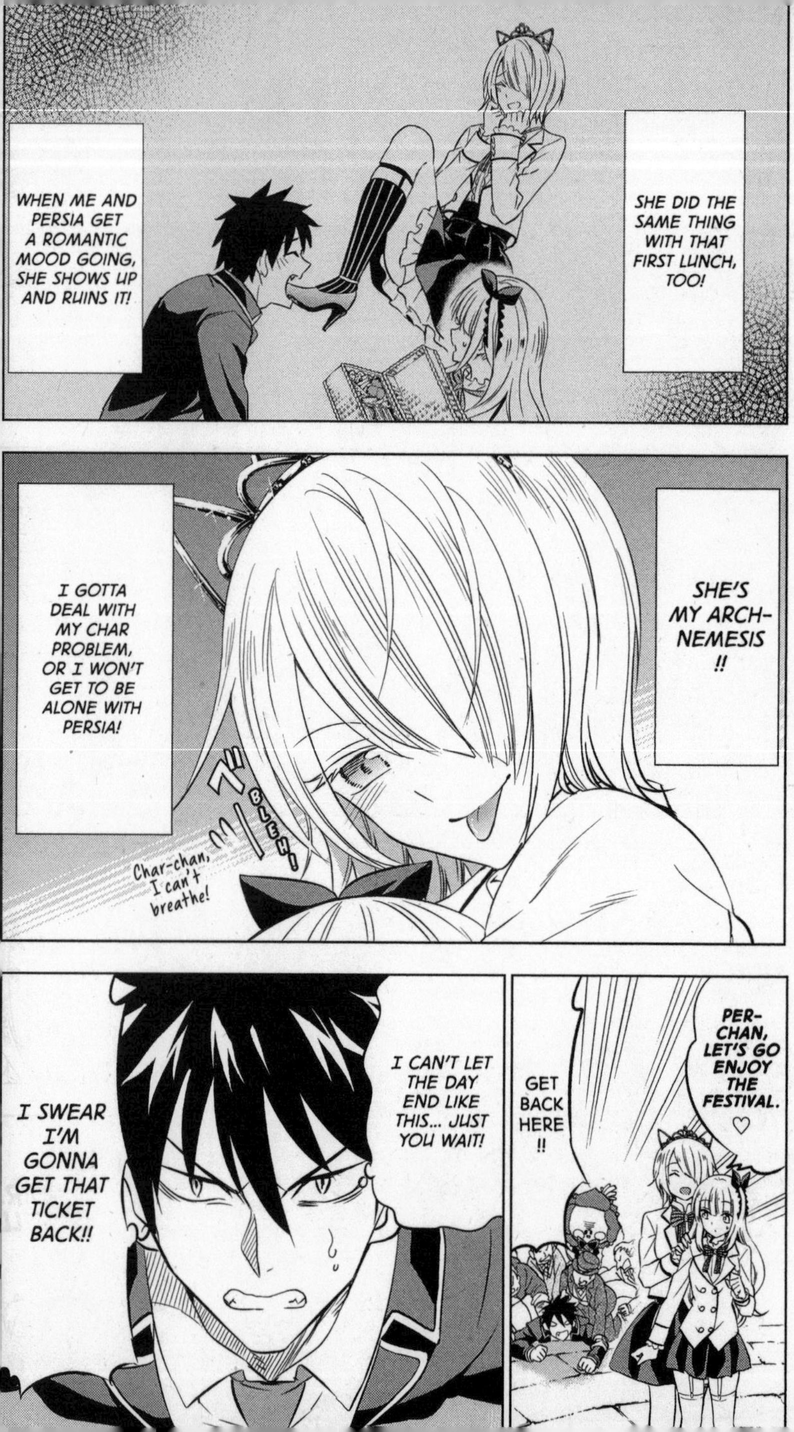
SHE DID THE SAME THING WITH THAT FIRST LUNCH, TOO!
WHEN ME AND PERSIA GET A ROMANTIC MOOD GOING, SHE SHOWS UP AND RUINS IT!
SHE'S MY ARCH-NEMESIS !!
ベー
BLEH!
Char-chan, I can't breathe!
I GOTTA DEAL WITH MY CHAR PROBLEM, OR I WON'T GET TO BE ALONE WITH PERSIA!
PER-CHAN, LET'S GO ENJOY THE FESTIVAL. ♡
GET BACK HERE !!
I CAN'T LET THE DAY END LIKE THIS... JUST YOU WAIT!
I SWEAR I'M GONNA GET THAT TICKET BACK!!

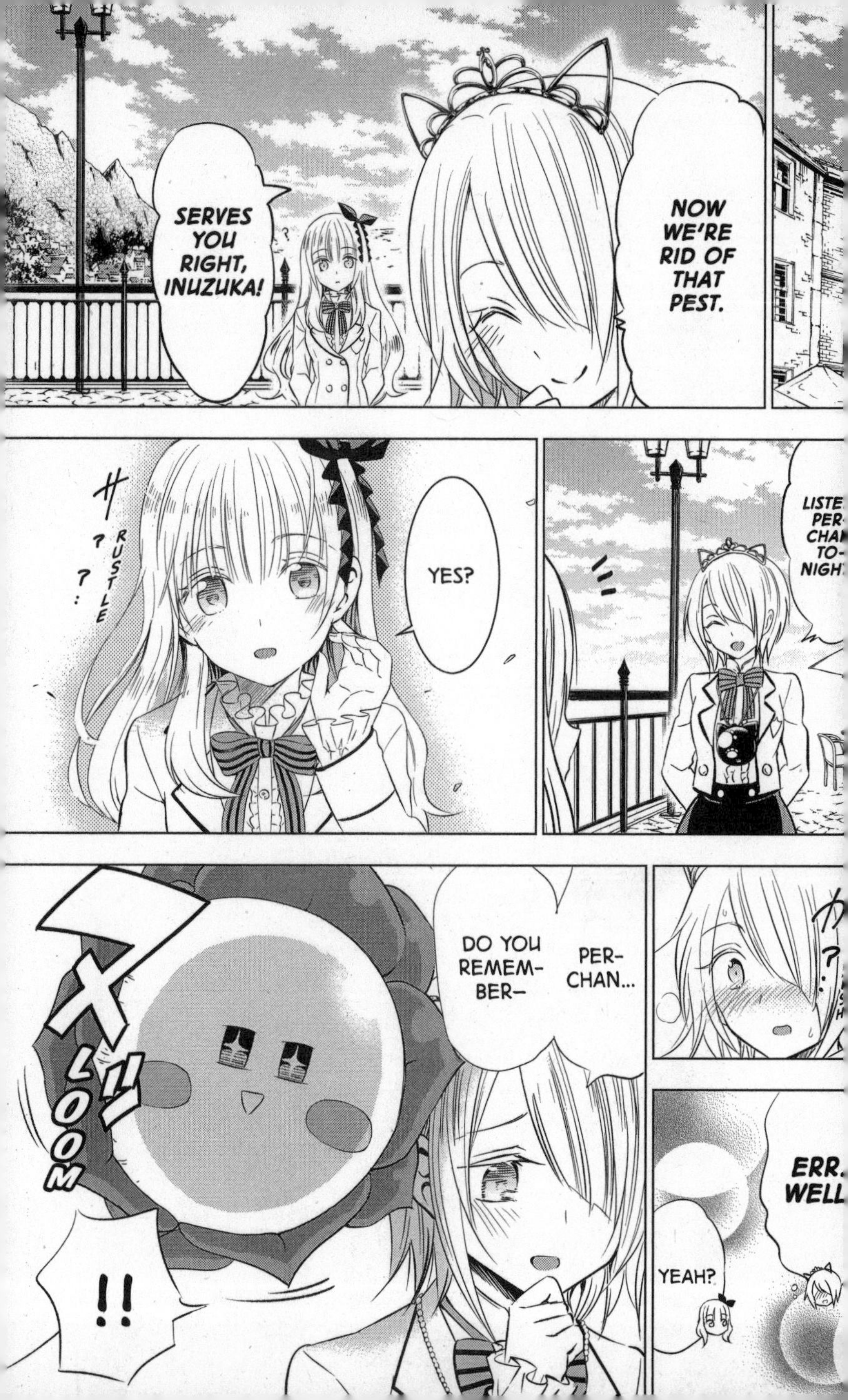
NOW WE'RE RID OF THAT PEST.
SERVES YOU RIGHT, INUZUKA!
YES?
RUSTLE
ERR.
WELL
YEAH?
PER-CHAN...
DO YOU REMEMBER—
VLOOOM
!!

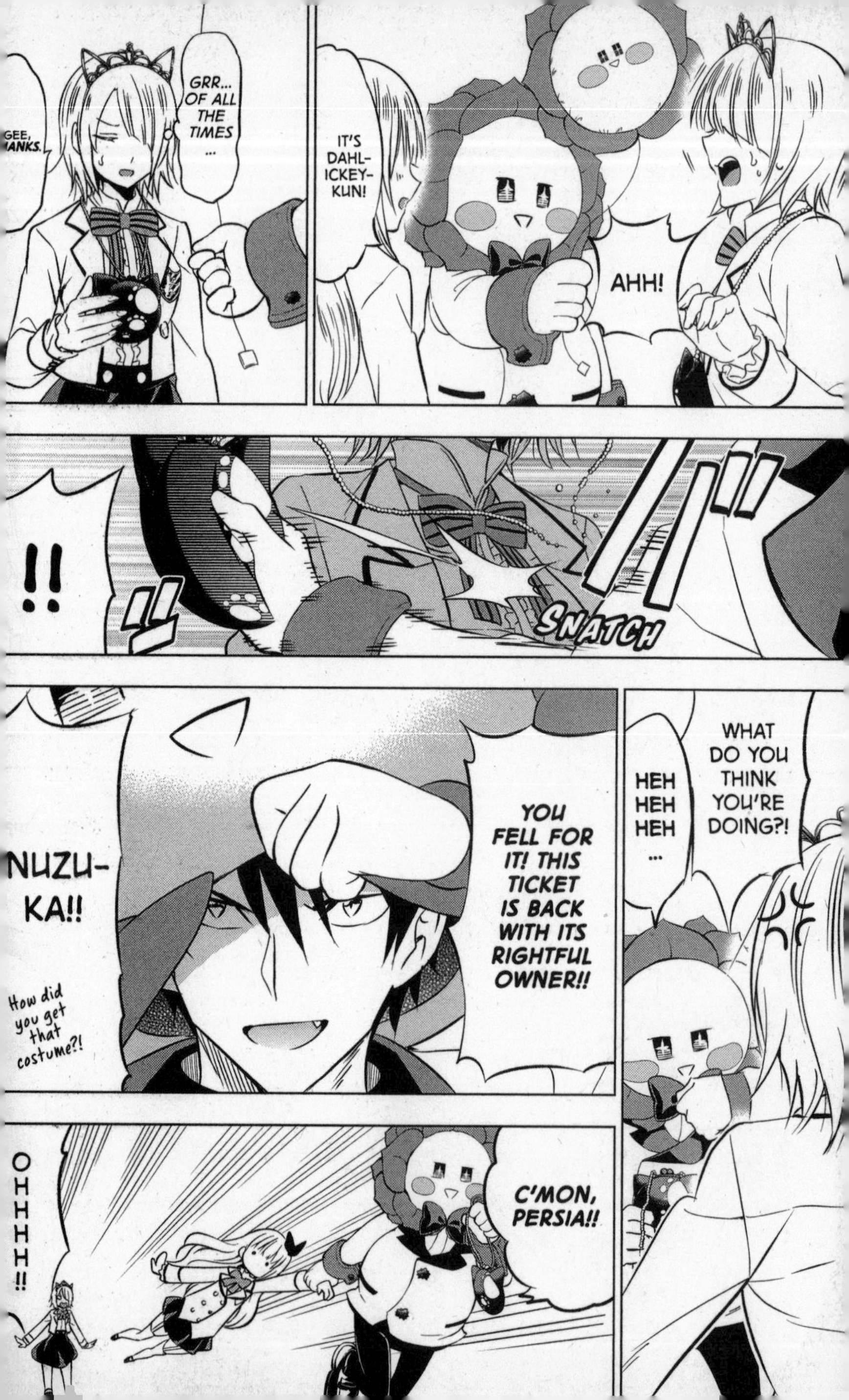
AHH!
IT'S DAHL-ICKEY-KUN!
GRR... OF ALL THE TIMES ...
GEE, HANKS.
!!
SNATCH
WHAT DO YOU THINK YOU'RE DOING?!
HEH HEH HEH ...
YOU FELL FOR IT! THIS TICKET IS BACK WITH ITS RIGHTFUL OWNER!!
NUZU-KA!!
How did you get that costume?!
C'MON, PERSIA!!
OHHHHH!!

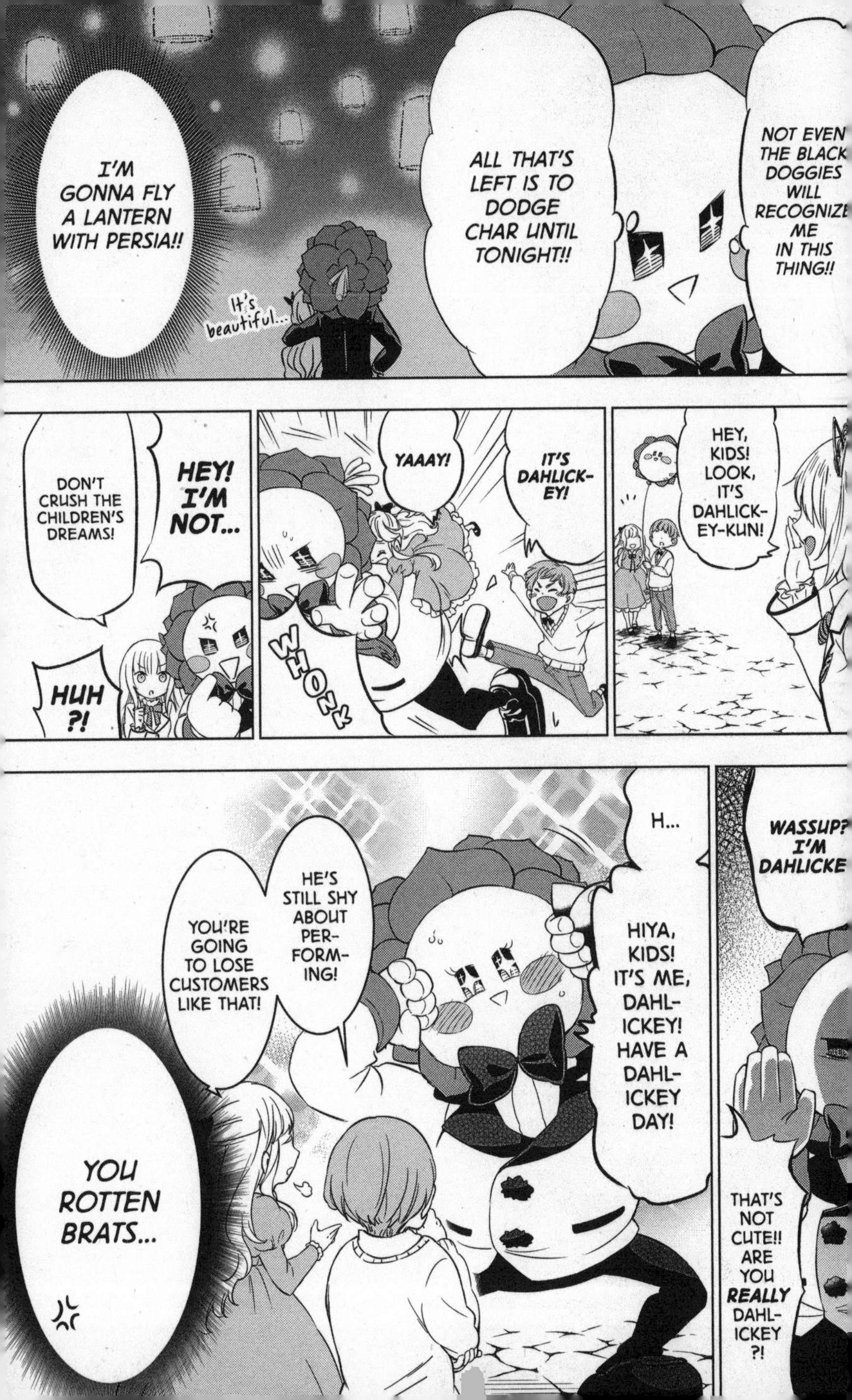
NOT EVEN THE BLACK DOGGIES WILL RECOGNIZE ME IN THIS THING!!
ALL THAT'S LEFT IS TO DODGE CHAR UNTIL TONIGHT!!
I'M GONNA FLY A LANTERN WITH PERSIA!!
It's beautiful...
HEY, KIDS! LOOK, IT'S DAHLICKEY-KUN!
IT'S DAHLICKEY!
YAAAY!
WHONK
HEY! I'M NOT...
DON'T CRUSH THE CHILDREN'S DREAMS!
HUH?!
WASSUP? I'M DAHLICKE
THAT'S NOT CUTE!! ARE YOU *REALLY* DAHLICKEY?!
H...
HIYA, KIDS! IT'S ME, DAHLICKEY! HAVE A DAHLICKEY DAY!
HE'S STILL SHY ABOUT PERFORMING!
YOU'RE GOING TO LOSE CUSTOMERS LIKE THAT!
YOU ROTTEN BRATS...

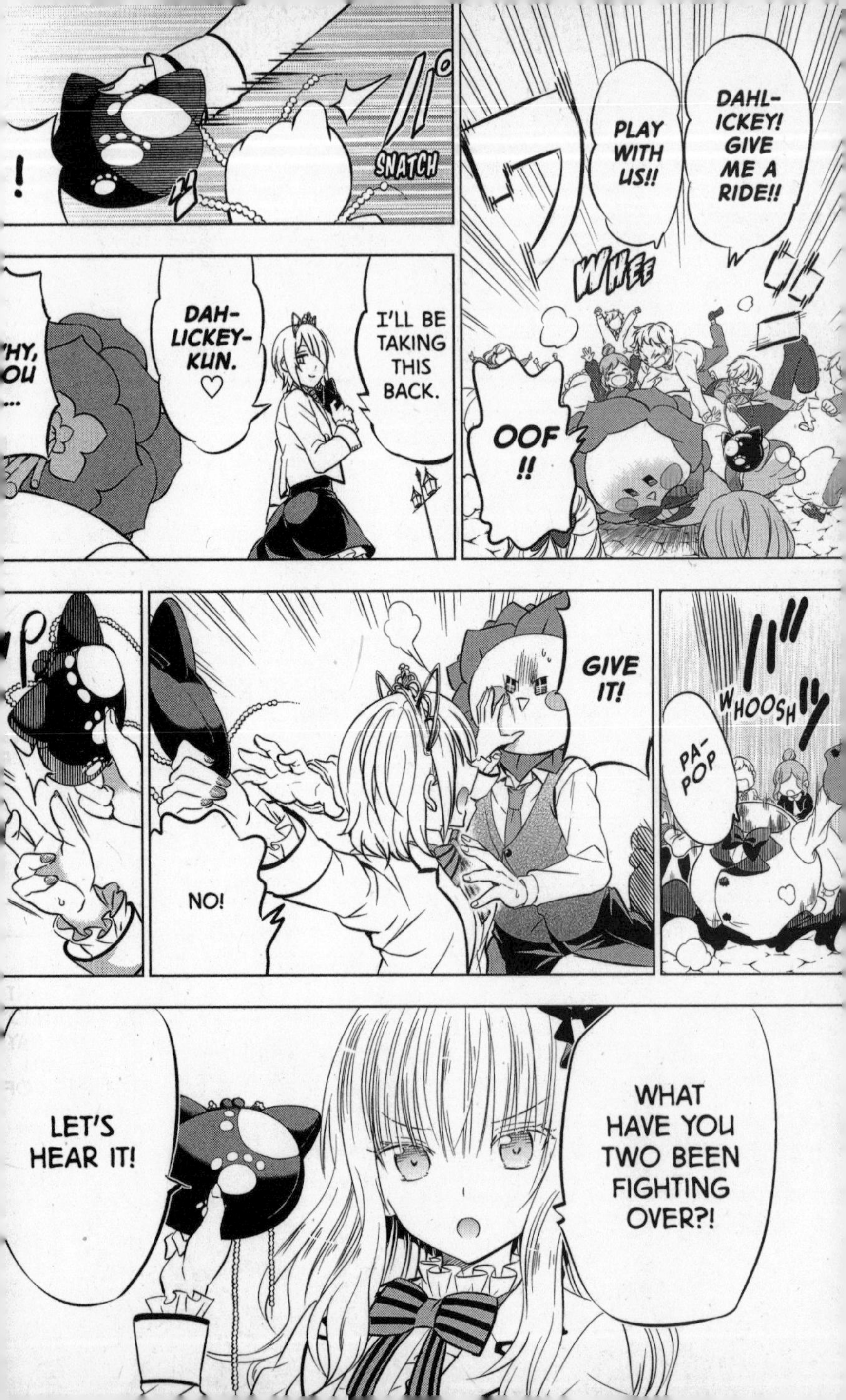
DAHL-ICKEY! GIVE ME A RIDE!!
PLAY WITH US!!
WHEE
OOF !!
SNATCH
!
I'LL BE TAKING THIS BACK.
DAH-LICKEY-KUN. ♡
WHOOSH
PA-POP
GIVE IT!
NO!
WHAT HAVE YOU TWO BEEN FIGHTING OVER?!
LET'S HEAR IT!

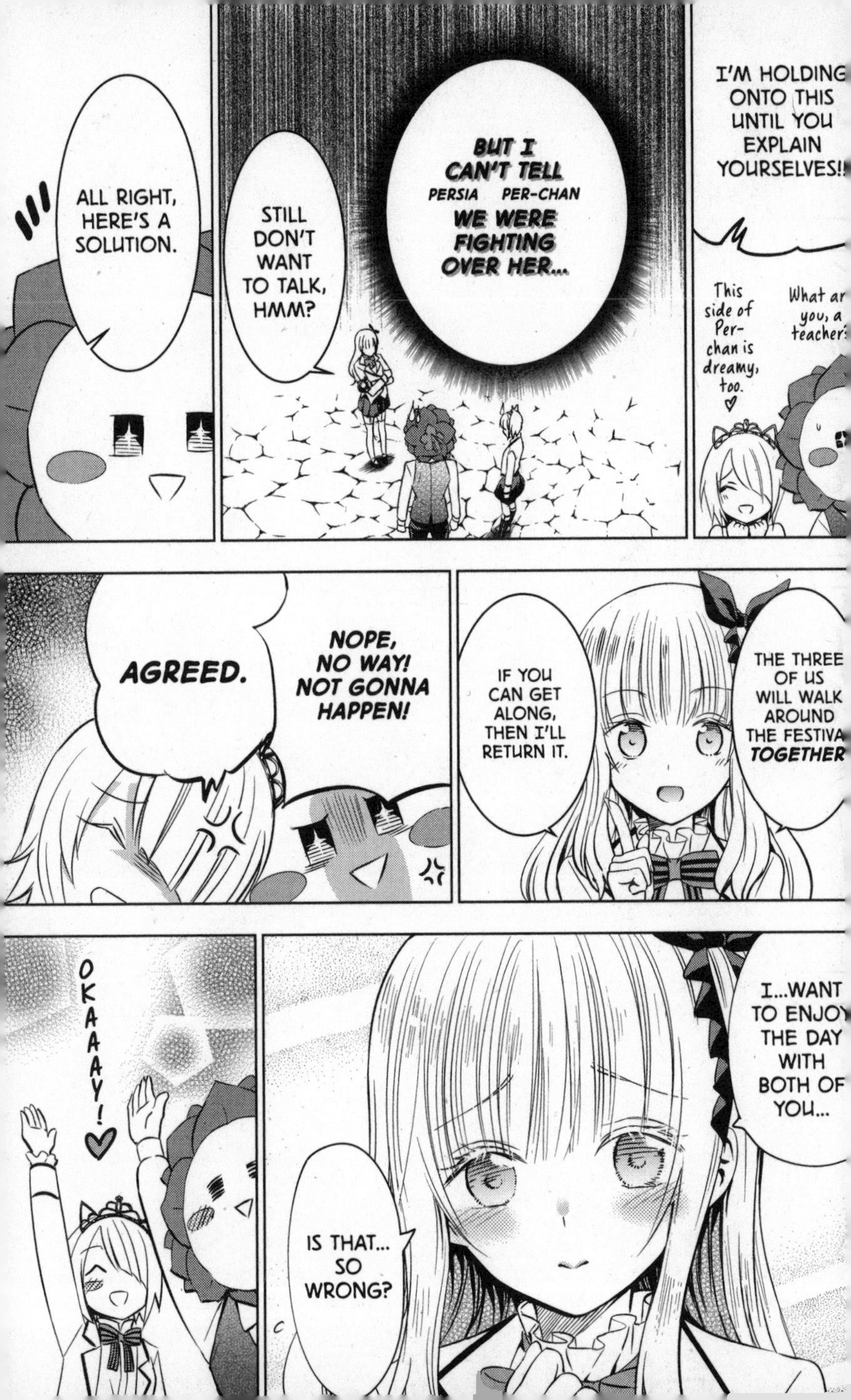
I'M HOLDING ONTO THIS UNTIL YOU EXPLAIN YOURSELVES!!
What ar you, a teacher
This side of Per-chan is dreamy, too. ♥
BUT I CAN'T TELL PERSIA PER-CHAN WE WERE FIGHTING OVER HER...
STILL DON'T WANT TO TALK, HMM?
ALL RIGHT, HERE'S A SOLUTION.
THE THREE OF US WILL WALK AROUND THE FESTIVA TOGETHER
IF YOU CAN GET ALONG, THEN I'LL RETURN IT.
NOPE, NO WAY! NOT GONNA HAPPEN!
AGREED.
I...WANT TO ENJO THE DAY WITH BOTH OF YOU...
IS THAT... SO WRONG?
OKAAAY! ♥

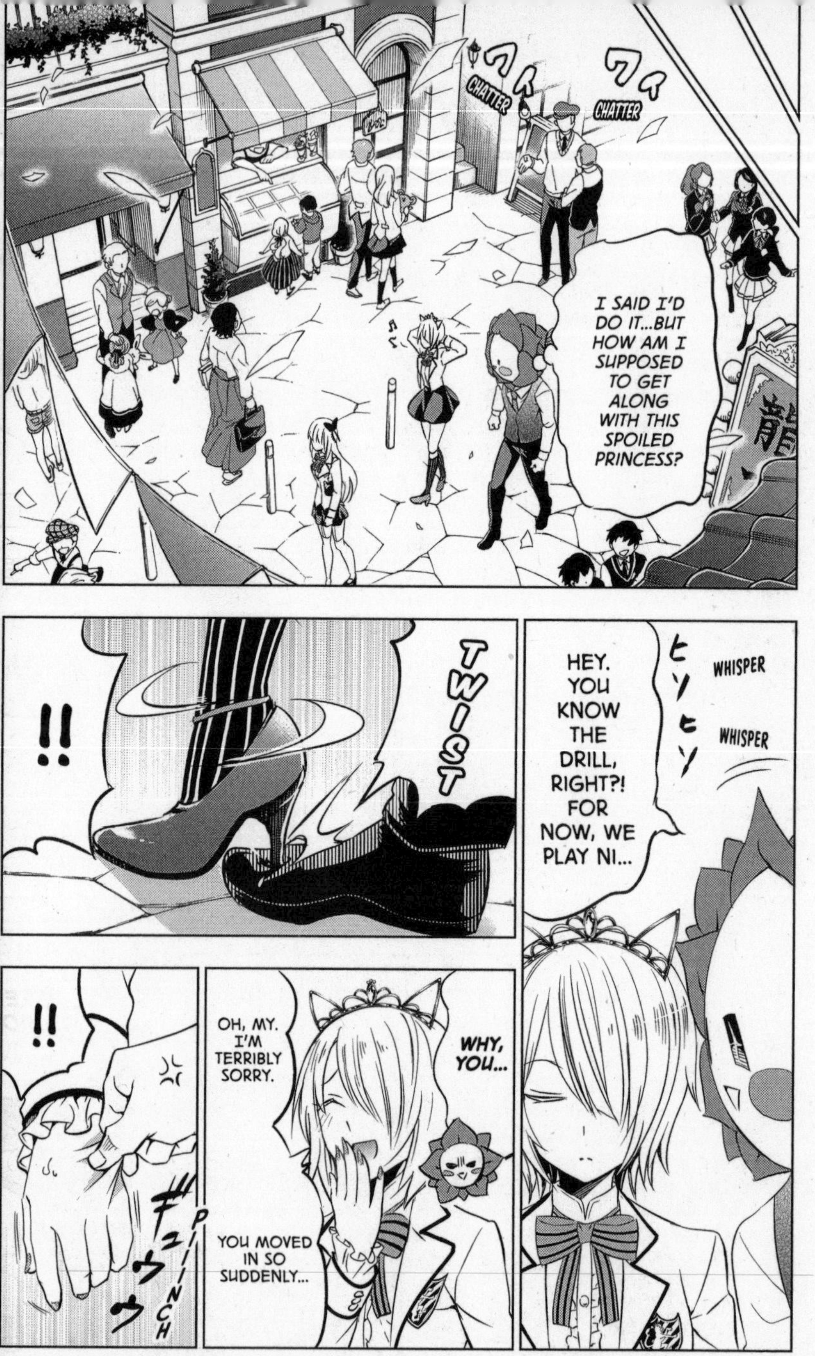

ワイワイ
CHATTER
CHATTER
I SAID I'D DO IT...BUT HOW AM I SUPPOSED TO GET ALONG WITH THIS SPOILED PRINCESS?
HEY. YOU KNOW THE DRILL, RIGHT?! FOR NOW, WE PLAY NI...
ヒソヒソ
WHISPER
WHISPER
TWIST
!!
OH, MY. I'M TERRIBLY SORRY.
WHY, YOU...
YOU MOVED IN SO SUDDENLY...
!!
ギュウウ
PIIINCH

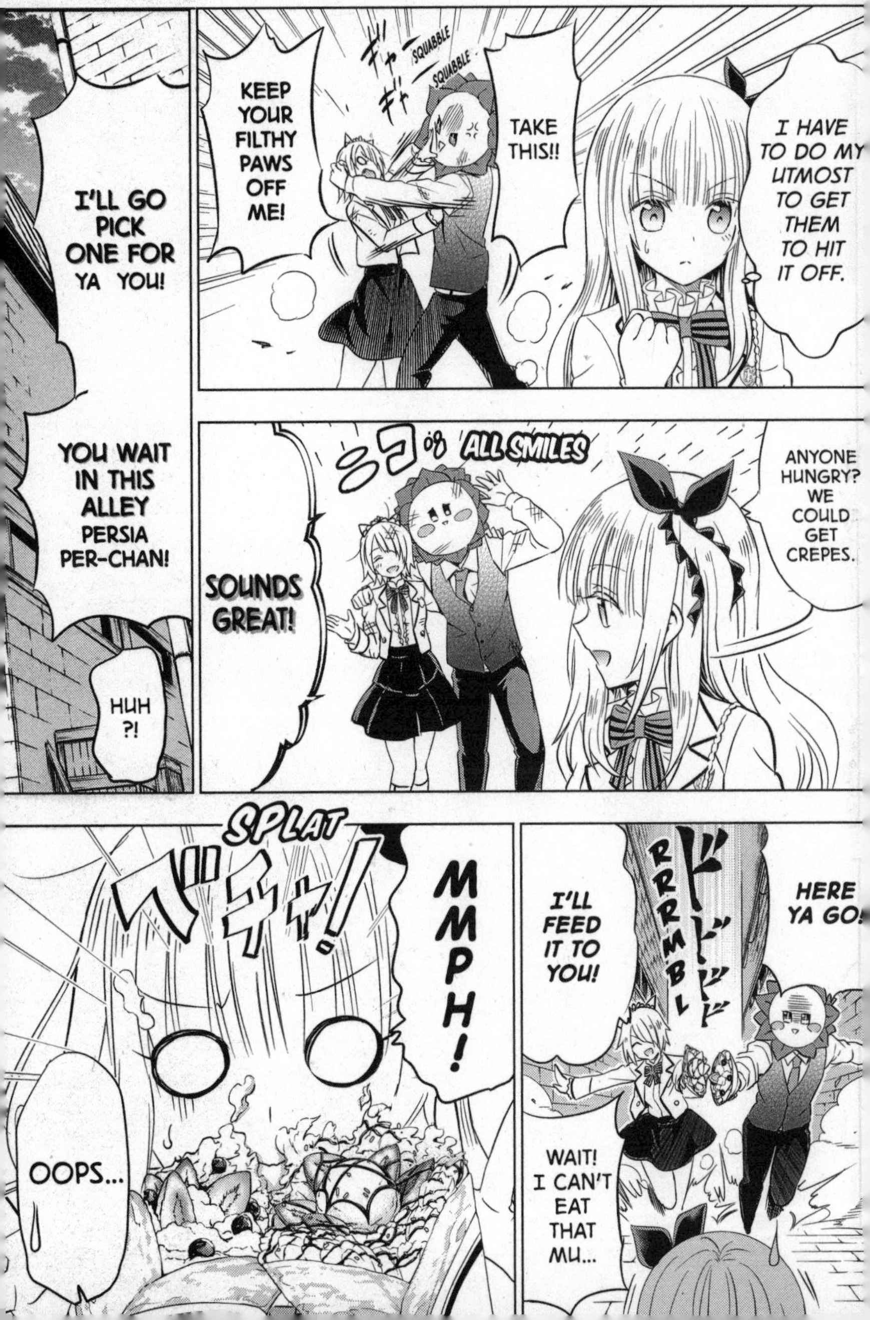
I HAVE TO DO MY UTMOST TO GET THEM TO HIT IT OFF.
TAKE THIS!!
SQUABBLE SQUABBLE
KEEP YOUR FILTHY PAWS OFF ME!
ANYONE HUNGRY? WE COULD GET CREPES.
ALL SMILES
SOUNDS GREAT!
I'LL GO PICK ONE FOR YA YOU!
YOU WAIT IN THIS ALLEY PERSIA PER-CHAN!
HUH ?!
HERE YA GO!
RRRMBL
I'LL FEED IT TO YOU!
WAIT! I CAN'T EAT THAT MU...
SPLAT
MMPH!
OOPS...

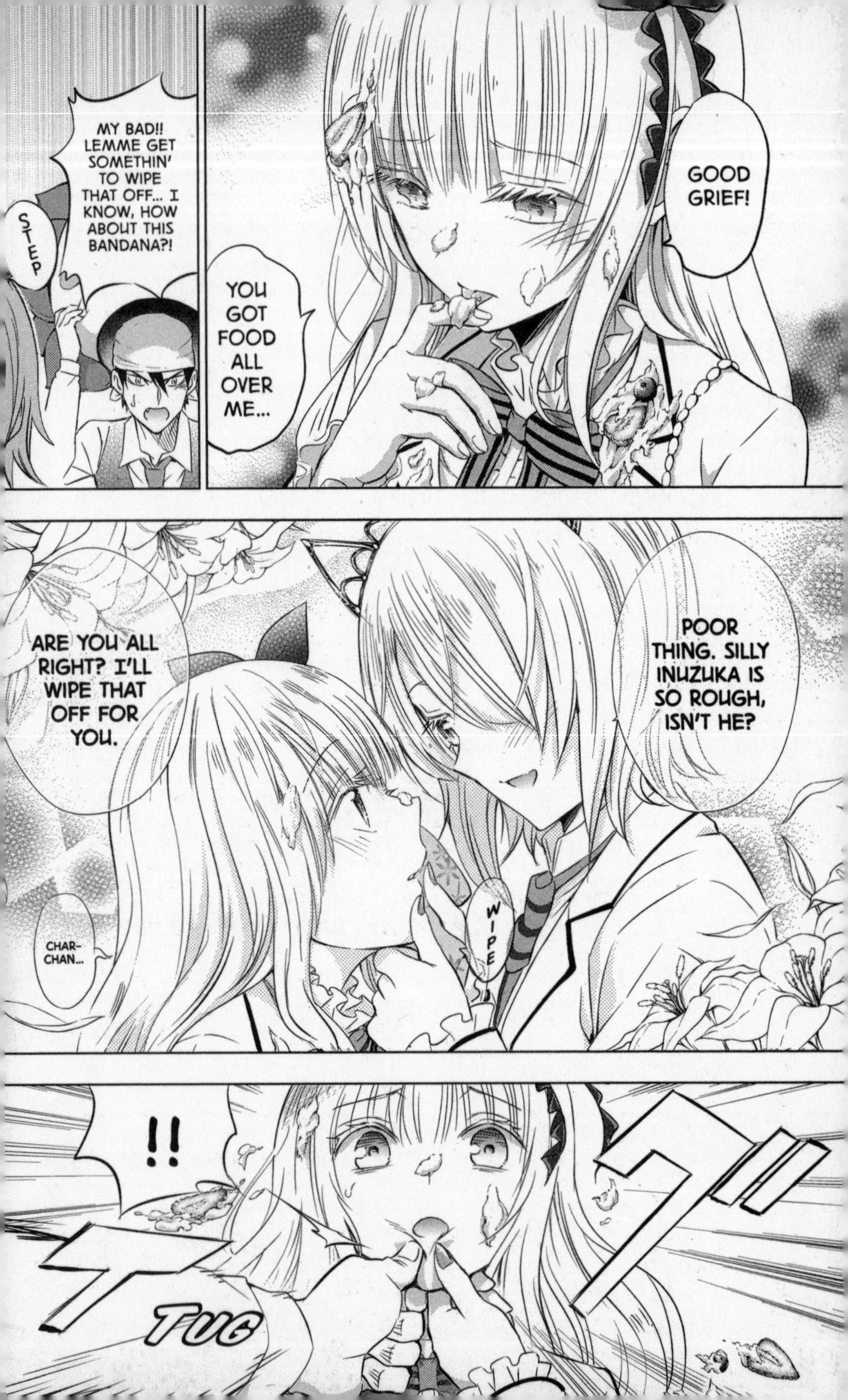
GOOD GRIEF!
YOU GOT FOOD ALL OVER ME...
MY BAD!! LEMME GET SOMETHIN' TO WIPE THAT OFF... I KNOW, HOW ABOUT THIS BANDANA?!
STEP
POOR THING. SILLY INUZUKA IS SO ROUGH, ISN'T HE?
ARE YOU ALL RIGHT? I'LL WIPE THAT OFF FOR YOU.
WIPE
CHAR-CHAN...
!!
TUG

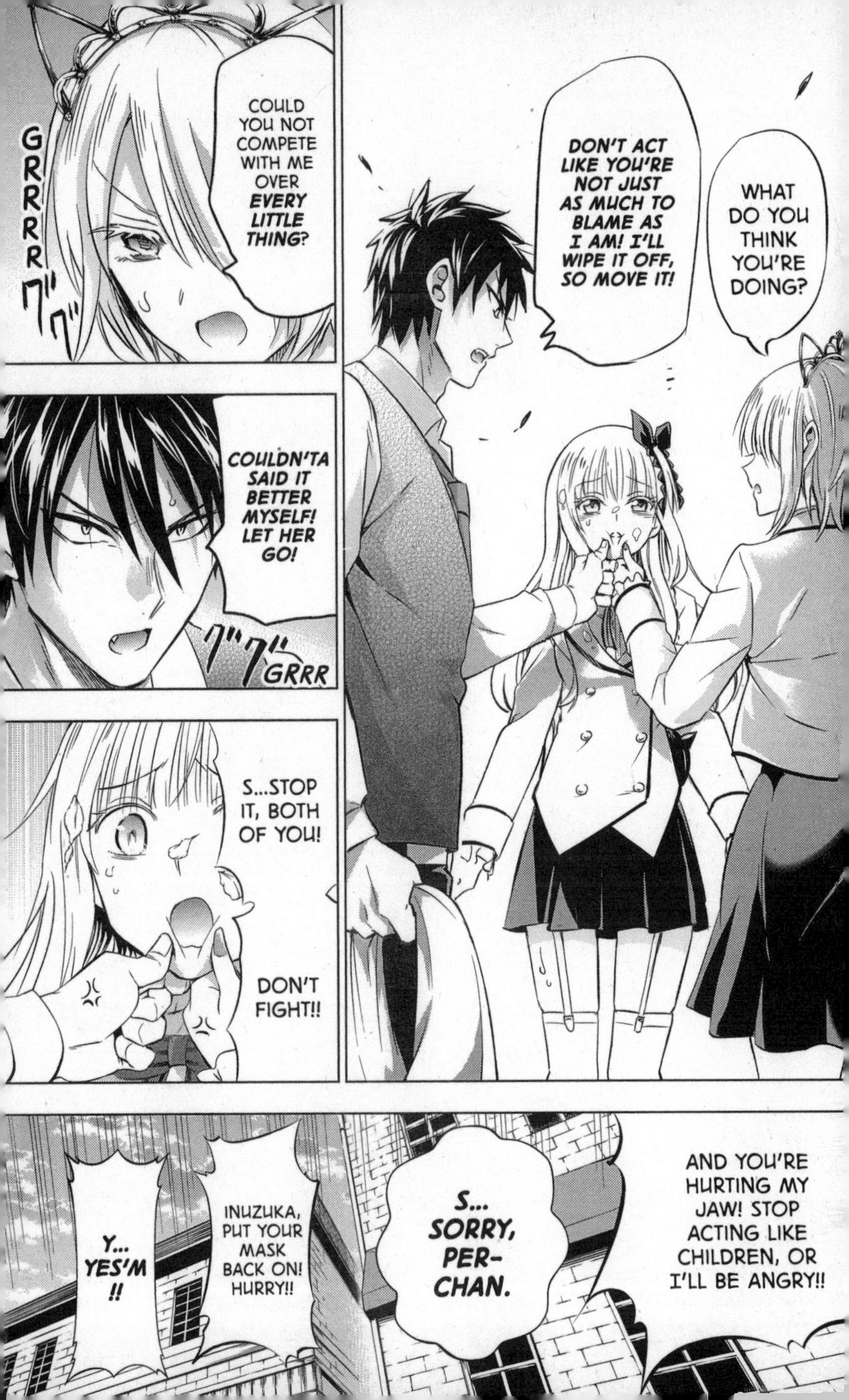
WHAT DO YOU THINK YOU'RE DOING?
DON'T ACT LIKE YOU'RE NOT JUST AS MUCH TO BLAME AS I AM! I'LL WIPE IT OFF, SO MOVE IT!
COULD YOU NOT COMPETE WITH ME OVER EVERY LITTLE THING?
GRRRR
ググ
COULDN'TA SAID IT BETTER MYSELF! LET HER GO!
ググ
GRRR
S...STOP IT, BOTH OF YOU!
DON'T FIGHT!!
AND YOU'RE HURTING MY JAW! STOP ACTING LIKE CHILDREN, OR I'LL BE ANGRY!!
S... SORRY, PER-CHAN.
INUZUKA, PUT YOUR MASK BACK ON! HURRY!!
Y... YES'M!!

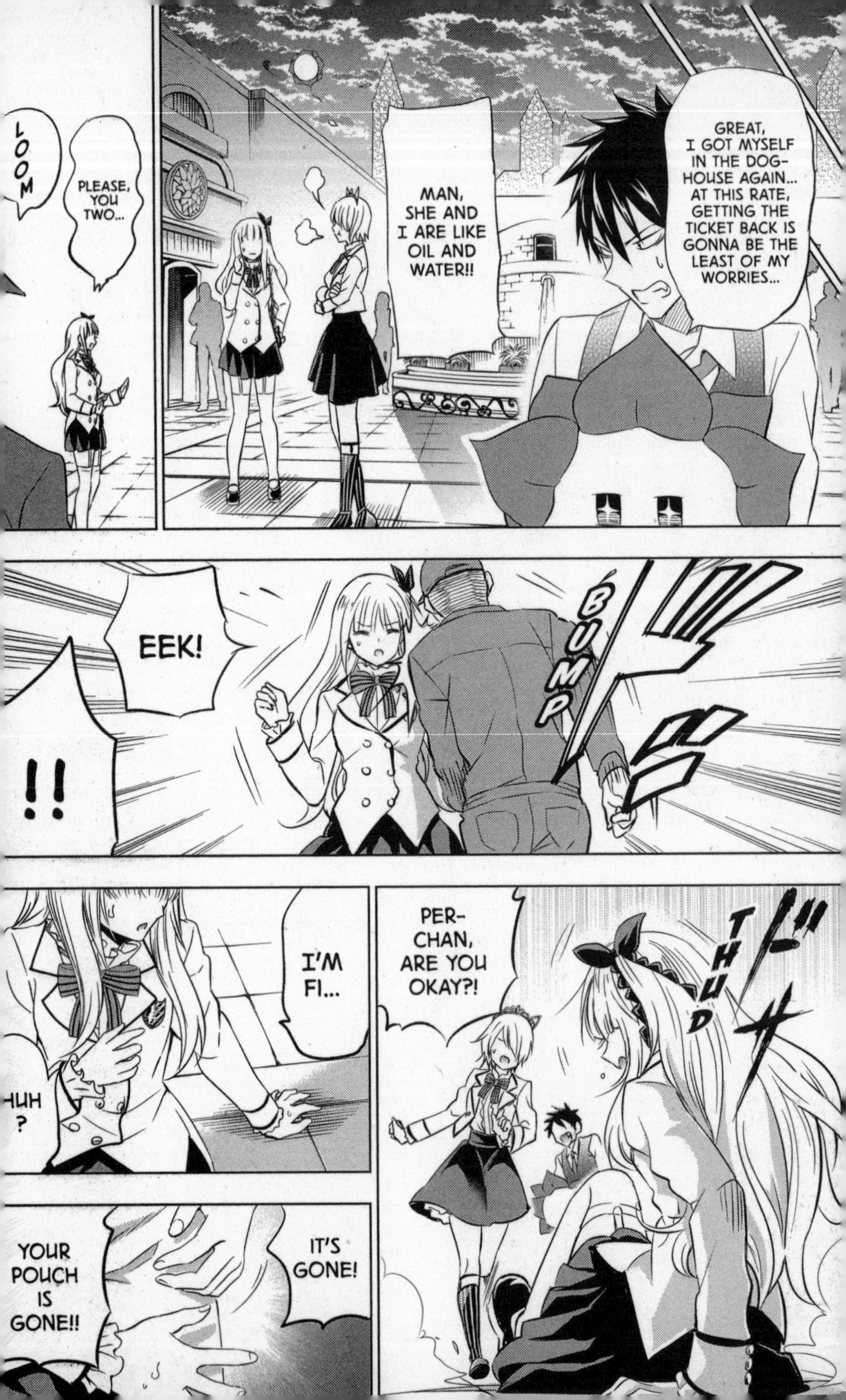
GREAT, I GOT MYSELF IN THE DOG-HOUSE AGAIN... AT THIS RATE, GETTING THE TICKET BACK IS GONNA BE THE LEAST OF MY WORRIES...
MAN, SHE AND I ARE LIKE OIL AND WATER!!
PLEASE, YOU TWO...
LOOOM
BUMP
EEK!
!!
PER-CHAN, ARE YOU OKAY?!
THUD
I'M FI...
HUH?
IT'S GONE!
YOUR POUCH IS GONE!!

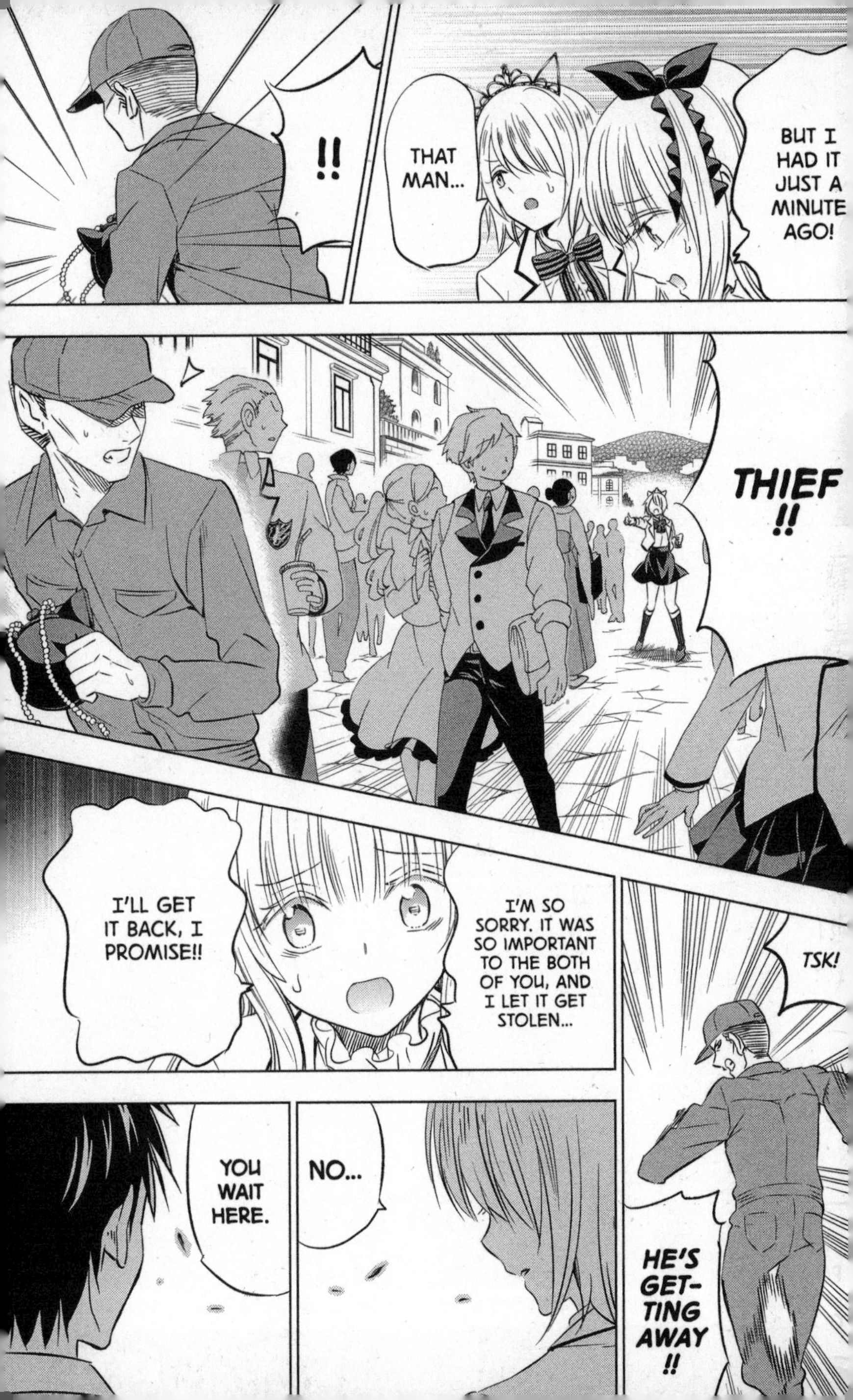
BUT I HAD IT JUST A MINUTE AGO!
THAT MAN...
!!
THIEF!!
TSK!
HE'S GET-TING AWAY!!
I'M SO SORRY. IT WAS SO IMPORTANT TO THE BOTH OF YOU, AND I LET IT GET STOLEN...
I'LL GET IT BACK, I PROMISE!!
NO...
YOU WAIT HERE.

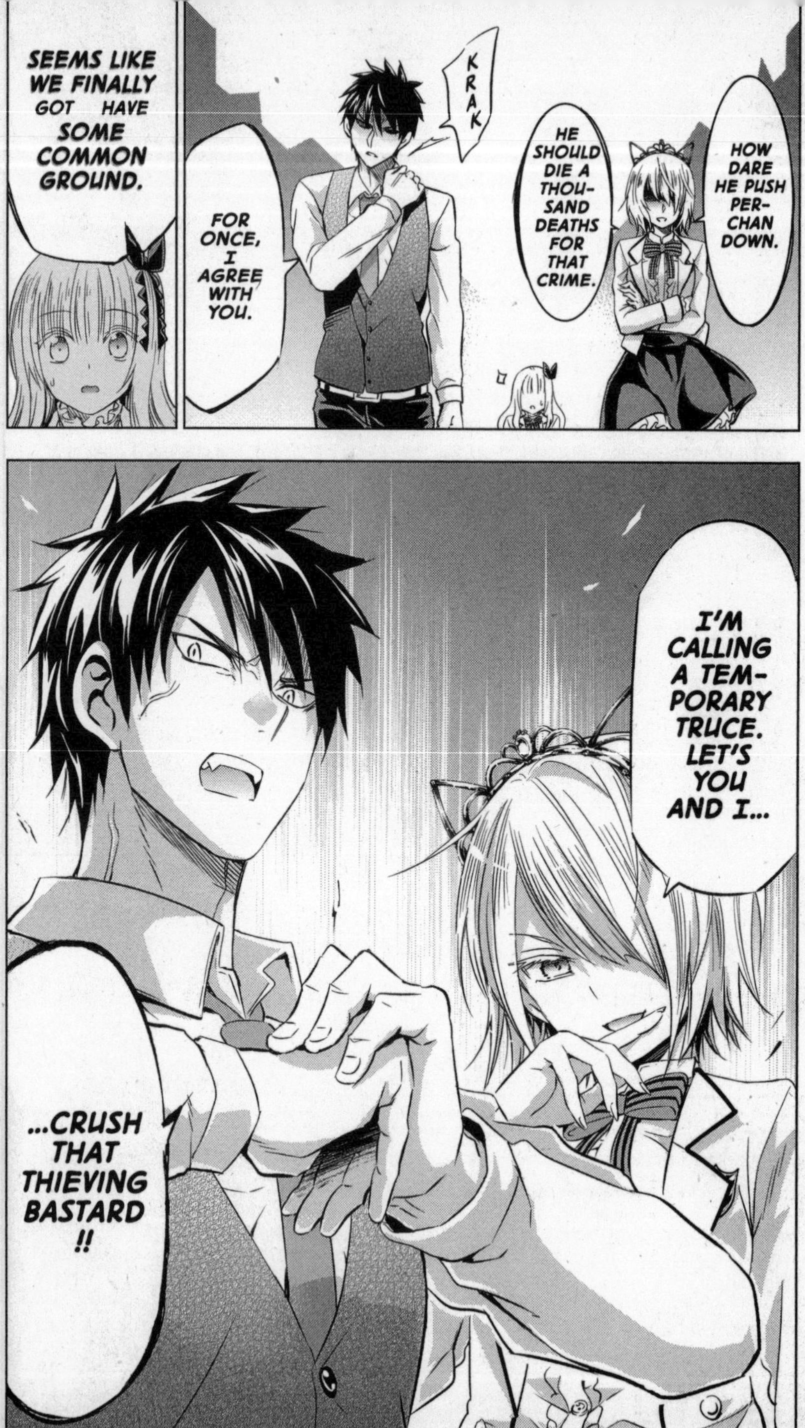
HOW DARE HE PUSH PER-CHAN DOWN.
HE SHOULD DIE A THOU-SAND DEATHS FOR THAT CRIME.
KRAK
FOR ONCE, I AGREE WITH YOU.
SEEMS LIKE WE FINALLY GOT HAVE SOME COMMON GROUND.
I'M CALLING A TEM-PORARY TRUCE. LET'S YOU AND I...
...CRUSH THAT THIEVING BASTARD!!

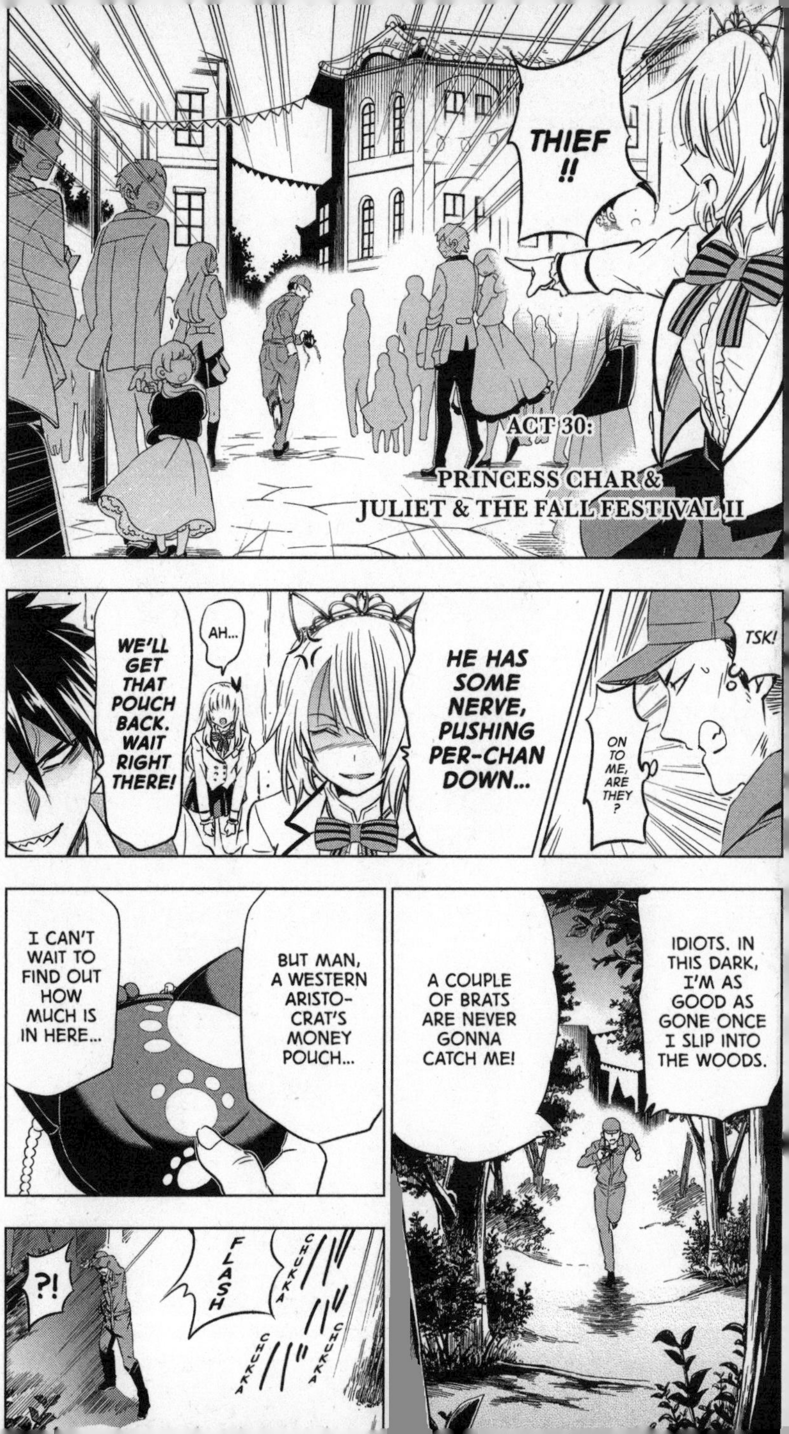
THIEF !!
ACT 30:
PRINCESS CHAR &
JULIET & THE FALL FESTIVAL II
TSK!
ON TO ME, ARE THEY?
HE HAS SOME NERVE, PUSHING PER-CHAN DOWN...
AH...
WE'LL GET THAT POUCH BACK. WAIT RIGHT THERE!
IDIOTS. IN THIS DARK, I'M AS GOOD AS GONE ONCE I SLIP INTO THE WOODS.
A COUPLE OF BRATS ARE NEVER GONNA CATCH ME!
BUT MAN, A WESTERN ARISTO-CRAT'S MONEY POUCH...
I CAN'T WAIT TO FIND OUT HOW MUCH IS IN HERE...
CHUKKA
CHUKKA
FLASH
CHUKKA
?!

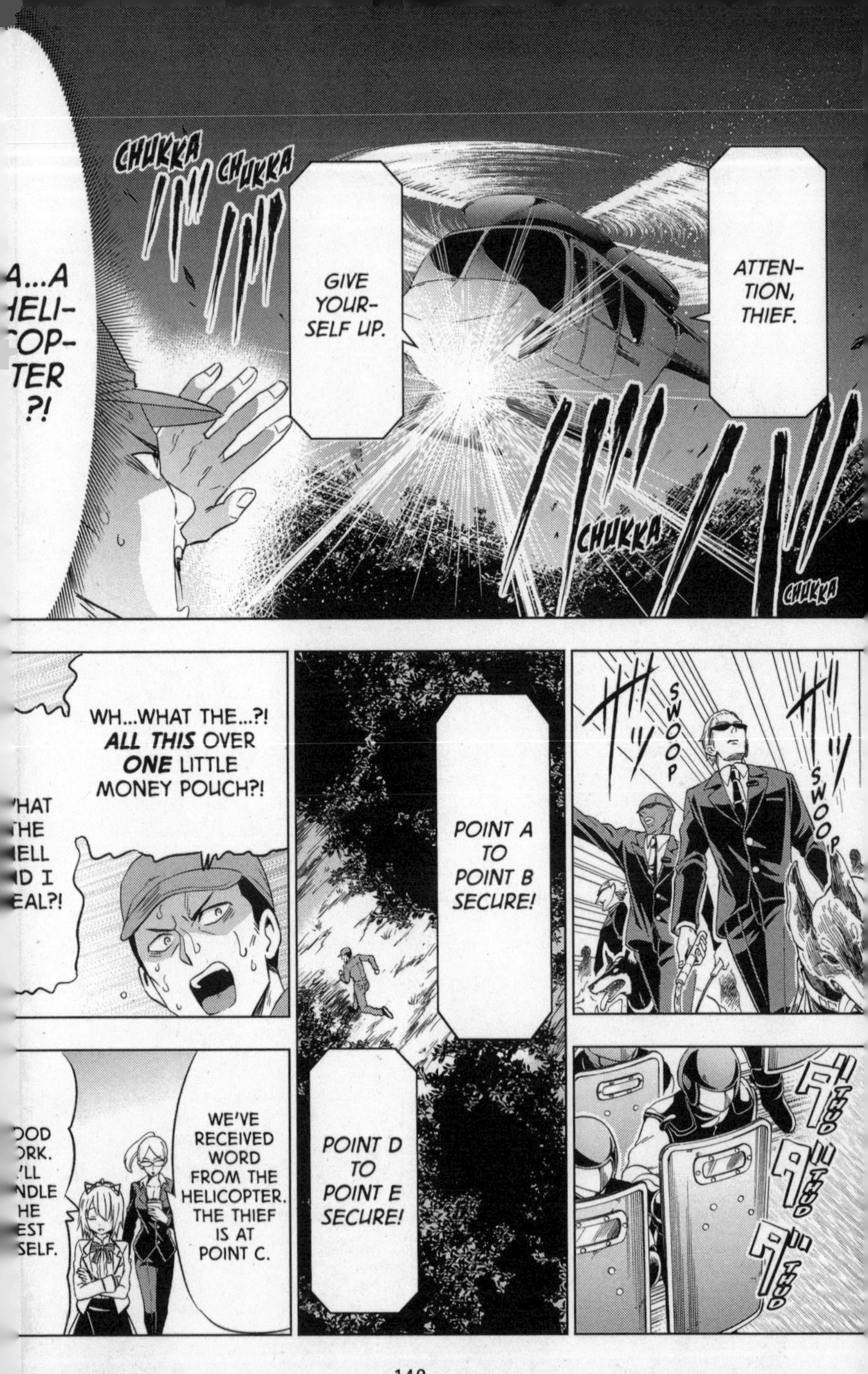
ATTENTION, THIEF.
GIVE YOURSELF UP.
CHUKKA CHUKKA
CHUKKA
CHUKKA
A...A HELI- COP- TER ?!
SWOOP
SWOOP
THUD THUD THUD
POINT A TO POINT B SECURE!
POINT D TO POINT E SECURE!
WH...WHAT THE...?! ALL THIS OVER ONE LITTLE MONEY POUCH?!
HAT THE ELL D I EAL?!
WE'VE RECEIVED WORD FROM THE HELICOPTER. THE THIEF IS AT POINT C.
OOD ORK. 'LL NDLE HE EST SELF.

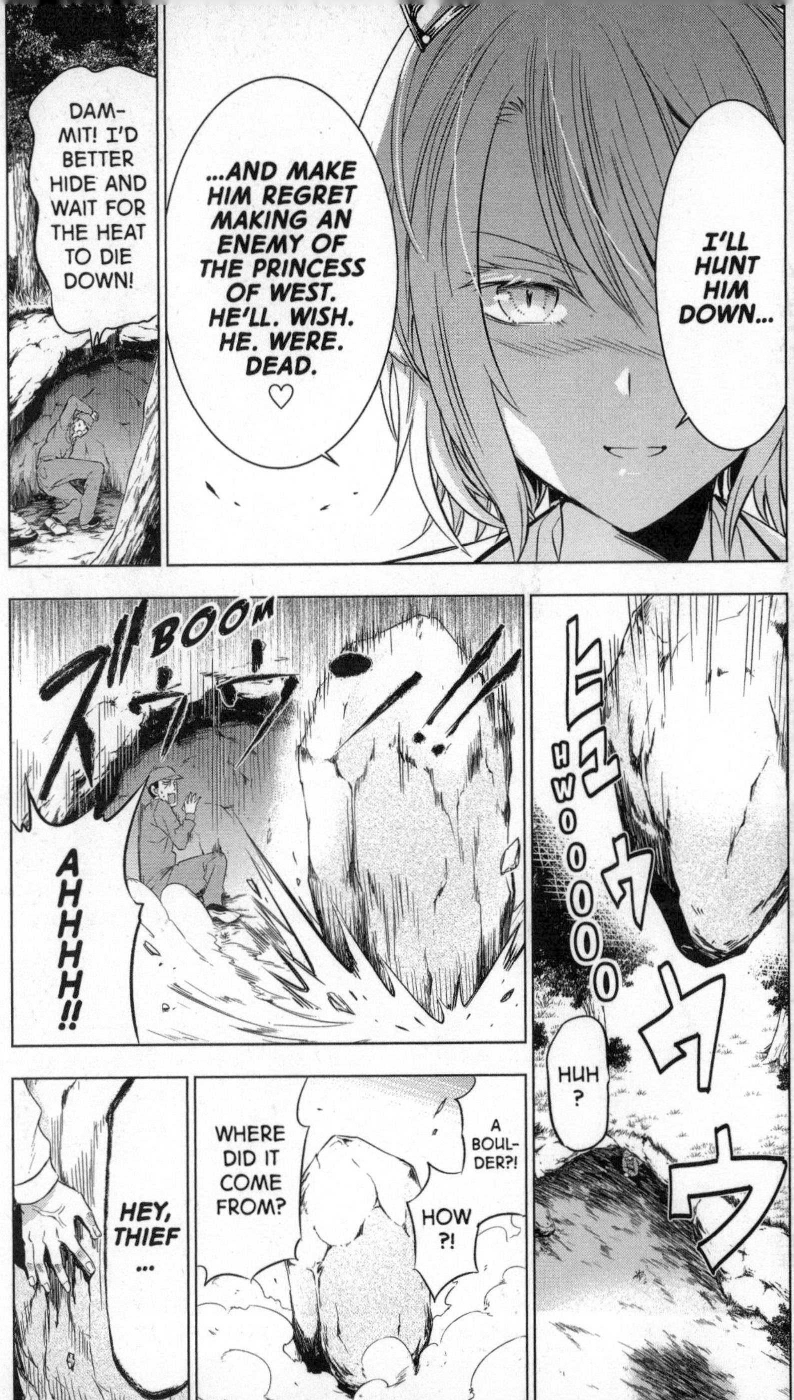
I'LL HUNT HIM DOWN...
...AND MAKE HIM REGRET MAKING AN ENEMY OF THE PRINCESS OF WEST. HE'LL. WISH. HE. WERE. DEAD. ♡
DAM-MIT! I'D BETTER HIDE AND WAIT FOR THE HEAT TO DIE DOWN!
ヒュウウ
HWOOOOOO
HUH?
ズゥゥ
BOOM
AHHHHH!!
A BOUL-DER?!
HOW?!
WHERE DID IT COME FROM?
HEY, THIEF ...

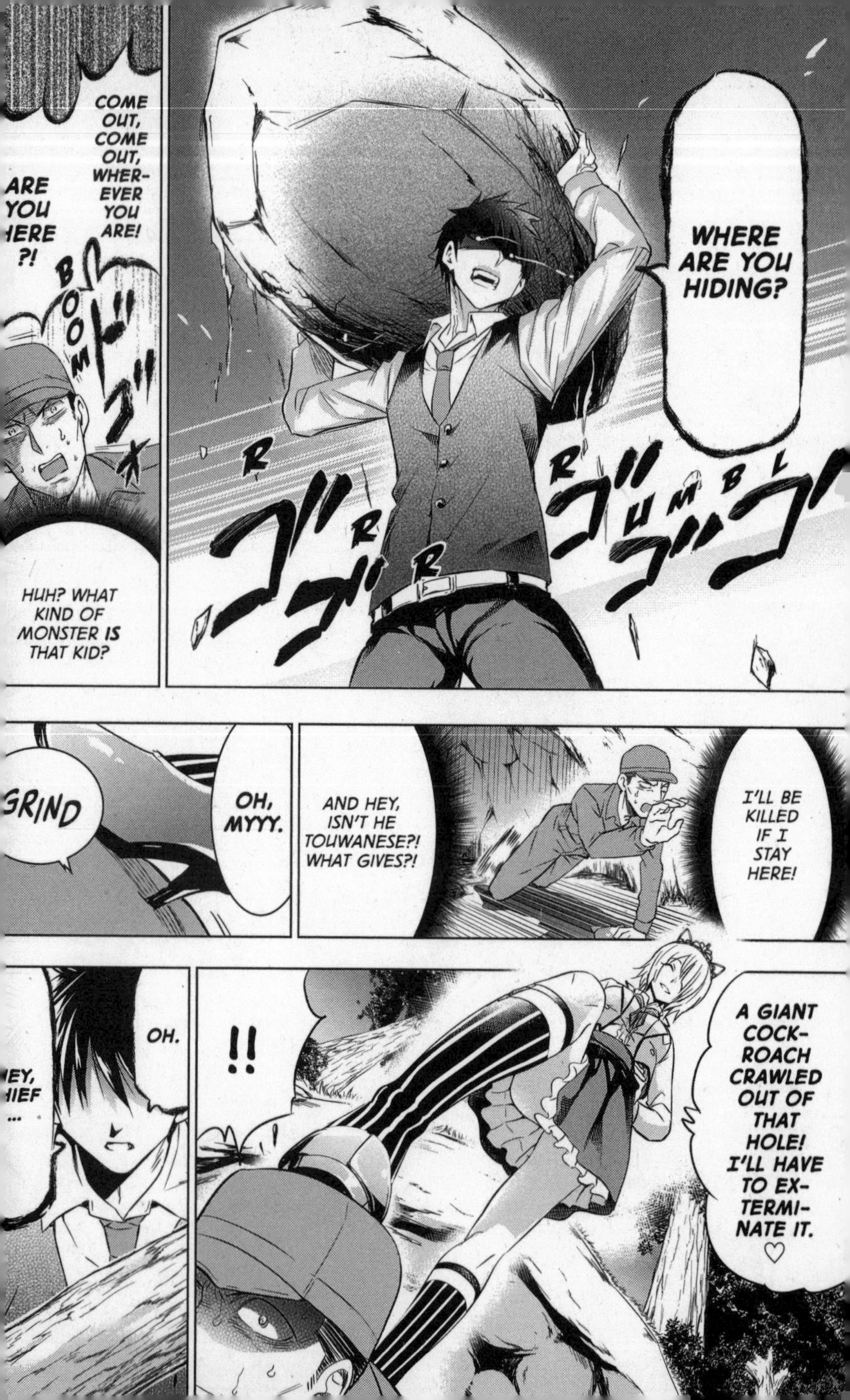
WHERE ARE YOU HIDING?
RRRRUMBL
COME OUT, COME OUT, WHEREVER YOU ARE!
ARE YOU HERE?!
BOOM
HUH? WHAT KIND OF MONSTER IS THAT KID?
I'LL BE KILLED IF I STAY HERE!
AND HEY, ISN'T HE TOUWANESE?! WHAT GIVES?!
OH, MYYY.
GRIND
A GIANT COCKROACH CRAWLED OUT OF THAT HOLE! I'LL HAVE TO EXTERMINATE IT. ♡
!!
OH.
EY, IEF ...

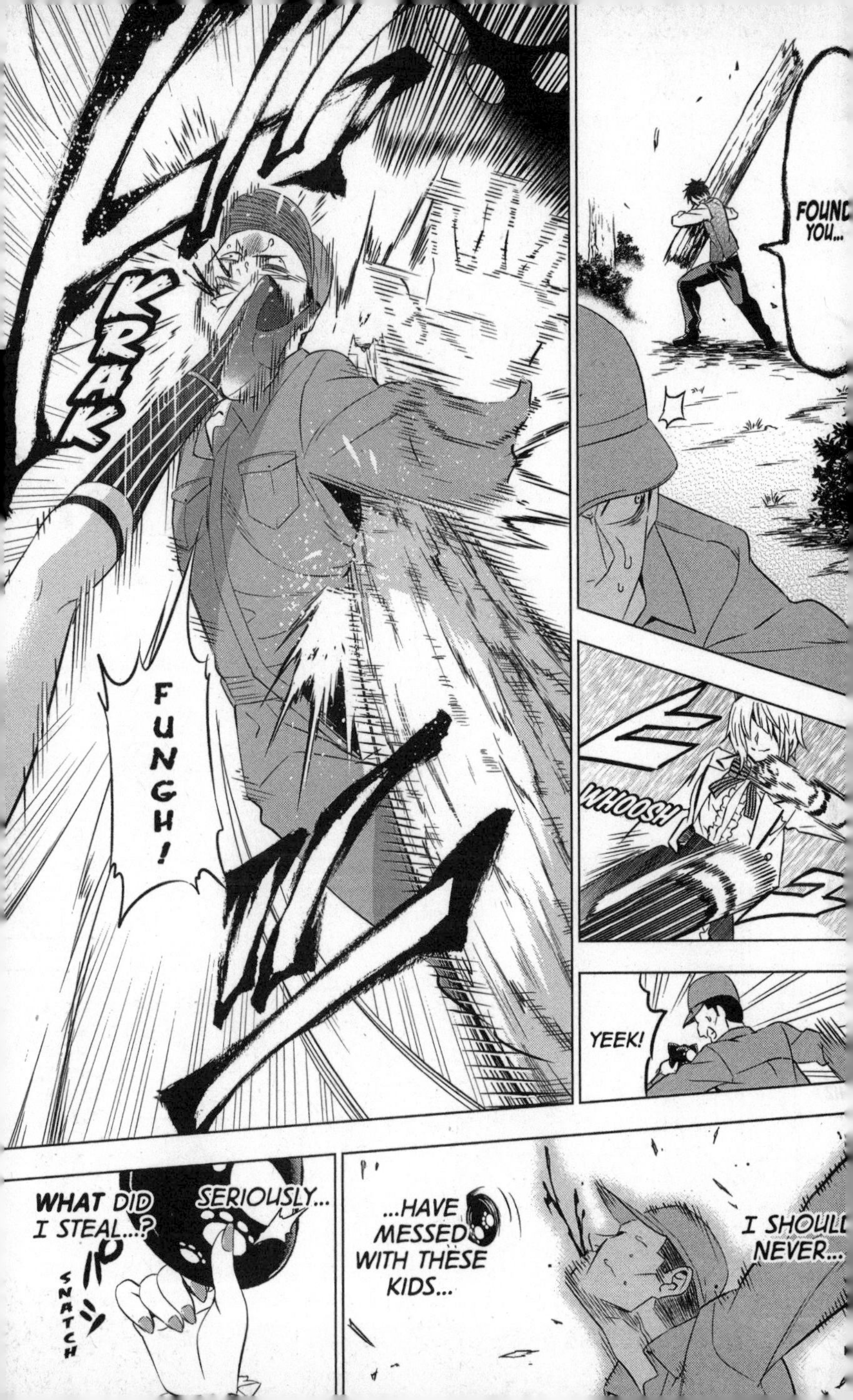
FOUND YOU...
WHOOSH
YEEK!
KRAK
FUNGH!
I SHOUL NEVER...
...HAVE MESSED WITH THESE KIDS...
SERIOUSLY...
WHAT DID I STEAL...?
SNATCH

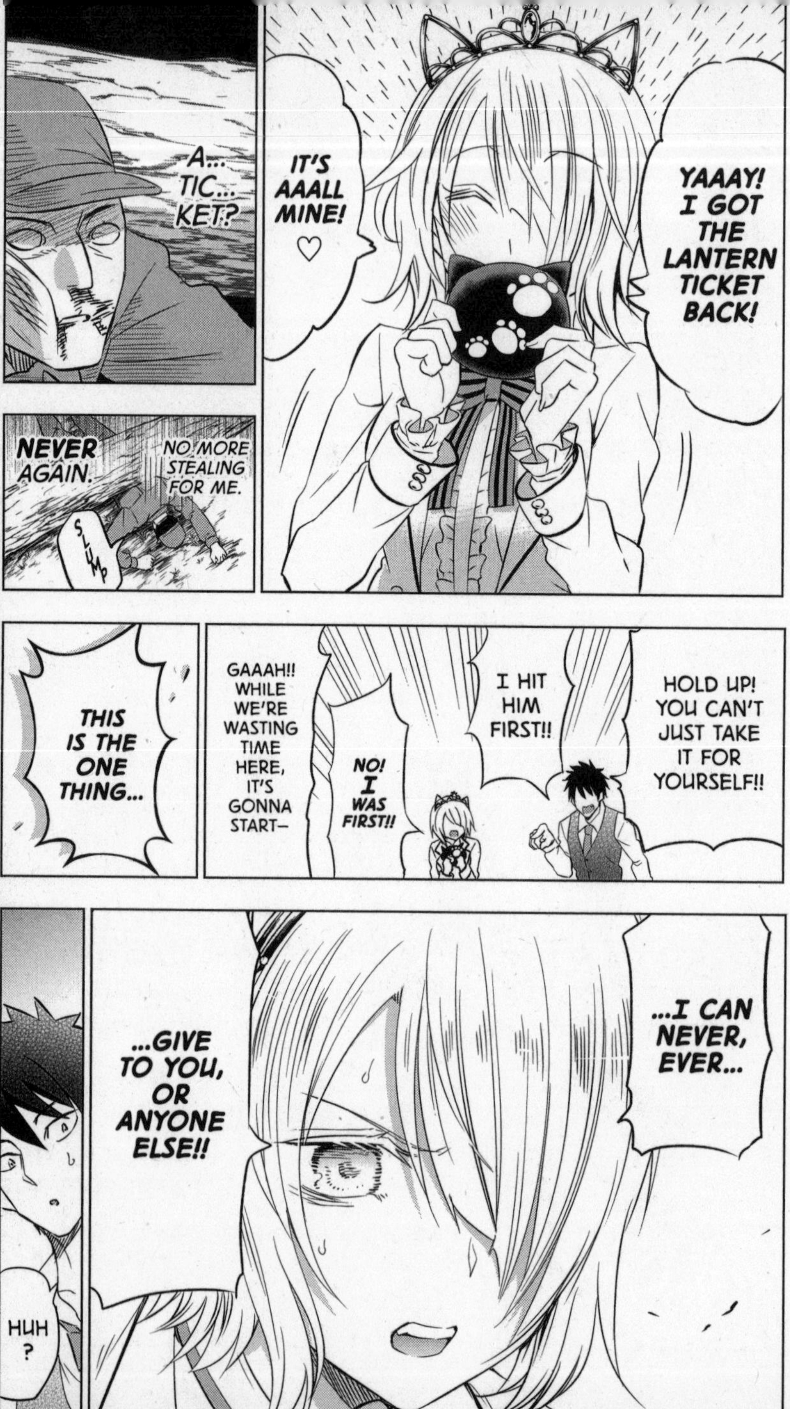
YAAAY! I GOT THE LANTERN TICKET BACK!
IT'S AAALL MINE! ♡
A... TIC... KET?
NO MORE STEALING FOR ME.
NEVER AGAIN.
SLUMP
HOLD UP! YOU CAN'T JUST TAKE IT FOR YOURSELF!!
I HIT HIM FIRST!!
NO! I WAS FIRST!!
GAAAH!! WHILE WE'RE WASTING TIME HERE, IT'S GONNA START—
THIS IS THE ONE THING...
...I CAN NEVER, EVER...
...GIVE TO YOU, OR ANYONE ELSE!!
HUH?

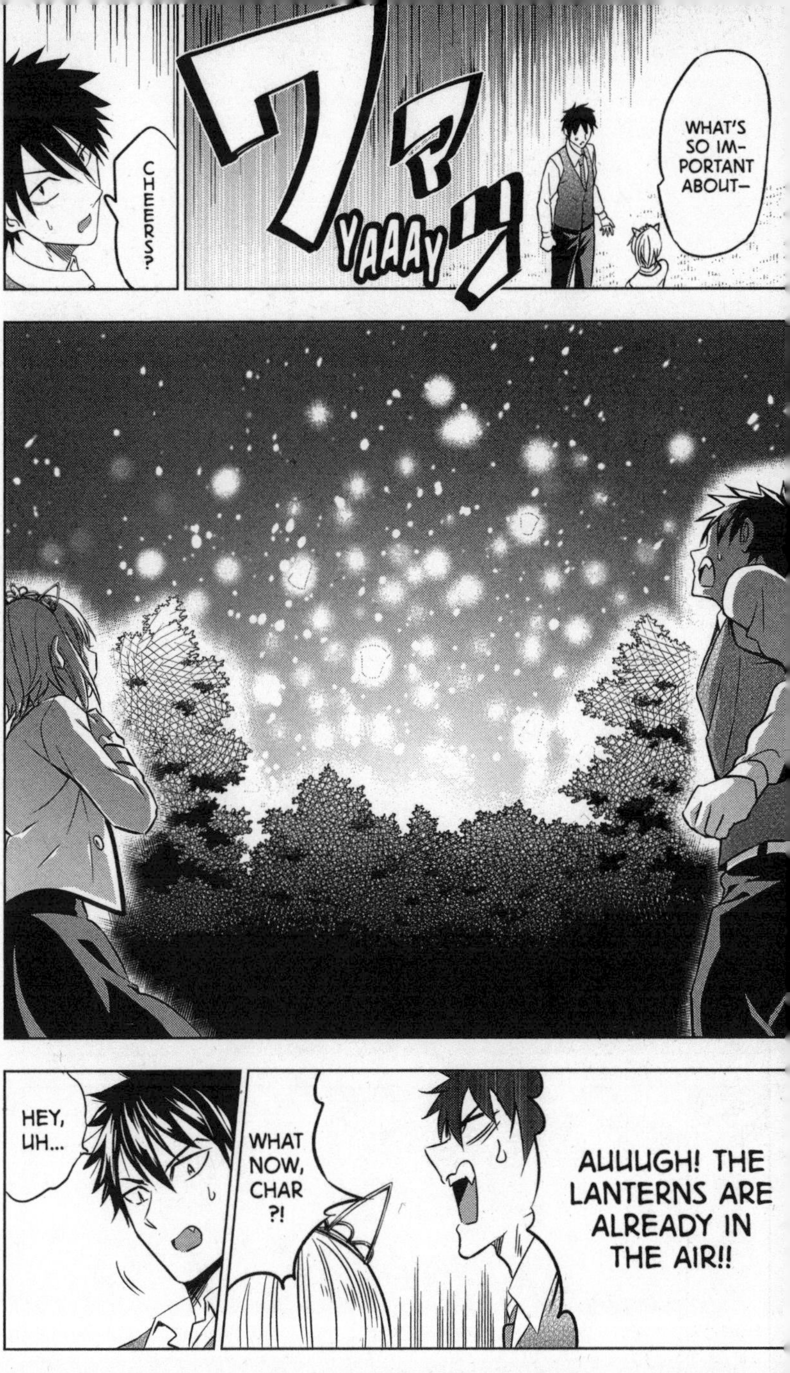
WHAT'S SO IM- PORTANT ABOUT—
YAAAY
CHEERS?
WHAT NOW, CHAR ?!
AUUUGH! THE LANTERNS ARE ALREADY IN THE AIR!!
HEY, UH...

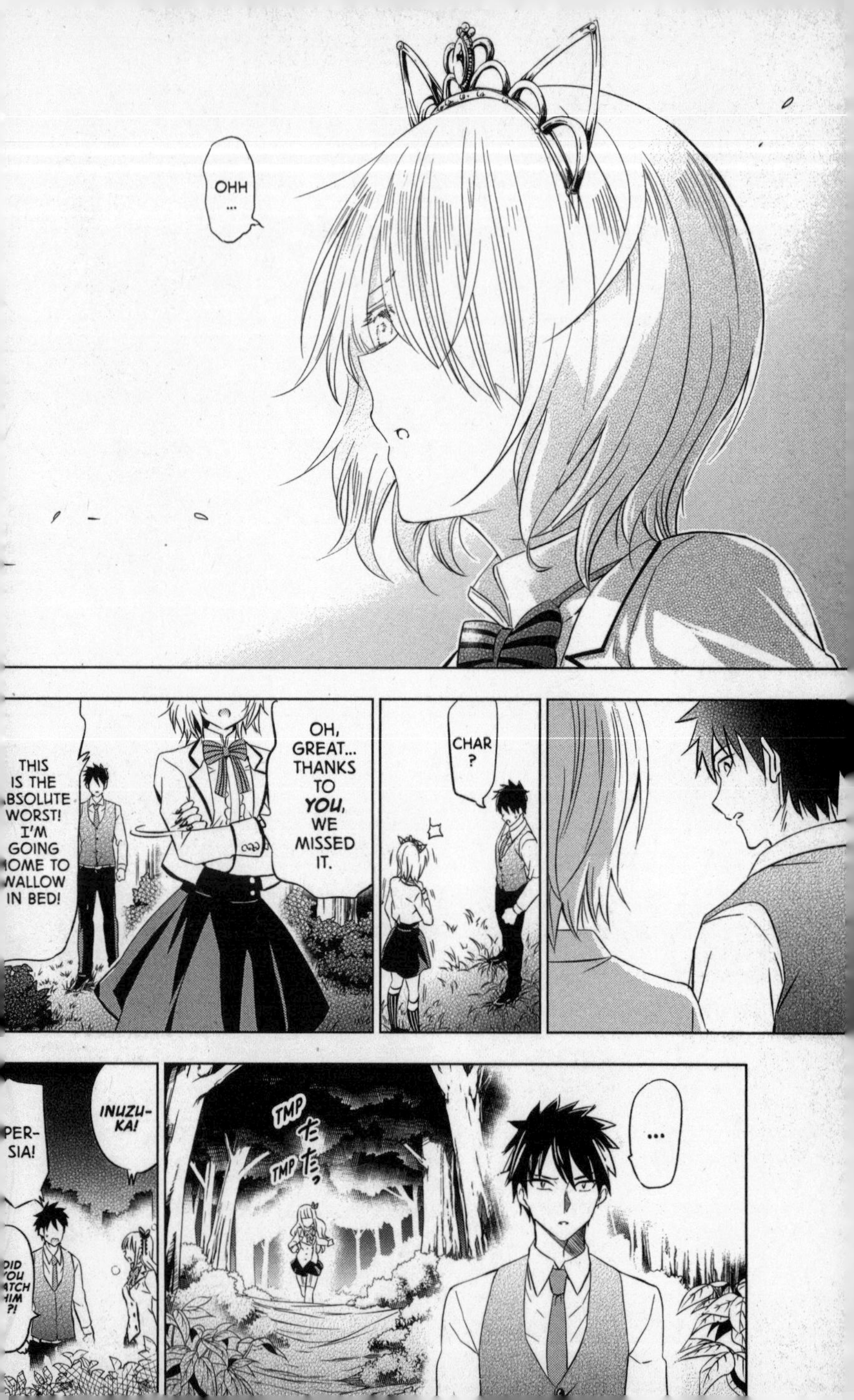
OHH ...
CHAR ?
OH, GREAT... THANKS TO YOU, WE MISSED IT.
THIS IS THE BSOLUTE WORST! I'M GOING OME TO WALLOW IN BED!
...
TMP たた TMP
INUZU-KA!
PER-SIA!
DID YOU ATCH HIM ?!

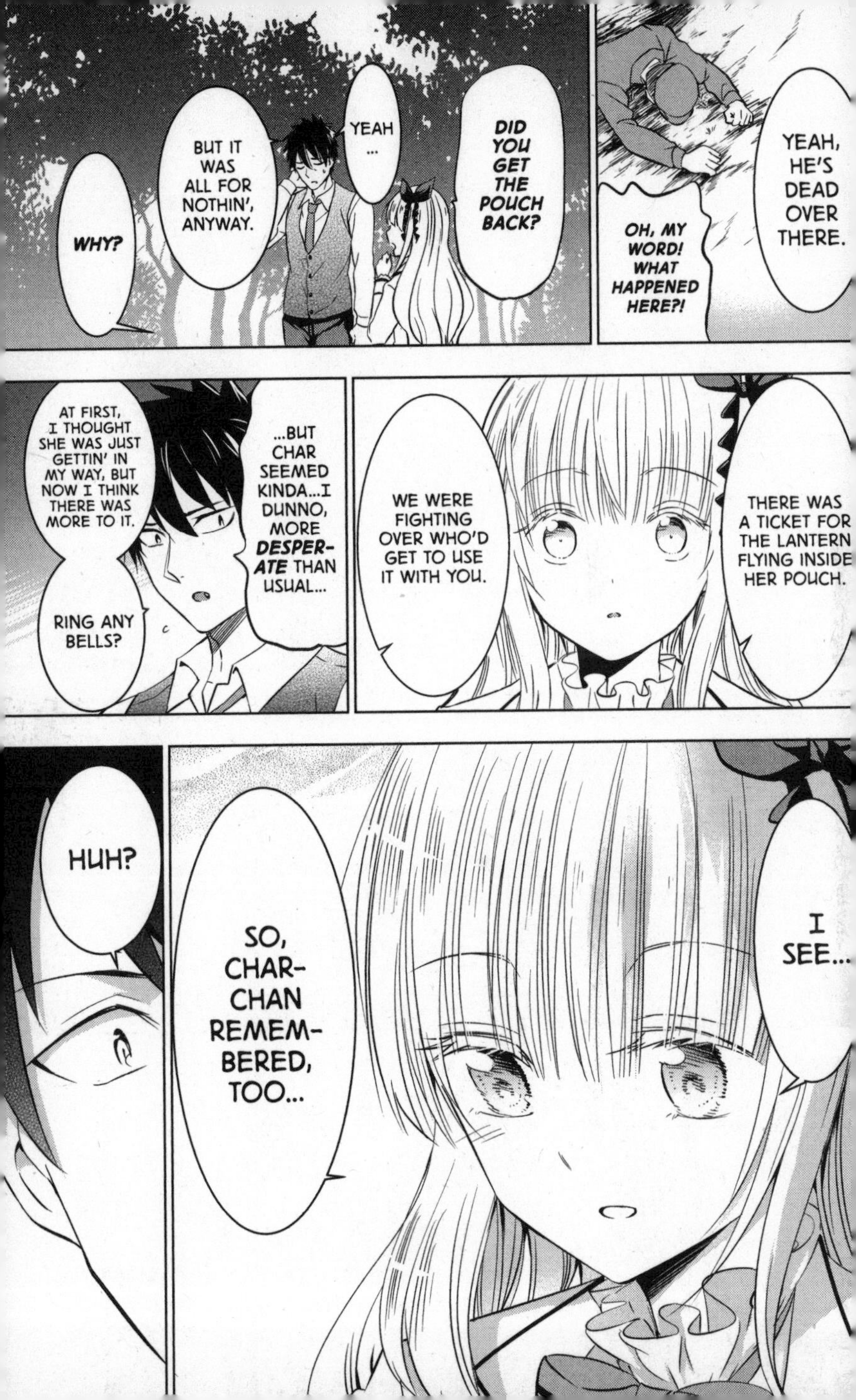
YEAH, HE'S DEAD OVER THERE.
OH, MY WORD! WHAT HAPPENED HERE?!
DID YOU GET THE POUCH BACK?
YEAH ...
BUT IT WAS ALL FOR NOTHIN', ANYWAY.
WHY?
THERE WAS A TICKET FOR THE LANTERN FLYING INSIDE HER POUCH.
WE WERE FIGHTING OVER WHO'D GET TO USE IT WITH YOU.
...BUT CHAR SEEMED KINDA...I DUNNO, MORE DESPERATE THAN USUAL...
AT FIRST, I THOUGHT SHE WAS JUST GETTIN' IN MY WAY, BUT NOW I THINK THERE WAS MORE TO IT.
RING ANY BELLS?
I SEE...
SO, CHAR-CHAN REMEMBERED, TOO...
HUH?

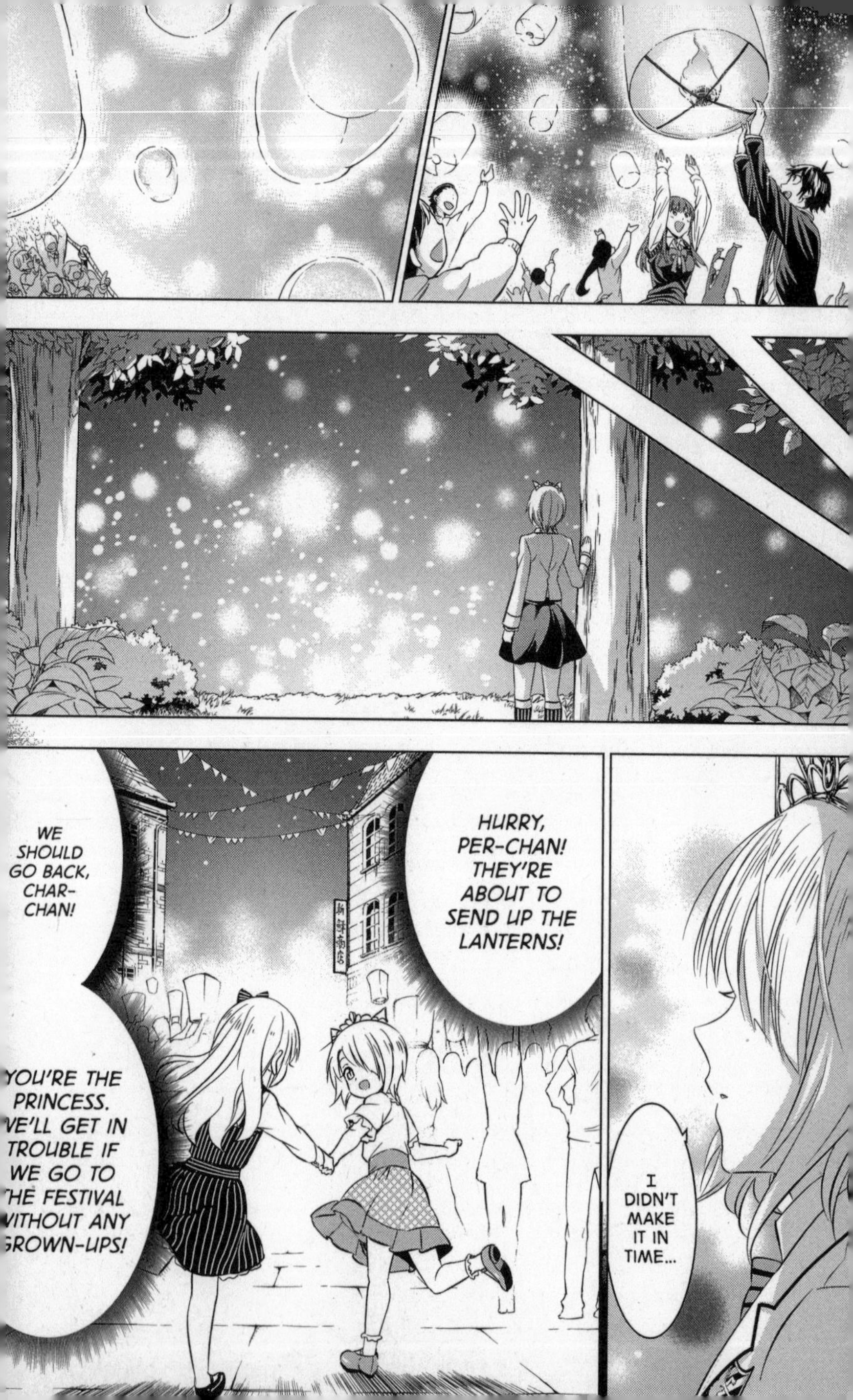
I DIDN'T MAKE IT IN TIME...
HURRY, PER-CHAN! THEY'RE ABOUT TO SEND UP THE LANTERNS!
WE SHOULD GO BACK, CHAR-CHAN!
YOU'RE THE PRINCESS. WE'LL GET IN TROUBLE IF WE GO TO THE FESTIVAL WITHOUT ANY GROWN-UPS!

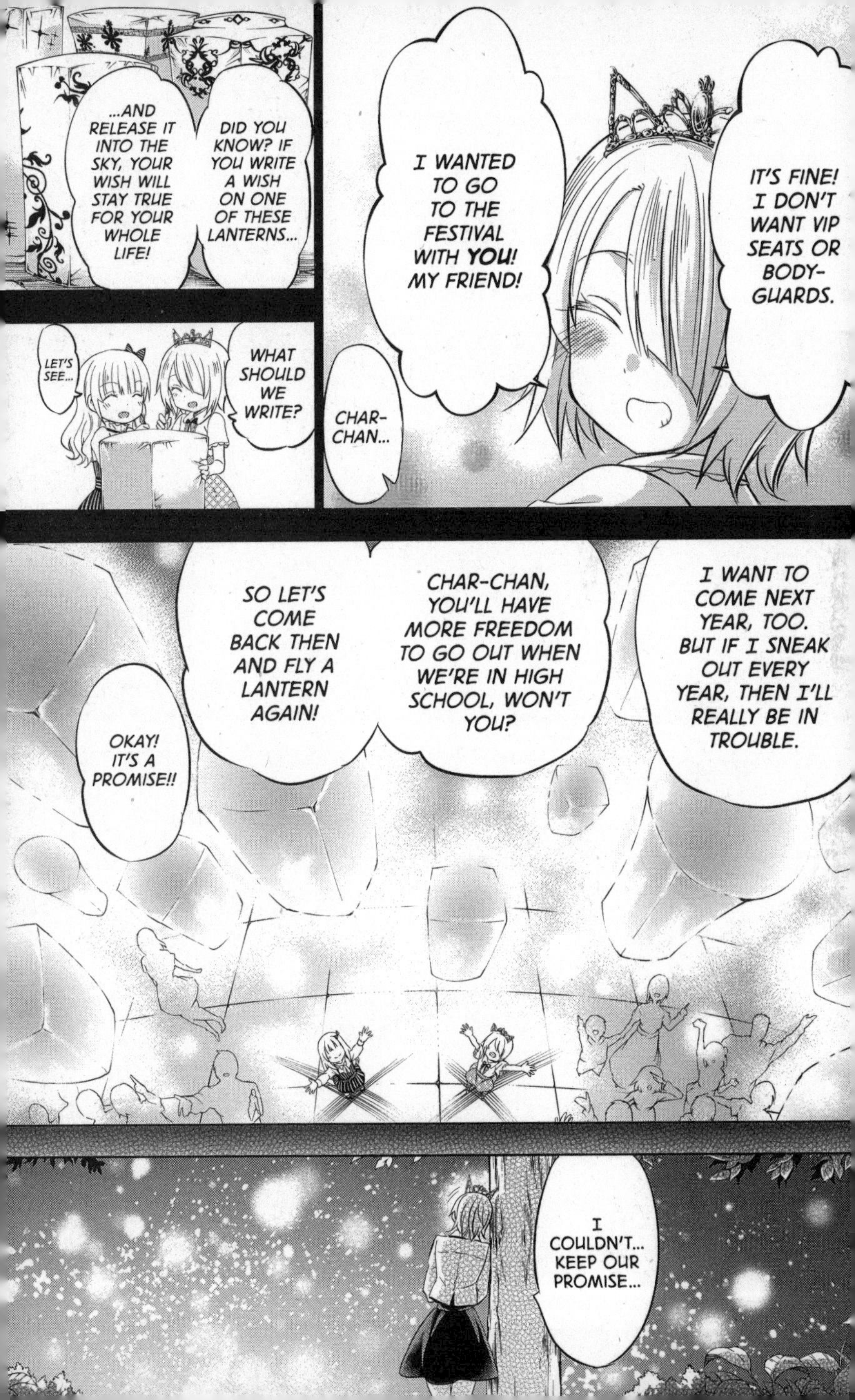
IT'S FINE! I DON'T WANT VIP SEATS OR BODY-GUARDS.
I WANTED TO GO TO THE FESTIVAL WITH **YOU**! MY FRIEND!
CHAR-CHAN...
DID YOU KNOW? IF YOU WRITE A WISH ON ONE OF THESE LANTERNS...
...AND RELEASE IT INTO THE SKY, YOUR WISH WILL STAY TRUE FOR YOUR WHOLE LIFE!
WHAT SHOULD WE WRITE?
LET'S SEE...
I WANT TO COME NEXT YEAR, TOO. BUT IF I SNEAK OUT EVERY YEAR, THEN I'LL REALLY BE IN TROUBLE.
CHAR-CHAN, YOU'LL HAVE MORE FREEDOM TO GO OUT WHEN WE'RE IN HIGH SCHOOL, WON'T YOU?
SO LET'S COME BACK THEN AND FLY A LANTERN AGAIN!
OKAY! IT'S A PROMISE!!
I COULDN'T... KEEP OUR PROMISE...

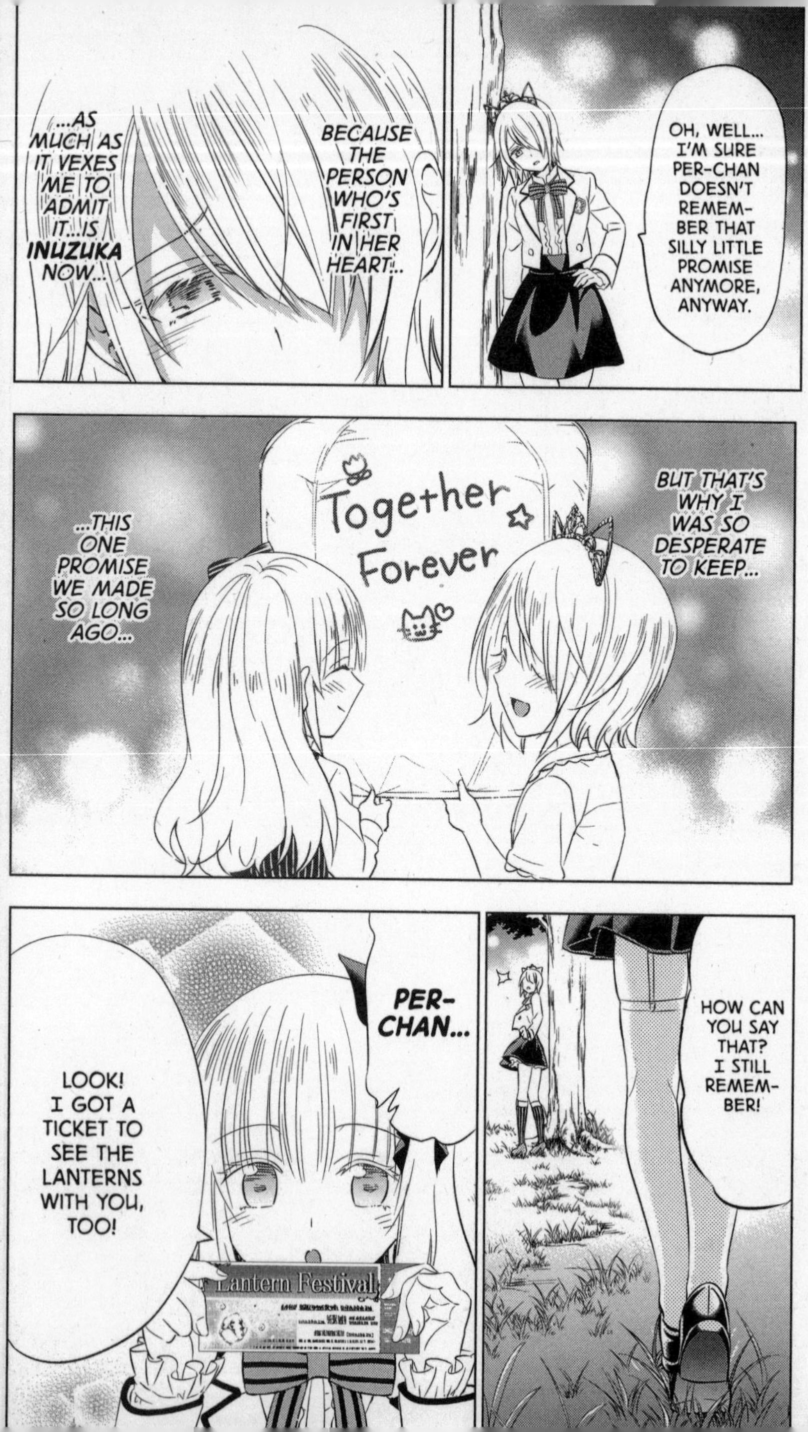
OH, WELL... I'M SURE PER-CHAN DOESN'T REMEMBER THAT SILLY LITTLE PROMISE ANYMORE, ANYWAY.
BECAUSE THE PERSON WHO'S FIRST IN HER HEART...
...AS MUCH AS IT VEXES ME TO ADMIT IT...IS **INUZUKA** NOW...
BUT THAT'S WHY I WAS SO DESPERATE TO KEEP...
Together Forever
...THIS ONE PROMISE WE MADE SO LONG AGO...
HOW CAN YOU SAY THAT? I STILL REMEMBER!
PER-CHAN...
LOOK! I GOT A TICKET TO SEE THE LANTERNS WITH YOU, TOO!
Lantern Festival

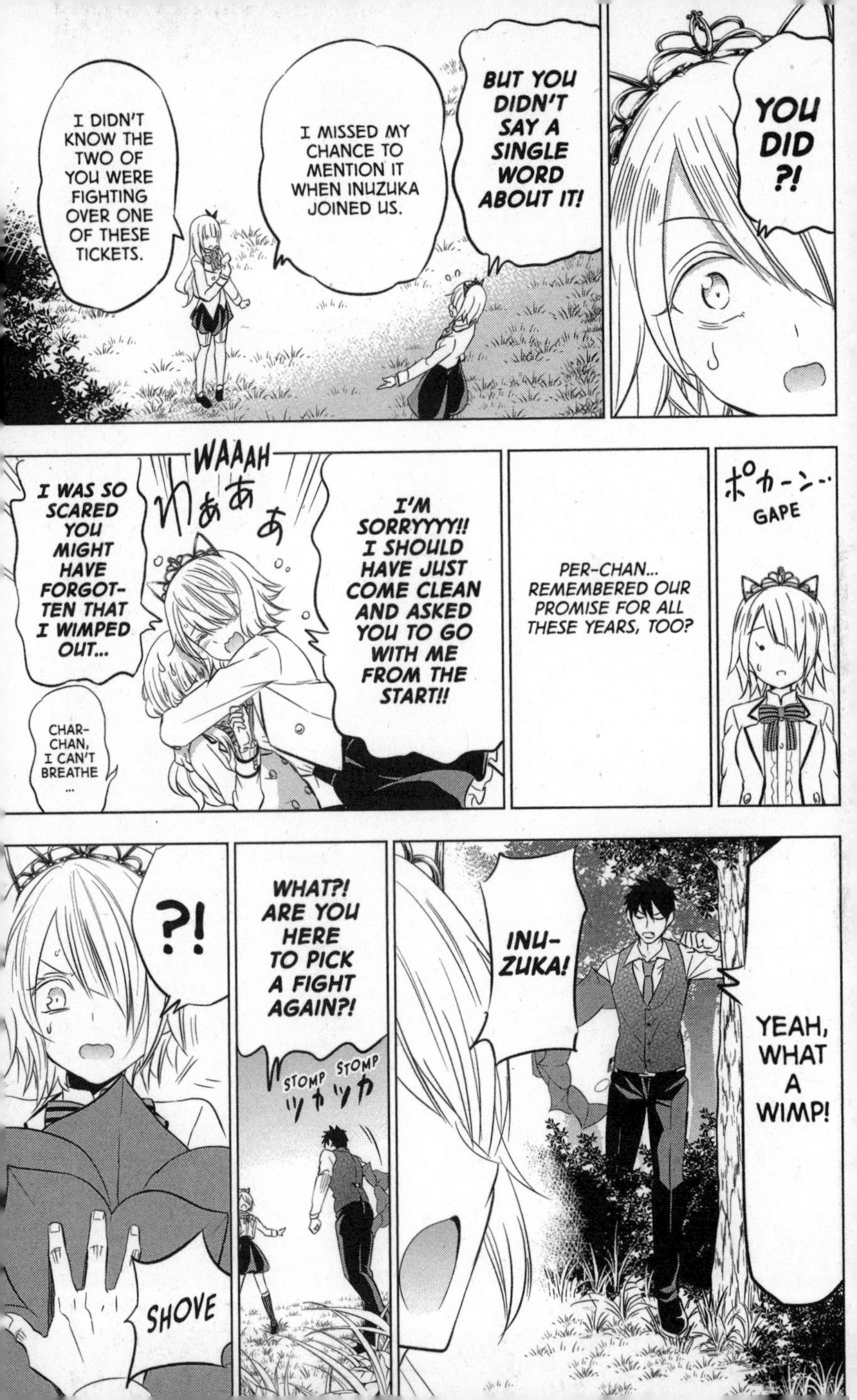
YOU DID ?!
BUT YOU DIDN'T SAY A SINGLE WORD ABOUT IT!
I MISSED MY CHANCE TO MENTION IT WHEN INUZUKA JOINED US.
I DIDN'T KNOW THE TWO OF YOU WERE FIGHTING OVER ONE OF THESE TICKETS.
ポカーン‥
GAPE
PER-CHAN... REMEMBERED OUR PROMISE FOR ALL THESE YEARS, TOO?
I'M SORRYYYY!! I SHOULD HAVE JUST COME CLEAN AND ASKED YOU TO GO WITH ME FROM THE START!!
WAAAH
わぁあぁ
I WAS SO SCARED YOU MIGHT HAVE FORGOT-TEN THAT I WIMPED OUT...
CHAR-CHAN, I CAN'T BREATHE ...
YEAH, WHAT A WIMP!
INU-ZUKA!
WHAT?! ARE YOU HERE TO PICK A FIGHT AGAIN?!
STOMP STOMP
ツカツカ
?!
SHOVE

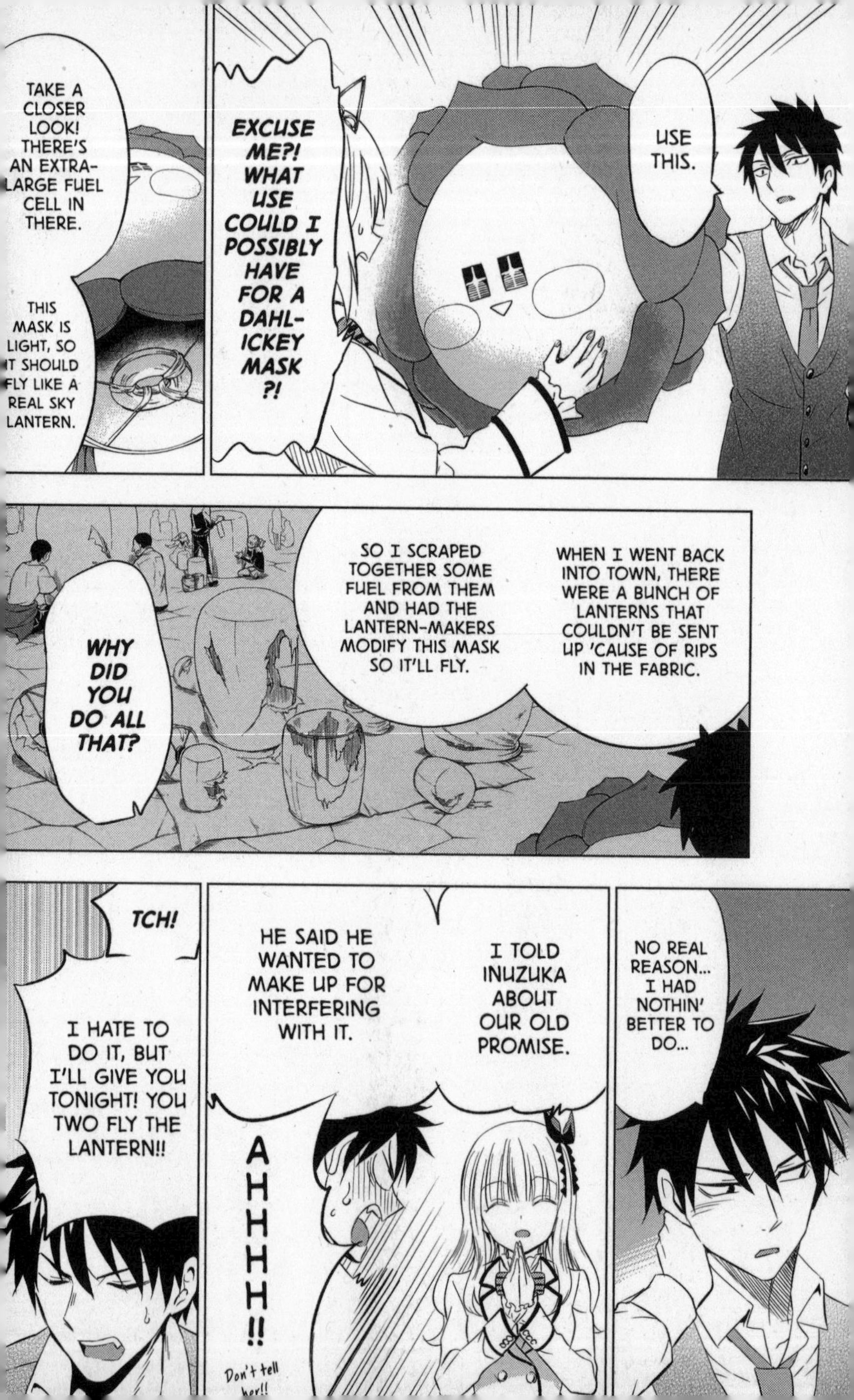
USE THIS.
EXCUSE ME?! WHAT USE COULD I POSSIBLY HAVE FOR A DAHL-ICKEY MASK?!
TAKE A CLOSER LOOK! THERE'S AN EXTRA-LARGE FUEL CELL IN THERE.
THIS MASK IS LIGHT, SO IT SHOULD FLY LIKE A REAL SKY LANTERN.
WHEN I WENT BACK INTO TOWN, THERE WERE A BUNCH OF LANTERNS THAT COULDN'T BE SENT UP 'CAUSE OF RIPS IN THE FABRIC.
SO I SCRAPED TOGETHER SOME FUEL FROM THEM AND HAD THE LANTERN-MAKERS MODIFY THIS MASK SO IT'LL FLY.
WHY DID YOU DO ALL THAT?
NO REAL REASON... I HAD NOTHIN' BETTER TO DO...
I TOLD INUZUKA ABOUT OUR OLD PROMISE.
HE SAID HE WANTED TO MAKE UP FOR INTERFERING WITH IT.
AHHHHH!!
Don't tell her!!
TCH!
I HATE TO DO IT, BUT I'LL GIVE YOU TONIGHT! YOU TWO FLY THE LANTERN!!

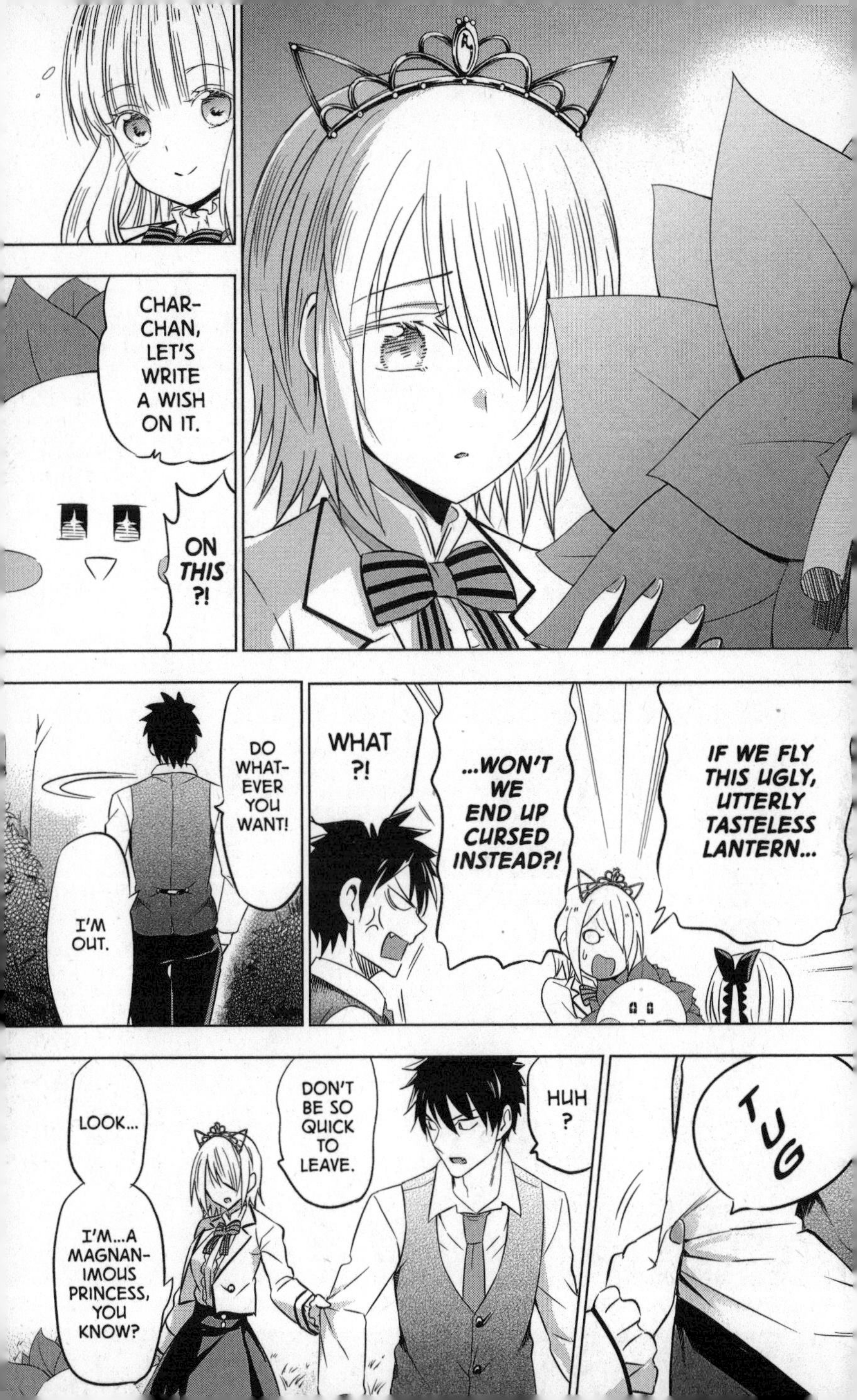
CHAR-CHAN, LET'S WRITE A WISH ON IT.
ON *THIS* ?!
IF WE FLY THIS UGLY, UTTERLY TASTELESS LANTERN...
...WON'T WE END UP CURSED INSTEAD?!
WHAT ?!
DO WHATEVER YOU WANT!
I'M OUT.
TUG
HUH ?
DON'T BE SO QUICK TO LEAVE.
LOOK...
I'M...A MAGNANIMOUS PRINCESS, YOU KNOW?

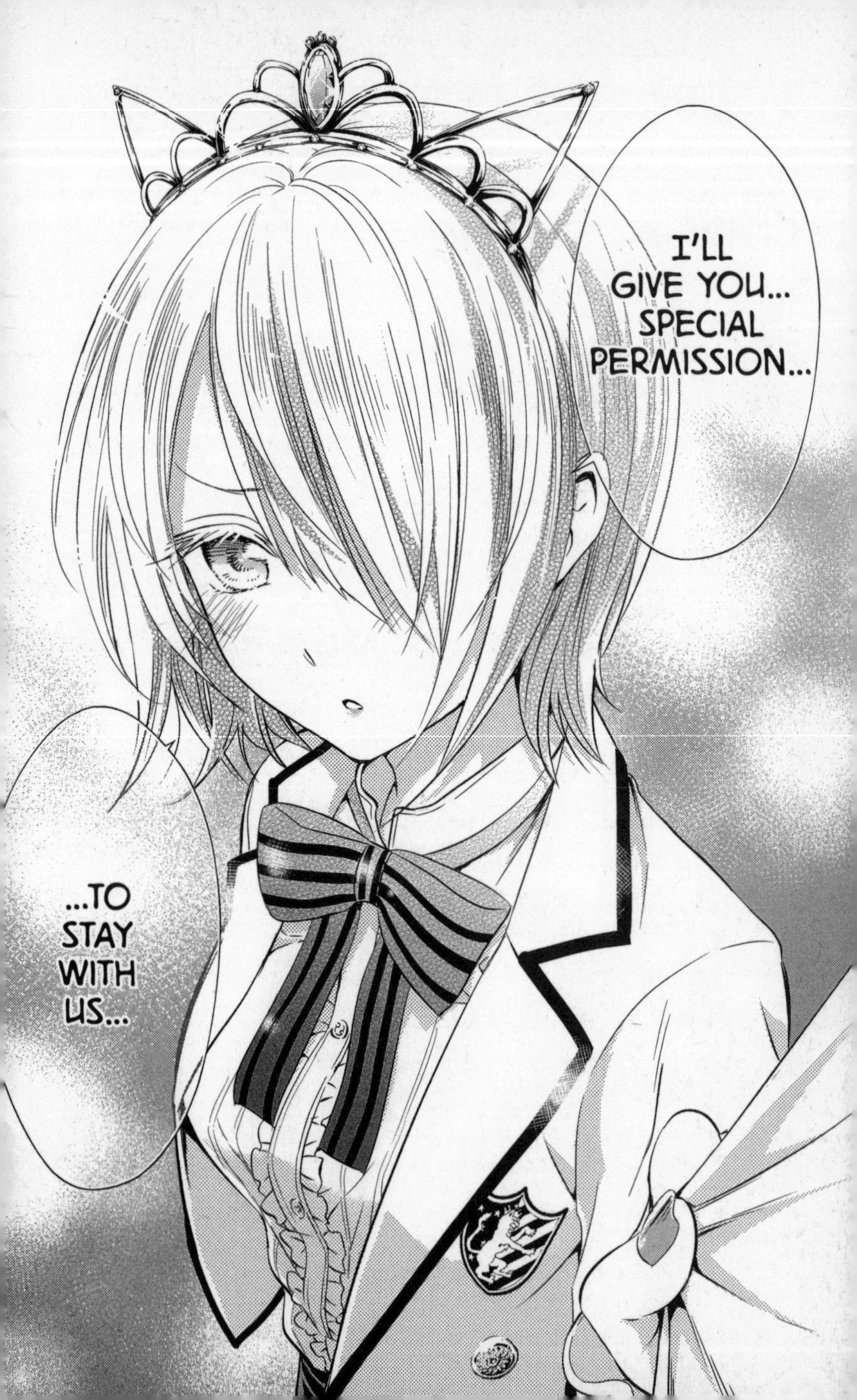
I'LL GIVE YOU... SPECIAL PERMISSION...
...TO STAY WITH US...

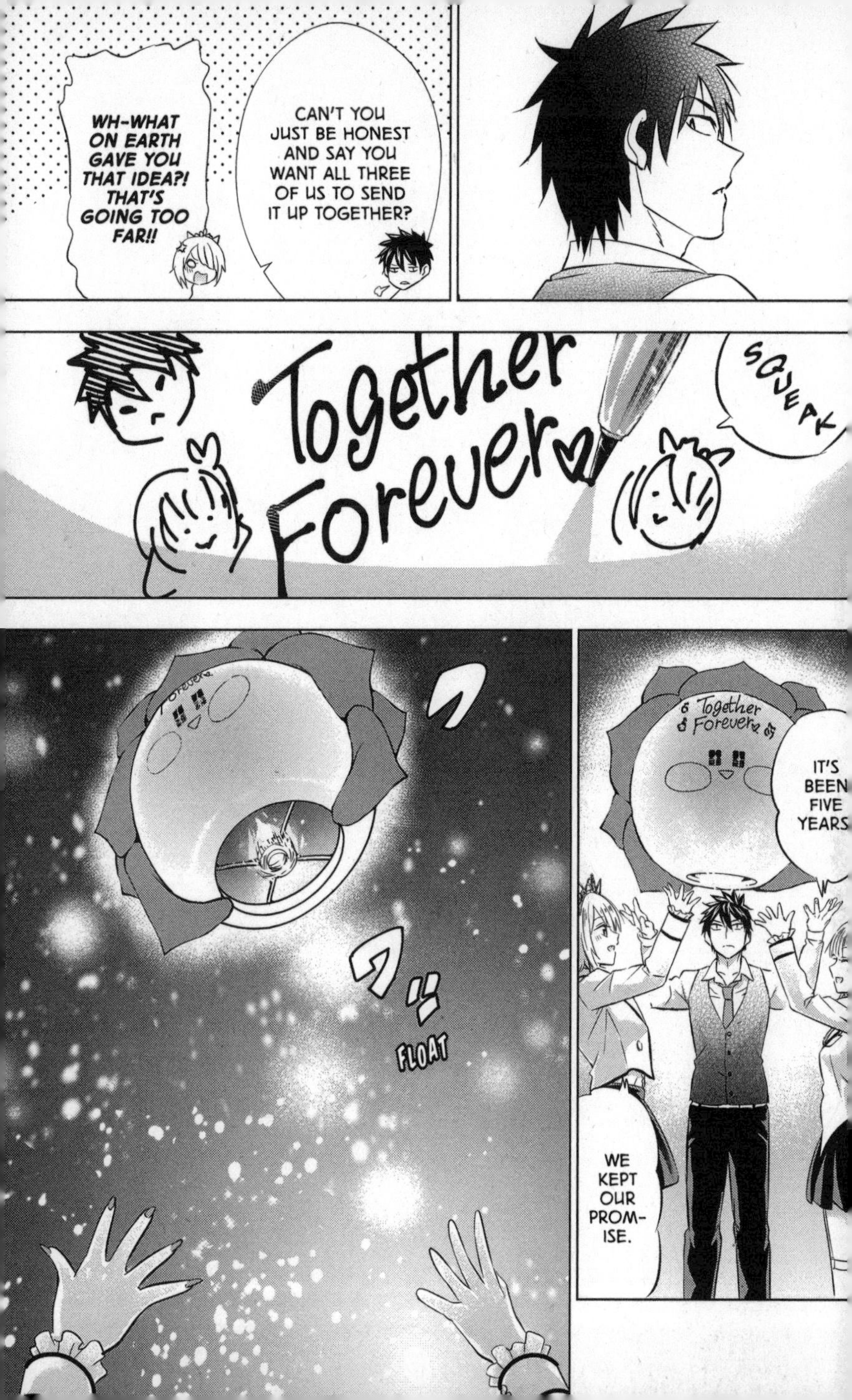
CAN'T YOU JUST BE HONEST AND SAY YOU WANT ALL THREE OF US TO SEND IT UP TOGETHER?
WH-WHAT ON EARTH GAVE YOU THAT IDEA?! THAT'S GOING TOO FAR!!
SQUEAK
Together Forever
Together Forever
IT'S BEEN FIVE YEARS
WE KEPT OUR PROM-ISE.
FLOAT

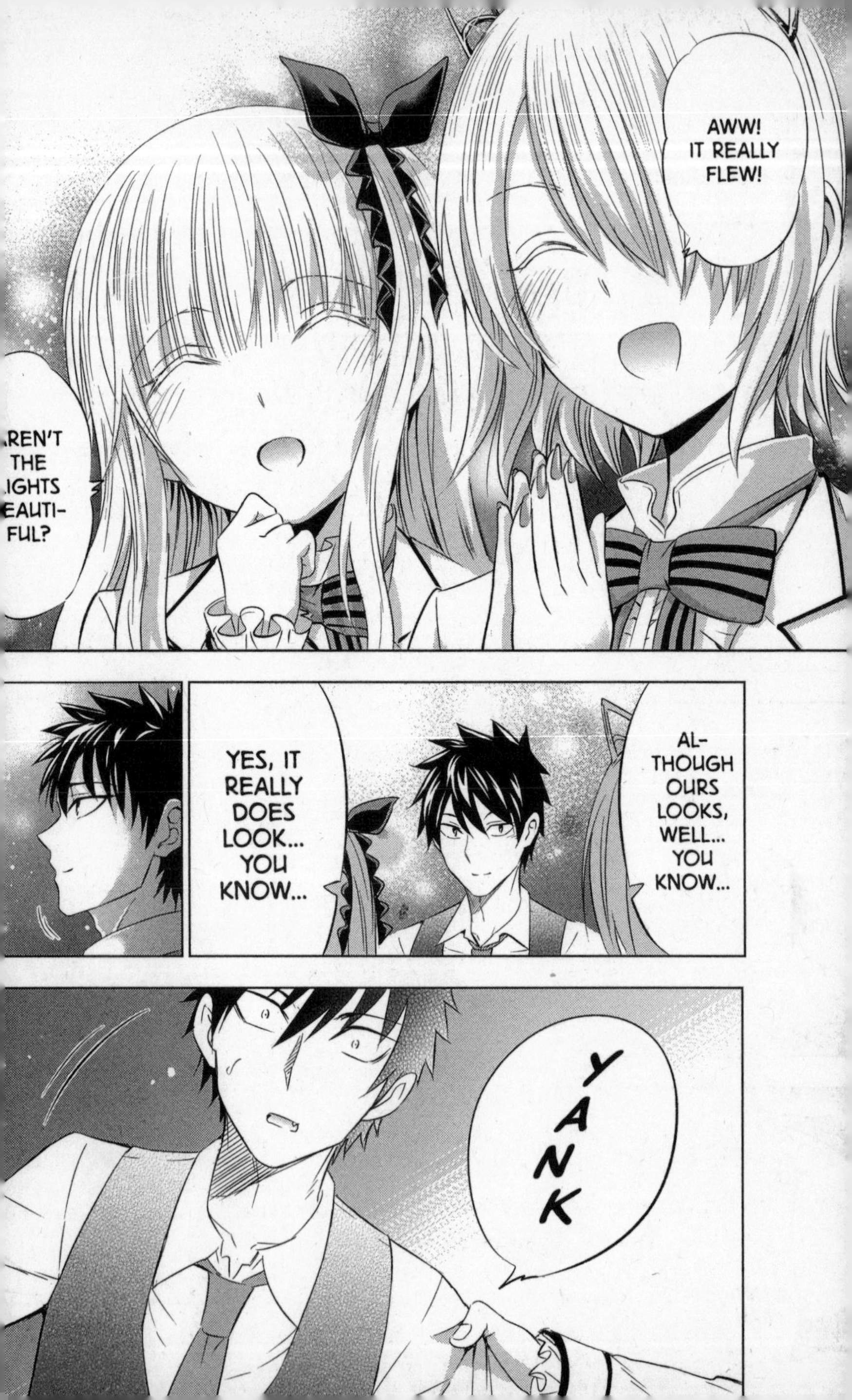
AWW! IT REALLY FLEW!
REN'T THE IGHTS EAUTI-FUL?
AL-THOUGH OURS LOOKS, WELL... YOU KNOW...
YES, IT REALLY DOES LOOK... YOU KNOW...
YANK

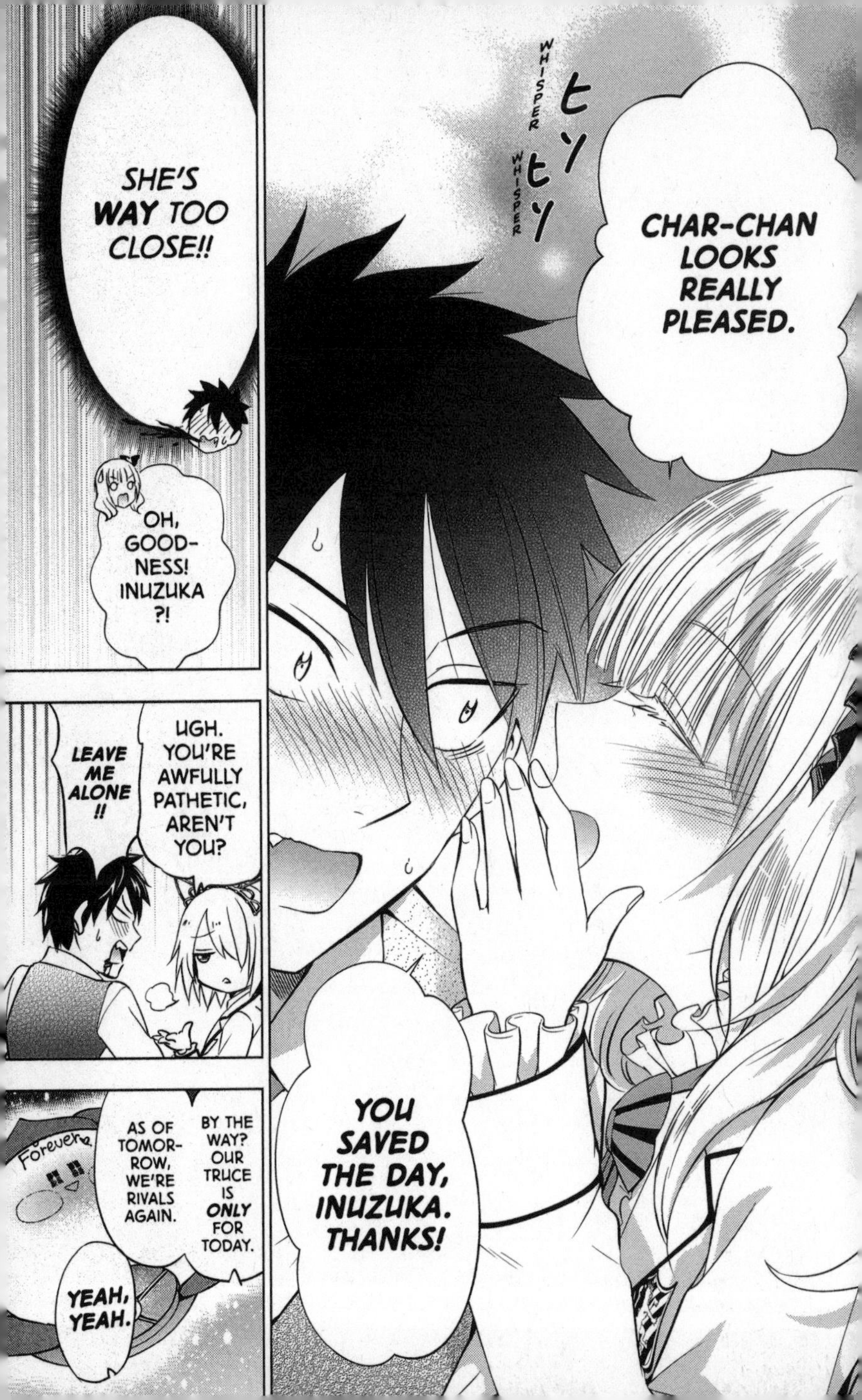
CHAR-CHAN LOOKS REALLY PLEASED.
ヒソヒソ WHISPER WHISPER
YOU SAVED THE DAY, INUZUKA. THANKS!
SHE'S WAY TOO CLOSE!!
OH, GOODNESS! INUZUKA?!
UGH. YOU'RE AWFULLY PATHETIC, AREN'T YOU?
LEAVE ME ALONE!!
BY THE WAY? OUR TRUCE IS ONLY FOR TODAY.
AS OF TOMORROW, WE'RE RIVALS AGAIN.
YEAH, YEAH.

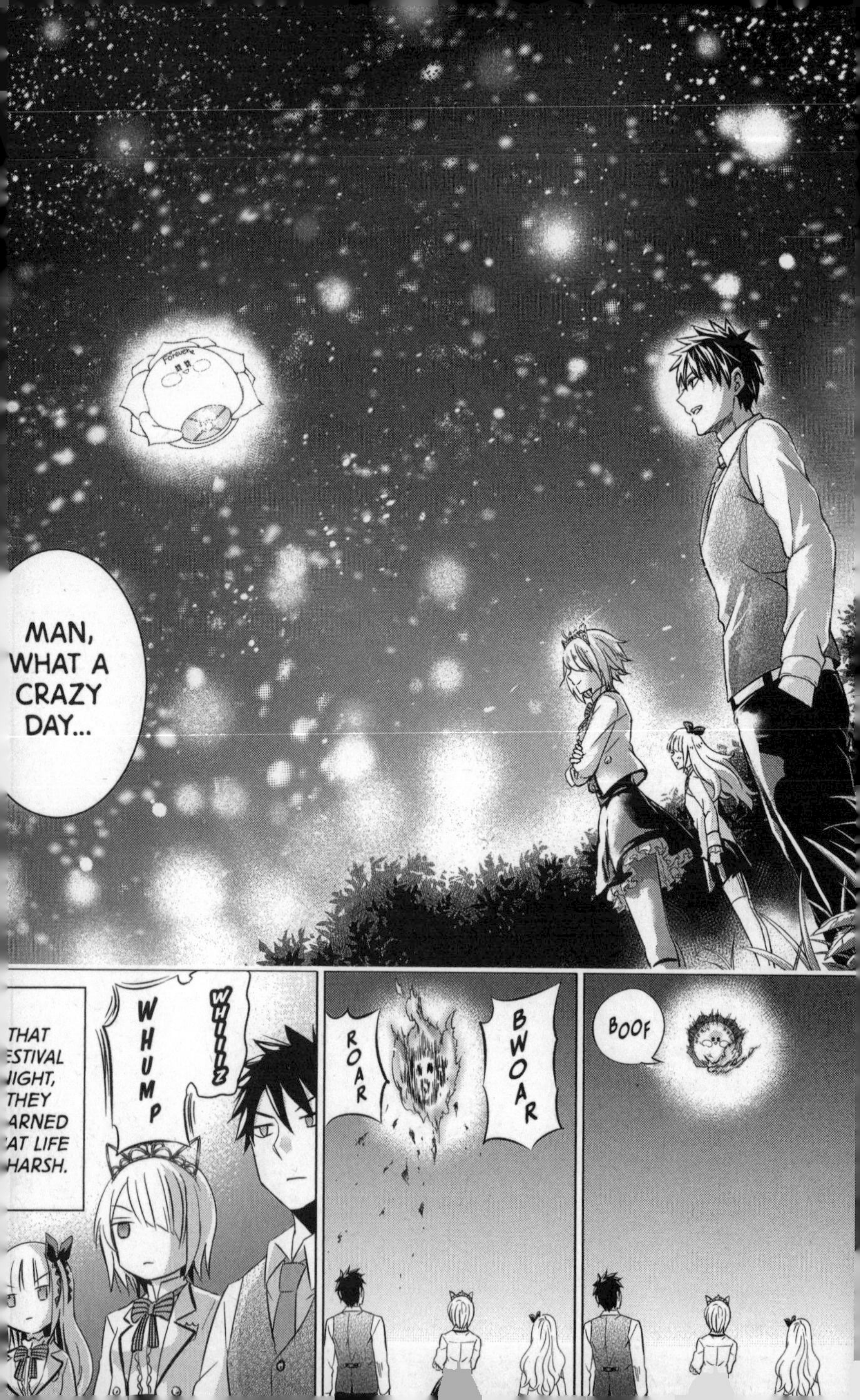
MAN, WHAT A CRAZY DAY...
BOOF
BWOAR
ROAR
WHIIIZ
WHUMP
THAT
ESTIVAL
IGHT,
THEY
ARNED
AT LIFE
HARSH.

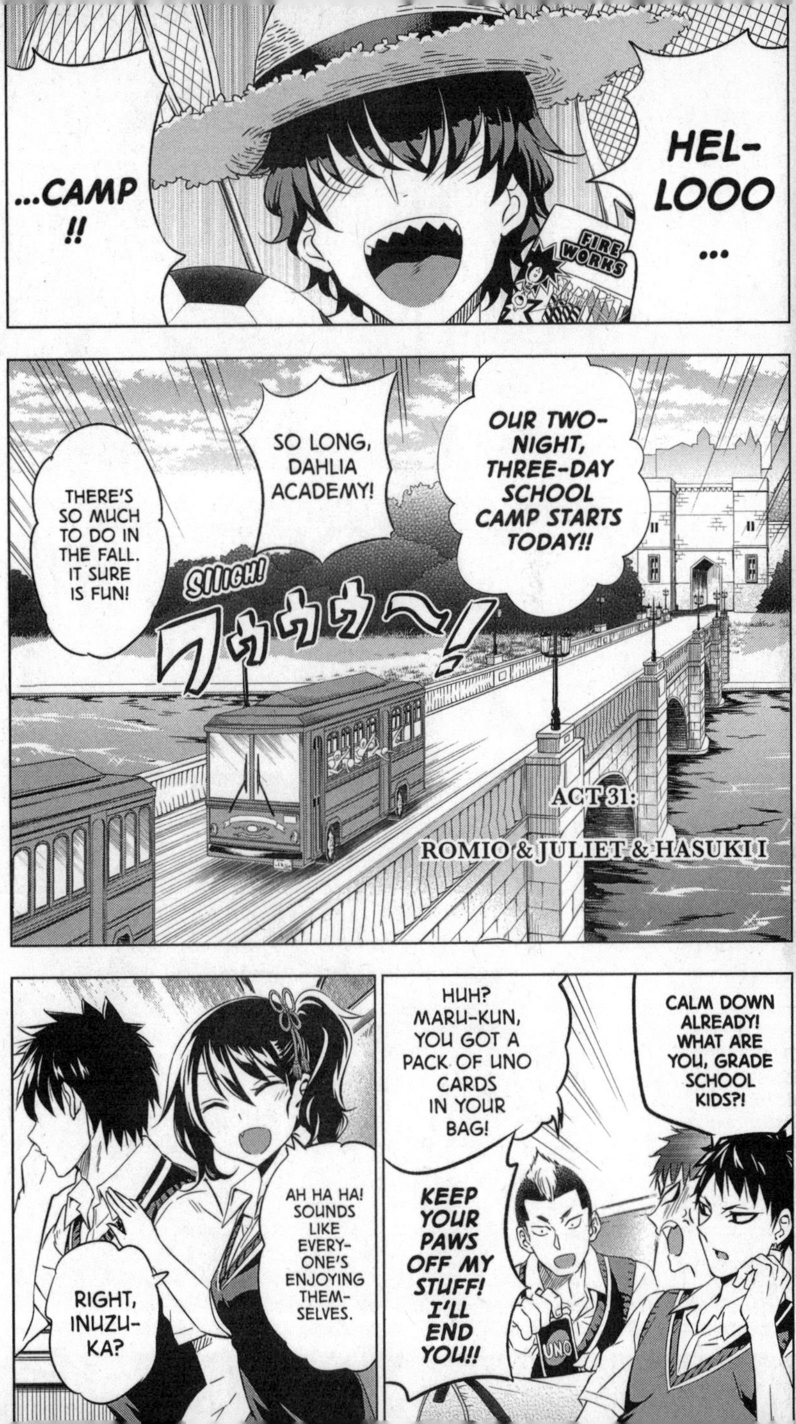
HEL-LOOO...
...CAMP!!
FIRE WORKS
OUR TWO-NIGHT, THREE-DAY SCHOOL CAMP STARTS TODAY!!
SO LONG, DAHLIA ACADEMY!
THERE'S SO MUCH TO DO IN THE FALL. IT SURE IS FUN!
SIIIGH!
フゥゥゥ〜!
ACT 31:
ROMIO & JULIET & HASUKI I
CALM DOWN ALREADY! WHAT ARE YOU, GRADE SCHOOL KIDS?!
HUH? MARU-KUN, YOU GOT A PACK OF UNO CARDS IN YOUR BAG!
KEEP YOUR PAWS OFF MY STUFF! I'LL END YOU!!
UNO
AH HA HA! SOUNDS LIKE EVERY-ONE'S ENJOYING THEM-SELVES.
RIGHT, INUZU-KA?

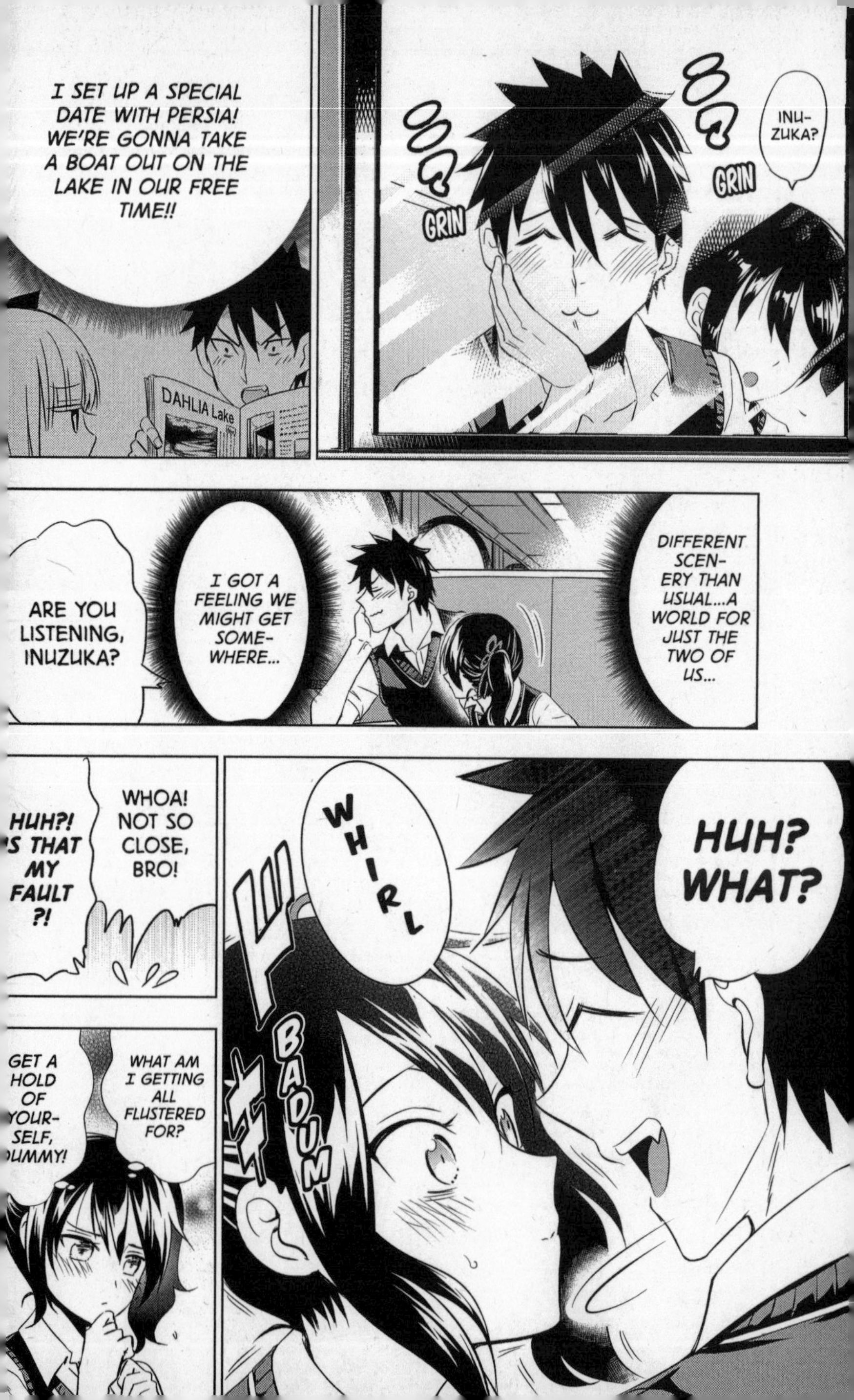
INU-ZUKA?
GRIN
GRIN
I SET UP A SPECIAL DATE WITH PERSIA! WE'RE GONNA TAKE A BOAT OUT ON THE LAKE IN OUR FREE TIME!!
DAHLIA Lake
DIFFERENT SCEN-ERY THAN USUAL...A WORLD FOR JUST THE TWO OF US...
I GOT A FEELING WE MIGHT GET SOME-WHERE...
ARE YOU LISTENING, INUZUKA?
HUH? WHAT?
WHIRL
BADUM
WHOA! NOT SO CLOSE, BRO!
HUH?! 'S THAT MY FAULT ?!
WHAT AM I GETTING ALL FLUSTERED FOR?
GET A HOLD OF YOUR-SELF, UMMY!

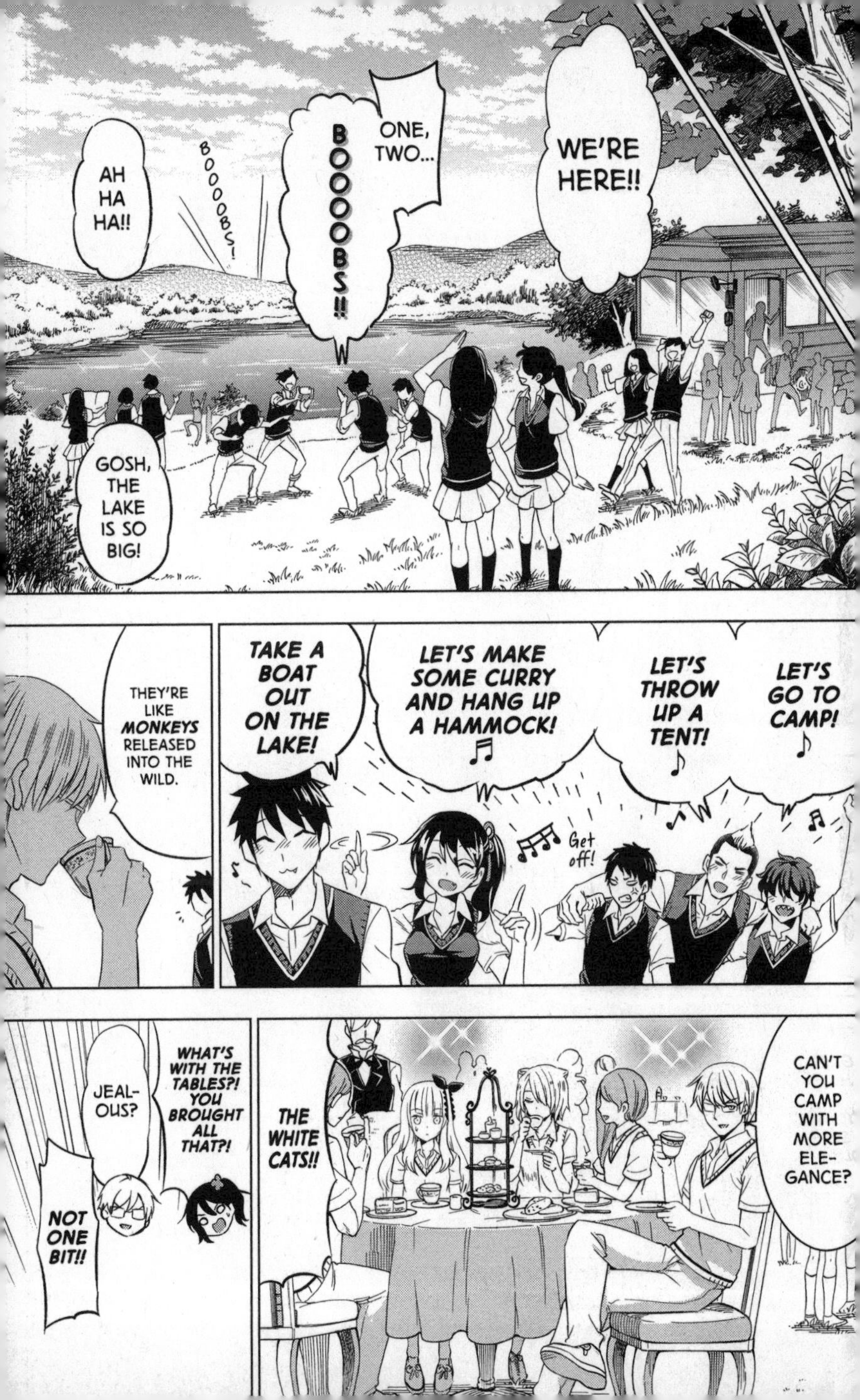
WE'RE HERE!!
ONE, TWO...
BOOOOOBS!!
BOOOOOBS!
AH HA HA!!
GOSH, THE LAKE IS SO BIG!
LET'S GO TO CAMP! ♪
LET'S THROW UP A TENT! ♪
LET'S MAKE SOME CURRY AND HANG UP A HAMMOCK! ♬
TAKE A BOAT OUT ON THE LAKE!
Get off!
THEY'RE LIKE MONKEYS RELEASED INTO THE WILD.
CAN'T YOU CAMP WITH MORE ELE-GANCE?
THE WHITE CATS!!
WHAT'S WITH THE TABLES?! YOU BROUGHT ALL THAT?!
JEAL-OUS?
NOT ONE BIT!!

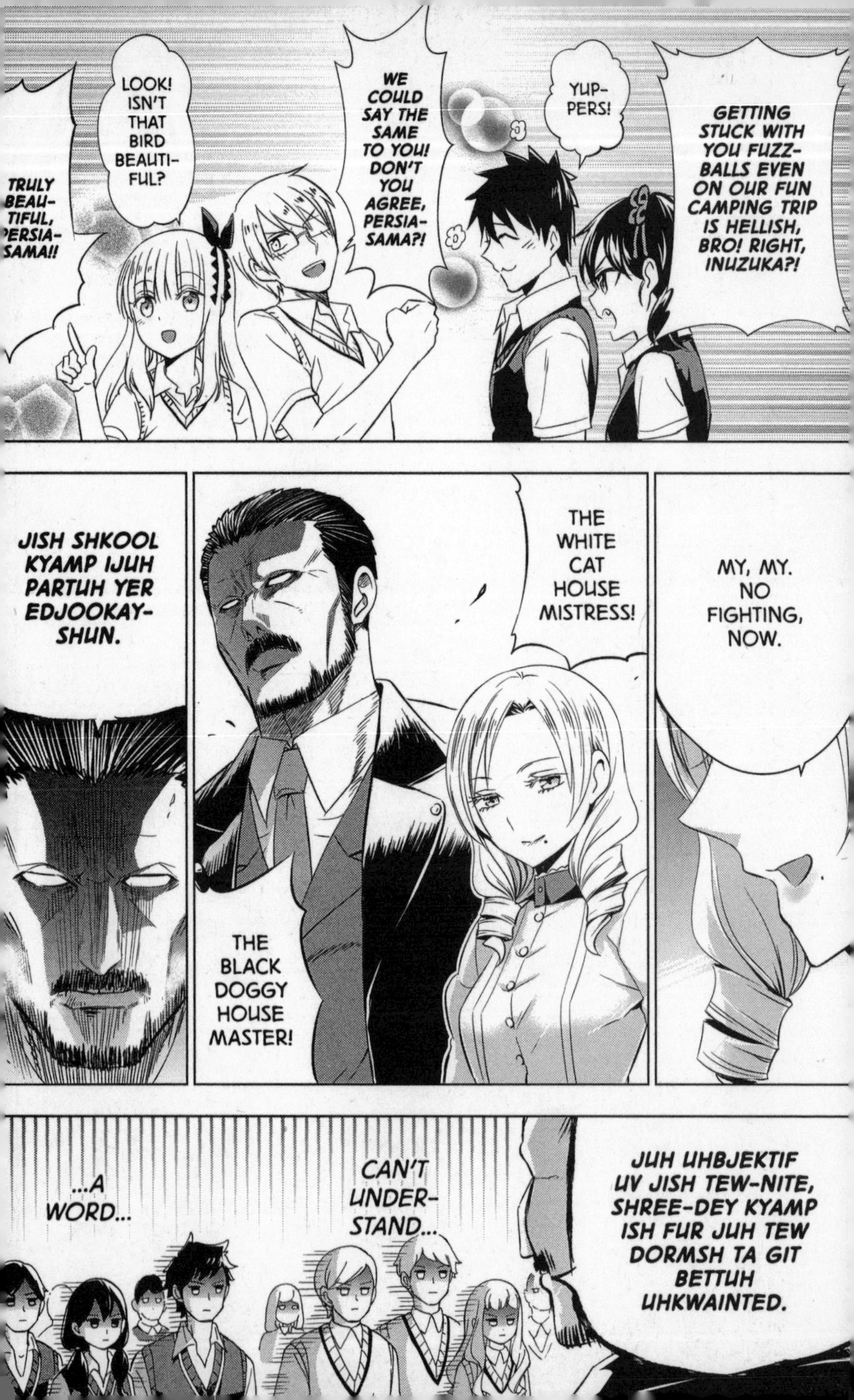
GETTING STUCK WITH YOU FUZZBALLS EVEN ON OUR FUN CAMPING TRIP IS HELLISH, BRO! RIGHT, INUZUKA?!
YUPPERS!
WE COULD SAY THE SAME TO YOU! DON'T YOU AGREE, PERSIA-SAMA?!
LOOK! ISN'T THAT BIRD BEAUTIFUL?
TRULY BEAUTIFUL, ERSIA-SAMA!!
MY, MY. NO FIGHTING, NOW.
THE WHITE CAT HOUSE MISTRESS!
THE BLACK DOGGY HOUSE MASTER!
JISH SHKOOL KYAMP IJUH PARTUH YER EDJOOKAYSHUN.
JUH UHBJEKTIF UV JISH TEW-NITE, SHREE-DEY KYAMP ISH FUR JUH TEW DORMSH TA GIT BETTUH UHKWAINTED.
CAN'T UNDERSTAND...
...A WORD...

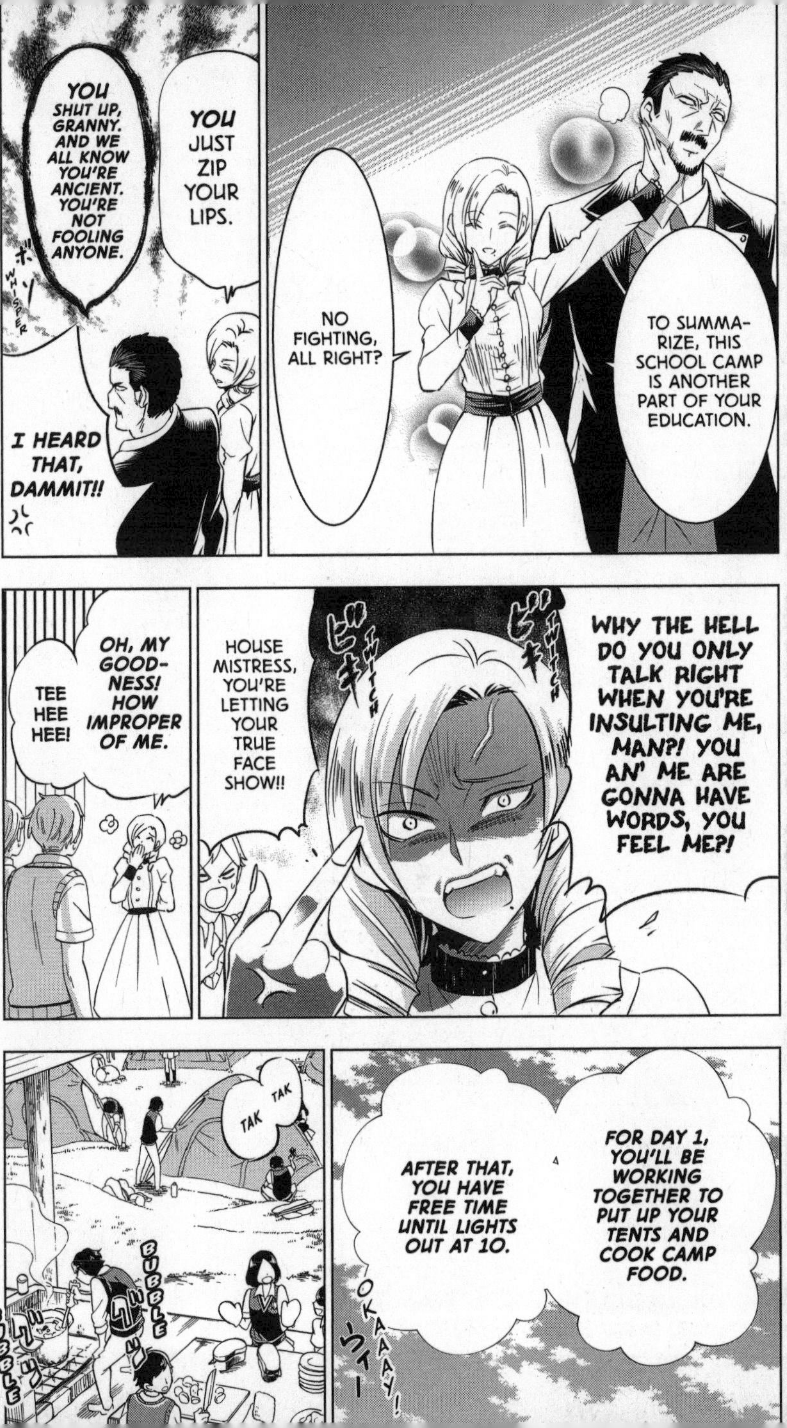
TO SUMMARIZE, THIS SCHOOL CAMP IS ANOTHER PART OF YOUR EDUCATION.
NO FIGHTING, ALL RIGHT?
YOU JUST ZIP YOUR LIPS.
YOU SHUT UP, GRANNY. AND WE ALL KNOW YOU'RE ANCIENT. YOU'RE NOT FOOLING ANYONE.
WHISPER
I HEARD THAT, DAMMIT!!
WHY THE HELL DO YOU ONLY TALK RIGHT WHEN YOU'RE INSULTING ME, MAN?! YOU AN' ME ARE GONNA HAVE WORDS, YOU FEEL ME?!
TWITCH
TWITCH
HOUSE MISTRESS, YOU'RE LETTING YOUR TRUE FACE SHOW!!
OH, MY GOODNESS! HOW IMPROPER OF ME.
TEE HEE HEE!
FOR DAY 1, YOU'LL BE WORKING TOGETHER TO PUT UP YOUR TENTS AND COOK CAMP FOOD.
AFTER THAT, YOU HAVE FREE TIME UNTIL LIGHTS OUT AT 10.
OKAAAY!
TAK TAK
BUBBLE
BUBBLE

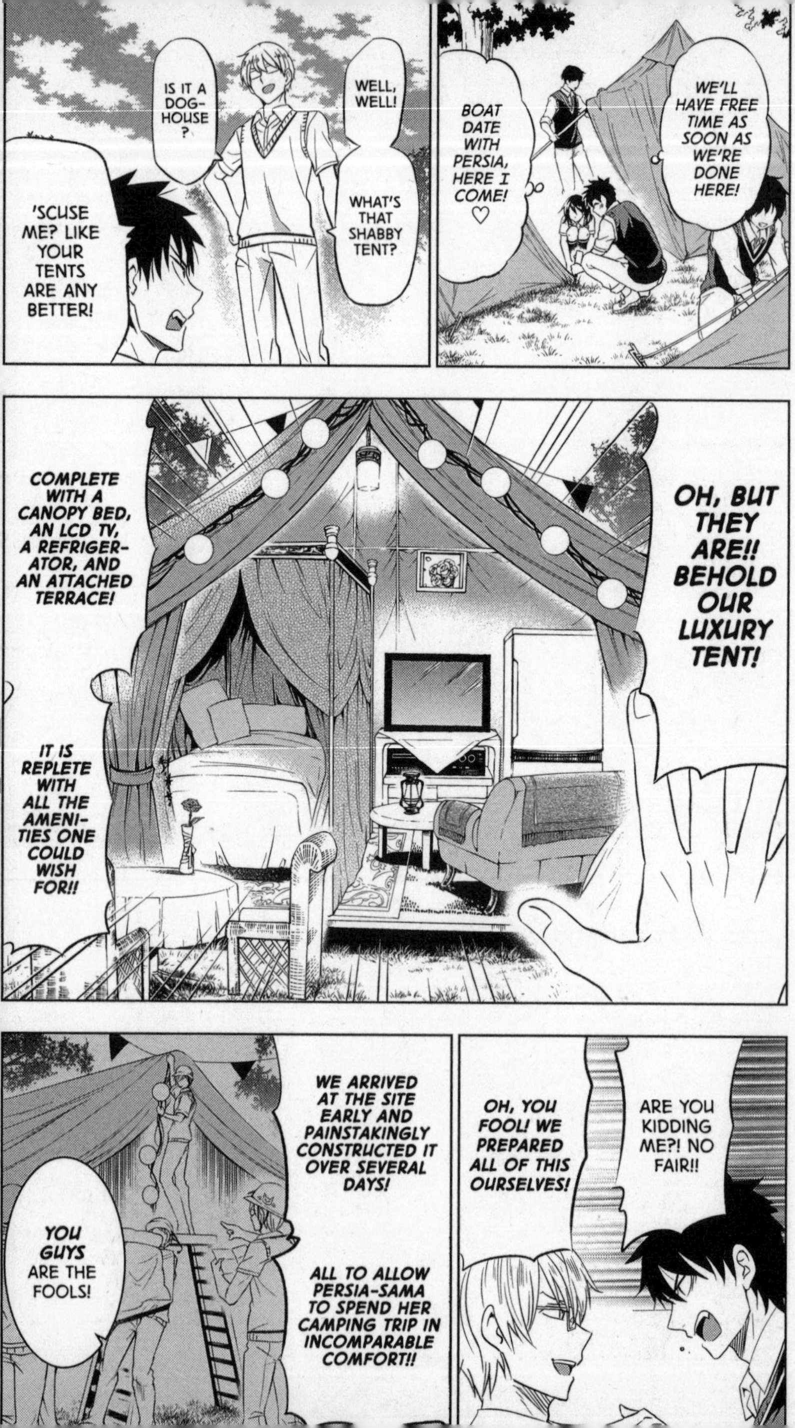
WE'LL HAVE FREE TIME AS SOON AS WE'RE DONE HERE!
BOAT DATE WITH PERSIA, HERE I COME! ♡
WELL, WELL!
WHAT'S THAT SHABBY TENT?
IS IT A DOG-HOUSE?
'SCUSE ME? LIKE YOUR TENTS ARE ANY BETTER!
OH, BUT THEY ARE!! BEHOLD OUR LUXURY TENT!
COMPLETE WITH A CANOPY BED, AN LCD TV, A REFRIGERATOR, AND AN ATTACHED TERRACE!
IT IS REPLETE WITH ALL THE AMENITIES ONE COULD WISH FOR!!
ARE YOU KIDDING ME?! NO FAIR!!
OH, YOU FOOL! WE PREPARED ALL OF THIS OURSELVES!
WE ARRIVED AT THE SITE EARLY AND PAINSTAKINGLY CONSTRUCTED IT OVER SEVERAL DAYS!
ALL TO ALLOW PERSIA-SAMA TO SPEND HER CAMPING TRIP IN INCOMPARABLE COMFORT!!
YOU GUYS ARE THE FOOLS!

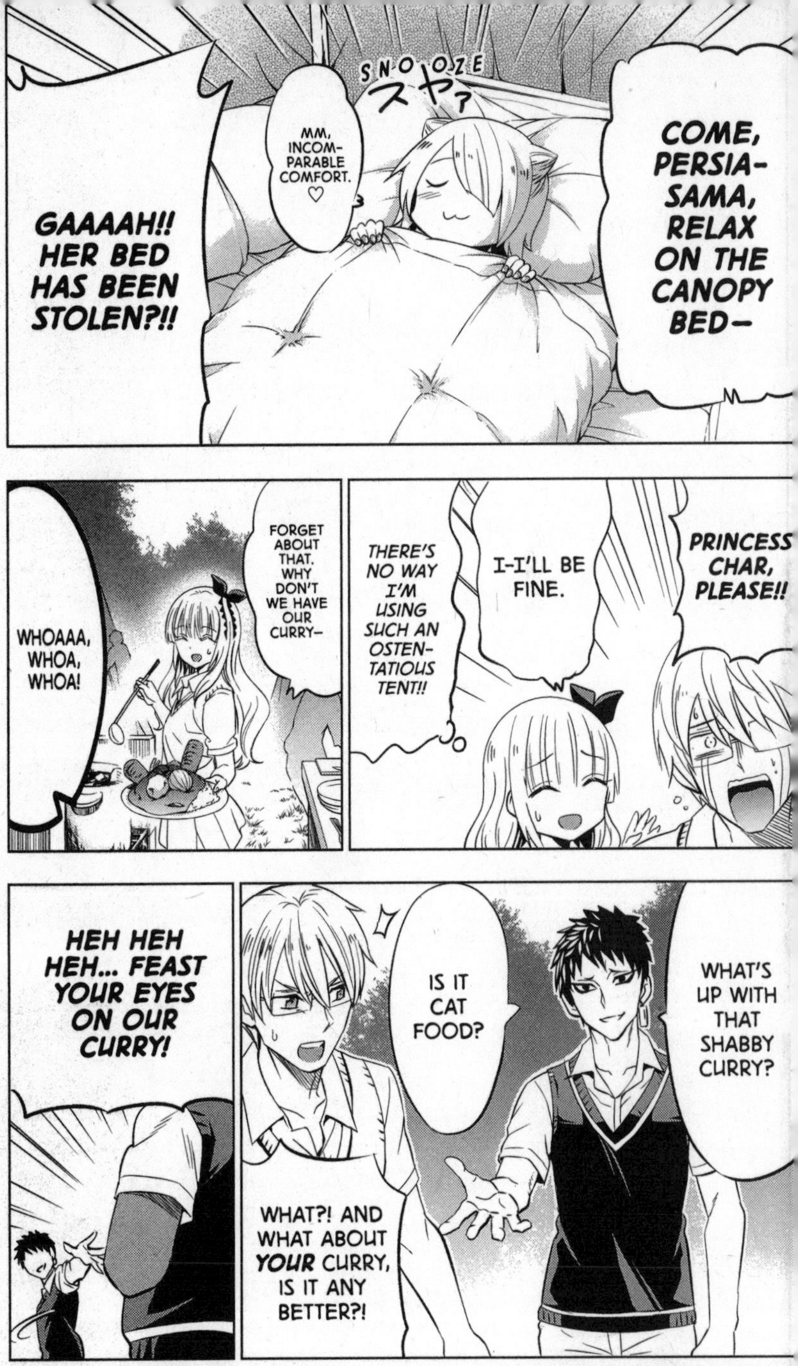
COME, PERSIA-SAMA, RELAX ON THE CANOPY BED—
SNOOZE
スヤァ
MM, INCOMPARABLE COMFORT. ♡
GAAAAH!! HER BED HAS BEEN STOLEN?!!
PRINCESS CHAR, PLEASE!!
I-I'LL BE FINE.
THERE'S NO WAY I'M USING SUCH AN OSTENTATIOUS TENT!!
FORGET ABOUT THAT. WHY DON'T WE HAVE OUR CURRY—
WHOAAA, WHOA, WHOA!
WHAT'S UP WITH THAT SHABBY CURRY?
IS IT CAT FOOD?
WHAT?! AND WHAT ABOUT YOUR CURRY, IS IT ANY BETTER?!
HEH HEH HEH... FEAST YOUR EYES ON OUR CURRY!

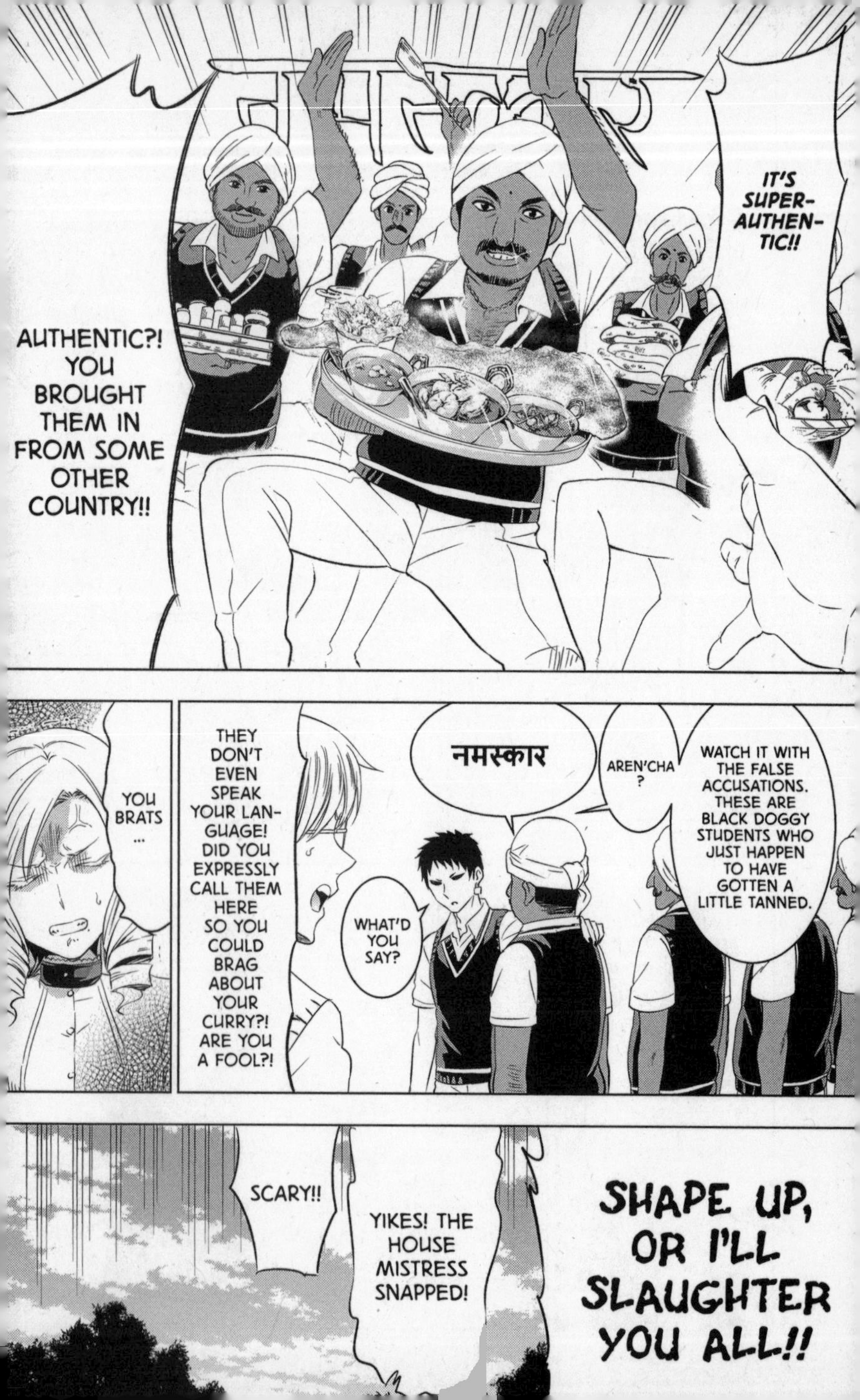

IT'S SUPER-AUTHENTIC!!
AUTHENTIC?! YOU BROUGHT THEM IN FROM SOME OTHER COUNTRY!!
WATCH IT WITH THE FALSE ACCUSATIONS. THESE ARE BLACK DOGGY STUDENTS WHO JUST HAPPEN TO HAVE GOTTEN A LITTLE TANNED.
AREN'CHA?
नमस्कार
THEY DON'T EVEN SPEAK YOUR LANGUAGE! DID YOU EXPRESSLY CALL THEM HERE SO YOU COULD BRAG ABOUT YOUR CURRY?! ARE YOU A FOOL?!
WHAT'D YOU SAY?
YOU BRATS...
SHAPE UP, OR I'LL SLAUGHTER YOU ALL!!
YIKES! THE HOUSE MISTRESS SNAPPED!
SCARY!!

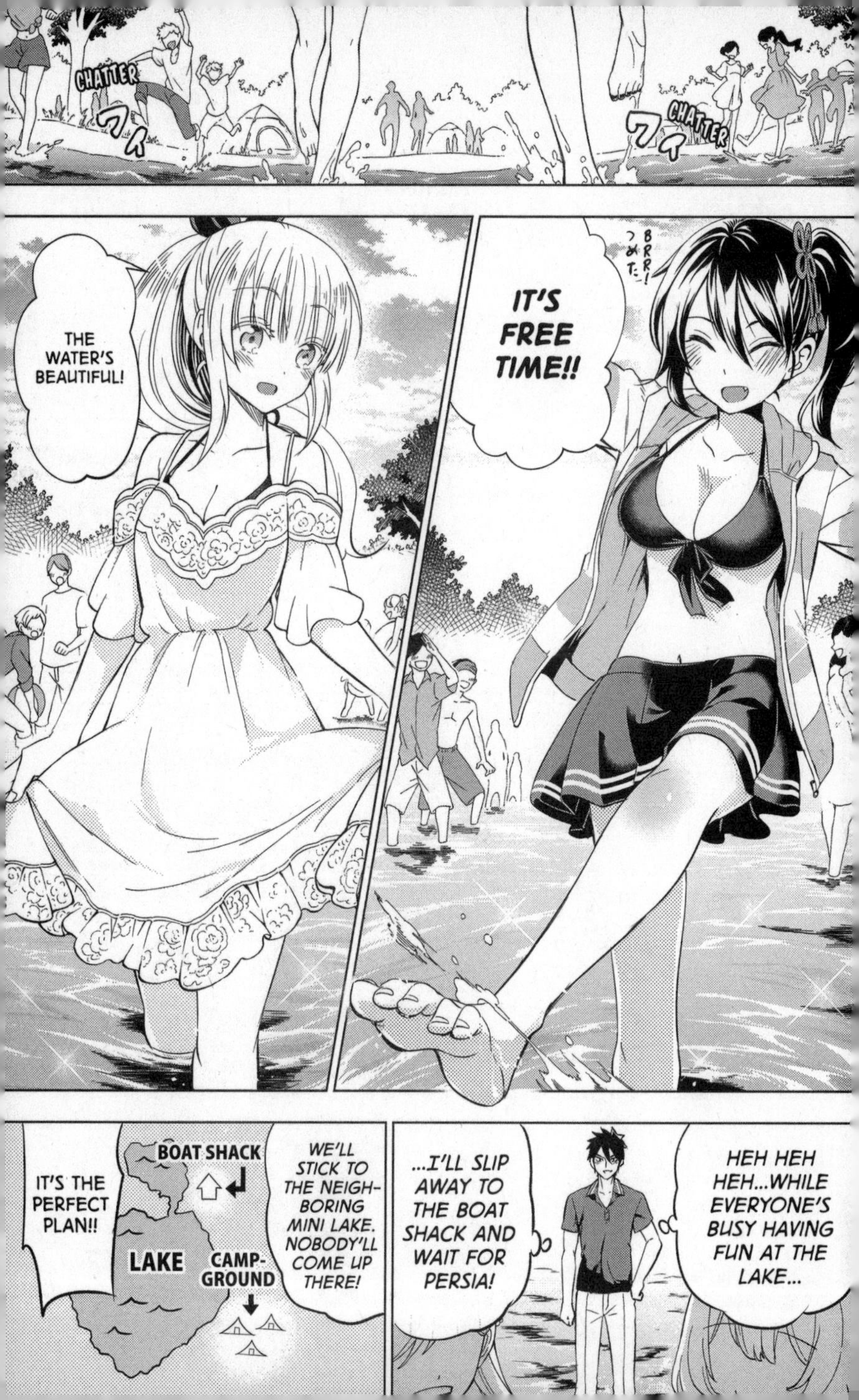
CHATTER
ワイ
CHATTER
ワイ
BRRR!
つめたー
IT'S FREE TIME!!
THE WATER'S BEAUTIFUL!
HEH HEH HEH...WHILE EVERYONE'S BUSY HAVING FUN AT THE LAKE...
...I'LL SLIP AWAY TO THE BOAT SHACK AND WAIT FOR PERSIA!
WE'LL STICK TO THE NEIGH-BORING MINI LAKE. NOBODY'LL COME UP THERE!
BOAT SHACK
LAKE
CAMP-GROUND
IT'S THE PERFECT PLAN!!

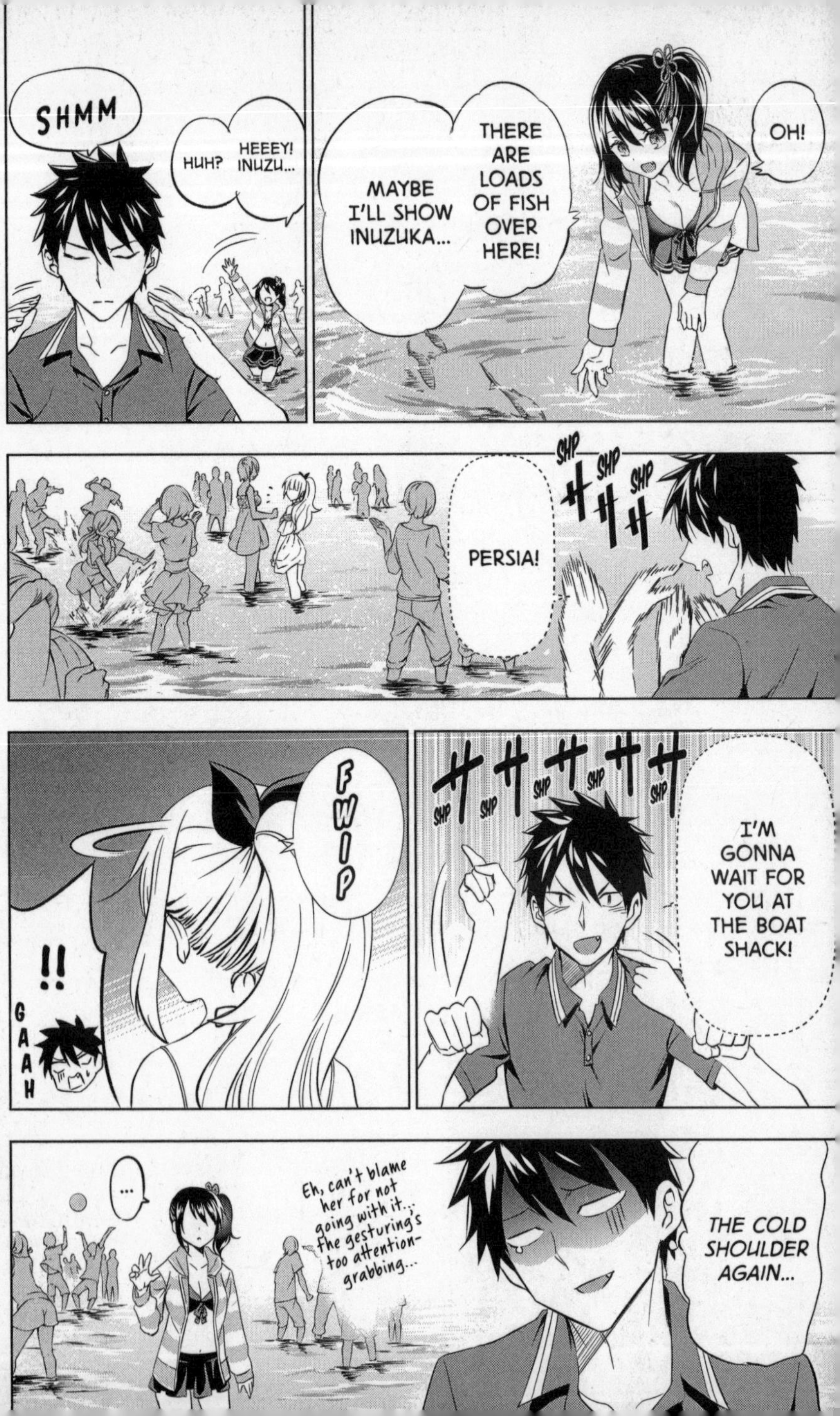
OH!
THERE ARE LOADS OF FISH OVER HERE!
MAYBE I'LL SHOW INUZUKA...
HEEEY! INUZU...
HUH?
SHMM
SHP SHP SHP
PERSIA!
I'M GONNA WAIT FOR YOU AT THE BOAT SHACK!
SHP SHP SHP SHP SHP
FWIP
!!
GAAH
THE COLD SHOULDER AGAIN...
Eh, can't blame her for not going with it... the gesturing's too attention-grabbing...
...

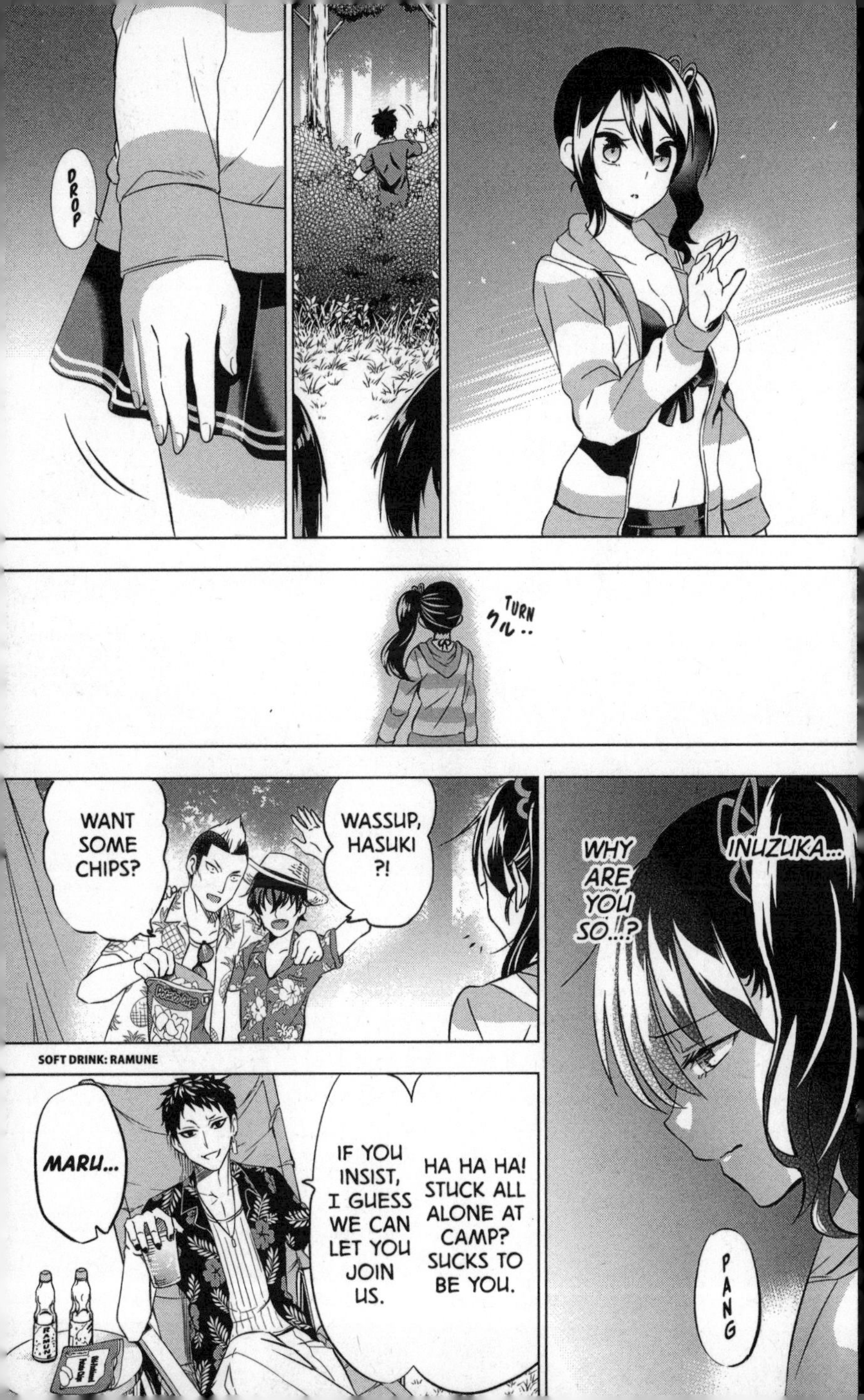
DROP
TURN
クル..
INUZUKA...
WHY ARE YOU SO...?
PANG
WASSUP, HASUKI ?!
WANT SOME CHIPS?
SOFT DRINK: RAMUNE
HA HA HA! STUCK ALL ALONE AT CAMP? SUCKS TO BE YOU.
IF YOU INSIST, I GUESS WE CAN LET YOU JOIN US.
MARU...

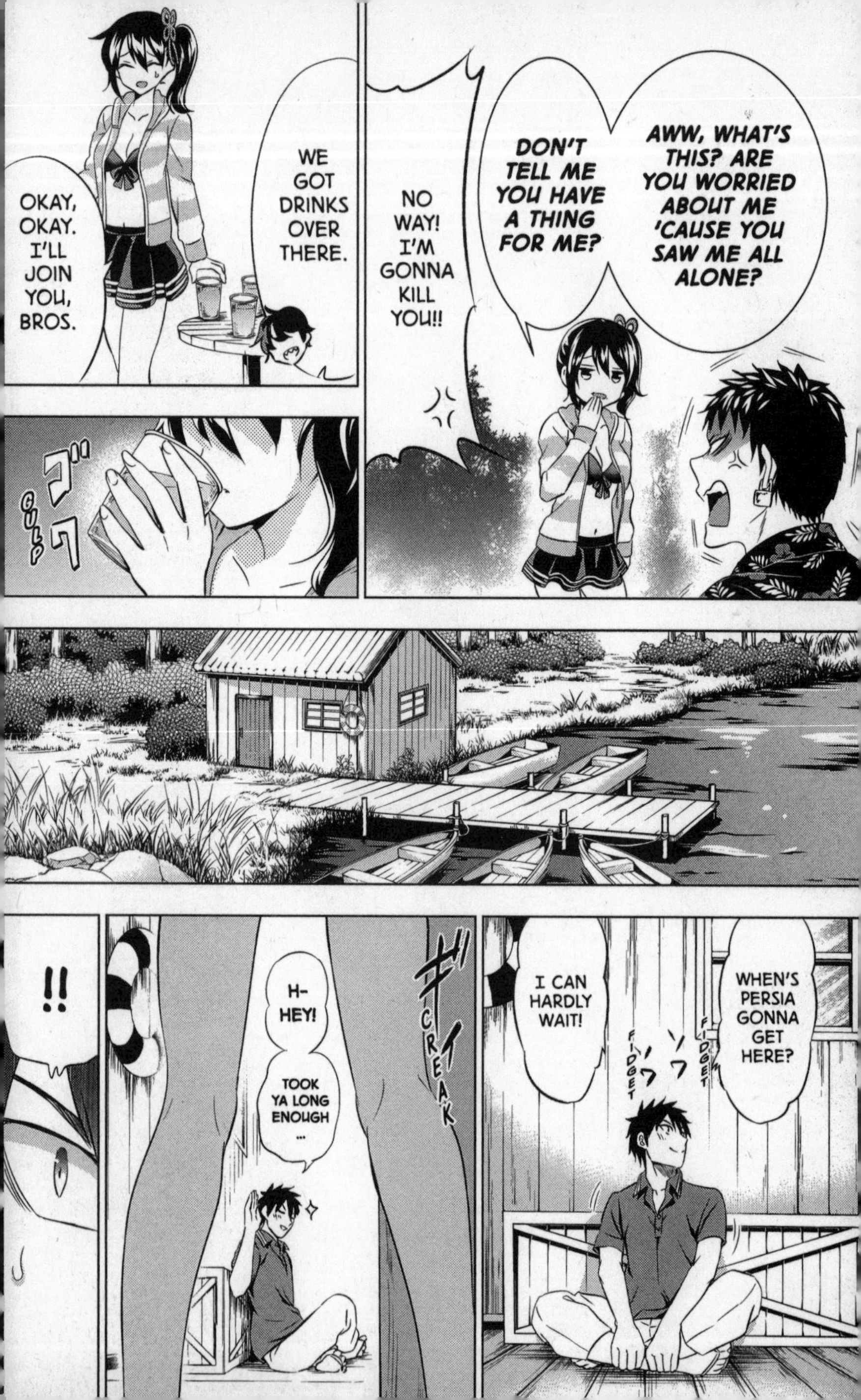
AWW, WHAT'S THIS? ARE YOU WORRIED ABOUT ME 'CAUSE YOU SAW ME ALL ALONE?
DON'T TELL ME YOU HAVE A THING FOR ME?
NO WAY! I'M GONNA KILL YOU!!
WE GOT DRINKS OVER THERE.
OKAY, OKAY. I'LL JOIN YOU, BROS.
GULP
WHEN'S PERSIA GONNA GET HERE?
FIDGET
FIDGET
I CAN HARDLY WAIT!
CREAK
H-HEY!
TOOK YA LONG ENOUGH...
!!

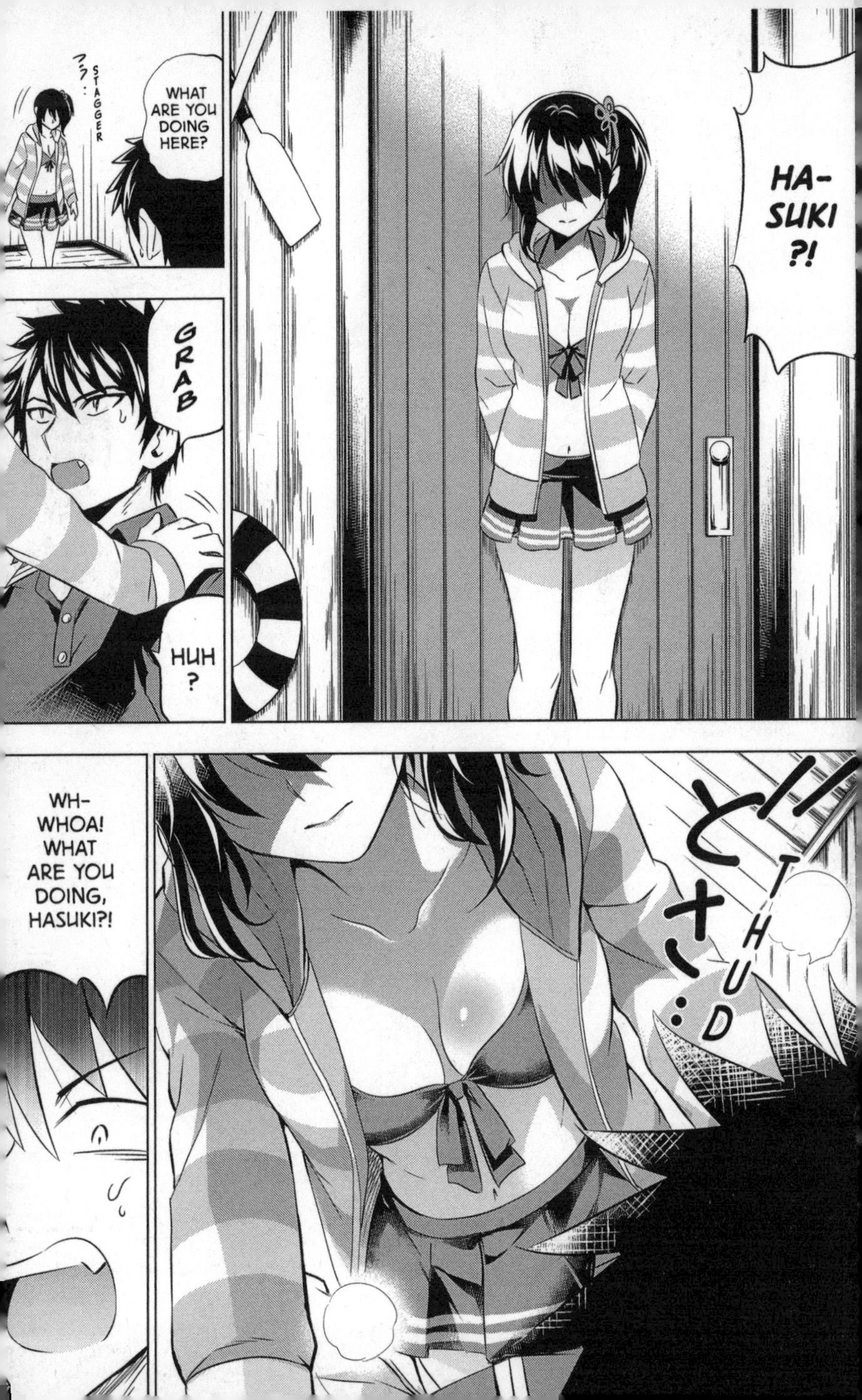
HA-SUKI?!
WHAT ARE YOU DOING HERE?
STAGGER
GRAB
HUH?
とさっ
THUD
WH-WHOA! WHAT ARE YOU DOING, HASUKI?!

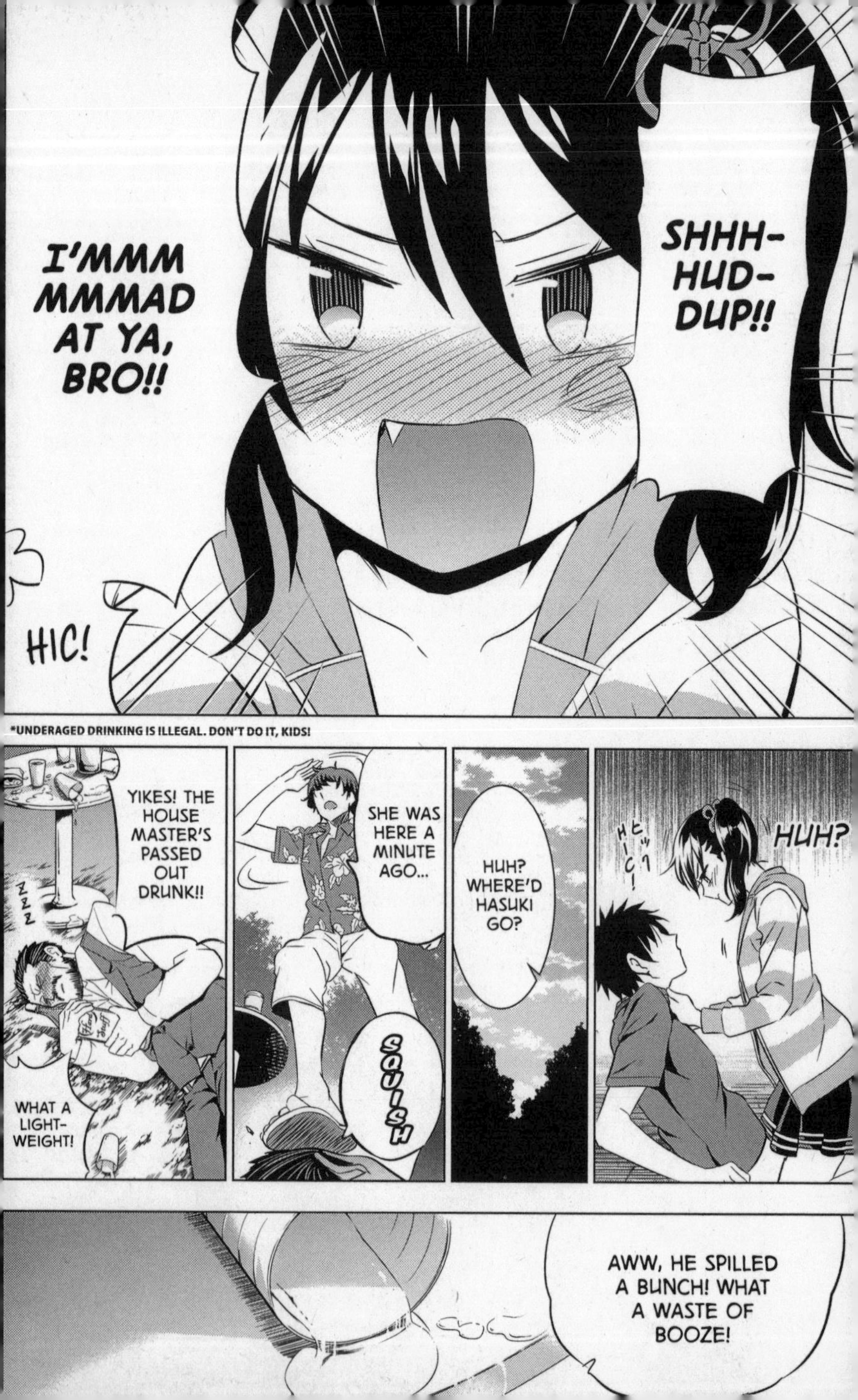
SHHH-HUD-DUP!!
I'MMM MMMAD AT YA, BRO!!
HIC!
HUH?
HIC!
HUH? WHERE'D HASUKI GO?
SHE WAS HERE A MINUTE AGO...
SQUISH
YIKES! THE HOUSE MASTER'S PASSED OUT DRUNK!!
ZZZ
WHAT A LIGHT-WEIGHT!
AWW, HE SPILLED A BUNCH! WHAT A WASTE OF BOOZE!
*UNDERAGED DRINKING IS ILLEGAL. DON'T DO IT, KIDS!

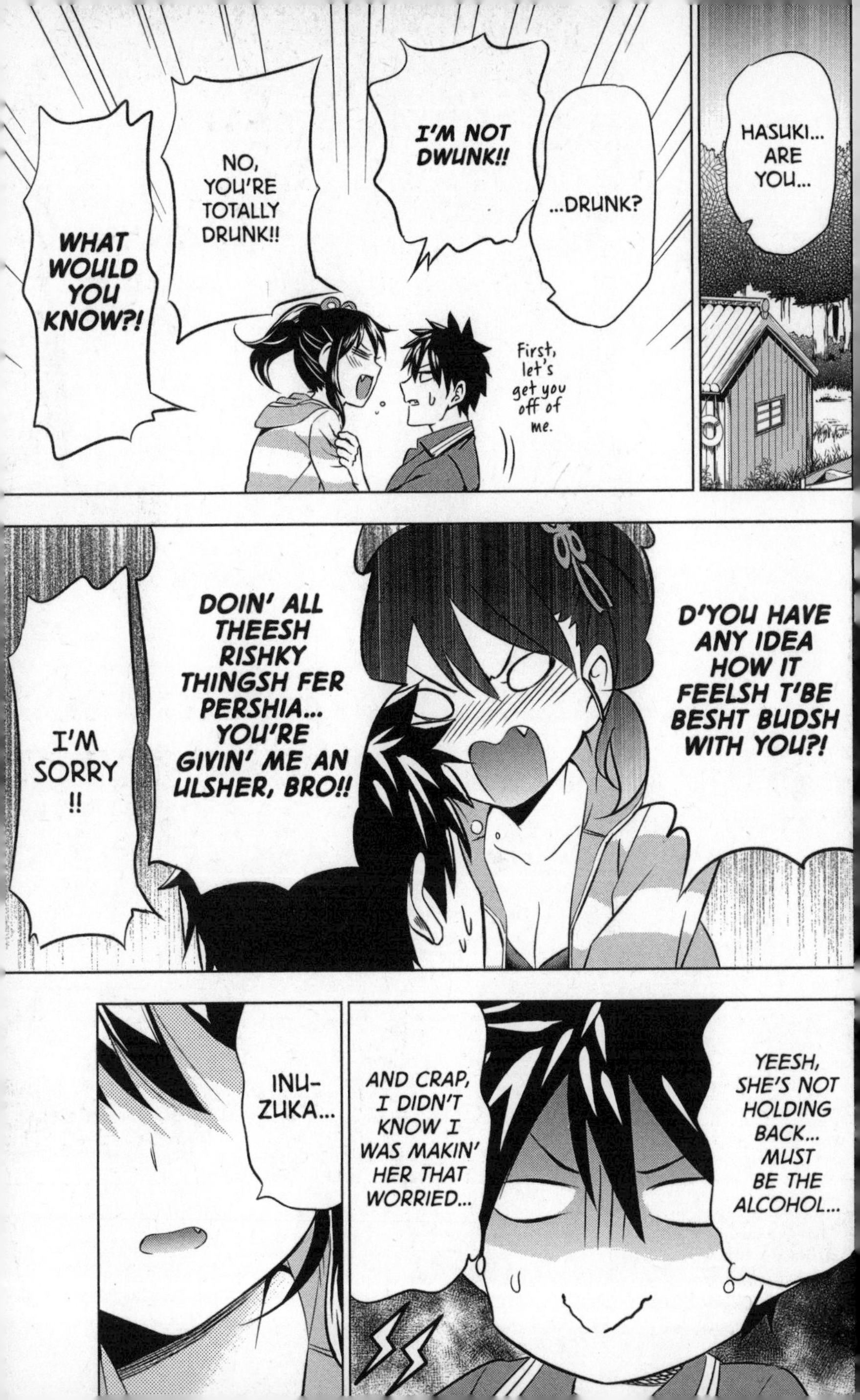
HASUKI... ARE YOU...
...DRUNK?
I'M NOT DWUNK!!
First, let's get you off of me.
NO, YOU'RE TOTALLY DRUNK!!
WHAT WOULD YOU KNOW?!
D'YOU HAVE ANY IDEA HOW IT FEELSH T'BE BESHT BUDSH WITH YOU?!
DOIN' ALL THEESH RISHKY THINGSH FER PERSHIA... YOU'RE GIVIN' ME AN ULSHER, BRO!!
I'M SORRY !!
YEESH, SHE'S NOT HOLDING BACK... MUST BE THE ALCOHOL...
AND CRAP, I DIDN'T KNOW I WAS MAKIN' HER THAT WORRIED...
INU-ZUKA...

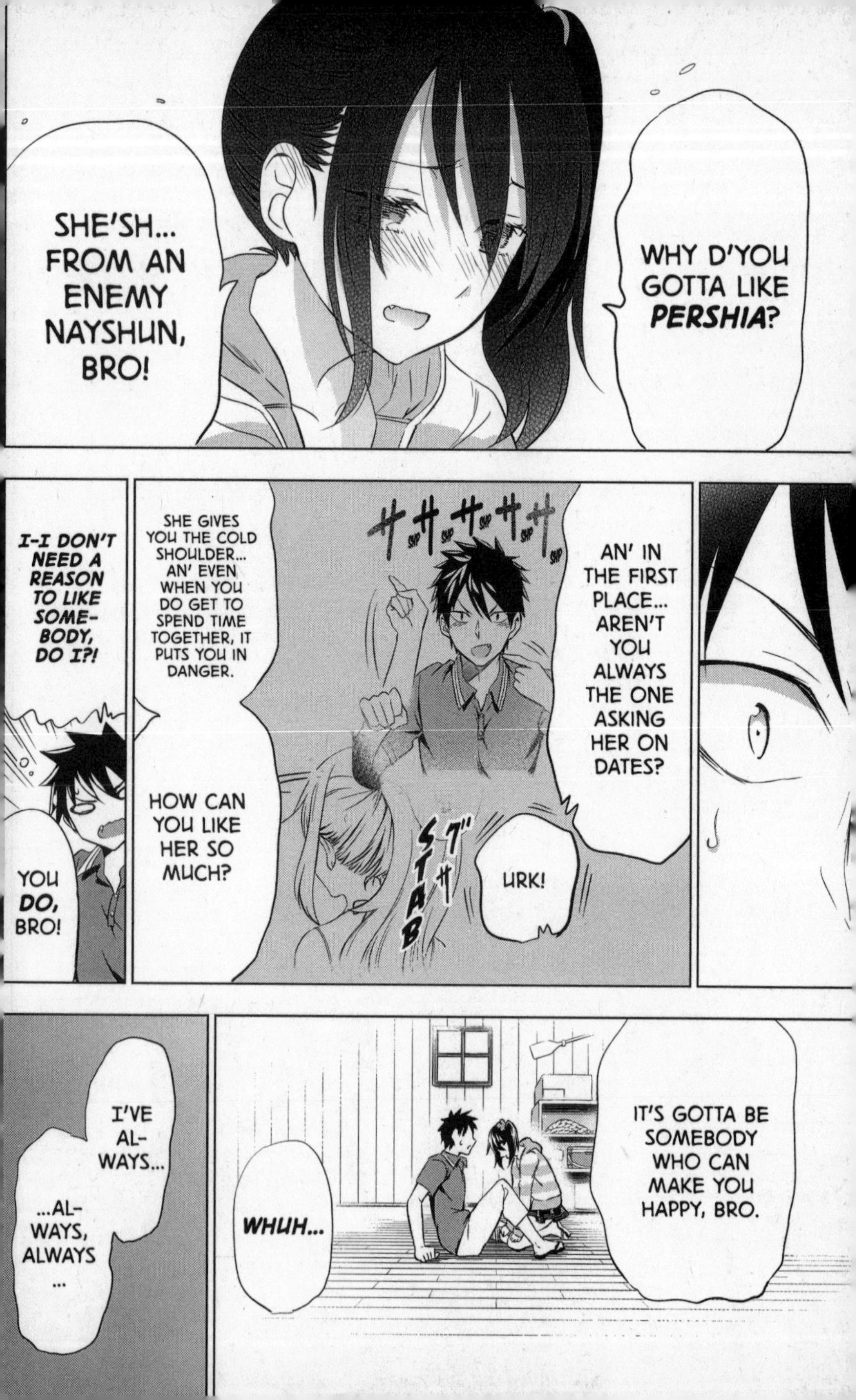
WHY D'YOU GOTTA LIKE *PERSHIA*?
SHE'SH... FROM AN ENEMY NAYSHUN, BRO!
AN' IN THE FIRST PLACE... AREN'T YOU ALWAYS THE ONE ASKING HER ON DATES?
SHP SHP SHP SHP SHP
SHE GIVES YOU THE COLD SHOULDER... AN' EVEN WHEN YOU DO GET TO SPEND TIME TOGETHER, IT PUTS YOU IN DANGER.
URK!
STAB
HOW CAN YOU LIKE HER SO MUCH?
I-I DON'T NEED A REASON TO LIKE SOME-BODY, DO I?!
YOU *DO,* BRO!
IT'S GOTTA BE SOMEBODY WHO CAN MAKE YOU HAPPY, BRO.
WHUH...
I'VE AL-WAYS...
...AL-WAYS, ALWAYS ...

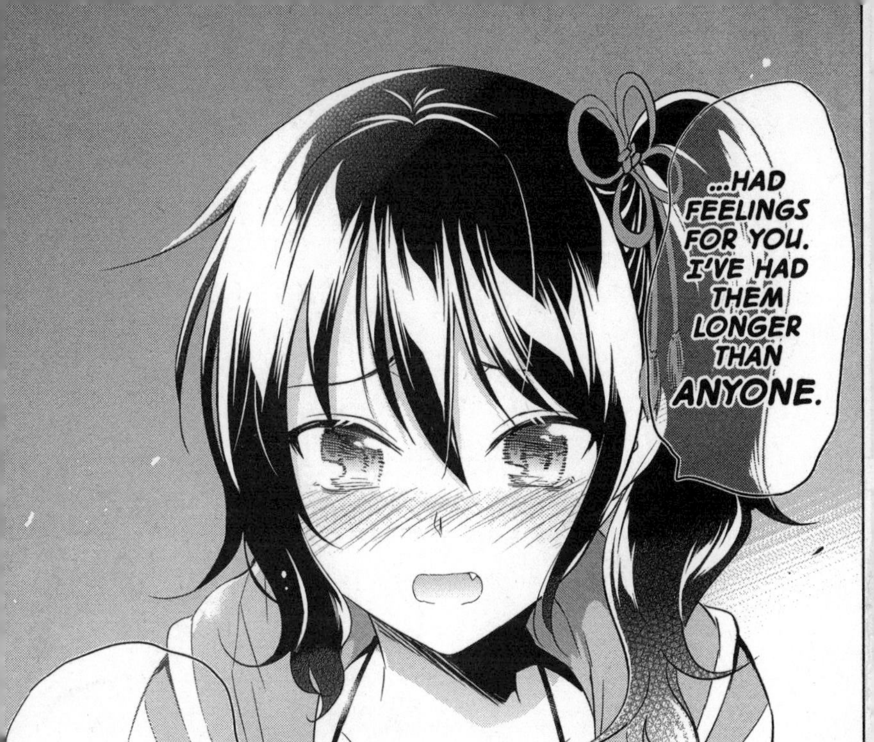
...HAD FEELINGS FOR YOU. I'VE HAD THEM LONGER THAN ANYONE.
THAT'S WHY I CAN'T... ACCEPT THINGS AS THEY ARE, BRO...

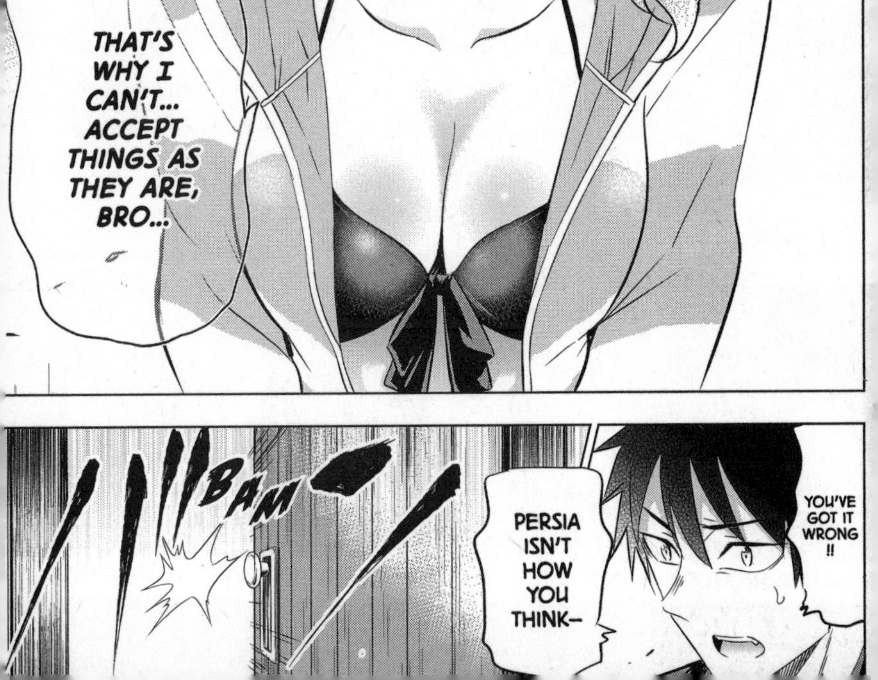
YOU'VE GOT IT WRONG !!
PERSIA ISN'T HOW YOU THINK–
BAM

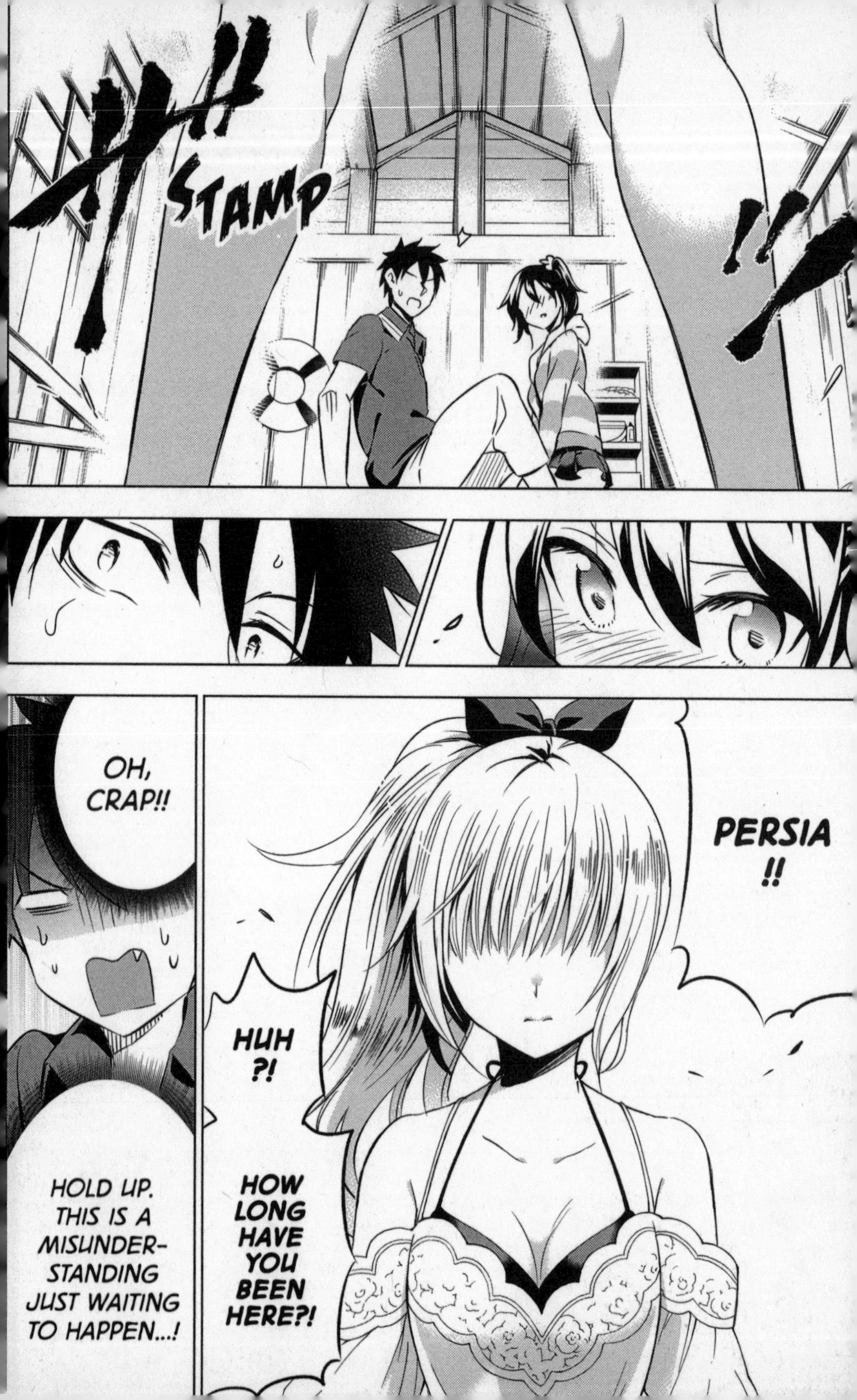
STAMP
PERSIA !!
HUH ?!
HOW LONG HAVE YOU BEEN HERE?!
OH, CRAP!!
HOLD UP. THIS IS A MISUNDER-STANDING JUST WAITING TO HAPPEN...!

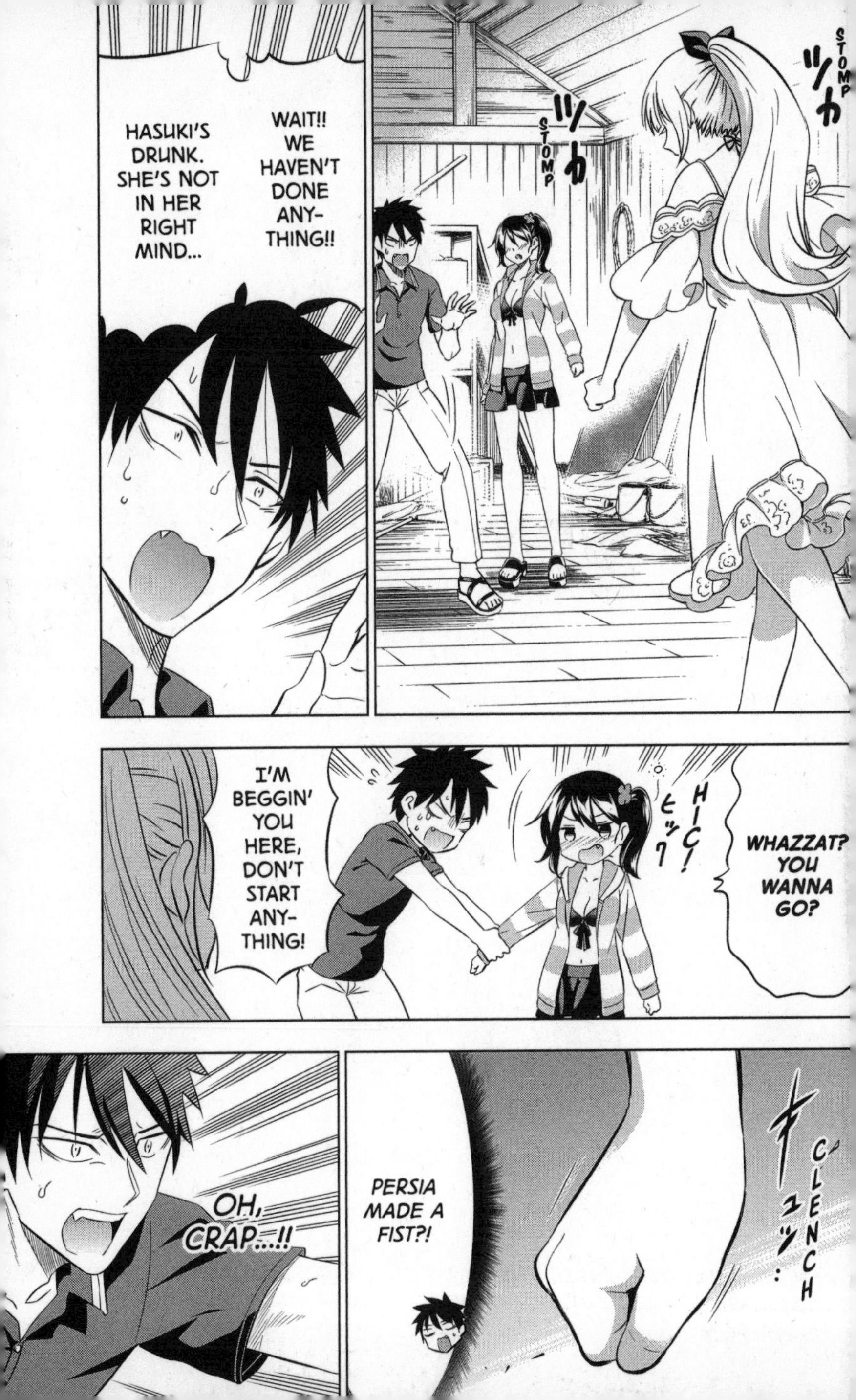
ツカ
STOMP
ツカ
STOMP
WAIT!! WE HAVEN'T DONE ANYTHING!!
HASUKI'S DRUNK. SHE'S NOT IN HER RIGHT MIND...
WHAZZAT? YOU WANNA GO?
ヒック
HIC!
I'M BEGGIN' YOU HERE, DON'T START ANYTHING!
ギュッ
CLENCH
PERSIA MADE A FIST?!
OH, CRAP...!!

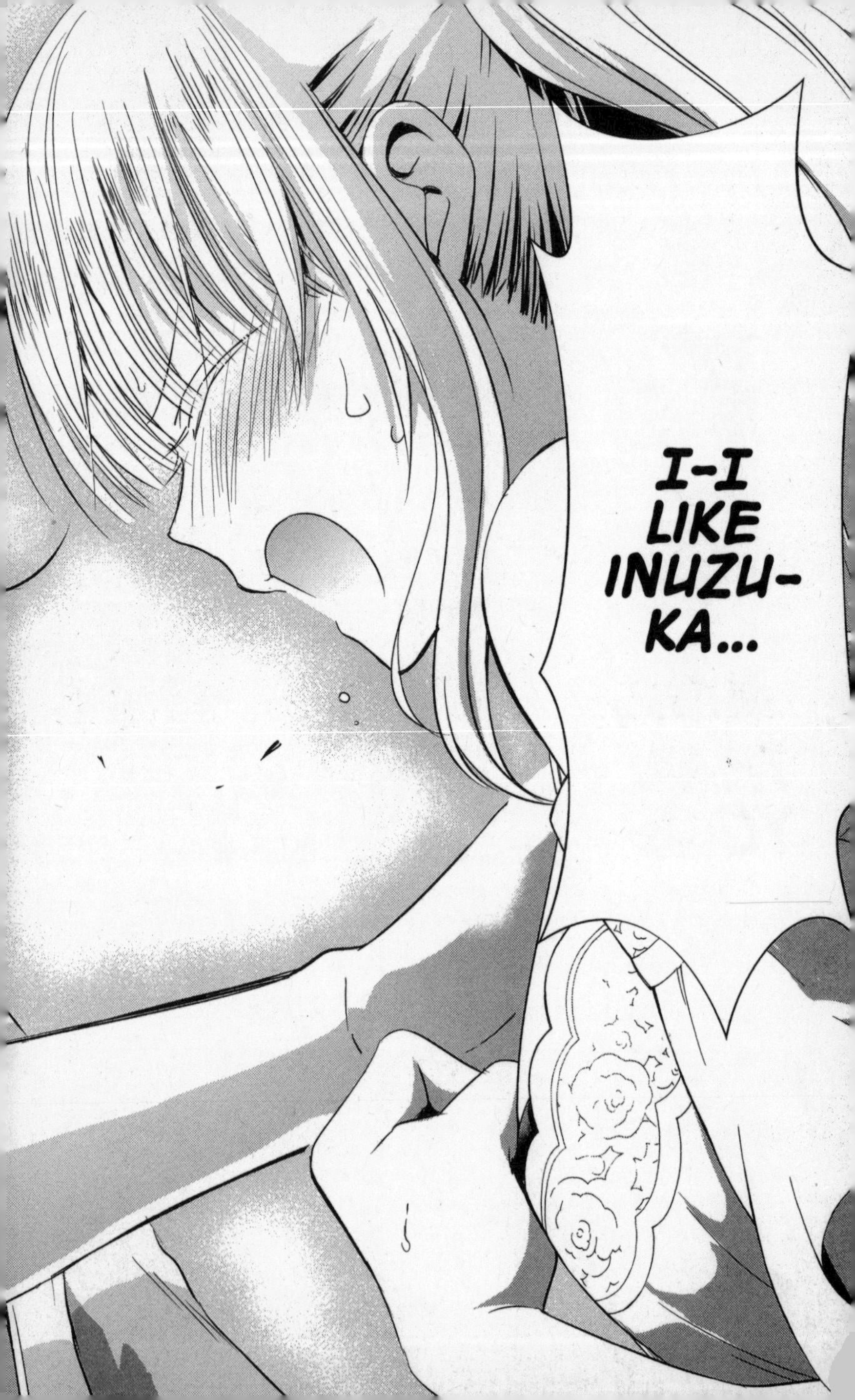
I-I LIKE INUZUKA...

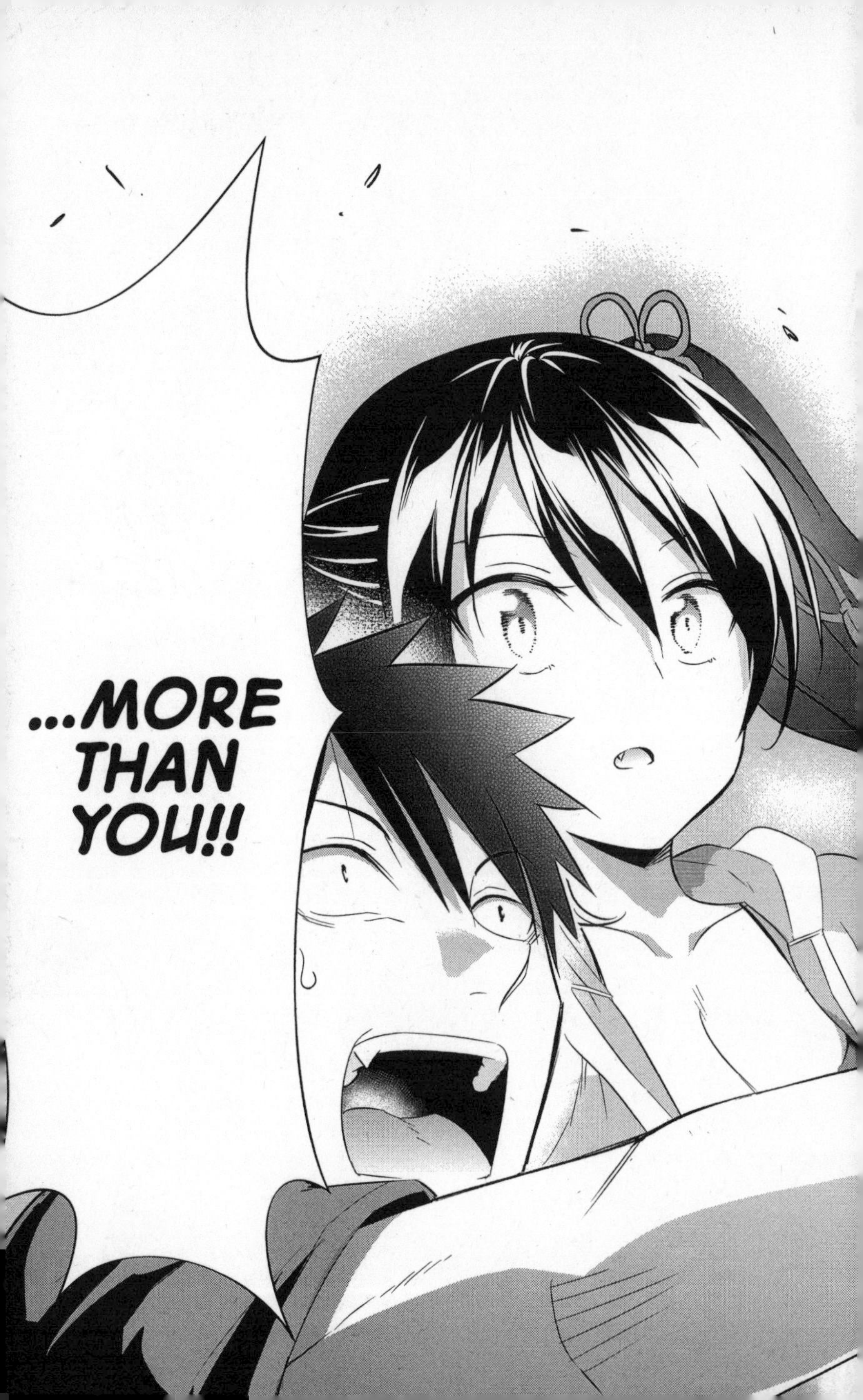
...MORE THAN YOU!!

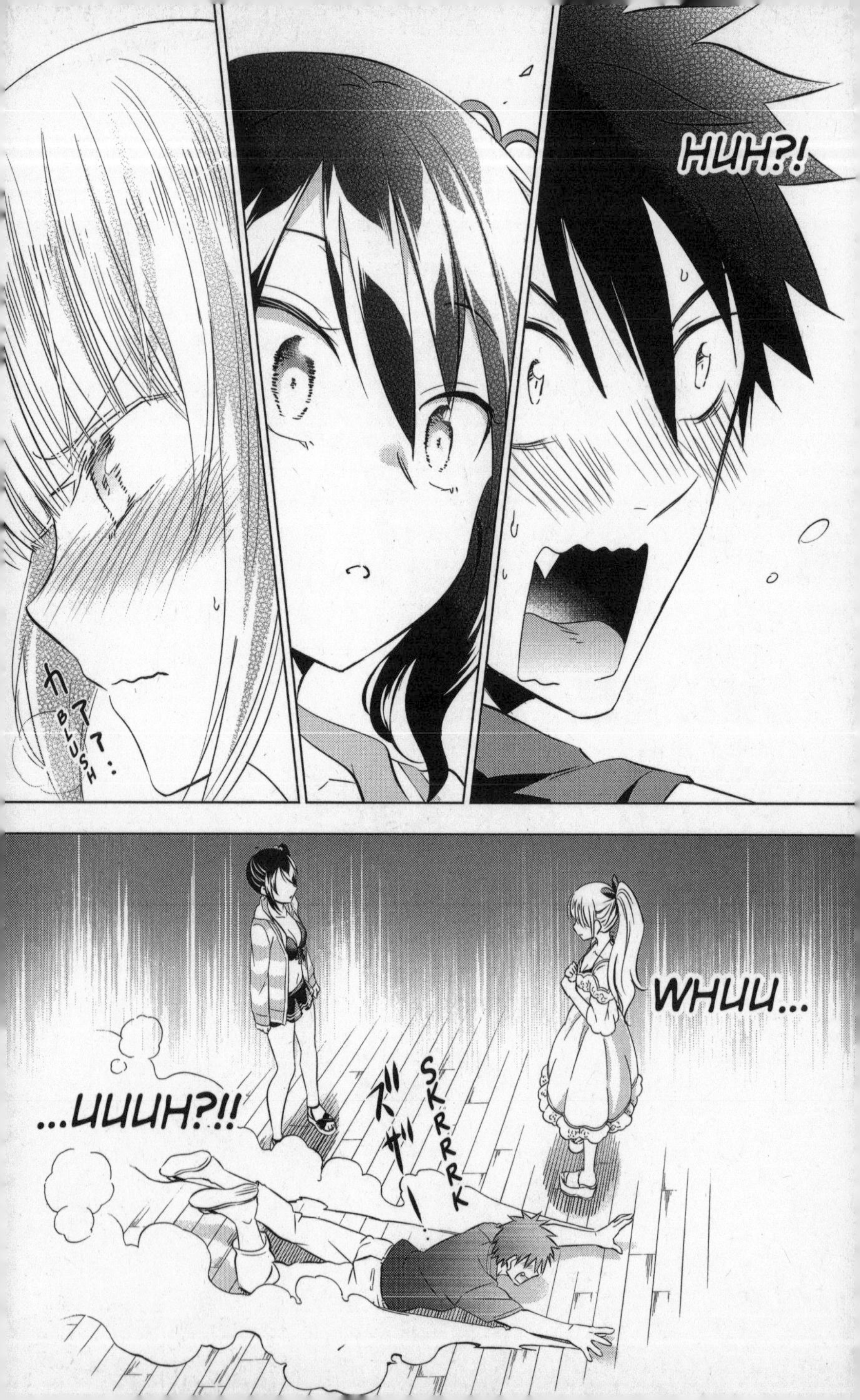
HUH?!
カアァ… BLUSH
WHUU...
ズザー!! SKRRRRK
...UUUH?!!

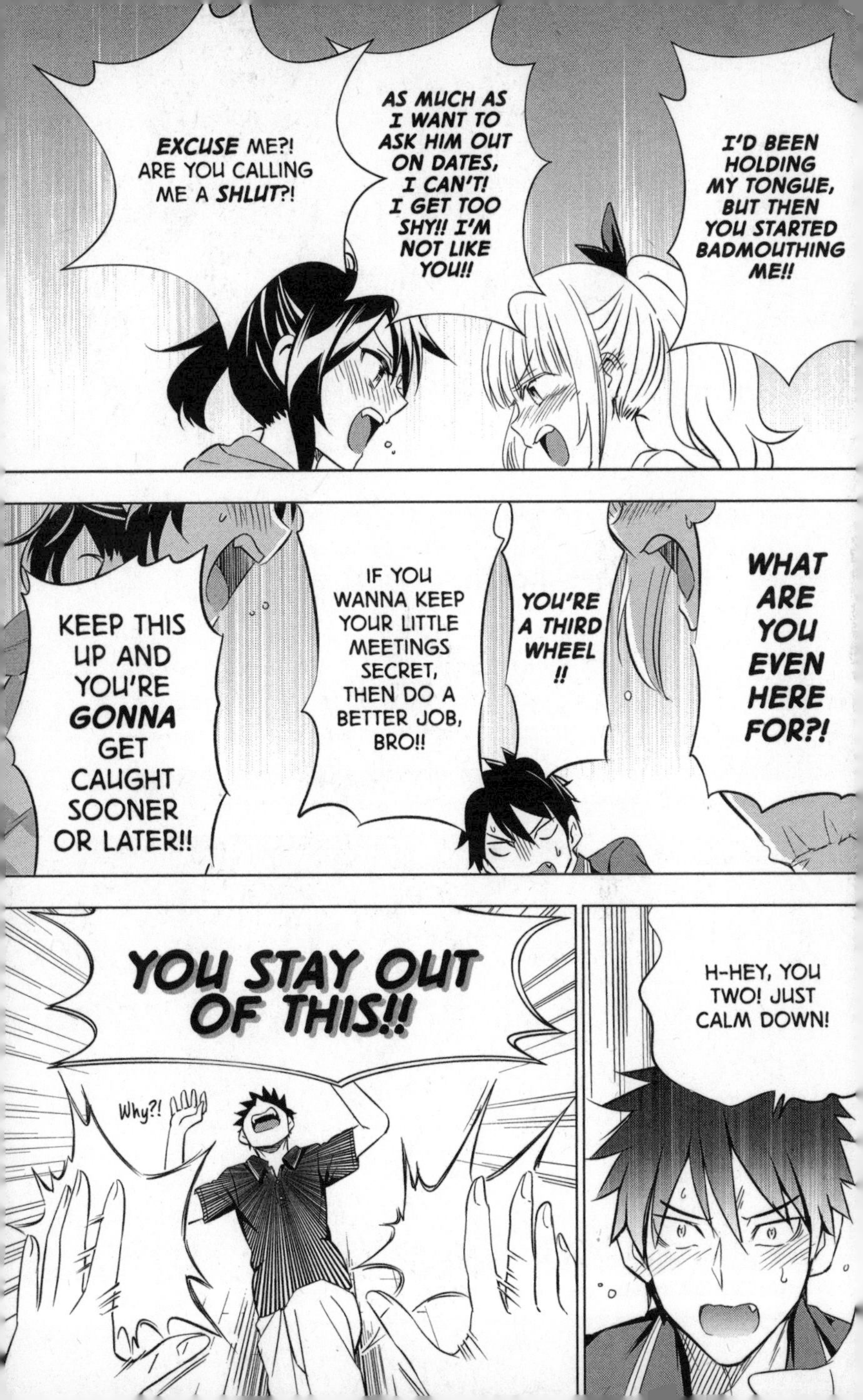
I'D BEEN HOLDING MY TONGUE, BUT THEN YOU STARTED BADMOUTHING ME!!
AS MUCH AS I WANT TO ASK HIM OUT ON DATES, I CAN'T! I GET TOO SHY!! I'M NOT LIKE YOU!!
EXCUSE ME?! ARE YOU CALLING ME A SHLUT?!
WHAT ARE YOU EVEN HERE FOR?!
YOU'RE A THIRD WHEEL !!
IF YOU WANNA KEEP YOUR LITTLE MEETINGS SECRET, THEN DO A BETTER JOB, BRO!!
KEEP THIS UP AND YOU'RE GONNA GET CAUGHT SOONER OR LATER!!
H-HEY, YOU TWO! JUST CALM DOWN!
YOU STAY OUT OF THIS!!
Why?!

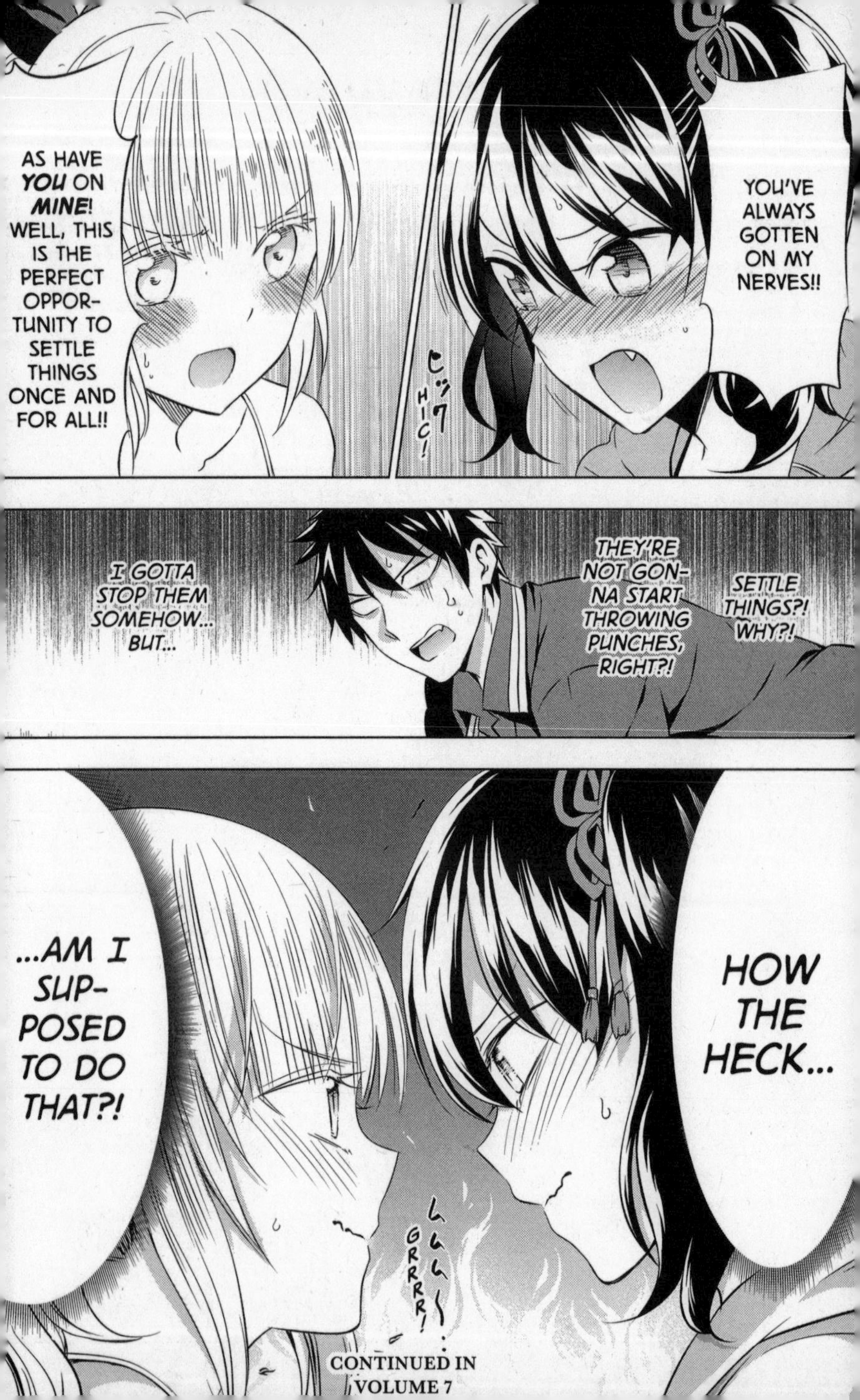
YOU'VE ALWAYS GOTTEN ON MY NERVES!!
HIC!
AS HAVE *YOU* ON *MINE*! WELL, THIS IS THE PERFECT OPPORTUNITY TO SETTLE THINGS ONCE AND FOR ALL!!
SETTLE THINGS?! WHY?!
THEY'RE NOT GONNA START THROWING PUNCHES, RIGHT?!
I GOTTA STOP THEM SOMEHOW... BUT...
HOW THE HECK...
GRRRR!
...AM I SUPPOSED TO DO THAT?!
CONTINUED IN VOLUME 7

AFTERWORD

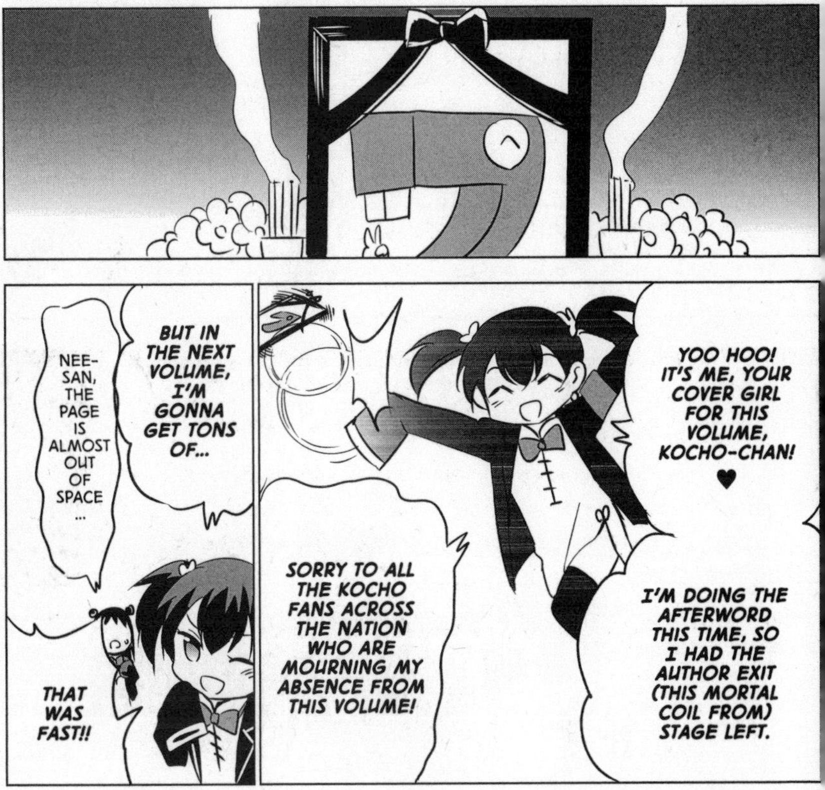
YOO HOO! IT'S ME, YOUR COVER GIRL FOR THIS VOLUME, KOCHO-CHAN! ♥
I'M DOING THE AFTERWORD THIS TIME, SO I HAD THE AUTHOR EXIT (THIS MORTAL COIL FROM) STAGE LEFT.
SORRY TO ALL THE KOCHO FANS ACROSS THE NATION WHO ARE MOURNING MY ABSENCE FROM THIS VOLUME!
BUT IN THE NEXT VOLUME, I'M GONNA GET TONS OF...
NEE-SAN, THE PAGE IS ALMOST OUT OF SPACE...
THAT WAS FAST!!

MY TWITTER ACCOUNT: @YOUSUKEKANEDA

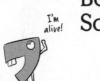

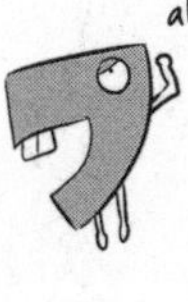
I'm alive!

Boarding School *Juliet*

VOL. 7 ON SALE SOON!

A Kodansha Comics Trade Paperback Original.

Boarding School Juliet volume 6 copyright © 2017 Yousuke Kaneda
English translation copyright © 2019 Yousuke Kaneda

All rights reserved.

Published in the United States by Kodansha Comics,
an imprint of Kodansha USA Publishing, LLC, New York.

Publication rights for this English edition arranged through
Kodansha Ltd., Tokyo.

First published in Japan in 2017 by Kodansha Ltd., Tokyo, as
Kishuku Gakkou no Jurietto volume 6

ISBN 978-1-63236-785-3

Printed in the United States of America.

www.kodanshacomics.com

9 8 7 6 5 4 3 2 1

Translation: Amanda Haley
Lettering: James Dashiell
Editing: Erin Subramanian and Tiff Ferentini
Kodansha Comics edition cover design: Phil Balsman